'An exceptional book. It is completely different from anything else currently available, refreshing, extremely well-written and original in so many ways . . . It is just the sort of book I would want my students to read . . . It is quite the best introductory book that I have ever come across.' **Philip Martin, De Montfort University**

'Fresh, surprising, never boring, and engagingly humorous, while remaining intellectually serious and challenging . . . This is a terrific book, and I'm very glad that it exists.' **Peggy Kamuf, University of Southern California, Los Angeles**

'This excellent book is very well-written and an outstanding introduction to literary studies. An extremely stimulating introduction.' **Robert Eaglestone, Royal Holloway College, University of London**

'I am convinced that Bennett and Royle have written a pathbreaking work and I suspect that this book – so full of laughter, suspense, secrets and pleasure – will have an appeal beyond a strictly academic audience.' **Alan Shima, University of Gothenberg**

'All the chapters in the volume are illuminating, informative and original.' **Robert Mills, King's College London**

'Bennett and Royle offer a different kind of introduction, which directly involves the reader in the problems and pleasures of thinking about literature – its distinctiveness, its strangeness, its power, its inexhaustibility . . . They succeed brilliantly in encouraging readers who are new to theory to appreciate its importance, enjoy its revelations, and understand some of its conceptual apparatus without diminishing the centrality of literary writing itself. This is a book which students in every introductory course on criticism and theory would benefit from having.' **Derek Attridge, University of York**

An Introduction to Literature, Criticism and Theory

Fourth edition

ANDREW BENNETT AND
NICHOLAS ROYLE

PEARSON
Longman

Harlow, England • London • New York • Boston • San Francisco • Toronto
Sydney • Tokyo • Singapore • Hong Kong • Seoul • Taipei • New Delhi
Cape Town • Madrid • Mexico City • Amsterdam • Munich • Paris • Milan

PEARSON EDUCATION LIMITED

Edinburgh Gate
Harlow CM20 2JE
United Kingdom
Tel: +44 (0)1279 623623
Fax: +44 (0)1279 431059
Website: www.pearsoned.co.uk

Fourth edition published in Great Britain in 2009

© International Book Distributors Limited 1995
© Andrew Bennett and Nicholas Royle 1995, 2009

The rights of Andrew Bennett and Nicholas Royle
to be identified as authors of this work have been asserted by
them in accordance with the Copyright, Designs and Patents Act 1988.

ISBN 978-1-4058-5914-1

British Library Cataloguing-in-Publication Data
A CIP catalogue record for this book can be obtained from the British Library

Library of Congress Cataloging-in-Publication Data

10 9 8 7 6 5 4 3 2 1
13 12 11 10 09

Set by 35 in 11/13pt Bulmer MT
Printed in Malaysia (CTP-VP)

The Publisher's policy is to use paper manufactured from sustainable forests.

Contents

21	God	188
22	Ideology	199
23	Desire	207
24	Queer	216
25	Suspense	226
26	Racial difference	234
27	The colony	242
28	Mutant	252
29	The performative	262
30	Secrets	270
31	The postmodern	279
32	Pleasure	289
33	War	299
34	The end	311
	Glossary	319
	Select bibliography of other introductory texts, reference works	
	and anthologies	328
	Literary works discussed	330
	Bibliography of critical and theoretical works	335
	Index	364

Acknowledgements

We are grateful to Michael Ayres for permission to reproduce his poem 'Bittersweet' published in *Poems, 1987–1992* by Odyssey Poets.

In some instances we have been unable to trace the owners of copyright material and we would appreciate any information that would enable us to do so.

Preface to the first edition

This is a new kind of book. It offers new ways of thinking about literature and about what is involved in reading critically. It is designed to be clear and accessible to those who are beginning to study literature, as well as to more advanced students. Although written with university students in mind, we dare to hope that it might also be of interest to other readers.

Literary theory is an unavoidable part of studying literature and criticism. But theory – especially when it takes the form of 'isms' – can often be intimidating or else, frankly, boring. We have tried to avoid simply giving potted summaries of *isms*. Instead we present brief essays on a range of key critical concepts all of which have more or less familiar names. We put these concepts into practice through readings of particular literary texts. Our primary focus, in other words, is on what is powerful, complex and strange about literary works themselves. Our aim is to explain, entertain, stimulate and challenge.

The book is divided into 24 chapters and looks as if it has a certain order or progression. It begins with 'The beginning' and ends with 'The end'. But it has been put together in such a way that it can also be read starting from any one chapter. 'The end', for example, is not a bad place to begin. Each chapter concludes with some suggestions for further reading. There is a glossary of critical and theoretical terms at the back of the book, plus a full bibliography of the texts discussed.

Preface to the second edition

This new edition of *An Introduction to Literature, Criticism and Theory* has been thoroughly revised and, we hope, improved. We have revised all existing chapters, updated and expanded the further reading sections, the glossary and the bibliography, and also added four new chapters: 'Monuments', 'Ghosts', 'Queer' and 'The colony'. These additional chapters reflect the importance of certain new or emerging areas of literary studies, such as queer theory, postcolonial theory, debates about 'the canon' and spectrality. We also hope, however, that the new chapters may complement and reinforce what we believe was already distinctive about the first edition of this book, namely its preoccupation with literature and the literary as such. Our foremost desire has been to explore and analyse the strange, protean forms and effects of the literary and of literature as an institution. This second edition, then, attempts to make explicit in new ways our continuing fascination with literary works themselves – with, for example, their monumental, ghostly, queer and colonizing power.

Preface to the third edition

For this third edition we have, once again, revised and updated the book as thoroughly as possible. Some of the revisions are so small that, we suspect, only Bennett and Royle will ever notice; others are more substantial. We have also added four new chapters: 'Creative writing', 'Moving pictures', 'Mutant' and 'War'. In each case, we have sought to acknowledge and engage with recent developments in literature, criticism and theory in what we hope are refreshing, informative and stimulating ways.

Preface to the fourth edition

For this new edition we have updated and made modest revisions through-out, and we have added two chapters. These new chapters offer ways of thinking through questions of the human in relation to the non-human world, focusing in particular on animals and the environment.

1. The beginning

When will we have begun?

Where – or when – does a literary text begin? This question raises a series of fundamental problems in literary criticism and theory. Does a text begin as the author puts his or her first mark on a piece of paper or keys in the first word on a computer? Does it begin with the first idea about a story or poem, or in the childhood of the writer, for instance? Or does the text only begin as the reader picks up the book? Does the text begin with its title, or with the first word of the so-called 'body' of the text?

We will try to begin with a poem. John Milton's great epic *Paradise Lost* (1667) begins by returning to the beginning:

> Of man's first disobedience, and the fruit
> Of that forbidden tree, whose mortal taste
> Brought death into the world, and all our woe,
> With loss of Eden, till one greater Man
> Restore us, and regain the blissful seat,
> Sing Heav'nly Muse, that on the secret top
> Of Oreb, or of Sinai, didst inspire
> That shepherd, who first taught the chosen seed,
> In the beginning how the heav'ns and earth
> Rose out of chaos: or if Sion hill
> Delight thee more, and Siloa's brook that flowed
> Fast by the oracle of God; I thence
> Invoke thy aid to my advent'rous song,
> That with no middle flight intends to soar
> Above th'Aonian mount, while it pursues
> Things unattempted yet in prose or rhyme.

This extraordinary opening sentence is all about beginnings. Thematically, it establishes the poem to be about the *first* disobedience of Adam and Eve which 'Brought death into the world, and all our woe'. But it is also about itself *as* a beginning: it assures us that this is the first time that such a project has been attempted ('Things unattempted yet in prose or rhyme'). It is as if the opening to a poem could be the equivalent of a moon-landing – one small step for John Milton . . . Rather differently, the opening sentence is about itself as a beginning in the sense that it is asking the 'Heav'nly Muse' for inspiration. It is about the way that poems are conventionally thought to begin – in inspiration. This produces a strange paradox of beginnings: the origin of the poem, inspiration, comes *after* the beginning of the poem. In other ways, too, Milton's opening unsettles any simple notion of opening or beginning. Not only does the poem talk about a beginning (the eating of the fruit of knowledge) but it also refers to a future return to a time before that beginning ('regain the blissful seat'), a restoration which will be both the beginning of a new age and a repetition of a previous state.

There is another way in which this beginning is not a beginning: it repeatedly refers us back to other texts. Milton refers to Moses ('That shepherd') in the belief that he 'taught' the children of Israel the creation story – in other words, that he wrote the opening books of the Old Testament. In this respect, the muse that Milton's poem addresses and invokes is a second-hand muse. Contrary to its claims to originality, this opening echoes and alludes to various other openings. 'Of man's first disobedience . . . Sing Heav'nly Muse' repeats the conventional apostrophe of such classical openings as Homer's *Iliad* and Virgil's *Aeneid*; 'In the beginning' repeats the opening to the Gospel according to St John ('In the beginning was the Word'), and so on. Finally, the very syntax of Milton's sentence displaces the beginning of the poem, in particular by holding back the main verb of the sentence – 'Sing' – until line six.

Despite the complications of Milton's opening, however, at least it tries (or pretends to try) to begin at the beginning, rather than in the middle. Beginning in the middle – *in medias res* – is the other way to begin. One of the most famous beginnings-in-the-middle is Dante's opening to *The Divine Comedy* (*c.* 1307–20):

> Nel mezzo del cammin di nostra vita
> mi ritrovai per una selva oscura,
> che la diritta via era smarrita.
> (Midway in the journey of our life I found myself in a dark
> wood, for the straight way was lost.)

There are at least three different middles here: the middle of 'our life', the middle of a dark wood, the middle of a narrative. Dante conflates life, journey and narrative, and suggests the uncanny terror of *beginning* at such a moment of middling. In particular, the uncanniness of 'mi ritrovai' suggests the hallucinatory terror of (re-)finding, of retrieving oneself. But Dante's opening might also suggest that there are *no* absolute beginnings – only strange originary middles. No journey, no life, no narrative ever really begins: all have in some sense already begun before they begin. But this is not to say that we can do without the concept of the beginning. Where would we be without a beginning? Where would a text be?

The paradox of the beginning having already begun is wittily presented by Laurence Sterne in the opening of his novel *The Life and Opinions of Tristram Shandy, Gentleman* (1759) in terms of both the beginning of a narrative and the beginning of a life:

> I wish either my father or my mother, or indeed both of them, as they were in duty both equally bound to it, had minded what they were about when they begot me; had they duly consider'd how much depended upon what they were then doing;—that not only the production of a rational Being was concern'd in it, but that possibly the happy formation and temperature of his body, perhaps his genius and the very cast of his mind;—and, for aught they knew to the contrary, even the fortunes of his whole house might take their turn from the humours and dispositions which were then uppermost:—Had they duly weighed and considered all this, and proceeded accordingly,—I am verily persuaded I should have made a quite different figure in the world, from that, in which the reader is likely to see me. (5)

This opening is a comic version of Philip Larkin's equivocal opening line to his poem 'This Be The Verse' (1974): 'They fuck you up, your mum and dad'. Tristram Shandy complains because his parents were thinking of something else at the moment of his conception and he is afraid that in consequence his whole life has been fucked up. As his uncle Toby remarks a few pages later, 'My Tristram's misfortunes began nine months before ever he came into the world' (7). *Tristram Shandy* famously confronts the intractable problem of how to end an autobiography: such a text can never catch up with itself because it takes longer to write about life than it takes to live it. In this sense, no autobiography can ever end. But *Tristram Shandy* is also about how to begin – how to begin at the beginning – and how we begin.

If beginnings always have a context and are therefore determined by what comes before, the opening to *Tristram Shandy* also makes it clear that, in turn, beginnings determine what comes after. This is true of literary as of other beginnings: beginnings augur, acting like promises for what is to come. Such is the force of many well-known literary beginnings. The opening to Jane Austen's *Pride and Prejudice* (1813) is apparently unequivocal: 'It is a truth universally acknowledged, that a single man in possession of a good fortune, must be in want of a wife' (1). This sets the stage for the whole novel. The topic is marriage, the tone is ironic. Austen proclaims the values of universalism ('a truth universally acknowledged'), while satirizing them: what is acknowledged as a truth for upper middle-class men in early nineteenth-century England is not necessarily acknowledged universally. Before going on to provide an 'Explanatory' note on its dialect, Mark Twain's *The Adventures of Huckleberry Finn (Tom Sawyer's Comrade)* (1885) begins with a 'notice':

NOTICE

Persons attempting to find a motive in this narrative will be prosecuted; persons attempting to find a moral in it will be banished; persons attempting to find a plot in it will be shot.

BY ORDER OF THE AUTHOR
PER G.G., CHIEF OF ORDNANCE

At once witty and baffling, the sentence is both an entrance and a barrier to the novel. It reads something like the sentence 'Do not read this sentence', in that it both acknowledges that readers *do* try to find motives and morals in narratives, and comically prohibits such a reading. Herman Melville's *Moby-Dick; or, The Whale* (1851) is also framed by a number of what Gérard Genette calls 'peritexts' (Genette 1987) – by a contents page, a dedication, an 'Etymology' (of the word 'Whale') and 'Extracts' (several pages of quotations about whales) – before it begins with the famous words 'Call me Ishmael'. Satirical prevarication and pedantry, combined with blustering assertiveness, characterize the whole novel. Virginia Woolf's *Orlando* (1928) opens (after a dedication, preface, contents page and list of illustrations) with a sentence that equivocates by appearing not to do so: 'He – for there could be no doubt of his sex, though the fashion of the time did something to disguise it – was in the act of slicing at the head of a Moor which swung from the rafters' (13). The sentence begins a book about a person of uncertain or variable gender in a tone of strange uncertainty, with a suggestive mixture of decapitation and castration. By appearing not to, this opening sentence, like the novel as a whole, subtly undermines conventional ideas about gender identity. The first sentence of Ford Madox Ford's *The Good Soldier* (1915) is sheer heart-tugging seduction: 'This is the saddest story I have ever heard' (7). It is the sort of sentence from which a novel might never recover. And Proust's famous understated opening to *Remembrance of Things Past* (1913–27) implies that there is no single beginning: 'Longtemps, je me suis couché de bonne heure' ('For a long time I used to go to bed early', 13). A studied reflection on the past, a sense of intimacy, the power of habit and repetition are what characterize Proust's 3,000-page novel. As these examples suggest, one of the peculiarities of literary openings is that they are never single. The openings to *Huckleberry Finn*, *Moby-Dick* and *Orlando* produce multiple beginnings through their 'peritexts', but the other examples also present more than one beginning: *The Good Soldier* suggests both a story and its retelling (as well as other stories that are not as sad), while Proust's opening gives a sense that narrative begins in repetition, that no single event can be said to be a beginning.

As we have begun to see, one of the ways in which a literary text multiplies its beginning is through the deployment of peritexts – titles, subtitles, dedications, epigraphs, introductions, 'notices' and so on. A classic example would be the opening of T.S. Eliot's *The Waste Land* (1922). Before we arrive at the first words of Eliot's poem we encounter a series of multilingual hurdles. To start with, there is the title. The title, like all titles, is uncertainly poised between inside and outside. It both names the poem, as if from outside, and forms part of that poem. 'The Waste Land' both refers to a place or predicament – post-1918 Europe, for example – and names the strange 'land' that Eliot's poem creates (like a waste land, the poem is full of debris from the past, fragmentary memories and quotations). Next we encounter the Latin and Greek of Petronius: 'Nam Sibyllam quidem Cumis ego ipse oculis meis vidi in ampulla pendere, et cum illi pueri dicerent: Σίβυλλα τί Θελεις; respondebat illa: ἀποθαυειυ Θέλω' ('For once I myself saw with my own eyes the Sibyl at Cumae hanging in a cage, and when the boys said to her "Sibyl, what do you want?" she replied, "I want to die"'). As an epigraph, this quotation too may be said to be both inside and outside the poem, both a commentary on and a part of the text. The next hurdle is a tribute in Italian to Ezra Pound: 'il miglior fabbro' ('the better craftsman'). Pound, as editor, was responsible for much of the final shape of Eliot's poem and therefore is in part the craftsman of what follows. Even this tribute is a quotation: it comes from Dante's *Purgatorio* and is in this sense too both part of Eliot's poem and not part of it. Finally, there is a subtitle: '1. The Burial of the Dead'. This is a quotation from the Anglican burial service. Then we have what appear to be the first words of the poem:

> April is the cruellest month, breeding
> Lilacs out of the dead land, mixing
> Memory and desire, stirring
> Dull roots with spring rain. (ll.1–4)

But in fact these lines are a pastiche or reworking of the opening to another poem, Chaucer's *The Canterbury Tales* (*c.* 1387–1400):

> Whan that April with his shoures sote
> The droghte of Marche hath perced to the rote,
> And bathed every veyne in swich licour,
> Of which vertu engendred is the flour. (ll. 1–4)

In these and other ways, Eliot's poem displaces its own beginning. The beginning of the poem is no longer the first stroke of the pen or keyboard. Through emphatic effects of intertextuality (including quotation, allusion, reference and echo), Eliot's poem suggests that originality, the notion of beginning as singular, definable, stable is severely problematic. To ask where or when Eliot's poem begins is to meet with a series of questions concerning the identity of the author, the text and reader, and finally of the Western literary tradition generally.

The Waste Land may seem to be unusually concerned with questions of origins and their displacement. But the kinds of effects of intertextuality that this opening explores are in fact fundamental to literary texts more generally. Literary texts, that is to say, are always constructed by and within a context or tradition. In his well-known essay 'Tradition and the Individual Talent' (1919), Eliot himself argues that 'No poet, no artist of any art, has his [*sic*] complete meaning alone': rather, what is important is the poet's 'relation to the dead poets and artists' (Eliot 1975, 38). A poem, novel or play that does not in some sense relate to previous texts is, in fact, literally unimaginable. The author of such a text would have to invent everything. It would be like inventing a new language from scratch, without any reliance on already existing languages. In this sense, intertextuality (the displacement of origins to other texts, which are in turn displacements of other texts and so on – in other words, an undoing of the very idea of pure or straightforward *origins*) is fundamental to the institution of literature. No text makes sense without other texts. Every text is what Roland Barthes calls 'a new tissue of past citations' (Barthes 1981, 39).

Two of the most compelling and most persistent myths of literary texts concern their origins. The first is the idea that the most important aspect of any reading is an imagined meeting of the reader's mind with that of the author – an idea that exemplifies what has been known, since a famous essay of that name (1946 rev. 1954), as the 'intentional fallacy' (the mistaken belief that what the author intended is the 'real', 'final' meaning of the work and that we can or should know what this is (see Wimsatt and Beardsley 1995)). But if we cannot know the beginnings of a text in terms of what is available to us on the page, how much more difficult it would be to discover the origins of the thought which impels the text. Does an author know where these thoughts come from? Are they in fact thoughts (conscious, coherent, consistent)? Whose 'thoughts' do we read when we read the beginning of *The Waste Land*? Eliot's, Chaucer's, Pound's, Petronius', Dante's? Are they still the poet's thoughts if the poet is said to be 'inspired'? The second common myth involves the priority given to an individual reader's first reading of a text. According to this myth, all literary criticism involves a corruption of the original 'experience' of reading. Once upon a time (so this myth goes) we were able to read a novel (by Charlotte Brontë, say, or J.K. Rowling) and have a completely unadulterated reading experience, unsullied by any critical thinking or complexity. But although we often talk about literary texts as though they have been subjected to only one reading, we all know that this is in many respects simply a convenient fiction. Roland Barthes, in his book *S/Z* (1970), makes a point about the act of rereading as 'an operation contrary to the commercial and ideological habits of our society' and suggests that it is 'tolerated only in certain marginal categories of readers (children, old people and professors)' (Barthes 1990b, 15–16). Professors – who are usually old people, very seldom children, though not infrequently an undecidable mixture of the two – include Roland Barthes, of course, and it is part of his aim to question the very idea of a single or first reading. Rereading, he argues,

> contests the claim which would have us believe that the first reading is a primary, naïve, phenomenal reading which we will only, afterwards, have to 'explicate', to intellectualize (as if there were a beginning of reading, as if everything were not already read: there is no *first* reading . . .). (Barthes 1990b, 16)

Once again, Eliot's *The Waste Land* suggests some of the complexities involved in a first reading. If the opening to Eliot's poem refers to Chaucer's, then when can we properly be said to read 'April is the cruellest month'? Surely we must reread it, once we have read it, with Chaucer's words in mind. In which case the first reading is inadequate. Less dramatically, perhaps, the same may be said of any other literary text: every reading (even a so-called 'first reading') is at least in part a learned or programmed response, conditioned by other and others' readings. In this respect, reading critically is, in T.S. Eliot's words, 'as inevitable as breathing' (Eliot 1975, 37).

The present book is, fundamentally, about questions of origins, about beginning. It is concerned with how we might begin to read, to think about and write about literary texts. In particular, the book is about those uncertain origins – the author, the reader and the text – none of which can ever be taken for granted. Neither author nor reader nor text finally or properly constitutes a beginning. As with 'beginning literary studies' (which we have begun now, haven't we?), the idea that everything begins with the author or with the reader or with one particular text is both deeply compelling and deeply false.

Further reading

The now classic exploration of literary beginnings is Edward Said's *Beginnings* (1975), a challenging but exuberant and theoretically astute exploration of openings, originality and origins in literature and theory. A more recent and perhaps more accessible book on beginnings is A.D. Nuttall's *Openings* (1992), which eschews theoretical discussion in favour of a concentrated focus on a small number of classic literary openings. On intertextuality, see Graham Allen's very readable *Intertextuality* (2000) and Mary Orr's rather more specialist *Intertextuality* (2003); and see Daniel Chandler's chapter on intertextuality in *Semiotics: The Basics* (2007), which is also available online at www.aber.ac.uk/media/Documents/S4B/sem09.html. There has been an enormous amount of work in recent years on questions of originality and plagiarism in literature, much of it rather specialized, but see, in particular, Margaret Russett's *Fictions and Fakes* (2006), Hillel Schwartz, *The Culture of the Copy* (1996), and Françoise Meltzer, *Hot Property* (1994). For a brilliant if sometimes polemically anti-theory approach to the question of allusion, see Christopher Ricks, *Allusion to the Poets* (2002). On the origins of creativity, see Timothy Clark's difficult but inspirational book, *The Theory of Inspiration* (1997).

2. Readers and reading

What do you do when you come across a poem like this?

I met a traveller from an antique land,
Who said—'Two vast and trunkless legs of stone
Stand in the desert . . . Near them, on the sand,
Half sunk a shattered visage lies, whose frown,
5 And wrinkled lip, and sneer of cold command,
Tell that its sculptor well those passions read
Which yet survive, stamped on these lifeless things,
The hand that mocked them, and the heart that fed;
And on the pedestal, these words appear:
10 My name is Ozymandias, King of Kings,
Look on my Works, ye Mighty, and despair!
Nothing beside remains. Round the decay
Of that colossal Wreck, boundless and bare
The lone and level sands stretch far away'.

In Percy Bysshe Shelley's famous sonnet 'Ozymandias' (1818) the narrator speaks of meeting a traveller who reports having seen a vast shattered statue strewn across the desert. The statue is of Ozymandias, the thirteenth-century BC King Rameses II of Egypt (Ozymandias is the Greek name for this king). All that remains of the King of Kings and of his 'works' are a few broken fragments, a couple of legs and an inscription which commands the reader to despair. The poem, then, is about monuments, survival and the transience of even the greatest of us. But we might also notice that the poem is about readers and reading – the traveller reads a piece of writing, an inscription on the pedestal of a fragmented statue. The inscription *commands* the reader. And, rather differently, the word 'read' appears in line six, referring to the way that the sculptor understood the 'passions' of Ozymandias and was able to immortalize them in stone. Both the traveller and the sculptor are explicitly figured as readers, and we might also think about the 'I' of the first line as another kind of reader – a listener to the traveller's tale.

The poem, then, concerns a series of framed acts of reading. The sculptor reads the face of the king, the traveller reads the inscription, the narrative 'I' listens to the tale and, finally, we read the poem. One of the things that we might do with this poem is to think about these acts of reading. The poem can be thought about as what Paul de Man calls an 'allegory of reading' (de Man, 1979): it is not only a poem which can be read, it is also a poem *about* reading. One of the crucial questions of reading, for example, is how we can justify any particular reading: how can we tell if a particular reading or interpretation is valid? This is a question that goes to the heart of almost every debate in criticism and theory. In this respect the poem presents a paradox in that the traveller says that only a few fragments of the statue remain, that this is all that is left of Ozymandias and his great works. But if this is the case, how can the traveller know that the sculptor read the king's passions 'well'? In this way Shelley's poem can be understood as telling a story or allegory about one of the central paradoxes of reading. To read 'well' is generally taken as meaning to read accurately or faithfully. But the question of which reading of a text is the most accurate is itself a question of reading.

'Ozymandias', then, opens up a series of questions concerning readers and reading. In addition to the crucial question of how we can validate any reading (how we can know whether it is true or faithful), the poem also engages with other questions. Who is this traveller who reads the inscription, for example? And who is the 'I' who listens to, or 'reads', his story? Is the sculptor's 'mocking' of the king's face a kind of reading? What do such questions lead us to think about the power relations of any reading? Is it in the king's power to command his readers to despair? Or to make them obey? Is the traveller's reading of the inscription different from how that inscription might have been read while the king was alive? And does reading therefore change over time – is reading historically determined? What does all of this suggest about reading more generally? In this chapter we shall begin to explore some of these questions, referring to Shelley's poem as a way of summarizing some important developments in literary criticism and theory of the last few decades.

Some of the most widely publicized developments in literary theory of the second half of the twentieth century went under the umbrella term 'reader-response criticism'. Such developments are usually understood as a reaction against Anglo-American 'new criticism' of the post-war period. Before we discuss reader-response criticism itself, then, it might be useful briefly to outline the position of new criticism with regard to readers and reading. Associated with such US critics as Cleanth Brooks, W.K. Wimsatt and Monroe Beardsley, and indebted also to the principles of 'practical criticism' associated with the British critics I.A. Richards and F.R. Leavis, new criticism involved a way of reading that emphasized form – the importance of considering 'the words on the page' – rather than factors such as the life of the author and his or her intentions, or the historical and ideological context in which the text was produced. New critics considered that such questions, while no doubt interesting, were irrelevant to a consideration of the text itself: they thought of literary texts as 'autonomous', as self-sufficient and self-contained unities, as aesthetic objects made of words. Correspondingly, new critics argued that to try to take account of readers' reactions or responses in the context of, for example, a poem, was to introduce an alien and fundamentally extraneous factor. They even invented a term for what they saw as the 'error' involved in talking about a reader's response in discussions of literary texts: they called it the 'affective fallacy'. For new critics, then, what was important was to pay scrupulous attention to the words of texts themselves, thus bypassing the subjective impressionism of the reader's response.

Like all critical movements, new criticism created its own special canon of literary works and authors. Shelley, notoriously, was not much in evidence in the new critical canon: in his influential book *Revaluation* (1936), F.R. Leavis had set the trend by caustically opining that Shelley was 'almost unreadable', and that the effect of his eloquence was 'to hand poetry over to a sensibility that has no more dealings with intelligence than it can help' (Leavis 1972, 171, 175). In his book *The Romantic Poets*, Graham Hough declared rather dismissively that '*Ozymandias* is an extremely clear and direct poem, advancing to a predetermined end by means of one firmly held image' (Hough 1967, 142). Dismissing the poem in this way is odd in view of the fact that irony, ambiguity and paradox are key elements in the new critical weaponry of reading, and that all three are dramatically at stake in lines 10 and 11 of the poem, the inscription on the pedestal. 'Look on my Works, ye Mighty, and despair!' is ironic, for example, from at least two perspectives. First, the line can be read as an example of 'hubris' or excessive pride on the part of Ozymandias, who is thus shown to be absurd. Second, it can be read as ironic from Ozymandias's point of view: knowing that even he will die, Ozymandias inscribes these words for future generations, reminding us that even the greatest will be forgotten in time. These conflicting ironies produce both ambiguity and paradox – ambiguity concerning which reading is more valid, and paradox in the fact that the inscription appears to say two conflicting things.

Beginning in the late 1960s and becoming increasingly influential in the 1970s and early 1980s, reader-response criticism directly questioned the principles of new criticism. For critics and theorists such as Wolfgang Iser, Stanley Fish and Michael Riffaterre, questions of the literary text and its meaning(s) cannot be disengaged from the role that the reader takes. Although these and other reader-response critics have widely different approaches to literary texts, they all agree that the meaning of the text is created through the process of reading. What they object to in new criticism is the notion that a certain quality or 'meaning' of a literary text simply lies there in the text waiting for the reader or critic to come along and identify it. Graham Hough's apparently objective assertion that 'Ozymandias' is 'extremely clear and direct', for example, elides the question of 'to whom?' Hough appears to generalize what is, in fact, his particular view of the poem. As we have tried to suggest, the poem may also be read very differently, as syntactically complex and semantically dense. The new critics' sense that the meaning of a poem is simply *there* involves thinking of meaning (in Terry Eagleton's memorable metaphor) as like a wisdom tooth, 'waiting patiently to be extracted' (Eagleton 1996, 77). Reacting against what we might characterize as the 'dentistry' school of criticism, reader-response critics recognize that the meanings of a text rely, in a dynamic way, on the work of the reader. Given that reading is a necessary dimension of any text, these critics attempt to plot the process of reading and the role of the reader.

Rather than closing down the questions of 'who reads?' and 'what is reading?', however, reader-response criticism has opened a postmodern Pandora's box. Critics such as Norman Holland and David Bleich, for example, are interested in investigating ways in which particular individuals respond to texts, and with exploring ways in which such responses can be related to those individuals' 'identity themes', to their personal psychic dispositions – the individual character of their desires, needs, experiences, resistances and so on. This is often referred to as 'subjective criticism' or 'personal criticism'. Such critics would not be interested in deciding which reading of line eleven of 'Ozymandias' is 'correct' because such correctness or accuracy is beside the point. Norman Holland, for example, argues that 'interpretation is a function of identity' and that 'all of us, as we read, use the literary work to symbolize and finally to replicate ourselves' (Holland 1980, 123, 124). To parody the logic of subjective criticism, we might suppose that a reader whose irregular potty-training has resulted in a pathological hatred of authority-figures will delight in the ironic treatment of the King of Kings in Shelley's poem, while another reader who has early come to associate father-figures with absence and unreliability will see the poem as a poignant confirmation of the inevitable disappearance of all fathers. Although Holland assures his reader that he is not 'positing an isolated solipsistic self' (Holland 1980, 131), this is precisely the danger that other critics have seen in this kind of criticism: such a reliance on the autonomy of the reader's thoughts and feelings seems to lead to a state of delusion epitomized by Ozymandias's hollow words.

Theorists such as Stanley Fish, on the other hand, argue that any individual reader is necessarily part of a 'community' of readers. Every reader, he suggests, reads according to the conventions of his or her 'interpretive community'. In other words, an individual reader's response, according to this model, is determined by the conventions of reading into which he or she has been educated within a particular socio-historical context. Our recognition of the equivocality of 'Ozymandias', for example, is determined by the fact that we have been taught to look and listen for ambiguity and polysemia in literary texts.

A third influential strand of reader-response criticism is exemplified by the work of Wolfgang Iser. Iser elaborates ways in which the work of reading involves an interaction between elements of the text and the act of reading itself. He explores ways in which the text is 'concretized' – given shape or meaning in the act of reading. For Iser, neither the text nor the reader should be studied in isolation. Rather, the text produces certain 'blanks' or 'gaps' that the reader must attempt to complete: the reader 'is drawn into the events and made to supply what is meant from what is not said' (Iser 1995, 24). For Iser, the fact that we know nothing about the traveller in Shelley's poem, for example, 'spurs the reader into action' (24). 'Who is this traveller?' we might ask. 'What does he or she think about what is described in the poem?' The text prompts us imaginatively to fill in or fill out such hermeneutic or interpretative 'gaps'.

During the 1980s and 1990s, the political dimensions of reading became increasingly central to critical debate. Literary texts have been read in terms of power relations, in accordance with Michel Foucault's suggestion that 'power is everywhere' (Foucault 1981, 93) – even in reading. 'Ozymandias', in fact, produces multiple representations of the relationship between power and reading. Most explicitly there is the sculptor's 'reading' of the power of the king. The crucial lines here are lines four to eight:

> Half sunk a shattered visage lies, whose frown,
> And wrinkled lip, and sneer of cold command,
> Tell that its sculptor well those passions read
> Which yet survive, stamped on these lifeless things,
> The hand that mocked them, and the heart that fed . . .

The word 'mocked' means both 'imitated' or 'copied' and 'ridiculed' (a *mis*representation that represents more accurately or more cruelly). The commanding power of the king – his power, not least, to make the sculptor 'read' his face and to copy it on to stone – is resisted in that very reading, in that mockery. The sculptor's 'reading' is both a copy, a faithful representation, and a reading which ridicules. Reading here is figured as *both* faithful, an action of subservience, *and* a subversive act of resistance to power, a transfer and transformation of power. Alternatively, we might consider ways in which the poem suggests that acts of reading are bound up in the historical specificity of power relations. The reading of the statue and the inscription, in this sense, changes over time. Someone contemporary with the King of Kings might read the commanding inscription – 'Look on my Works, ye Mighty, and despair!' – as a statement of omnipotence. By contrast, a reader who, like the traveller, reads the inscription surrounded by the 'lone and level sands', by the *absence* of those works, their *non*-survival, can only read them ironically. What has remained, what has survived, is the work of the sculptor, the *represented* 'passions' of the king (itself a kind of reading), not his works. The power relations of text and reader have shifted decisively over time. Reading, in this sense, is not always and everywhere the same. As Robert Young comments, Shelley's poem 'demonstrates that meaning, like power, is not stable or fixed, and that even power cannot guarantee a tyranny of meaning: although authors may have intentions when they write, once they have written they cannot control and fix the meaning of any reading' (Young 1991a, 238). Finally, we might extrapolate from this to think about the way in which any reading produces a certain relation of power. Shelley's poem might itself be read as a kind of 'cold command' – a command to read. But any reading of the poem must constitute a form of resistance to such a command, a 'mockery' of that command, by the imposition or 'stamping' of its own interpretation on the poem. Reading *survives* the command of the text.

As part of this emphasis on power-relations, recent criticism has also given increased attention to questions of gender and race. Judith Fetterley, for example, has argued that female readers of classic US fiction (and, by implication, of other literary texts) have been 'immasculated', by which she means that they have traditionally been taught to read 'as men' (Fetterley 1978). Writing in the late 1970s, Fetterley argues that women should begin to liberate themselves from the notion of a 'universal' reader (who is implicitly male) and from an identification with male viewpoints in reading, and to develop specifically female models of reading. At stake here is, in Jonathan Culler's terms, the question of what it would mean to read 'as a woman' (Culler 1983, 43–64): how might 'reading as a woman' be different from 'reading as a man'?

And do we know what it means to read 'as a man'? It might be possible to think about Shelley's poem in terms of gendered reading. If we can assume that the traveller is male (after all, few solitary European travellers were female in the early nineteenth century), then one can see that the poem is not only about male pride, but also about male reading. The poem, indeed, is overwhelmingly masculine, a text from which women have been excluded. Yet few critics have been troubled by questions of sexual difference in relation to 'Ozymandias': in this respect, we might suggest, the critical response has been 'immasculated'. From Fetterley's perspective, we might ask how a non-immasculated reading would respond to the masculine power-play of Shelley's poem.

Critics concerned with questions of race and ethnicity have also developed specific strategies of reading and talking about reading. Theorists such as Gayatri Chakravorty Spivak, Henry Louis Gates Jr and Edward Said, for example, have transformed the nature of contemporary literary studies through their emphasis on questions of colonization, ethnic difference, racial oppression and discrimination, the position of the subaltern, the West and its construction of the 'other', imperialism and Orientalism. Edward Said, for instance, argues for what he calls 'contrapuntal reading' whereby, in reading a text, one 'open[s] it out both to what went into it and to what its author excluded' (Said 1993, 79). Our reading of *Jane Eyre* in terms of race and slavery in Chapter 24 suggests one such 'contrapuntal' reading. Similarly, Henry Louis Gates makes questions of reading central to black literary criticism and theory when he argues that black people in the United States have had to develop particular strategies of reading and interpretation for survival:

> Black people have always been masters of the figurative: saying one thing to mean something quite other has been basic to black survival in oppressive Western cultures. Misreading signs could be, and indeed often was, fatal. 'Reading', in this sense, was not play; it was an essential aspect of the 'literacy' training of a child. (Gates 1984, 6)

A reading concerned with questions of race might start from the fact that this English poem deals with a racial other – Egyptian or African – and explore the way in which such otherness is inscribed in the poem. The fact that the land is referred to as 'antique', for example, entirely effaces any possibility of a contemporary civilization and culture there. There is nothing beside the barrenness of the 'lone and level sands'. For this poem, Africa apparently only signifies in terms of a mythical past.

The recent emergence of ecocriticism has allowed for important new ways of reading such a poem (see Chapter 16, below). From this perspective,

'Ozymandias' is concerned with the relationship between the human, specifically in this case an ancient human culture, and the environment. Once you think of the poem in this context, its force immediately alters. It is no longer a poem only about the relationships between *people* – the pharaoh, the sculptor, the traveller, the speaker and his addressee, the poet, the reader – but also about the effect that a civilization has had on its environment, on what is now the wasted landscape so poignantly described. According to such a reading, Shelley's poem would be understood to respond to the ecological destruction caused by monumental human arrogance. This desolate landscape ('boundless and bare / The lone and level sands stretch far away') can be seen not as 'natural' but as having been produced by human intervention (perhaps by over-cultivation, or through the redirection of water for irrigation or by other geo-engineering endeavours). After all, we can safely assume that in *Ozymandias*'s time, the land surrounding the statue was able to sustain the life that this poem represents only in its absence. An ecocritical reading would pay attention not only to the poem's engagement with political and aesthetic questions, then, but also to the wider ramifications of its stark analysis of the eco-destruction that has typified human 'civilization' down the ages.

Finally, a poststructuralist or deconstructive reading of 'Ozymandias' might, in addition to these concerns, trace the dispersal or dissolution of the reader's identity in the act of reading and question the very possibility of interpretive mastery. For poststructuralists, there is a dynamic significance in the question of which comes first – the text or the reader? Is reading simply something that happens to a text as if by chance, something which leaves a text fundamentally unaltered? If so, then the role of the reader would appear to be determined by the text itself: each literary text would be like a set of instructions, a kind of recipe, for how it should be read. By contrast, the text may be understood as fundamentally incomplete, to be effected in the act of reading. In this case the text is remade in every reading. Rather than choosing between these two hypotheses, deconstructive theories of reading argue that *both* models are operative, in a peculiar double bind of reading: the reader makes the text and the text makes the reader. Deconstruction explores the space between these two possibilities and it seeks to highlight ways in which every reading and every text is unpredictable. Thus deconstruction is interested in the fact that while any text demands a 'faithful' reading, it also demands an *individual* response. Put differently, reading is at once singular (yours and nobody else's) and general (conforming to patterns of meaning dictated by the text – a text that does not require *you* in order to function). Through analysis of these and other paradoxes, critics such as Paul de Man and J. Hillis Miller suggest ways in which reading is strange, unsettling, even 'impossible'.

How should we read the word 'appear' in line nine of Shelley's poem ('And on the pedestal, these words appear'), for example? What makes these words appear? The word 'appear' might be shown to challenge all conventional preconceptions concerning reading. In particular, it challenges us to rethink the relationship between a text on the one hand simply *appearing*, simply being there like a monument, to be read, appearing from nowhere, and on the other hand a text appearing in the sense of 'seeming', an apparition, made in reading. Is the text *there*, or do we make it appear, do we imagine it? Jacques Derrida has referred to the *delireium* of reading, a pun or 'portmanteau' word which combines the French 'lire' ('to read') with 'delirium', to suggest ways in which reading can be delirious or hallucinatory (Derrida 1979, 94, quoting Blanchot). Just as we can never know how 'well', how accurately or faithfully the sculptor has read the king's passions, neither can we escape the dynamics of reading and delirium. In short, we can never stop reading because we can never finally know if what 'appears' in this poem is us reading or us being read. This is not to suggest we should therefore give up, either in despair or in indifference. Our very lives and identities are at stake. If, as we have argued, 'Ozymandias' is as much about readers and reading as about anything else, then we might see that the relation between reading and being read is strangely twisted: not only do we read the poem but the poem reads us. Like Ozymandias himself, we are fragmented, mute and transient: our 'passions' are read, and perhaps mocked, by the sculptor, in the form of the poem itself. After all, in reading this poem, we perhaps cannot avoid a ventriloquistic articulation, silent or not, of the king's words –

> My name is Ozymandias, King of Kings,
> Look on my Works, ye Mighty, and despair!

How do you read *that*? What happens to you, to your name?

Further reading

Karin Littau's *Theories of Reading* (2006) is a fascinating book that is alert to the history and to theories of reading. For collections of essays on the theory of reading see Andrew Bennett, ed., *Readers and Reading* (1995) and Suleiman and Crosman, eds, *The Reader in the Text* (1980); Sara Mills, ed., *Gendering the Reader* (1994) approaches reading theory from the perspective of gender and feminism. For an accessible and entertaining history of reading practices and theories from the earliest records to the present, see Alberto Manguel, *A History of Reading* (1997); two collections of essays which consider reading in history are Raven, Small and Tadmor, eds, *The Practice and Representation of Reading in England* (1995) and James L. Machor, ed., *Readers in History* (1993). For a more focused cultural history of reading and publishing practices in the late eighteenth and early nineteenth centuries, see William St Clair, *The Reading Nation in the Romantic Period* (2007). St Clair's book is in the relatively new discipline of book history: for an important collection of essays in the field, see Finkelstein and McCleery, eds, *The Book History Reader* (2006). A concise and accessible summary of what might now be called 'classic' reader-response criticism and theory is Elizabeth Freund's book *The Return of the Reader* (1987). On a more challenging level, for a brilliant discussion of how reading is figured in literary texts, see Paul de Man's *Allegories of Reading* (1979), and see J. Hillis Miller's *The Ethics of Reading* (1987) for a consideration of the act of reading as a response to an ethical call. Two important books from a psychoanalytically oriented feminist perspective are Mary Jacobus's *Reading Woman* (1986) and Shoshana Felman's *What Does a Woman Want? Reading and Sexual Difference* (1993). For introductions to poststructuralism, see Robert Young, 'Poststructuralism: The Improper Name', in *Torn Halves* (1996), and Colin Davies, *After Poststructuralism* (2004). On close reading, see Lentricchia and DuBois, eds, *Close Reading* (2003). For a powerful if highly idiosyncratic take on reading, see Harold Bloom's *How to Read and Why* (2000).

3.   The author

If you really want to hear about it, the first thing you'll probably want to know is where I was born, and what my lousy childhood was like, and how my parents were occupied and all before they had me, and all that David Copperfield kind of crap, but I don't feel like going into it. (5)

The opening sentence of J.D. Salinger's *The Catcher in the Rye* (1951) suggests a number of ways of thinking about the figure of the author. It is at once compellingly straightforward and strangely cryptic. The sentence gives the impression of a spontaneous, candid speaking voice, directly addressing us and showing a specific concern for our wishes and desires ('If you really want . . . you'll probably want'). We are being addressed very much *on the level* – nothing pretentious here, none of 'that David Copperfield kind of crap'. Despite appearances, however, this opening sentence gives little away, rather it is furtive and evasive: 'I don't feel like going into it'. The most important word in this famous opening sentence may indeed be the word 'it': 'it' is the emphatic but equivocal subject ('If you really want to hear about it . . . I don't feel like going into it'). Is the 'it' at the beginning of the sentence the same as the 'it' at the end?

The ambiguity of 'it' corresponds to another kind of uncertainty. For what is also unclear from this opening sentence is *who is speaking* or, more accurately, *who is writing*. After all, despite the seductiveness of the confiding, colloquial voice here, it would be somewhat naive to pretend that this is *not* writing. The sentence is playing a type of literary game with conventions of novel-openings. Of course, we quickly learn that the 'I' here is a 16-year-old American boy called Holden Caulfield, but this is not something that is made clear in the first sentence. All we can presume at this point is that we are reading that particular kind of text called a novel and that it has been written by J.D. Salinger. The literary game that is set in motion by this opening sentence has to do with the relationship between fiction (a novel) and truth (biography or autobiography), as well as between an author and a narrator. This is suggested by the apparently deprecating reference to David Copperfield ('all that David Copperfield kind of crap'). There is, then, a metafictional dimension in this seemingly simple opening sentence – metafictional in the sense that it explicitly refers to itself and draws attention to the fact that a story is being told. The narrator invokes the protagonist of one of the 'classic' English nineteenth-century novels and implies, even by denying it, a correlation with *another* literary text.

Both *David Copperfield* and *The Catcher in the Rye* offer a mixing of novel and (auto)biography. In doing so, they provoke a series of fundamental questions about the relationship between literary texts, narrators, characters and authors. Above all, they provoke the question: who is speaking? In presenting us with the voice of a fictional speaker, these texts draw attention to the figure of the author as a sort of concealed or cryptic, haunting but unspecified presence. Who is behind this 'I'? The opening of *The Catcher in the Rye* thus introduces a general question for literary criticism and theory, the question of the presence of another 'I' – the haunting absent-presence of the 'I' who writes, of the author. The author is a kind of ghost. Salinger's novel provides more than one illustration of this. A few pages further on, for example, Holden Caulfield tells us:

> What really knocks me out is a book that, when you're all done reading it, you wish the author that wrote it was a terrific friend of yours and you could call him up on the phone whenever you felt like it. That doesn't happen much, though. I wouldn't mind calling this Isak Dinesen up. And Ring Lardner, except that D.B. [Holden's brother] told me he's dead. You take that book *Of Human Bondage*, by Somerset Maugham, though. I read it last summer. It's a pretty good book and all, but I wouldn't want to call Somerset Maugham up. I don't know. He just isn't the kind of a guy I'd want to call up, that's all. I'd rather call old Thomas Hardy up. I like that Eustacia Vye. (22)

Again, this passage is delightfully straightforward and yet extraordinarily suggestive. It presents us with what is in many respects an undeniable truth, as well as with what constitutes one of the curious effects of literature: literary texts can generate powerful feelings of identification, not only between reader and character but also, perhaps more enigmatically, between reader and author. You really can be drawn into the feeling that the author is 'a terrific friend of yours' or that your appreciation and understanding of an author is so intense it touches on the telepathic. Holden's reference to getting on the phone to the author is uncannily apposite: the rapport that exists between you and your favourite author is indeed a sort of linguistic tele-link. The author is an absent presence, both there and not there. You may feel that you understand like nobody else what it is that the author is saying; and you may be willing to acknowledge that this author can express your opinions, thoughts and feelings as well as or even better than you yourself could. This is, in fact, precisely how the greatness of Shakespeare is often described. It is what William Hazlitt says, for example, in his 1818 lecture 'On Shakespeare and Milton': 'the striking peculiarity of Shakespeare's mind' is 'its power of communication with all other minds' (Hazlitt 1910, 47).

At the same time, however, this passage from *The Catcher in the Rye* prompts us to reflect on at least two other points. First, it is not (not usually, anyway) a two-way friendship that a reader enjoys with an author. Indeed, this one-waywardness is part of the fantasy of reading: the 'author' is generally *not* someone whose telephone number you can readily acquire and with whom you really can become terrific friends in the way that Caulfield is suggesting. The author, in other words, is not so much an 'actual' author at all: rather, it is your personal projection, *your idea* of the author. Second, it is also the case that the author not only *may be* dead, but in some respects *is* dead, even when alive. Part of the irony and humour of this passage from Salinger's novel consists in the blurring of the distinction between living authors and dead ones. For despite his concern with the problem of giving Ring Lardner a ring, given that Ring Lardner cannot be rung (since he is dead), Holden Caulfield concludes his 'call-an-author' fantasy by saying he would like to 'call old Thomas Hardy up' – as if Hardy, though 'old', still lived. As we might all be reasonably expected to know, Thomas Hardy is (and was, well before 1951) in his grave. (Or to be more precise, in two graves: his heart is buried with the body of his first wife, in Stinsford churchyard, Dorset; the rest of him is in Westminster Abbey.)

A lot has been said and written over the past few decades about 'the death of the author'. This paradoxical idea refers not to the empirical or literal death of a given author, but to the fact that, in a radical sense, the author is absent from the text. 'The death of the author' became a catch-phrase primarily on account of an essay of that title, written by the French poststructuralist Roland Barthes and first published in 1967. Barthes's essay is flamboyant and provocative. In part, he is arguing against the very common ascription of authority to the figure of the author. People often ask, for example: 'Is that what Shakespeare (or Brontë or Dickens) really meant? Is that what the author intended?' Such questions reflect what W.K. Wimsatt and Monroe Beardsley described, in an essay first published in 1946 (rev. 1954), as 'the intentional fallacy' (Wimsatt and Beardsley 1995). In what became a conceptual corner-stone of Anglo-American New Criticism, they argued that 'the design or intention of the author is neither available nor desirable as a standard for judging the success of a literary work' (Wimsatt and Beardsley 1995, 90). All we have, they argued, is the text itself, and the work of criticism has no business inquiring into the quite separate question of its author's intentions. Indeed, Wimsatt and Beardsley contend that any answer to the question of what, for example, T.S. Eliot meant by 'Prufrock' 'would have nothing to do' with the poem itself (Wimsatt and Beardsley 1995, 99). Even if we were to go to a living author and ask what he or she meant by a particular text, all we would get would be another *text* (his or her answer), which would then, in turn, be open to interpretation. Just because it comes 'from the horse's mouth' does not mean that the horse is telling the truth, or that the horse *knows* the truth, or indeed that what the horse has to say about the 'words on the page' is necessarily more interesting or illuminating than what anyone else might have to say. As anyone who has read an 'interview with the author' will know, the words you get from the horse's mouth often tell us more about the horse than about the text we were trying to read: an author interview tends to take us away from the strange specificity of the literary work into the labyrinths of bio-graphy, projection and fantasy.

We could also ponder the question of 'authorial intention' in the light of psy-choanalysis. 'Conscious intention', in this respect, can always be considered as subject to the unconscious workings of the mind. With psychoanalysis, it is no longer possible simply to privilege consciousness as the sombre judge of what is intended. The jurisdiction of 'authorial intention' falters here: what is not meant can still (in another sense) be meant. 'I didn't mean to hurt you' might, after all, mean 'I did'. In the wake of psychoanalysis, in particular, it is difficult if not impossible to suppose that intention can ever be pure and unambiguous. Correspondingly, it is important to acknowledge some of the implications of twentieth-century linguistics (Saussure, Chomsky, Pinker) as regards this question of the author and his or her authority. Rather than say that the author is in control of the language that he or she uses, we might con-sider the idea that the language is as much in control of the author. In this respect, language can be thought of as a kind of system within which any writer must take a designated place: the system and rules of language inevitably dic-tate the possibilities of what someone can say. An author is not God, after all.

Barthes's essay provides a strong sense of the ways in which we need, if not to ridicule, at least to be sceptical about the idea of the author as the origin and end of the meaning of a text. But rather than solving the problem of interpretive authority, 'The Death of the Author' in certain respects simply transfers it. Barthes ends his essay by declaring that 'the death of the author' coincides with 'the birth of the reader' (Barthes 1977a, 118). But as we suggest in the preceding chapter, such a claim is manifestly problematic: after all, the critique of the notion of the Author (to which Barthes wittily gives a capital 'A', thus highlighting the putatively god-like attributes of this figure) is just as valid as a critique of the notion of the reader (who, in effect, simply acquires in Barthes's account a capital 'R' instead). Nevertheless his essay does offer some crucial and succinct remarks on the idea of the author and it remains a valuable account. Barthes writes:

> We know now that a text is not a line of words releasing a single 'theological' meaning (the 'message' of the Author–God) but a multi-dimensional space in which a variety of writings, none of them original, blend and clash. The text is a tissue of quotations drawn from the innumerable centres of culture . . . Once the Author is removed, the claim to decipher a text becomes quite futile. To give a text an Author is to impose a limit on that text, to furnish it with a final signified, to close the writing. (Barthes 1977a, 146)

In a sense the problem here is evident simply from the two words which frame the above quotation: 'Barthes writes'. We are still talking in terms of the author and there could be little more persuasive indication of the idea that the author is *not* dead (though Roland Barthes, sadly, is) than the use of the present tense: Barthes *writes*. But at the same time we need to be careful here. The 'death of the author', in Barthesian terms, is explicitly figurative or metaphorical, and we could say, by way of a sort of corrective to possible misreading in this context, that the author cannot die precisely because, as we've been suggesting, the author is – always has been and always will be – a ghost. Never fully present or fully absent, a figure of fantasy and elusiveness, the author only ever haunts. It is also important to stress that Barthes is not in fact talking about 'the author' but 'the Author'. Insofar as the metaphorical death makes sense, then, it is the death of a particular *concept* of the Author that is at stake. In this respect Barthes's essay has to be seen in its cultural and historical context, as providing a simplified but forceful articulation of a variety of intellectual positions that emerged in the 1960s, in France and elsewhere.

Barthes's essay should be read alongside Michel Foucault's 'What Is an Author?' (1969), an essay that is undoubtedly more systematic and rigorous in many respects. More drily but more carefully than Barthes, Foucault provides a forceful and luminous impression of the figure of the author as a *historical construction*. The idea of the author is not a timeless given: the figure and significance of the author varies across time, and from one culture to another, from one discourse to another and so on. As regards works of literature, Foucault is concerned to criticize the notion of the author as 'the principle of a certain unity of writing' (Foucault 1979, 151). In other words, like Barthes, he calls into question the idea that the author is a god-like or (in more Foucauldian terms) saint-like figure, that the author is the presiding authority or principle of coherence for the understanding of a text. He does this primarily by focusing on the historical and ideological determinations of the notion of the author. He notes, for example, that

> There was a time when the texts that we today call 'literary' (narratives, stories, epics, tragedies, comedies) were accepted, put into circulation, and valorized without any question about the identity of their author; their anonymity caused no difficulties since their ancientness, whether real or imagined, was regarded as a sufficient guarantee of their status. (Foucault 1979, 149)

And he emphasizes that, more recently, literary authorship has been integrally bound up with changes in law and questions of copyright and ownership of texts. Finally, like Barthes, Foucault is interested in the potentially revolutionary effects of writing. 'What Is an Author?' affirms the jubilatory – because anti-authoritarian (here the correlations between 'author' and 'authority' become explicit) – energies of a writing or discourse freed of the conventional impositions of authorship. Foucault emphasizes the paradox that, while we think of the author as 'a perpetual surging of invention', in fact 'we make him [or her] function in exactly the opposite fashion'. While we think of the author as endlessly creative, in other words, our practice of reading and criticism makes him or her into a locus of authority which confines meaning and significance to a single univocal strand. Foucault thus concludes: 'The author is therefore the ideological figure by which one marks the manner in which we fear the proliferation of meaning' (159). We want there to be an identifiable author for a text because this comforts us with the notion that there is a particular sense to that text.

Barthes and Foucault, among many others, are interested in thinking about literature in ways that do not depend on regarding the author as the origin of the meaning of a text or as the authoritative 'presence' in that text. Contemporary literary theory draws together threads from psychoanalysis (the 'I' is in many ways *by definition* not in control of itself, since it is determined by what it cannot control, in other words, by the unconscious), linguistics (language *speaks us* as much as we speak language), ethnology (creativity, authorship, etc. are differently constructed and conceived in different cultures) and feminism (the Author with a capital A is in many respects clearly – and oppressively – male: God, the Father, the patriarchal Presence). Nevertheless, the figure of the author remains a decisive force in contemporary culture – for all kinds of reasons, some of them entirely admirable. Thus in women's writing, for example, or in the study of supposedly non-mainstream (i.e. non-white, non-US-or-European, non-middle-class, non-heterosexual) writing, there has been and continues to be an emphasis on the person of the author, an emphasis that is in some ways quite conventional and 'conformist'. This emphasis is particularly characteristic of what has come to be known as identity politics. Such 'conformism' is understandable especially if, as theorists of such writing sometimes claim, it is presented as the initial step in a longer-term strategy of disturbing, dislocating and transforming anthropocentric, patriarchal, white, bourgeois or 'straight' values. In truth, however, the literary works that endure are those which exceed or elide all or any of the constraints imposed by identity politics.

At the same time it is also true that what we think about a particular text, how we read and understand it, can probably never be simply dissociated from what we know (or think we know) of its author. The fact that we know (assuming that we do) that John Keats died of tuberculosis at the tragically early age of 25 cannot but affect the way we read those prophetically poignant lines from 'Ode to a Nightingale' (1819), written only two years before his death:

> Now more than ever seems it rich to die,
>> To cease upon the midnight with no pain,
>>> While thou art pouring forth thy soul abroad
>>>> In such an ecstasy!
> Still wouldst thou sing, and I have ears in vain—
>> To thy high requiem become a sod.

Similarly, the fact that Ezra Pound made Fascist propaganda broadcasts on Italian radio cannot but affect the way that we read his *Cantos*. But it is still important to bear in mind that there is something deeply problematic about any straightforward reduction of a text to what we think we know of the author's life, thoughts, habits or ideas. In particular, the attempt to settle questions of interpretation through appeals to the intentions of the author cannot but be viewed with suspicion. It is not a question of simply denying or ignoring authorial intention: some hypothesis of what an author intends is an important element in reading and sense-making. But reading and sense-making invariably overflow 'mere' authorial intention. Correspondingly, we could say, it is not a question (as Barthes polemically argued) of simply 'removing' the author, but rather of acknowledging that s/he has a less central and authoritative, in some ways more ghostly role. In this respect, we might say, the author was dead from the start. Specifically, as Jacques Derrida has argued, an author is 'dead insofar as his [or her] text has a structure of survival even if he [or she] is living' (Derrida 1985a, 183). Like any piece of writing (even a text-message), a literary work is capable of outliving its author. This capacity for the text to live on is part of its structure, of what makes it a text. This is not something that the author can control. More generally, no author owns the meanings or the readings of his or her text.

As we have attempted to show, then, the idea of an author-centred reading is in various ways flawed. No doubt it will never be possible to give up the sense of phantasmatic identification with an author ('I love Emily Brontë', 'John Webster is my hero'). Nor, indeed, are we likely to stop reading literary biographies and being interested in the apparently tangential issues of authors' love affairs, their compositional practices or even, if all else fails, their shopping lists. But the relationship between life and work is highly complex and highly mediated, and a key to the authorial life is by no means necessarily a key to the literary text. Our identifications with and ideas about authors are, in the final analysis, themselves forms of fiction. We may speculate, fantasize and tell ourselves stories about an author; but the author is a sort of phantom. In keeping with the notion that the author is necessarily a ghost, we could suggest that the greatest literary texts are indeed those in which the author appears most spectral. The most powerful works of literature are those which suggest that they are singular, that no one else could have written them, *and yet* that their authorship is, in more than one sense, a phantom issue. One need think only, for example, of Chaucer's *Canterbury Tales*, the plays of Shakespeare, Emily Brontë's *Wuthering Heights*, Toni Morrison's *The Bluest Eye* or of course J.D. Salinger's *The Catcher in the Rye*, to realize that in a sense they tell us nothing about their authors, even if they are texts in which we feel their elusive presence in an especially forceful way. What Keats says of the poet is true of authors generally. The poet as poet has no identity (Keats 1958, 1:387): he or she lives, and lives on, in the strange space of writing.

Further reading

For a general introduction to author theory, see Andrew Bennett, *The Author* (2005). The brief essay entitled 'The Intentional Fallacy' (Wimsatt and Beardsley 1995) remains a valuable critical reference point for thinking about authorial intention. For a concise and thought-provoking more recent essay on 'Intention', see Annabel Patterson (1995), and see Irwin (1999). On the figure of the author more generally, Roland Barthes's 'The Death of the Author' (1977a) is vigorous and entertaining but should perhaps be read alongside his somewhat later essays, 'From Work to Text' (Barthes 1977b) and 'Theory of the Text' (in Young 1981), as well as Michel Foucault's classic essay 'What Is an Author?' (1979). For wide-ranging collections of critical and other material on the author, see Seán Burke, ed., *Authorship: From Plato to the Postmodern* (1995), Maurice Biriotti and Nicola Miller, eds, *What is an Author?* (1993), and William Irwin, ed., *The Death and Resurrection of the Author?* (2002). For collections of essays on authorship in film theory, see Caughie, ed. (1980), Gerster and Staiger, eds. (2003) and Wexman, ed. (2003). Mark Rose's *Authors and Owners* (1993) is an influential study of the introduction of copyright law and its influence on the 'invention' of the author in the eighteenth century. Similarly, for a study that challenges poststructuralist thinking on authorship, see Seán Burke's *The Death and Return of the Author* (2nd edn, 1998).

4. The text and the world

All of the chapters in this book are, in different ways, about the relationship between texts and the world. How do texts represent the world? Where does a text begin and end? Is an author an inhabitant of the world or the creation of a literary text? To what extent is history a kind of text? And what implications does this have for thinking about literature? Can literary texts do things to the world as well as simply describe it? These are some of the questions with which we engage in this book.

The relation between literary texts and the world has been a central problem in criticism and theory at least since the fourth century BC when Plato banished poets from his imaginary Republic for allegedly misrepresenting the world. The very phrase 'the text and the world', however, immediately presents a questionable distinction: its very formulation presupposes a difference between a text on the one hand and the world on the other. This distinction is, of course, a very common way of thinking about literature: it is implicit in a certain understanding of mimesis or imitation, and in notions of realism and naturalism, and of representation, as well as in metaphors which suggest that literary texts offer a window onto the world or (in Hamlet's words) hold a mirror up to nature. All of these ways of thinking about literary texts start from an assumed separation of the literary work, the text, from the world. They imply that a literary text is not, in essence, part of the world. Actually, over the centuries, writers have been trying to drive a stake into the heart of this assumption: the text–world dichotomy is like a vampire that will not lie down. The latest and most persistent of these vampire-killers are called post-structuralists. Poststructuralism (including new historicism, deconstruction, certain forms of feminism, postcolonialism and queer theory) consistently undermines the very terms of this text–world dichotomy. Michel Foucault puts the point in a Nietzschean way: 'if language expresses, it does so not in so far as it is an imitation and duplication of things, but in so far as it manifests . . . the fundamental will of those who speak it' (Foucault 1970, 290). Poststructuralists ask what it means to say that a literary text is different from, separate from the world. Shouldn't we say, rather, that such texts actually make up our world? How can an act of inscription or an act of reading *not* be part of the world? Is there a world without such acts? In a later chapter, we look at the ways in which texts may be considered as performative, as acts of language which themselves *do* things, as well as just talk about things. In this chapter, we shall explore the idea that literary texts are acts that destabilize the very notion of the world and that disturb all assumptions about a separation between world and text.

In order to consider this proposition, we shall discuss Andrew Marvell's poem 'To His Coy Mistress' (1681). The poem presents itself as a work of seduction. The speaker addresses his 'coy mistress' and attempts to persuade her to go to bed with him:

> Had we but world enough, and time,
> This coyness, lady, were no crime.
> We would sit down, and think which way
> To walk, and pass our long love's day.
> 5 Thou by the Indian Ganges' side
> Shouldst rubies find: I by the tide
> Of Humber would complain. I would
> Love you ten years before the flood:
> And you should, if you please, refuse
> 10 Till the conversion of the Jews.
> My vegetable love should grow
> Vaster than empires, and more slow.
> An hundred years should go to praise
> Thine eyes, and on thy forehead gaze.
> 15 Two hundred to adore each breast:
> But thirty thousand to the rest.
> An age at least to every part,
> And the last age should show your heart:
> For, lady, you deserve this state,
> 20 Nor would I love at lower rate.
>
> But at my back I always hear
> Time's wingèd chariot hurrying near:
> And yonder all before us lie
> Deserts of vast eternity.

25   Thy beauty shall no more be found;
     Nor, in thy marble vault, shall sound
     My echoing song: then worms shall try
     That long-preserved virginity:
     And your quaint honour turn to dust;
30   And into ashes all my lust.
     The grave's a fine and private place,
     But none, I think, do there embrace.

     Now, therefore, while the youthful hue
     Sits on thy skin like morning dew,
35   And while thy willing soul transpires
     At every pore with instant fires,
     Now let us sport us while we may,
     And now, like amorous birds of prey,
     Rather at once our time devour,
40   Than languish in his slow-chapped power.
     Let us roll all our strength, and all
     Our sweetness, up into one ball:
     And tear our pleasures with rough strife,
     Thorough the iron gates of life.
45   Thus, though we cannot make our sun
     Stand still, yet we will make him run.

As soon as we ask even the simplest questions about this poem we come up against the problem of representation, the problem of the relationship between the text and the world. Perhaps the most obvious question that we would want to ask is whether the poem should be read as *really* a poem of seduction: is the speaker the same as the poet and, if so, is this text really addressed to a woman Andrew Marvell knew? Or should we understand the speaker to be a fictional construction and the 'real' addressee to be another reader – us, for example – a reader or readers not explicitly addressed but nevertheless implied by the text? Most readings of the poem assume that the latter is the case, that rather than attempting to seduce a woman, this poem presents a fictional dramatization of such an attempt. In this sense, it may seem that the poem is categorically separate from the 'real' world and from 'real' people. But this poetic attempt at seduction does not just take place between a fictive woman and speaker. In various ways, 'To His Coy Mistress' challenges our thinking on fiction and the real. For example, regardless of whether the mistress is conceived as real or fictive, the poem has effects on us. In particular, such a poem can be considered as performative – in the sense that it performs an act not so much of sexual as of textual seduction. It tries to entice us to read and to read on and to draw us into another world – a world of reading that is both fictional and real.

But Marvell's poem does not stop here. It can be shown to engage with the world through the use of a number of specific discourses. The seduction is mediated not only by reference to other kinds of literary texts (poems of seduction, love poems, the *blazon*, the *carpe diem* or *memento mori* motif and so on), but also in terms of other kinds of discourse (biblical, classical, colonial, philosophical, scientific, military). In this respect, the poem could be seen as an example of what the Russian critic M.M. Bakhtin calls 'heteroglossia', in that it embraces a series of overlapping codes and discourses. This complex jumble of discourses positions the text in relation to 'the world' – even if we try to read the poem as simply fictional.

Indeed, rather than thinking of texts on one side and 'the world' on the other, we might reflect on the idea that everything human that happens in the world is mediated by language. Language, as Jean-Jacques Lecercle puts it, 'always reminds us that it, and no one else, is speaking, that whenever we believe we rule over our words, we are in the grip of an unavoidable but nevertheless delusive illusion' (Lecercle 1990, 265). In this context we could attempt to clarify the notoriously controversial statement by Jacques Derrida, in his book *Of Grammatology* (1976, 158, 163), that 'There is nothing outside the text'. This much quoted and much misunderstood slogan is, in fact, a misleading translation of the French sentence 'Il n'y a pas de hors-texte', which is perhaps better rendered as 'There is no outside-text'. The latter version is preferable because it is easier to see that it is saying something credible. When Derrida makes this statement he is talking about reading. His point is not that there is no such thing as a 'real world' but that there is no access to the real world of, for example, Marvell's poem, except through the language of the poem. In other words, there is no reading of 'To His Coy Mistress' that is not dependent, precisely, on language: the 'real world' of the poem is the poem. We cannot go beyond or transcend the text to Marvell's coy mistress since our only access to her is through the poem. But Derrida is also making a larger, more difficult claim, arguing that there is no way to conceive, imagine or even perceive 'the world' without stubbing our toes on the question of language. Put very crudely, Derrida suggests there is no access to 'the world' except, in the broadest sense, through language. 'Language' here need not be simply verbal, but may include everything that works as a system of signs. Even without words, for example, seduction is an affair of language – there is the language of eyes, gestures, touch, a complex olfactory system, and so on. Derrida and other theorists of deconstruction, then, regard the text–world opposition as untenable if also perhaps unavoidable. In this respect, those critics of Derrida who argue that his is a 'pure' textualism which cannot account for power or politics are simply failing to recognize – or choosing to ignore – the extent to which political, social, economic and historical forces are bound up in language, in discourse, in representation.

Some of these points may become clear if we take a closer look at a few details of Marvell's poem. The poem explicitly plays upon an opposition between text and world. It begins by claiming that if there were 'world enough, and time', the speaker would spend many hundreds of years praising the woman's beauty. Thus the opening verse-paragraph immediately establishes an opposition between words and deeds, between talking and making love, between language and the body – between the text and the world. And, in a self-consuming rhetorical gesture, the poem argues against any more discourse, any more talk. It argues for the disposal or rejection of speech in favour of action – the action of the joining of two bodies. In this sense, the whole poem may be read in terms of a conflict played out between the text and the world, an attempt to go beyond its own discourse to the body of the woman. At the same time, however, and paradoxically, the poem appears to suggest that this separation of text and world is itself impossible. The poem culminates in a rejection of speech or discourse and in a militaristic metaphor for the violent exchange between two bodies ('Let us roll all our strength, and all / Our sweetness, up into one ball: / And tear our pleasures with rough strife / Thorough the iron gates of life'). But this final rejection of speech in favour of action simply results in silence, the end of the poem: it does not, cannot, go beyond talk to the body of the woman. For the speaker, there is no escape from talk, language, discourse, no pure body without, outside of, this poem.

Nevertheless, at various points in the poem, the speaker does attempt to point beyond language, to refer to the woman's body – here and now. At the beginning of the third verse-paragraph, for example, he describes a blush which suffuses the woman's body:

> Now, therefore, while the youthful hue
> Sits on thy skin like morning dew,
> And while thy willing soul transpires
> At every pore with instant fires,
> Now let us sport us while we may . . .

What we might call the poem's 'fiction of immediacy' (the sense that the speaker is addressing a woman who is present and that the action of this poem takes place in 'real time') becomes fully apparent at this point, when the speaker refers directly to the altering state of the woman's body. In addition to the insistent deixis of 'Now . . . Now', this sense of immediacy is generated through complex *rhetorical* strategies. For example, the blush or sweat which 'transpires / At every pore' is read as a sign of the inner 'fires' produced by the 'willing soul' of the woman. In its most direct reference to the woman's body, at this 'instant', here and now, the poem is highly figurative. The complicated metaphoricity of these lines, their sheer insistent textuality, dissolves any illusion of corporeal presence. Moreover, as we have suggested, the speaker *interprets* the woman's blush just as we interpret his lines. The fiction of immediacy in Marvell's poem, the reiterated force of the 'now', is derived above all perhaps from the extraordinary turn that occurs at the start of the second verse-paragraph: 'But at my back I always hear / Time's wingèd chariot hurrying near'. This 'always' evokes the constant imminence of something, an unceasing urgency and apprehension that is always there, always 'hurrying near', regardless of whether we are reading or making love, writing or fighting.

'The text and the world' names a false opposition. Texts cannot but be part of the world. To talk about texts as 'representing' reality simply overlooks ways in which texts are already part of that reality, and ways in which literary texts *produce* our reality, make our worlds. In this respect we may be prompted to ask what is at stake not only in the narrator's but in Marvell's and in Western culture's representations of the female body. In particular, we might ask what is involved in the violence embedded within Marvell's figuration of the woman as a body and as dead – as a corpse. What is the relationship between aesthetic and erotic contemplation in this representation on the one hand and its imagining of the woman's death on the other? In her influential book *Over Her Dead Body: Death, Femininity and the Aesthetic* (1992), Elisabeth Bronfen has explored the multiple ways in which patriarchy figures the conjunction of femininity with death and the aesthetic, and the fact that the female body as an object of aesthetic contemplation is also bound up with a certain violence towards femininity, towards women. According to this thinking, the very status of Marvell's poem as a classic, as a showcase poetic urn in the imaginary museum of English literary history, its reproduction in classrooms, lecture theatres, anthologies and in books such as our own, produces and reinforces the cultural construction of 'woman' as allied with death and with the aesthetic. Indeed, Bronfen would argue that such a poem and its reception have a crucial social and cultural function since, like other representations of the death of a beautiful woman, the poem exemplifies patriarchy's repression of the fact of the (male) subject's own death by the displaced representation of that death in the 'other' (the woman). The linguist Roman Jakobson famously defines the 'poetic function' of language as 'a focus on the message for its own sake' (Jakobson 1960, 365), and the critical tradition has tended to respond to

Marvell's poem in just this way, reading it as a self-reflexive, autonomous work of art which transcends the interests of the world. But if instead we read it as a powerful and influential expression of the cultural construction of femininity, we see that the distinction that is embedded in our chapter title – between the text and the world – has dissolved.

Further reading

Edward Said's *The World, the Text, and the Critic* (1983), especially the title essay, persuasively argues the case for saying that 'a text in being a text is a being in the world'. An earlier and now classic argument for a similar position is contained in the work of Raymond Williams, whose 1961 book *The Long Revolution* (1992) has been deeply influential for British cultural materialism in particular. Roland Barthes's classic book *Mythologies* (1972) demonstrates the cultural construction of 'reality' or 'nature' in fascinating analyses of anything from soap powder to wrestling. Roger Fowler's *Linguistic Criticism* (1986) takes a linguistic perspective on questions raised in this chapter. Whiteside and Issacharoff, eds, *On Referring in Literature* (1987) collects a number of essays on the problem of reference in relation to literary texts. For a challenging but brilliant exploration of questions of mimesis and the materiality of writing, see Tom Cohen's *Anti-Mimesis from Plato to Hitchcock* (1994). Alongside and rather more accessible than Bronfen's *Over Her Dead Body* (1992) is Peter Brooks's lucid and thought-provoking *Body Work* (1993), which also considers the representation of bodies – especially female bodies – in nineteenth- and twentieth-century art and literature. For two powerful and very different accounts of writing and/through the body of a woman, see Luce Irigaray, 'This Sex Which is Not One' (1985) and Hélène Cixous, 'The Laugh of the Medusa' (1990). Another way in which the 'world' is articulated in literature is investigated in ecocrticism: see Chapter 16, below, on this question and see especially Coupe, ed., *The Green Studies Reader* (2000), for debates on the question of representation in this context.

5.   The uncanny

Literature is uncanny. What does this mean? To try to define the uncanny is immediately to encounter one of its decisive paradoxes, namely that it has to do with a *troubling* of definitions, with a fundamental disturbance of what we think and feel. The uncanny has to do with a sense of strangeness, mystery or eeriness. More particularly it concerns a sense of unfamiliarity which appears at the very heart of the familiar, or else a sense of familiarity which appears at the very heart of the unfamiliar. The uncanny is not just a matter of the weird or spooky, but has to do more specifically with a disturbance of the familiar. Such a disturbance might be hinted at by way of the word 'familiar' itself. 'Familiar' goes back to the Latin *familia*, a family: we all have some sense of how odd families can seem (whether or not one is 'part of the family'). The idea of 'keeping things in the family' or of something that 'runs in the family', for instance, is at once familiar and potentially secretive or strange. As an adjective 'familiar' means 'well acquainted or intimate', 'having a thorough knowledge', etc., but as a noun it carries the more unsettling, supernatural sense of 'a spirit or demon supposed to come to a person *esp* a witch, etc, at his or her call' (*Chambers Dictionary*). We might think here, for example, of the demonic 'familiar' that is said to haunt Bertha Mason in Charlotte Brontë's *Jane Eyre* (1847) or, more comically, of the 12-year-old Maud's 'supernatural companion' in Elizabeth Bowen's superb novel *A World of Love* (1955).

Here are a couple of examples of the uncanny. First: you walk into a room in a house you have never visited before and suddenly you have the sense that you *have* been there before and that you even seem to know what will happen next. This kind of experience has even developed its own name, *déjà vu*. Or, second example: you are in some public place (a shop perhaps or a train) and you catch sight of someone whom you think looks rather disturbing, and then you realize that you have caught sight of this person reflected in a window or a mirror and that this person is yourself.

These examples could be described as so-called 'real life' occurrences. But are they in fact 'real life'? If, as we shall see, the uncanny is especially relevant to the study of literature, it also has to do with how the 'literary' and the 'real' can seem to merge into one another. On the one hand, uncanniness could be defined as occurring when 'real', everyday life suddenly takes on a disturbingly 'literary' or 'fictional' quality. On the other hand, literature itself could be defined as the discourse of the uncanny: literature is the kind of writing which most persistently and most provocatively engages with the uncanny aspects of experience, thought and feeling. In some ways this is in keeping with the sort of conception of literature theorized by the Russian formalists of the early twentieth century, especially Viktor Shklovsky. Literature, for the Russian formalists, has to do with *defamiliarization* (*ostranenie*): it makes the familiar strange, it challenges our beliefs and assumptions about the world and about the nature of 'reality'. Bertolt Brecht's argument that theatre should produce 'alienation effects' is an obvious analogy here. For Brecht, no actor is supposed to identify completely with the character he or she plays. Likewise the spectator is encouraged to feel dissociated, uneasy, alienated. In accordance with this, Brecht's concern is to demonstrate that the 'real' is not something that is simply a *given*: it is not something definite and immutable, but is constructed through human perception, language, beliefs and assumptions, and consequently it is something that can be changed. In Brechtian terms, the alienating or defamiliarizing power of drama – and art and literature more generally – lies in its capacity to transform us and the world around us. In this chapter we shall argue that these ideas about the power of art to disturb, defamiliarize or shake our beliefs and assumptions are intimately bound up with the uncanny. The uncanny – in particular as first elaborated by Freud, in his essay of that title (Freud 1985b) – is central to any description of the literary.

The uncanny has to do with making things *uncertain*: it has to do with the sense that things are not as they have come to appear through habit and familiarity, that they may challenge all rationality and logic. Let us nevertheless suggest, thirteen unlucky forms that the uncanny can take:

1. Repetition. For example, strange repetition of a feeling, situation, event or character. Two obvious examples of the uncanny, in this respect, would be the experience of *déjà vu* (the sense that something has happened before), and the idea of the double (or *doppelgänger*).

2. Odd coincidences and, more generally, the sense that things are *fated* to happen. Something might happen, for example, that seems 'too good to be true' or that suggests, despite the fact that you do not believe in God, that someone or something is pulling the strings.

3. Animism. This is the rhetorical term referring to a situation in which what is inanimate or lifeless is given attributes of life or spirit. In the last sentence of Emily Brontë's *Wuthering Heights* (1847), for example, we read of 'the soft wind breathing through the grass' – a potentially uncanny instance of animism.

4. Anthropomorphism – that is to say, a more specific (because specifically human) form of animism. It is the rhetorical figure that refers to a situation in which what is not human is given attributes of human form or shape: the legs of a table or the face of a cliff would be examples of anthropomorphism, though they might not immediately or necessarily provoke a feeling of uncanniness. In a similar fashion, children's toys and fairy tales present many possibilities for thinking about anthropomorphism: we may think of such things (dolls or household utensils coming to life and talking) as decidedly *not* uncanny, but there is perhaps also a strange, potential slipperiness here. It is perhaps not by chance that children and children's toys loom large in certain books and films about the supernatural. (A fairy tale is not as far from a horror story as we might initially suppose.) An uncanny story frequently involves a mingling of such elements. It is crucial to the strange and disturbing atmosphere of Charlotte Perkins Gilman's story *The Yellow Wallpaper* (1892) that the room in which the narrator is confined is a former children's nursery. More immediately and more obviously uncanny, however, would be the anthropomorphic character of the wallpaper in this room. There is, for example, the moment when the narrator tells us about the 'kind of sub-pattern' in the wallpaper: 'in the places where [the wallpaper] isn't faded and where the sun is just so – I can see a strange, provoking, formless sort of figure, that seems to skulk about behind' (18).

5. Automatism. This is a term that can be used when what is human is perceived as merely mechanical: examples of this would be sleepwalking, epileptic fits, trance-states and madness. The narrator of *The Yellow Wallpaper* would clearly fit into this category (especially when she is 'creeping' round and round her room at the end), but a sufficiently careful reading of, say, Keats's trance-like 'Ode to a Nightingale' (1819) might also prove interesting in this context. The question at the end of Keats's poem is about trance and, perhaps, madness. In a sense it is a question that haunts literature in general: 'Do I wake or sleep?' To suggest briefly

one other example, the writing of D.H. Lawrence is full of people in states of trance and seizure. Towards the end of 'The Rocking-Horse Winner' (1912), for instance, there is a description of Paul and his mother: 'The Derby was drawing near, and the boy grew more and more tense. He hardly heard what was spoken to him, he was very frail, and his eyes were really uncanny. His mother had sudden seizures of uneasiness about him' (745). Robots and other automata (such as Terminator), on the other hand, are also potentially uncanny, for the opposite reason: what is perceived as human is in fact mechanical.

6. A sense of radical uncertainty about sexual identity – about whether a person is male or female, or apparently one but actually the other. This is made dramatically clear, for instance, in the uncanny revelation in the course of Neil Jordan's film *The Crying Game* (1992), when an apparently female character turns out to have the genitalia of a man; but we could also think of the uncanniness of gender in, for example, Virginia Woolf's *Orlando* (1927), Jeanette Winterson's *Sexing the Cherry* (1989) and *Written on the Body* (1992), and Jeffrey Eugenides's *Middlesex* (2002).

7. A fear of being buried alive. This may seem a somewhat refined example of the uncanny, but it is relevant insofar as it is related more broadly to images or experiences of claustrophobia, of being unexpectedly and unpleasantly stuck (for instance in an elevator, or in a swamp, or simply in a room with the last person in the world you would like to be left alone with). An extreme but fascinating instance of the uncanny in this context would be Edgar Allan Poe's story 'The Premature Burial' (1844) – about a man who has an obsessive fear of being buried alive and goes to great trouble and expense to have his family crypt designed in such a way as to allow him to escape, in the (one might have thought laughably unlikely) event of being buried alive by mistake. In a broader sense, however, we could reflect on the uncanny feelings encountered in all the aspects of being locked in, of enclosure and confinement, in Brontë's intensely claustrophobic *Wuthering Heights* or in Tennyson's short but extraordinarily evocative poem 'Mariana' (1830).

8. Silence. Intriguingly, this is an example proposed by Freud, though he himself is effectively silent on the subject of what makes it uncanny. The potentially uncanny qualities of silence are particularly evident in a work such as Henry James's *The Turn of the Screw* (1898). There is, for example, the strangely silent encounter on the stairs, between the governess and the dead Peter Quint:

> It was the dead silence of our long gaze at such close quarters that gave the whole horror, huge as it was, its only note of the unnatural. If I had

met a murderer in such a place and at such an hour we still at least would have spoken. Something would have passed, in life, between us; if nothing had passed one of us would have moved. The moment was so prolonged that it would have taken but little more to make me doubt if even *I* were in life. I can't express what followed it save by saying that the silence itself . . . became the element into which I saw the figure disappear. (135)

9. Telepathy. This is an uncanny idea not least because it involves the thought that your thoughts are perhaps not your own, however private or concealed you might have assumed them to be. Literature is pervaded by examples of the telepathic. Alongside some of the texts already mentioned, such as *Jane Eyre, Wuthering Heights*, 'The Rocking-Horse Winner' and *The Turn of the Screw*, we might think, for instance, of George Eliot's *The Lifted Veil* (1878) – the very title of which gestures towards uncanny relevation. Eliot's narrator, Latimer, describes how he suddenly becomes capable of reading others' thoughts. In this way he presents an uncanny example of one of the most fundamental characteristics of narrative fiction: he becomes a telepathic narrator.

10. Death. In particular, death as something at once familiar – 'all that lives must die', as Gertrude puts it (*Hamlet*, I, ii, 72) – and absolutely unfamiliar, unthinkable, unimaginable. As the Anglican *Book of Common Prayer* declares: 'In life we are in the midst of death.'

11. The death drive. This term, initially deriving from Sigmund Freud's remarkable essay of 1920, 'Beyond the Pleasure Principle' (Freud 1984), refers to the idea that everyone at some level (consciously or unconsciously) is driven by a desire to die, to self-destruct, to return to a state of inanimacy. By a sort of uncanny reversal or displacement of perspective, then, life would not be about living, progressing and developing, about pleasure, vitality and staying healthy. Instead, and without our even necessarily realizing it, life is about what W. B Yeats calls the 'longing for the tomb' (Yeats 1977), in other words an uncannily strange return or recurrence (the desire to return to non-being, the desire *not to be*). Literature is packed with examples. We might think, once again, of *Wuthering Heights*, 'The Rocking-Horse Winner', 'Ode to a Nightingale', 'Mariana' or, of course, *Hamlet*.

12. Ghosts. In some ways, perhaps, this is the uncanny par excellence. The notion of the ghost unsettles all distinctions between being alive and being dead, the real and the unreal, the familiar and the unfamiliar. A ghost is the very embodiment of strange repetition or recurrence: it is a revenant, it *comes back*. (For more on this particular form of uncanniness, see Chapter 18.)

13. Language. The word 'uncanny' is singular: it is not just a case of something being 'weird', 'spooky', or 'eerie'. An uncanny feeling or experience
is intimately bound up with language, and more particularly perhaps
with a kind of *crisis in relation to language*. We call it 'uncanny' but we are
also rather at a loss, we experience uncertainty, we encounter (however
fleetingly) the sense of something *beyond language*, unnamable.

In sum, then, the uncanny can be described as the thoughts and feelings
that may arise on those occasions when the homely becomes unhomely,
when the familiar becomes uncomfortably strange or the unfamiliar becomes
strangely familiar. Alternatively, the uncanny is – in the words of the German
philosopher F.W.J. Schelling – that which 'ought to have remained . . . secret
and hidden but has come to light'. Schelling's definition of the uncanny is
quoted by Sigmund Freud in his essay, published in 1919, entitled 'The
"Uncanny"' ('Das Unheimliche'). In fact, most of the account of the uncanny
which we have given so far is indebted to this extraordinary text. When Freud
chose to write an essay on the uncanny he was opening up a very strange can
of worms.

Freud's essay is largely focused on literature and in particular on a reading of E.T.A. Hoffmann's story 'The Sand-Man' (1816). In this respect it
is slightly unusual, since Freud wrote comparatively little that could be
described as literary criticism or literary theory. But few of Freud's essays have
had a more pervasive impact on literary studies. What is especially fascinating
about Freud's essay is the way in which it prompts us to ask various questions
about *boundaries* and *limits*: How much of Freud's essay is psychoanalysis
and how much is literature? Where does reason become imagination and
imagination reason? Where does science become fiction and fiction science?
Where does literature end and literary criticism or literary theory begin?

It has become something of a truism to note that Freud's writings can be
thought about in at least two basic and quite different ways. First, there is the
Freud of the so-called popular imagination: Freud the patriarchal, bourgeois,
nineteenth-century Viennese Jew, who believed that everything has to do with
sex. This Freud has very firm views and spouts these in the form of rather
mechanically predictable theories, the most celebrated and fundamental
of which is perhaps the Oedipus complex. Second, however, there is the other
Freud, a Freud who did not fully realize what he was saying, who was for
various reasons (historical as much as personal) unable to see or develop the
implications of what he was saying, not least because these implications regularly exceed or interfere with his own proposed themes and assumptions.
This second Freud is a Freud who is, we could say, different from himself, and

who constitutes what is sometimes referred to as 'the new Freud' or 'French Freud' (in acknowledgement of the work done by the French psychoanalyst Jacques Lacan and others), a result in other words of what has been called 'the rereading of Freud' or 'the return to Freud'.

Freud's 'The "Uncanny"' provides one of the most dramatic and stimulating manifestations of these two Freuds. On the one hand there is the Freud who believes (and in some sense *needs* to believe) that literature and psychoanalysis can be simply and clearly separated off from each other, and that psychoanalysis can significantly contribute towards a scientific and objective understanding of literary texts. On the other hand, there is the Freud who shows (often only inadvertently) that the 'literary' is stranger and more disturbing than psychoanalysis, science or rationalism in general may be able or willing to acknowledge. The essay gives us two Freuds, or a kind of double-Freud, and this double spends the essay investigating the importance among other things of the idea of the double. What makes the double uncanny? According to Freud's essay, the double is paradoxically both a promise of immortality (look, there's my double, I can be reproduced, I can live forever) and a harbinger of death (look, there I am, no longer me here, but there: I am about to die, or else I must be dead already). The notion of the double undermines the very logic of identity.

All of this is suggested, in fact, by the English title of Freud's essay, where the word 'uncanny' is in quotation marks. This putting-into-quotation-marks itself constitutes potential breeding grounds for the uncanny – for the 'uncanny' is in a sense always in quotation marks. The uncanny might thus be thought of as a kind of ghost-effect that haunts all words, however self-evident or 'familiar' they may appear to be. We could illustrate this most easily perhaps by trying to imagine what it would be like if proper names (such as 'London', 'Hillary Clinton', 'God') were suddenly used only in quotation marks – thus giving a new sense to the phrase 'scare quotes'. Language itself, then, becomes uncanny. Indeed, very often the more *familiar* a word, the more uncanny it can become. Every 'word', for example, is capable of being put into quotation marks and the act of putting it into quotation marks makes that word a little strange, as if different from itself, referring to something or somewhere else. This is a general point, also, about repetition: repetition of a word ('Words, words, words', as Hamlet says) can give rise to a sense of hollowness, strangeness, even spookiness.

Repetition is a key aspect of the uncanny, as Freud's essay makes clear. The uncanny is not simply a matter of the mysterious, bizarre or frightening: as we have tried to suggest, it involves a kind of *duplicity* (both doubling and deception) within the familiar. This logic of the uncanny, whereby the familiar turns into, or becomes contaminated by, the unfamiliar, is evident in the word 'uncanny' (or, in German, '*unheimlich*') itself. 'Uncanny' is the opposite of 'canny', meaning 'skilful', 'shrewd', 'knowing' (from Old English *kunnan*, 'to know', especially in the sense 'to know how to be able to do something'). But the word 'canny' shades into its opposite: in Scottish English in particular, 'canny' can suggest *unnatural* or *excessive* skilfulness, shrewdness or knowing. This capacity for a word to contain or to turn into its opposite is what Freud elsewhere talks about as the 'antithetical' meanings of 'primal words' (see Freud 1957a). We consider another example of this in Chapter 30, where 'pleasure' can be seen – at least in certain contexts – to entail its opposite ('pain'). Masochism is the term conventionally used to gloss this contradictory logic according to which pain can be pleasure or pleasure pain.

Analysis of the word 'uncanny' seems ineluctably, even fatalistically, bound up with an experience *of* the uncanny, an experience which disturbs any attempt to remain analytically detached and objective. This is strikingly clear from the early pages of Freud's essay, in which he seeks to show how the German word for 'homely' ('*heimlich*'), with its connotations of 'private', 'hidden', 'secret', inevitably conceals its opposite – the 'unhomely' or *unheimlich*. From this it may be concluded that the uncanny cannot readily be avoided or denied: ultimately, the uncanny is aligned with death. As a form of strange disruption, questioning and uncertainty, the idea of the uncanny may be frightening, but it also continues to be a crucially important and productive area for literary study.

The uncanny, then, is an experience – even though this may have to do with the unthinkable or unimaginable. It is not a theme which a writer uses or which a text possesses. The uncanny is not something simply present like an object in a painting. It is, rather, an effect. In this respect it has to do with how we read or interpret (interestingly, it makes no difference here whether we are talking about something in a book or something in the so-called outside world). In other words, the uncanny has to do, most of all, with effects of reading, with the experience of the reader. The uncanny is not so much *in* the text we are reading: rather, it is like a foreign body within ourselves.

Further reading

For a book-length study dealing with many of the concerns of this chapter, see Nicholas Royle's *The Uncanny* (2003). For two accessible and rather different discussions of the uncanny in literature, see Terry Apter's chapter in *Fantasy Literature* (1982) and J. Hillis Miller's essay on the uncanny and *Wuthering Heights*, in his *Fiction and Repetition* (1982). On the historical background to the concept of the uncanny, see Terry Castle's *The Female Thermometer* (1995) and Mladen Dolar's ' "I Shall Be with You on Your Wedding-night" ' (1991). Hillel Schwartz's *The Culture of the Copy* (1996) offers some fascinating perspectives on doubles and dual-thinking, from 'identical twins' to 'parallel universes'. For a good collection of essays on various aspects of the uncanny, including the first English translation of Ernst Jentsch's 'On the Psychology of the Uncanny' (1906), see *Home and Family* (1995), ed. Sarah Wood. On defamiliarization, the classic essay is Shklovsky's 'Art as Technique' (1965), but for an earlier engagement with similar ideas, see Shelley's crucial and widely reprinted 1821 essay 'A Defence of Poetry'. On theatre and alienation, 'A Short Organum for the Theatre' (Brecht 1978) is terse and stimulating. On fairy tales and the uncanny, see Jack Zipes (1988). On telepathy and the uncanny, see Royle's *Telepathy and Literature* (1991). Freud's 'The "Uncanny" ' remains an extremely rich and surprising text (see Freud 1985b, as well as the new Penguin translation in Freud 2003). For some of the more challenging readings of Freud's essay, see Samuel Weber (1973, 2000), Hélène Cixous (1976), Neil Hertz (1979) and Jane Marie Todd (1986). On 'the return to Freud', see Samuel Weber's fine study of that title (1992). For especially good general introductions to psychoanalysis and literature, see Ellmann, ed., *Psychoanalytic Literary Criticism* (1994) and Wright, *Psychoanalytic Criticism: A Reappraisal* (1998).

6.   Monuments

Thou art a monument without a tomb,
And art alive still while thy book doth live,
And we have wits to read, and praise to give.

Ben Jonson's poem 'To the Memory of My Beloved, The Author, Mr. William Shakespeare, And What He Hath Left Us' was originally published as a preface to the First Folio edition of Shakespeare's collected plays in 1623, just seven years after the Bard's death. In these lines Jonson addresses the topic of this chapter: the nature of the literary monument and the way in which the writings of living authors are posthumously transformed into monuments to those authors' lives and work. The poet is, in Jonson's seemingly paradoxical formulation, a 'monument without a tomb', and is 'alive still' despite his death. The paradox that Jonson explores involves the idea that the poet is both alive and dead: after his death the poet still 'lives' through the 'life' of his 'book', which itself lives just as long as we read it and praise it. Exploring this paradox of the literary afterlife, the poem is performative. It *performs* an act of monumentalization, since it is designed not only to remind the reader of the value of Shakespeare's work (the word 'monument', we may remind ourselves, originates in the Latin *monere*, to remind) but also, in so doing, to establish that value. In fact, the publishing venture to which Jonson contributes his poem plays a crucial part in the monumentalization of the poet: the publication of a posthumous 'Collected Works' is itself a sign of the importance of the dead poet's work, an index of his genius. Contrary to Dryden's sense that the poem was 'an insolent, sparing, and invidious panegyric' (quoted in Donaldson 1988, 718), Jonson's intention seems to have been to 'honour' Shakespeare. This is the first stage in the poet's transcendence of his time and in his establishment as a 'classic'. Shakespeare 'was not of an age', Jonson asserts, 'but for all time!' (l.43).

The Second Folio of Shakespeare's plays, published nine years later in 1632, included an anonymous sixteen-line poem (written in fact by John Milton) entitled 'An Epitaph on the Admirable Dramatic Poet, W. Shakespeare'. Like Jonson's poem, Milton's begins by remarking on the fact that the poet had been buried in Stratford rather than, as might be thought more appropriate, Westminster Abbey (where, as Jonson notes, Chaucer, Spenser and Francis Beaumont are buried). Milton also plays on the opposition of life and death in the idea that Shakespeare has built for himself a 'live-long monument'. But he develops Jonson's notion of the relationship between reading and monumentalization by exploring the idea that we, readers, through our 'wonder and astonishment' at Shakespeare's art, are made 'marble with too much conceiving'. For Milton, we ourselves are monuments to the poet's genius, his living tomb:

> What needs my Shakespeare for his honoured bones
> The labour of an age in piled stones,
> Or that his hallowed relics should be hid
> Under a star-ypointing pyramid?
> Dear son of memory, great heir of fame,
> What need'st thou such weak witness of thy name?
> Thou in our wonder and astonishment
> Hast built thyself a live-long monument.
> For whilst to the shame of slow-endeavouring art,
> Thy easy numbers flow, and that each heart
> Hath from the leaves of thy unvalued book,
> Those Delphic lines with deep impression took,
> Then thou our fancy of itself bereaving,
> Dost make us marble with too much conceiving;
> And so sepulchred in such pomp dost lie,
> That kings for such a tomb would wish to die.

Both Jonson and Milton, then, articulate a series of questions around the idea of the monument, around the idea of the monumentalization of literary texts. How does an author enter the 'canon'? What is the relationship between monumentalization and reading? Do literary texts become static, frozen into their own tombs of eternity, or do they change with time and with each new generation? What is at stake in the literary critical process of canonization and monumentalization? What is gained and what lost? Literary texts, as the epitaphs by Jonson and Milton suggest, are themselves places where such questions are inaugurated, first posed and first pondered.

As we have seen, Jonson and Milton both express a certain ambivalence in their sense of the value of the monument and the process of monumentalization. They assert that Shakespeare needs no physical tomb, a structure that is at once a reminder of life and signifier of death. The third and fourth lines of Milton's poem sneer at the idea that Shakespeare's 'hallowed relics should be hid / Under a star-ypointing pyramid'. The lines suggest that the act of remembering, of monumentalizing the poet, is also an act of hiding, disguising, defacing him, and they remind us that this is precisely what we do when we bury the dead: by burying them we honour them but at the same time we hide them from sight, as if they are as much objects of terror and taboo as they are of veneration and awe. As Jonson and Milton recognize, the acts of monumentalization in which they are engaged when they write on Shakespeare are also acts of burial. And it might be argued that we are engaged in a similar dynamic whenever we read, talk and write about literary texts – not least, of course, when we write works of literary criticism. As Paul de Man has argued in an essay on Shelley, the transformation of literary texts into 'historical and aesthetic objects' involves a certain burial of those texts: what we do with dead poets, he remarks, 'is simply to bury them, to bury them in their own texts made into epitaphs and monumental graves' (de Man 1984, 121). The impulse to honour the dead, that is to say, is at the same time an impulse to bury them, to do away with them, to forget them, to be done with them. This, it might be said, is the fundamental tension of the institution of literary studies, an irreducible conflict between at once remembering and forgetting the dead.

The paradox is broached rather differently in Frank Kermode's *The Classic* (1975), a book that has itself become a minor classic in discussions of literary value, the canon and the nature of the institutionalization of literature. Kermode comments on the tension between endurance and changeability that constitutes the canon: 'the books we call classic possess intrinsic qualities that endure, but possess also an openness to accommodation which keeps them alive under endlessly varying dispositions' (Kermode 1975, 44). Just as Jonson defines Shakespeare as 'not of an age but for all time', so Kermode is attempting to think about the way that such a text or such an oeuvre 'speaks' to all generations and is as such 'timeless'. But he also suggests that it can only be 'timeless' by signifying differently at different times, so that it is, as such, time-bound. For Kermode, it is the possibility of a certain 'openness' to interpretation, what he terms the text's 'accommodation', which allows what we call a 'classic' to survive. Kermode evokes a sense of the classic as the living dead, surviving endlessly on or in new readers. His account has certain implications for notions of authorial intention and for ideas about the limits of interpretation: if a literary text can be read and reread at different times, in accordance with their varying (conscious *and* unconscious) interests, prejudices, ideas and conventions, then it would seem that the text cannot be limited to a single or univocal interpretation. If this position is correct, Kermode comments, we must somehow 'cope with the paradox that the classic changes, yet retains its identity'. And this has the further consequence that the text must be 'capable of saying more than its author meant', even if it were the case that saying 'more than he meant was what he meant to do'. Strange as it might seem, a 'classic' author may have meant what he or she cannot have known that he or she meant. Ultimately, Kermode suggests, 'the text is under the absolute control of no thinking subject' and is 'not a message from one mind to another' (Kermode 1975, 80, 139).

These ideas about the canon, about literary survival and about the nature of the 'classic', bring us back to questions of meaning, interpretation and authorial intention which we address elsewhere in this book. But here we are also concerned with another question, one that is equally fundamental to this book and to the practice and discipline of literary criticism more generally: the question of literary value. Readers will no doubt have noticed the way in which Bennett and Royle repeatedly employs terms of valuation: we refer, for example, to Milton's 'great epic poem' in Chapter 1, to Elizabeth Bowen's 'superb' novel in Chapter 5, to the opening paragraph of *Middlemarch* as 'extraordinary' in Chapter 8, to Sheridan's *The School for Scandal* as 'one of the greatest eighteenth-century English comedies' in Chapter 12. We also repeatedly use such terms as 'haunting', 'powerful', 'disturbing', 'singular' to suggest our positive valuation of texts, and seem to ascribe value, more or less explicitly, to aspects of texts that we see as funny, complex, undecidable, unsettling, and so on. In other words, Bennett and Royle, like any other work of literary criticism or theory, is benetted and embroiled in value judgements. This situation is unavoidable: even if we were to exclude value-laden terms from our critical vocabulary, we (have to) choose certain texts to read and talk about and such choices can in themselves be taken to imply judgements of value. Indeed, it may be said that the primary aim of critical discourse, the impulse for talking about books, is to persuade someone else to appreciate what the critic finds valuable about a literary text.

The bases on which judgements about literary value are made, however, are not easy to define. One of the most intriguing things about T.S. Eliot's classic essay 'What is a Classic?' (1945) is the way that he repeatedly uses the word 'mature' as a kind of talisman to express what he sees as valuable in literary texts. Indeed, for Eliot, in this essay at least, it amounts to the very definition of a classic: 'If there is one word on which we can fix, which will suggest the maximum of what I mean by the term "a classic", it is the word *maturity*' (Eliot 1975, 116). He then goes on to use the words 'mature' (as adjective and verb) and 'maturity' a total of 23 times in the same paragraph: ripeness is certainly all, it would seem, as far as Eliot is concerned. Eliot's essay was written in 1944. He was 56 in that year, which might be one reason why maturity seemed so attractive to him. It's possible, of course, that four years of world war also had some influence on this thinking – if only because maturity was at a premium, so many of the young having died in battle. Either way, it would seem strange now, in the twenty-first century, to find a critic so confident about the values to be ascribed to the notion of 'maturity'. In general, it might be said, 'mature' is no longer part of the critical vocabulary of value. And what strikes us now about Eliot's use of the word is the fact that he nowhere says what he means by it, what he means when he says that a literary text is 'mature'. We can all tell when a peach is ripe but can we tell a mature poem from an immature one? What do we do with it – squeeze it? Is Shelley's *Adonais* mature? Is it more or less mature than Pope's *Essay on Man*, or Spenser's *Epithalamion*, or Eliot's *The Waste Land*? Is maturity even seen as valuable any more? As a critical term, 'mature' has become almost risible. And yet, for Eliot, it is crucial to his project of exploring the notion of the 'classic' and to his concept of literary value. This is not to say that Eliot was foolish or irresponsible in his terminology: rather, it exemplifies the fact that critical vocabularies change over time while always being in any case somewhat porous, unstable, contentious. In the eighteenth century, the vocabulary of value included ideas of proportion, probability and propriety; the Romantics developed a vocabulary of the sublime, imagination and originality; while nearer to our time, the New Critics valued complexity, paradox, irony and tension in poems, and postmodern critics valorize disjunction, fragmentation, heteroglossia, aporia, decentring.

Alongside changes in critical vocabulary, there are changes in how literary monuments are perceived and valued. The most obvious example would be the reception of Shakespeare himself. While Jonson and Milton declared, very soon after his death in 1616, that Shakespeare had earned a place in the literary canon, in fact his reputation developed much more slowly and patchily than this would suggest. Indeed, during much of the eighteenth century his work was criticized as brilliant but faulty: he was seen as a poet of 'nature' rather than learning, and was faulted for his versification and diction, his endless punning, his handling of plot and characterization, the improbability of his narratives, for not obeying the unities of time and place, and so on (see Vickers 1981, 1–86). It was only towards the end of the eighteenth century that an unalloyed and arguably uncritical sense of Shakespeare's monumental and timeless genius became commonplace. Indeed, throughout the eighteenth and even into the nineteenth century his plays were regularly rewritten to iron out his faults and make him more amenable to contemporary tastes. Thus *King Lear* was never performed on the English stage in its original form during the eighteenth century because its ending was held to be too gloomy – a happier, more appropriate ending was written for it by Nahum Tate in 1681 and became the standard acting text. In the present day, the perception and valuation of Shakespeare remains deeply indebted to the Romantic conception of his work as sublime, even sacred. At the same time, this conception of Shakespeare has undergone radical demystification and deconstruction in the work of such critics as Terence Hawkes, Jonathan Dollimore, Joel Fineman, Catherine Belsey, John Drakakis, Margreta de Grazia and others.

In recent years, much attention has been given to the construction of the literary canon. In particular, critics have explored the ways in which the canon is bound up with questions of education, class, economics, race, ethnicity, colonization, sexual and gender difference, and so on. This has led to a large-scale reassessment of both the canon itself and how evaluations take place. The notion of literary value as an inviolable essence has disintegrated. Our sense of the apparently impersonal and autonomous realm of the aesthetic has been irrevocably complicated. More than ever we are made aware of how far our own individual judgements are subject to social, political and institutional constraints. More than ever we are made aware of how far the canon is a fabrication. Thus, for example, critics have devoted much energy in recent years to discovering or rediscovering women writers and writers from different racial and ethnic backgrounds whose work has been neglected. In the case of women writers, it is often argued that such authors have been overlooked precisely because they are women, since, with a few notable exceptions (Austen, the Brontës, Woolf, Plath, for example), the patriarchal ethos of the literary critical establishment has tended to efface or marginalize women's writing in general. The publication of such anthologies as Gilbert and Gubar's *Norton Anthology of Literature by Women* (1985), Roger Lonsdale's *Eighteenth-Century Women Poets* (1989), Andrew Ashfield's *Romantic Women Poets* (1995, 1998), and Angela Leighton and Margaret Reynolds's *Victorian Women Poets: An Anthology* (1995), have altered the shape of the canon in and beyond the academy. More generally, what Elaine Showalter calls 'gynocriticism' and publishing ventures such as Virago and the Woman's Press have altered our literary historical maps by rediscovering numerous forgotten (or never recognized) authors, and critics have devoted a great deal of energy to the work of re-editing their writings, as well as to the critical, biblio- and biographical tasks of new evaluations.

Such reassessments and rediscoveries force us to face a series of difficult and complex questions concerning literary value and critical evaluation. Is literary value eternal and unchanging or is it contingent and dependent on readers and the institutions of criticism? Are we simply constructing new, exclusive canons when we discover 'neglected' writers, or are we rethinking the whole idea of 'the canon' and canonization? Is there such a thing as literary value? If so, how can it be described and defined? What are we doing when we make such judgements? Is there, as Steven Connor argues, an 'imperative' or 'necessity' of value (Connor 1992, 8)?

The recent rethinking of the canon, then, involves both a reassessment of which texts should be in the canon and a rethinking of the idea of the canon itself. Such reassessments have hardly gone unchallenged. One of the most stubbornly provocative challenges to what, in his view, has become the modern critical orthodoxy, is Harold Bloom's *The Western Canon* (1994). Bloom's 'single aim' is to 'preserve poetry as fully and purely as possible' against the politicizing of what he calls the 'school of resentment'. For Bloom, the school of resentment is typified by those critics who argue that the literary critical institution has valorized the work of 'dead white males' at the expense of the work of marginalized writers – women, say, or Afro-Caribbeans or Hispanics or gays or the working classes (Bloom 1994, 18). For these 'resentful' critics, the work of criticism cannot be disengaged from the work of social and political critique since the traditional canon operates as an ideological justification of the values (often racist, heterosexist, patriarchal, colonial and elitist) of the male, Western, establishment figures which it enshrines. For Bloom, by contrast, literature is and should be an antisocial body of work. Literary texts, he argues, even work *against* political and social improvement: indeed, for Bloom, great writers 'are subversive of all values'. Reading their work with a view to forming our 'social, political, or personal moral values' would merely make us 'monsters of selfishness and exploitation' (29). The canon, for Bloom, is elitist and discriminatory or it is nothing. Accordingly, his book is itself elitist. Bloom lists the 3,000 books and authors that he claims make up the Western canon. He then narrows this down to 26 books/authors to which his volume is devoted. In the final analysis, though, Bloom's canon comes down to a single author by whose work all else must be judged. We will not be surprised by now to learn that that author is William Shakespeare. Bloom's argument for the Western canon relies, finally, on Shakespeare's unique genius:

> Shakespeare's eminence is, I am certain, the rock upon which the School of Resentment must at last founder. How can they have it both ways? If it is arbitrary that Shakespeare centres the Canon, then they need to show why

the dominant social class selected him rather than, say, Ben Jonson, for that arbitrary role. Or if history and not the ruling circles exalted Shakespeare, what was it in Shakespeare that so captivated the mighty Demiurge, economic and social history? Clearly this line of inquiry begins to border on the fantastic; how much simpler to admit that there is a *qualitative* difference, a difference in kind, between Shakespeare and every other writer, even Chaucer, even Tolstoy, or whoever. Originality is the great scandal that resentment cannot accommodate, and Shakespeare remains the most original writer we will ever know. (Bloom 1994, 25)

Bloom is compelling. The apparent continuity in the valuation of Shakespeare from the eighteenth century to the present does indeed seem to validate such a judgement of his work as a unique and uniquely original phenomenon, and this is confirmed by what seems to be our instinctive sense on reading him that we are encountering something original, unique, 'for all time'. It is hard to get round our sense, our intuitive sense, on reading Shakespeare, that his work is simply, unquestionably richer, more complex, more endlessly fertile, than that of other writers, even of other 'canonical' writers.

And yet, and yet . . . Still we might have nagging doubts. How do we know that our 'intuition' is not itself a learned response, that our 'instinctive' sense of Shakespeare's genius is not, itself, a result of our schooling? If we see our appreciation of Shakespeare as an effect of social conditioning, we might feel that his work does not have the eternal qualities we thought it did. Moreover, we might notice that Bloom's 'explanation', his offering of the case of Shakespeare as a final arbiter for his judgement about aesthetic judgement, tells us nothing about the grounds for such claims: indeed, the questions that Bloom poses for the 'school of resentment' might also be asked of his own work, since his account of Shakespeare as *different*, as *original* and so on, is no more an explanation than the 'history' or 'class' which his opponents offer. Bloom's is, finally (and proudly), a monumentalizing gesture: his very language allies Shakespeare with the material of the tomb itself in its metaphor of the 'rock', and eternalizes him and abstracts him from history in its comment that he is 'the most original writer we will ever know'. We are led back, then, to the question with which we began this chapter: is that what we want of our writers? Monuments?

It might seem ironic that what would appear to be the deeply conservative, reactionary, elitist position of Harold Bloom should find confirmation in the writings of that monument of socialism, Karl Marx. And yet Marx himself affirms the sense that, as far as art goes, the crucial question is not how artists reflect on or are influenced by their time but rather just the strange fact of their survival:

the difficulty lies not in understanding that the Greek arts and epic are bound up with certain forms of social development. The difficulty is that they still afford us artistic pleasure and that in a certain respect they count as a norm and as an unattainable model. (Marx 1973, 111; Quoted in Guillory 1993, 322)

This, then, is what remains to be explained: the way that literary works remain with us, haunt us, still, beyond the conditions of their production, whatever may be our legitimate concerns for human and social justice. Just this remaining, this endurance of the haunting singularity of the literary text, is what keeps us coming back to it as our preoccupations, desires, prejudices and commitments change. What baffles and enthrals – what Bloom is responding to in his flawed but deeply productive defence of the canon – is the singularity and uncanny *force* of the literary. It is this characterization of Shakespeare as a 'monument without a tomb' – a monumentalizing *and* anti-monumentalizing phrase – that Bloom shares with Jonson. And it is the undecidable nature of such gestures, the sense that we bury poets as we raise monuments of reading to them and our sense that, still, they hold over us an uncanny, haunting power, which brings us to them, brings us back to them.

Further reading

Much, often highly polemical work, has been published on the so-called 'canon wars' in the last few years, evincing the high institutional and pedagogical stakes involved in how canons are formed and regarded. Barbara Herrnstein Smith's *Contingencies of Value* (1988) offers a persuasive proposal for a pragmatic sense of literary value and the canon. John Guillory's *Cultural Capital* (1993) is a densely argued polemic for the 'inevitability of the social practice of judgement' and of the inextricability of aesthetic and economic 'value'; Guillory is influenced by the work of the French sociologist Pierre Bourdieu, whose *Distinction: A Social Critique of the Judgement of Taste* (1984) offers an important account of the social, cultural, economic and political issues embedded in decisions about the value of literary and other works. Henry Louis Gates's *Loose Canons* (1992) engages with issues raised in this chapter, especially regarding racial and ethnic difference. On postcolonialism and the canon see John Thieme, *Postcolonial Con-texts* (2001). For studies of the creation of the English canon, see Kramnick, *Making the English Canon* (1998) and Ross, *The Making of the English Literary Canon* (1998). On the canonization of Shakespeare, see Michael Dobson, *The Making of the National Poet* (1992), and Gary Taylor, *Reinventing Shakespeare* (1990).

Within the specifically English critical tradition of the twentieth century, perhaps the most influential and opinionated work is that of F.R. Leavis, who is happy in, for example, *The Great Tradition* (1948), sweepingly to dismiss great swathes of literature (an author such as Laurence Sterne is relegated to a dismissive footnote) and to try to reduce the novel tradition to just four writers: an amusing and enlightening book to read, still, for insights into the rhetoric of *doxa* and unreflective prejudice in canon formation.

7. Narrative

Stories are everywhere: in movies, sitcoms, cartoons, commercials, poems, newspaper articles, novels, computer games and websites. We all make use of stories every day and our lives are shaped by stories – stories about what happened in our dreams or at the dentist, stories about how we fell in love or the origins of the universe, stories about war and about peace, stories to commemorate the dead and to confirm a sense of who we are. In this chapter, we propose to circle around the following propositions:

1. Stories are everywhere.
2. Not only do we tell stories, but stories tell us: if stories are everywhere, we are also in stories.
3. The telling of a story is always bound up with power, with questions of authority, property and domination.
4. Stories are multiple: there is always more than one story.
5. Stories always have something to tell us about stories themselves: they always involve self-reflexive and metafictional dimensions.

Roland Barthes suggests that falling in love involves telling ourselves stories about falling in love: in this sense, he argues, 'mass culture is a machine for showing desire' (Barthes 1990c, 136). Disagreements, arguments, even wars, are often the result of conflicting stories concerning, for example, the rights to a piece of land: the real reason for both the first Gulf War (1991) and the second Gulf War (2003–) may have been oil, but the technical justification for going to war turned on the story of who owned or should own a particular piece of Kuwait in the first instance and the existence or otherwise of weapons of mass destruction in the second. Academic, 'objective' or 'scientific' discourses are constructed as stories. The historian Hayden White has given special emphasis to the fact that history is written in the form of certain kinds of narrative, that the task of the historian is to 'charge . . . events' with 'a comprehensible plot structure' (White 1978, 92). Science is composed of stories: astronomy attempts to narrate the beginnings of the universe; geology seeks to tell the story of the formation of mountains and plains, rivers, valleys and lakes; and like Rudyard Kipling's *Just So Stories*, evolutionary psychology purports to tell us the story of how we came to be as we are. For many centuries, millions of people have come to understandings about their place in the world, the meaning of their lives and the nature of politics, ethics and justice through stories about the lives of Christ, Buddha or the prophet Muhammad. The narrative of class struggle and emancipation from peasant society to the dictatorship of the proletariat has had a profound influence in the past 150 years. And in the twentieth century, Sigmund Freud produced a new and scandalous story about the nature of childhood. To say that Christianity, Buddhism, Islam, Marxism and psychoanalysis involve stories is not to suggest that they are merely fictive. Rather, it is to register the fact that there are few aspects of life which are not bound up with strategies and effects of narrative.

The simplest way to define narrative is as a series of events in a specific order – with a beginning, a middle and an end. We might think about James Joyce's short story 'The Dead', from *Dubliners* (1914), to illustrate the point. Put very simply, the story begins with the arrival of Gabriel and his wife Gretta at a party, tells of the events of the party and the couple's walk home, and ends as they fall asleep in their hotel. What is important in this description is the temporal ordering of what happens. By contrast, lyric poems, for example, are not typically thought to express or depict a series of temporally ordered series of events. One of the ways in which lyric poetry is defined, in fact, is by the absence of any such representation of events – lyric poems characteristically use the present tense and exploit a sense of the presence of the speaker in the act of meditating or speaking. Percy Bysshe Shelley's 'To a Sky-Lark' (1820) recounts no events, but is an effusion of the poet's sense of the bird's 'unpremeditated art' which he attempts both to define and in some ways to reproduce. Similarly, while Seamus Heaney's 'bog poems' from *North* (1975) might dig up buried narratives of victimization, sacrifice and atonement, their lyric tone gives a sense of an individual poet responding, now, to what he sees. Narrative, however, is characterized by its foregrounding of a series of events or actions which are connected in time. What happens at the end of 'The Dead' is determined by what happened earlier. The events are recounted more or less chronologically in Joyce's story, in that the order of the telling follows the order of the told: first we learn of Gabriel and Gretta's arrival, then of the party, and finally of what happens back at the hotel. But narratives also invariably involve what the narratologist Gérard Genette has called anachronisms – flashbacks, jumps forwards (or prolepses), the slowing down and speeding up of events and other distortions of the linear time-sequence (Genette 1986). Texts such as Virginia Woolf's 'The Mark on the Wall' (1921) dislodge our sense of temporal sequence. The story begins: 'Perhaps it was the middle of January in the present year' (Woolf 1982, 41). This suggests that the events recounted span a number of months, but by the end we have the sense that the story follows the wanderings of the narrator's consciousness over only a number of minutes or, at most, hours. Despite this and many other distortions of chronological order, however, Woolf's text is only readable insofar as it exploits our *expectations* of narrative sequence. Indeed, these distortions themselves can only be conceived against a background of linear chronological sequence.

Time, then, is crucial to narrative. But as the novelist E.M. Forster recognizes in *Aspects of the Novel* (1927), the temporal ordering of events is not the whole story. Forster makes a memorable distinction between 'The king died and then the queen died' on the one hand, and 'The king died, and then the queen died of grief' on the other (Forster 1976, 87). While the first 'narrative' includes two events related in time, he proposes, the second includes another 'connection', the crucial element of causality. The first simply lists two events, while the second provides the thread of a narrative by showing how they are related. The logical or causal connections between one event and another constitute fundamental aspects of every narrative. An obvious example would be detective stories. Detective stories rely, above all, on our expectation and desire for connection. They produce quite complex routes to a revelation of whodunnit, routes both determined and detected by the logic of cause and effect.

The beginning–middle–end sequence of a narrative also tends to emphasize what is known as a teleological progression – the *end* (in Greek, *telos*) itself as the place to get to. A lyric poem does not seem to rely on its ending to provide coherence: the end is not typically the place where all will be resolved. By contrast, we often think of a good story as one that we just cannot put down, a novel we compulsively read to find out what happens at the end. The narrative theorist Peter Brooks has studied ways in which readers' desires are directed towards the end, ways in which narratives are structured towards, or as a series of digressions from, an ending:

> we are able to read present moments – in literature and, by extension, in life – as endowed with narrative meaning only because we read them in

anticipation of the structuring power of those endings that will retrospect-ively give them the order and significance of plot. (Brooks 1984, 94)

Likewise, Brooks has elaborated the paradoxical ways in which the dénoue-ment or tying up of a story is worked towards through the paradox of digres-sion. Thus, for example, while we may find a novel, film or play frustrating if it contains too many digressions from the main plot, we enjoy the suspense involved in delaying a denouement. 'Suspense' movies, thrillers and so on, in particular, exploit this strangely masochistic pleasure that we take in delay. One of the paradoxical attractions of a good story, in fact, is often understood to be its balancing of digression, on the one hand, with progression towards an end, on the other.

But what is this end which we so much desire? (We may find out in more detail below, in Chapter 34.) Brooks and others have suggested that narratives move from a state of equilibrium or stasis through a disturbance of this stabil-ity, and back to a state of equilibrium at the end. The end of a narrative, the state of equilibrium, occurs when the criminal is discovered, when the lovers get married, or when the tragic hero dies. In addition, this end is characteris-tically the place of revelation and understanding. A part of the equilibrium that endings apparently offer is the satisfaction of epistemophilia, the reader's desire to know (from the Greek *episteme*, knowledge, and *philia*, love). And because of the conventional emphasis on hermeneutic discovery at the end, endings tend to be particularly over-determined places: we look to the end to provide answers to questions that the text has raised. In modernist narratives such as Woolf's 'The Mark on the Wall', however, these answers tend to be withheld or else treated ironically. The ending of Woolf's story is paradoxical, in fact, in that it resolves the question with which the story starts out – what is the mark on the wall? – by telling us that it is a snail. But this 'answer' to the question simply parodies those conventional realist endings that seem to clear up our confusions and satisfy our curiosity. So what if it is a snail? To say that the mark is a snail is an example of what is called an aporia – an impassable moment or point in narrative, a hermeneutic abyss. If we ask what Woolf's story is 'about', we realize that it is about itself as a story. The ending tells everything, it gives us 'the answer', and it tells us nothing: it is not for this 'answer' that we have read the story. Our epistemophilia proves to be perverted.

One of the most fundamental distinctions in narrative theory is that between 'story' and 'discourse'. As Jonathan Culler has suggested, a funda-mental premise of narratology is that narrative has a double structure: the level of the told (story) and the level of telling (discourse) (Culler 1981). These levels have been given different names by different theorists – the Russian formalists call them *fabula* and *sjuzhet*; the French structuralists call them either *récit* (or *histoire*) and *discours*, and so on. 'Story', in this sense, involves the events or actions which the narrator would like us to believe occurred, the events (explicitly or implicitly) *represented*. 'Discourse', on the other hand, involves the way in which these events are recounted, how they get told, the organization of the *telling*. In fact, of course, these two levels can never be entirely separated, and much narrative theory has been concerned to describe ways in which they interact. Thus Charlotte Brontë's *Jane Eyre* and Joyce's 'The Dead', for example, present the events of the narrative more or less in the order that they are alleged to have occurred. By contrast, texts such as Emily Brontë's *Wuthering Heights* and Woolf's 'The Mark on the Wall' move forward and backward in time and shift from the level of telling to that of the told in complex and unnerving ways. Many modernist and postmodernist texts experiment with the relation between these two levels, to denaturalize or defamiliarize our sense of how narratives function. A text such as Robert Coover's short story 'The Babysitter' from *Pricksongs and Descants* (1969), for instance, presents several slightly different accounts of what appears to be the same evening from a number of different perspectives: the contradictions and dislocations produced within and between these accounts, however, make it impossible, finally, to determine the precise nature or order of the evening's events. Alain Robbe-Grillet's novels, such as *The Voyeur* (1955) and *Jealousy* (1957), also recount the 'same' series of events over and over again, but from the 'same' narratorial perspective: each telling, however, is subtly different, thus dissolving our sense of any one, true, narrative of events. Rather than reading such texts simply as exceptions or aberrations, we might consider ways in which they metafictionally reflect on the multiplicity of any narrative – its susceptibility to different readings, its differing narrative perspectives, its shifting senses of place and time.

Everything that we have said about narrative up to this point has concerned the sense of its linearity: narrative involves a linear series of actions connected in time and through causality. In addition to this linearity, we might consider another important aspect of narrative, namely the relation between teller and listener or reader. Indeed, rather than appealing to the idea of a sequence of events, Barbara Herrnstein Smith has argued that we need to ground our understanding of narrative in terms of 'someone telling someone else that something happened' (Smith 1981, 228). The significance of this proposition is that it redirects our focus from the events or actions themselves to the relationship between the author or teller and the reader or listener. As Jonathan Culler has put it, 'To tell a story is to claim a certain authority, which listeners grant' (Culler 1997, 89). Much of the work in narrative theory has involved attempts to discriminate among different kinds of narrators (first person or third person, objective or subjective, reliable or unreliable, so-called 'omniscient' or not, together with questions concerning his or her 'point of view', his or her 'voice' and so on). Our understanding of a text is pervaded by our sense of the character, trustworthiness and objectivity of the figure who is narrating. Moreover, it is often very important to discriminate between the narratorial point of view and that of the so-called implied author – a particularly important distinction in certain ironic texts, for example. Although Jonathan Swift's essay 'A Modest Proposal' (1729) would not usually be considered as a narrative, it does provide one of the classic examples of narratorial irony. In this essay, the narrator proposes that in order to deal with poverty and hunger in Ireland and to prevent children of the poor from being a burden to their parents, such children should be sold to the rich as food – a solution that would be 'innocent, cheap, easy, and effectual' (509). The narrator appears to make his proposal seriously but we necessarily conceive of an 'implied author' who has very different views and motives, and who is making a political point about the immorality of the English government in its attitude towards poverty in Ireland. Our understanding of the ironic force of the text necessitates a discrimination between the two voices or personae of the narrator and the implied author.

A consideration of the relationship between teller and listener or reader leads in turn to questions of power and property. One of the most famous storytellers is Scheherazade from *A Thousand and One Nights* (a collection of tales that originated in the Middle East in the ninth–tenth centuries). In these classical Arabic narratives, Scheherazade has been sentenced to death by the king but is able to stave off her execution by telling him stories. By ending her story each night at a particularly exciting point, she is able to delay her death for another day because the king wants to find out what happens next. What makes *A Thousand and One Nights* so intriguing for narrative theorists has to do with its enactment of forms of power. As Ross Chambers proposes, 'To tell a story is to exercise power' (Chambers 1984, 50). Chambers argues that storytelling is often used, as in the case of Scheherazade, as an 'oppositional' practice, a practice of resistance used by the weak against the strong: 'oppositional narrative', he claims, 'in exploiting the narrative situation, discovers a power, not to change the essential structure of narrative situations, but to *change its other* (the "narratee" if one will), through the achievement and maintenance of authority, in ways that are potentially radical' (Chambers 1991, 11). In this respect, we might consider the motives and effects of Gretta's story of her dead lover in 'The Dead': perhaps the ending of Joyce's narrative should be understood in terms of the diffusion of Gabriel's egoistic, domineering and even rapacious desire for his wife by Gretta's narration of her love story. Gretta, subject to patriarchal society's insistence on the husband's rights to the wife's body, displaces her husband's unwanted attention by telling him a story. The violence of Gabriel's desire is expressed in references to his longing 'to be master of her strange mood . . . to cry to her from his soul, to crush her body against him, to overmaster her' (248). By the middle of Gretta's narration, Gabriel sees himself, by contrast with the lover of her story, as a 'ludicrous figure . . . idealizing his own clownish lusts' and a 'pitiable fatuous fellow' (251). And by the end, all lusts and all passions and anger, all mastery and desire, have dissolved: 'Gabriel held her hand for a moment longer, irresolutely, and then shy of intruding on her grief, let it fall gently and walked quietly to the window' (253). This conflict of stories – Gabriel's about himself and Gretta's about her dead lover – results in a disturbance of power relations. In this sense, just as much as 'The Mark on the Wall', or the stories of Coover and Robbe-Grillet, 'The Dead' is self-reflexively about the power of stories. More often, of course, it is the dominant ideology which is able to tell stories about, for example, how it got to be the dominant ideology. In the Soviet Union, it was the Bolsheviks and later the Stalinists who got to write the history books. In present-day China, the 1989 Tiananmen Square 'massacre' (as it is called in the West) is not in the history books at all and literary works that attempt to represent it, such as Ma Jian's *Beijing Coma* (2008), are officially banned. At the same time, Chairman Mao still figures in textbooks as a largely benevolent and wise figure (despite what are acknowledged in China as his 'excesses' and what are generally regarded in the West as his 'atrocities'), since his 'thought' continues to be the basis for current doctrine and policy of the ruling Chinese Communist Party (see http://english.cpc.people.com.cn/66095/4471924.html).

The power exerted by Scheherazade and by Gretta is a specifically *narrative* power. The only way that these storytellers can avoid death on the one hand and violent passion on the other is by making their stories good, by making them compelling to the point of distraction. By contrast, as far as the Soviet Union was concerned, for example, the Stalinist version of history did not even have to be plausible, because its lessons would be enforced in other ways. *Narrative* power, then, may be the only strategy left for the weak and dispossessed: without narrative power, they may not be heard. The social and political importance of stories is eloquently expressed by the old man in Chinua Achebe's novel *Anthills of the Savannah* (1987): 'The sounding of the battle-drum is important; the fierce waging of the war itself is important; and the telling of the story afterwards – each is important in its own way' (123–4). But, the man continues, the story is 'chief among his fellows':

'The story is our escort; without it we are blind. Does the blind man own his escort? No, neither do we the story; rather it is the story that owns us and directs us. It is the thing that makes us different from cattle; it is the mark on the face that sets one people apart from their neighbours.' (124)

Stories own us, and tell us, Achebe suggests, as much as we own or tell stories.

There are many questions of narrative, then, which may be considered in relation to literature: temporality, linearity and causality, so-called omni-science, point of view, desire and power. But most of all, perhaps, it is the relation between narrative and 'non-' or 'anti-narrative' elements that fascinate and disturb. Aspects such as description, digression, suspense, aporia and self-reflection, temporal and causal disorders are often what are most com-pelling in narrative. A text such as Woolf's 'The Mark on the Wall', indeed, *has* no narrative outside of description and aporetic reflections on the nature of narrative. Correspondingly, Joyce's 'The Dead' depends to a large extent on moments of what Joyce refers to elsewhere as 'epiphany', moments of revel-ation or understanding, moments that appear to stand outside time, outside of narrative. As Gabriel watches his wife listening to a piece of music as they prepare to leave the party, there is just such a moment – a moment of revelation which is also a moment of mystery. Gretta, standing listening to a song is, for Gabriel, full of 'grace and mystery . . . as if she were a symbol of something' (240). Like Scheherazade's, Joyce's storytelling holds off, and hangs on, death. And as the snow falls on the world outside the hotel window at the end of the story, as Gabriel falls into unconsciousness and the narrative slips away, there is another moment of epiphany, a dissolution of time, of space, of life, of identity, desire and narrative.

Further reading

Wallace Martin, *Recent Theories of Narrative* (1986), Shlomith Rimmon-Kenan, *Narrative Fiction* (2002) and H. Porter Abbott, *The Cambridge Introduction to Narrative* (2002) all provide good, clear introductions to narrative theory, while David Herman, ed., *The Cambridge Companion to Narrative* (2007) is a useful collection of clear and helpful accounts of various dimensions of the topic. See also Herman, Manfred John and Marie-Laure Ryan, eds, *The Routledge Encyclopaedia of Narrative Theory*, for a compre-hensive survey of the field, and Gerald Prince, *A Dictionary of Narratology* (2004) for concise accounts of its principal concepts. J. Hillis Miller's essay 'Narrative' (1990) is a concise and accessible summary of a number of paradoxes in narrative. Gérard Genette's *Narrative Discourse* (1986) is an influential systematic account of the structure of narrative. Another modern classic which takes as its focus questions of narrative perspective is Dorrit Cohn's *Transparent Minds* (1978). Peter Brooks's *Reading for the Plot* (1984) explores ways in which narrative may be thought about in relation to readers' desires; on the 'epistemophilic urge' in narrative, see his *Body Work* (1993). A good short summary of feminist perspectives on narrative theory is Margaret Homans's 'Feminist Fictions and Feminist Theories of Narrative' (1994); see also Lidia Curti, *Female Stories, Female Bodies* (1998). James Phelan has collected some useful and provocative essays on narrative and its relationship to issues of reading in *Reading Narrative* (1989) and in his more recent co-edited collection (with Peter Rabinowitz), *A Companion to Narrative Theory* (2005). Seymour Chatman's *Coming to Terms* (1990) is an incisive summary of narrative theory in relation to literary texts and film, and is especially useful in its discussion of ideas of narrative perspective and point of view. For a critique of traditional narratology from a poststructuralist perspective, see Andrew Gibson, *Towards a Postmodern Theory of Narrative* (1996). For a valuable and wide-ranging collection of essays on narrative theory, from Plato to Trin Minh-Ha, focusing in particular on 'classic' structuralist approaches and poststructuralist provocations, see Martin McQuillan, ed., *The Narrative Reader* (2000).

8.   Character

Characters are the life of literature: they are the objects of our curiosity and fascination, affection and dislike, admiration and condemnation. Indeed, so intense is our relationship with literary characters that they often cease to be simply 'objects'. Through the power of identification, through sympathy and antipathy, they can become part of how we conceive ourselves, a part of who we are. More than two thousand years ago, writing about drama in the *Poetics*, Aristotle argued that character is 'secondary' to what he calls the 'first essential' or 'lifeblood' of tragedy – the plot – and that characters are included 'for the sake of the action' (Aristotle 1965, 40). Considerably more recently in an essay on the modern novel, 'The Art of Fiction' (1884), the novelist Henry James asked, 'What is character but the determination of incident? What is incident but the illustration of character?' (James 1986, 174). While Aristotle makes character 'secondary' to plot, James suggests that the two are equal and mutually defining. Indeed, the novels and plays we respond to most strongly almost invariably have forceful characters as well as an intriguing plot. Our memory of a particular novel or play often depends as much on our sense of a particular character as on the ingenuities of the plot. Characters in books have even become part of our everyday language. Oedipus, for example, has given his name to a condition fundamental to psychoanalytic theory, whereby little boys want to kill their fathers and sleep with their mothers. Mrs Malaprop in Sheridan's play *The Rivals* (1775) has given us the word 'malapropism' when someone uses, for example, the word 'illiterate' to mean 'obliterate' (see I.2.178). A 'romeo' denotes a certain kind of amorous young man resembling the hero of Shakespeare's *Romeo and Juliet* (*c.* 1595). When we refer to someone as a 'scrooge', we mean a miser, but when we do so we are alluding, knowingly or not, to the protagonist of Charles

Dickens's *A Christmas Carol* (1843), for whom Christmas is a fatuous waste of time and money. Vladimir Nabokov's novel *Lolita* (1958) has given us a term for what the *OED* defines as 'a sexually precocious schoolgirl', as well as a word which especially through the Internet has acquired an association with the sexual abuse of children. There is even a day named after a fictional character, 'Bloomsday' (16 June), after Leopold Bloom in James Joyce's *Ulysses* (1922).

But what is a person or a character in a literary work? What does it mean to talk about a character as 'vivid' or 'life like'? How do writers construct characters and produce the illusion of living beings? What is the relationship between a person in a literary text and a person outside it? As we shall try to demonstrate, these are questions that books themselves – in particular plays, novels and short stories – consistently explore. In this chapter, we shall focus, in particular, on the nineteenth-century realist tradition. It is, we suggest, this tradition which has culminated in the kinds of assumptions that we often hold about people and characters today. And it is against such preconceptions that modernist and postmodernist texts tend to work.

Charles Dickens's novels are indisputably from the nineteenth century. Whether or not they can be described as 'realist', though, is very definitely a matter of dispute. But this very uncertainty makes the novels particularly intriguing for a discussion of character since they tend both to exploit and to explode 'realist' conventions of characterization. *Great Expectations* (1860–1) opens with the orphan-hero, Pip, examining the writing on his parents' gravestones in order to attempt to determine the 'character' of his mother and father:

> As I never saw my father or my mother, and never saw any likeness of either of them (for their days were long before the days of photographs), my first fancies regarding what they were like, were unreasonably derived from their tombstones. The shape of the letters on my father's, gave me an odd idea that he was a square, stout, dark man, with curly black hair. From the character and turn of the inscription, '*Also Georgiana Wife of the Above*', I drew a childish conclusion that my mother was freckled and sickly. (35)

The comedy of this passage is partly produced by the double sense of 'character' – as the shape of an inscribed letter on a tombstone and as the personality of a human being. The text implies that our knowledge of people is determined by writing, by the character of written words. Although he is 'unreasonable', in taking the shape of letters to denote character, Pip is not simply mistaken in recognizing that our sense of our self and of other people is developed through language. For as this passage clearly indicates, we construct ourselves through and in words, in the image-making, story-generating power of language. In this respect, it is significant that the opening to *Great*

Expectations explores one of the major themes of literary texts: the question 'Who am I?' One fascination of characters in fiction and drama, as well as one of their most 'characteristic' activities, is to suggest answers to this question, not only for themselves, but also for us.

To talk about a novel such as *Great Expectations* as 'realist' is in part to suggest that its characters are 'lifelike', that they are like 'real' people. But what does this mean? The first requirement for such a character is to have a plausible name and to say and do things that seem convincingly like the kinds of things people say and do in so-called 'real life'. The second requirement is a certain complexity. Without this complexity, a character appears merely 'one-dimensional', cardboard or (in E.M. Forster's terms) 'flat' (Forster 1976, 73). To be lifelike, a fictional character should have a number of different traits – traits or qualities which may be conflicting or contradictory: he or she should be, to some extent, unpredictable, his or her words and actions should appear to originate in multiple impulses. Thirdly, however, these tensions, contradictions, multiplicities should cohere in a single identity. Thus 'lifelikeness' appears to involve both multiplicity and unity at the same time. In the classic nineteenth-century realist novel *Middlemarch* (1871–2), for example, there is a character called Lydgate of whom George Eliot observes: 'He had two selves within him', but these selves must 'learn to accommodate each other' in a 'persistent self' (182). It is this tension, between complexity and unity, that makes a character like Lydgate both interesting and credible. The importance of such unity in realist texts is made clear by works like Robert Louis Stevenson's *The Strange Case of Dr Jekyll and Mr Hyde* (1886) or, less melodramatically, Joseph Conrad's 'The Secret Sharer' (1910): these narratives can be called 'limit texts' in that they use the framework of lifelike or realistic characters to explore what happens when the self is demonically split or doubled. In doing so, such texts challenge the basis of realism itself.

Realist characterization presupposes a 'mimetic' model of literary texts whereby what is primary or original is a real person, and a character in a book is simply a copy of such a person. Such a model does not allow for a reversal of this relationship: it does not allow for the possibility that, for example, a person in 'real life' might be convincing to the extent that he or she resembles a person in a book. On the face of it, such a reversal may sound rather strange or counter-intuitive: we would normally want to give priority to a 'person' and say that characters in books are more or less like 'real' people. In fact, however, as the example of *Great Expectations* suggests, it is easy to demonstrate that things also work the other way round. Indeed, literary history contains various dramatic instances where 'life' copies fiction. After the publication of Goethe's *The Sorrows of Young Werther* in Germany in 1774, for example, there was a fashion among young men in Europe for suicide, an act modelled on the suicide of the eponymous hero of that novel. Similarly, J.D. Salinger's novel *The Catcher in the Rye* (1951) was held responsible for the antisocial behaviour of numerous young men in the United States in the 1950s and early 1960s who identified with the disaffected hero Holden Caulfield. The young, in fact, are often considered (by the old) to be in danger of mimetic dissipation, to endanger themselves, their families and society because they identify with and then copy the actions and attitudes of disreputable people in books or, more recently, in films, on TV, in videos or computer games.

This paradox of character whereby people in books are like 'real' people who are, in turn, like people in books, is suggested by the words 'person' and 'character' themselves. We have been using these words more or less interchangeably, though with an implicit and conventional emphasis on the 'reality' of a person and the 'fictionality' of a character. But the words are worth examining in more detail. According to *Chambers Dictionary*, 'person' signifies both 'a living soul or self-conscious being' and 'a character represented, as on the stage'. Indeed, 'person' goes back to the Latin word *persona*, the mask worn by an actor in a play on the classical stage. The English language uses the word 'persona' to signify a kind of mask or disguise, a pretended or assumed character. The word 'person', then, is bound up with questions of fictionality, disguise, representation and mask. To know a person, or to know who a person is, involves understanding a mask. In this respect, the notion of person is inseparable from the literary. This is not to say that 'real' people are actually fictional. Rather it is to suggest that there is a complex, destabilizing and perhaps finally undecidable interweaving of the 'real' and the 'fictional': our lives, our *real* lives, are governed and directed by the stories we read, write and tell ourselves.

There is a similar enigma about the word 'character': just as the word 'person' has a double and paradoxical signification, so 'character' means both a letter or sign, a mark of writing, and the 'essential' qualities of a 'person'. Again, the etymology of the word is suggestive: from the Greek word *kharattein*, to engrave, the word becomes a mark or sign, a person's title and hence a distinguishing mark – that which distinguishes one person from another – and from this a 'fictional' person or a person on stage. Pip's characterological reading of his parents' tombstones, then, is perhaps not so far off the mark. And in *Hamlet*, when Polonius tells his son Laertes that he should remember his 'precepts' or advice, he plays on this double sense, using 'character' as a verb: 'And these few precepts in thy memory / Look thou character' (I.iii.58–9). In this way, Shakespeare's play suggests how intimately 'character' is bound up with inscription, with signs, with writing.

We have argued that the realist novel tends to rely on a particular conception of what a person is – that a person is a complex but unified whole. We might develop this further by suggesting that the realist model of character involves a fundamental dualism of inside (mind, soul or self) and outside (body, face and other external features). The 'inside' that we associate with being human has many different forms. In the nineteenth century this was often described in terms of 'spiritual life' or 'soul'. More recently, it has just as often (and perhaps more helpfully) been understood in terms of the unconscious. The following extracts from the first paragraph of George Eliot's novel *Middlemarch* will allow us to explore this in more detail:

> Miss Brooke had that kind of beauty which seems to be thrown into relief by poor dress. Her hand and wrist were so finely formed that she could wear sleeves not less bare of style than those in which the Blessed Virgin appeared to Italian painters; and her profile as well as her stature and bearing seemed to gain the more dignity from her plain garments, which by the side of provincial fashion gave her the impressiveness of a fine quotation from the Bible, – or from one of our elder poets, – in a paragraph from today's newspaper. She was usually spoken of as being remarkably clever, but with the addition that her sister Celia had more common-sense. Nevertheless, Celia wore scarcely more trimmings; and it was only to close observers that her dress differed from her sister's, and had a shade of coquetry in its arrangements; for Miss Brooke's plain dressing was due to mixed conditions, in most of which her sister shared. The pride of being ladies had something to do with it: the Brooke connections, though not exactly aristocratic, were unquestionably 'good' [. . .] Young women of such birth, living in a quiet country-house, and attending a village church hardly larger than a parlour, naturally regarded frippery as the ambition of a huckster's daughter. Then there was well-bred economy, which in those days made show in dress the first item to be deducted from, when any margin was required for expenses more distinctive of rank. Such reasons would have been enough to account for plain dress, quite apart from religious feeling; but in Miss Brooke's case, religion alone would have determined it [. . .] and to her the destinies of mankind, seen by the light of Christianity, made the solicitudes of feminine fashion appear an occupation for Bedlam. She could not reconcile the anxieties of a spiritual life involving eternal consequences, with a keen interest in guimp and artificial protrusions of drapery. [. . .] (29–30)

This extraordinary opening paragraph, with its ironic insistence on the importance of clothes despite Dorothea Brooke's spiritual aspirations, clearly acknowledges that physical appearance (outside) works as a sign of character (inside). What is indicated here is an opposition that is fundamental in realist texts: that there is an inside and an outside to a person, that these are separate, but that one may be understood to have a crucial influence on the other. The opening to *Middlemarch* concentrates almost obsessively on Dorothea's clothes because it is her clothes that allow us insight into her character. As this suggests, another convention of characterological realism is that character is hidden or obscure, that in order to know another person – let alone ourselves – we must decipher the outer appearance. Eliot constantly manipulates and plays with the mechanisms of such realism, above all with that form of telepathy or mind-reading whereby a narrator can describe a character from the outside but can also know (and keep secrets about) that character's inner thoughts and feelings, conscious or unconscious. At the same time, by evoking Dorothea's appearance in terms of how 'the Blessed Virgin appeared to Italian painters' and by comparing her 'plain garments' to 'the impressiveness of a fine quotation', Eliot subtly foregrounds a sense of the painterly and the textual. We are drawn and caught up in intriguing uncertainties about where representation (a picture or text) begins or ends.

From Dorothea's clothes, then, Eliot weaves a fine and intricate web of character – in terms of the familial, social and political, and in terms of the moral and religious. Indeed, one of the most striking sentences of the excerpt focuses ironically on this concern with clothes: 'She could not reconcile the anxieties of a spiritual life involving eternal consequences, with a keen interest in guimp and artificial protrusions of drapery.' The passage as a whole makes it clear, however, that Dorothea's puritan plainness is simply the reverse side of a 'keen interest in guimp'. Her preference for 'plain dressing' is itself a complex and considered statement of fashion. It is at this point, in particular, that Eliot's ironic presentation of Dorothea involves a subtle questioning of the conventional opposition between a 'spiritual life' on the one hand and the 'artificial protrusions of drapery' on the other. The passage suggests that this opposition is itself artificial, that whatever people 'really' are cannot be separated from how they appear. It suggests that people are constituted by an interplay of inner and outer, but that it is not a question of one being the truth and the other mere surface. So while realist conventions of character may rely on the opposition between inner and outer, mind or spirit and body, and so on, Eliot's description of Dorothea also shows how this opposition can be questioned from within the realist tradition itself.

This brings us to one of the central questions raised by many novels: How can we know a person? As we have seen, realist novels such as George Eliot's attempt to answer this question by presenting people as knowable by a number of 'outward' signs of 'inner' worth. Appearances, however, can be deceptive. Indeed, many novels and plays are concerned with the problem of deception or disguise, with discriminating between an appearance that is a true sign of inner value and one that is not. The realist tradition often relies on the possibility of such deception, while also presupposing the possibility of finally discovering the worth or value of a person by reading the outward signs. The exposure, despite appearances, of Bulstrode's hypocrisy, for example, and the final validation of Lydgate's good character are central to the plot of *Middlemarch*. But the fact that a 'person' is itself, in some sense, a 'mask', means that even if we think we 'know' the soul or self of a person, his or her true identity, there is always a possibility, even if that person is ourself, that such an identity is itself a form of mask. This irreducible uncertainty may partly account for realism's obsessive concern with the question: 'Who am I?'

The stories of Raymond Carver (1938–88), like many so-called post-modern texts, relentlessly play with such conventions of characterological construction and perception. In 'Cathedral' (1983), for example, the somewhat obtuse, belligerent, intolerant, discriminatory narrator finds it both comic and unnerving to think about how a blind man, a friend of his wife who has come to visit, looks – even while (or because) he cannot look. The narrator is struck by the fact that the blind man does not wear dark glasses. This disturbs him, since although at first sight the blind man's eyes 'looked like anyone else's eyes', on closer inspection (and the narrator takes the opportunity for a lengthy session of unreciprocable inspection) they seem 'creepy': 'As I stared at his face, I saw the left pupil turn in toward his nose while the other made an effort to keep in one place. But it was only an effort, for that eye was on the roam without his knowing it or wanting it to be' (297). The story culminates in a dope-smoking session in which the blind man teaches the narrator the advantages of drawing with closed eyes, of the necessary visual imagination of the blind. On one level, the story performs a conventional reversal of the blind and the seeing, figuring the blind man as the seer. But on another level, Carver explores conventions of characterological construction by querying the equation of the look of someone with their identity (the eyes, conventionally the most telling indicator of character are, for our view of the blind man, just 'creepy' signifiers of mechanical dysfunction, disconnected from intention, emotion, will), and by prompting an awareness that in this story it is the one who is *not* seen – either by us as readers or by the blind man – who most fully exposes himself, exposes his 'character', in all its belligerence, intolerance and obtuseness.

As we have seen, it is difficult in an absolute sense to separate real from fictional characters. To read about a character is to imagine and create a character in reading: it is to create a person. And as we have tried to show, reading characters involves learning to acknowledge that a person can never finally be singular – that there is always multiplicity, ambiguity, otherness and unconsciousness. Our final point concerns what it means to 'identify' with characters in fiction. It seems difficult, if not impossible, to enjoy a novel or play without, at some level, identifying with the characters in it. In fact, the most obvious definition of the 'hero' or 'heroine' of a novel or play would be the person with whom we 'identify', with whom we sympathize or empathize, or whose position or role we imaginatively inhabit. The anti-hero, by contrast, is the character with whom we might identify, but only in wilful resistance to prevailing codes of morality and behaviour. 'Identification' in any case is never as simple as we might think. To identify with a person in a novel or play is to identify *oneself*, to produce an identity for oneself. It is to give oneself a world of fictional people, to start to let one's identity merge with that of a fiction. It is, finally, also to create a character for oneself, to create oneself as a character.

Further reading

A good place to start in thinking more about literary character is Uri Margolis's lucid cognitive-psychological essay 'Character' (2007). For an alternative and reasonably accessible account, see Harold Bloom, 'The Analysis of Character' (1990). A classic if somewhat reductive account of character may be found in Chapters 3 and 4 of Forster's *Aspects of the Novel* (1976), first published in 1927. For a good discussion of character in the nineteenth- and early twentieth-century novel, see Martin Price, *Forms of Life* (1983). A very different and more challenging approach is Thomas Docherty's *Reading (Absent) Character* (1983), which focuses in particular on the *nouveau roman* and postmodern writing generally, in order to move beyond a 'mimetic' theory of character to one in which characterization is seen as 'a process of reading and writing'. For an excellent, if difficult, argument for the deconstruction of character which challenges the humanist perspective of a unified self and argues for 'an esthetic and ethic of the fragmented self', see Leo Bersani's important book *A Future for Astyanax: Character and Desire in Literature* (1978); see also Hélène Cixous's 'The Character of "Character" ' (1974). J. Hillis Miller's chapter on 'Character' in *Ariadne's Thread* (1992) brilliantly weaves literary with critical, theoretical and philosophical reflections on character. On the question of identification in psychoanalysis and literature, see Diana Fuss, *Identification Papers* (1995).

9. Voice

Nothing is stranger, or more familiar, than the idea of a voice. In George Eliot's *Daniel Deronda* (1876), a character called Mrs Meyrick observes that 'A mother hears something like a lisp in her children's talk to the very last' (423). In Shakespeare's *King Lear* (1605), the blinded Gloucester recognizes Lear from his voice: 'The trick of that voice I do well remember; / Is't not the King?' (IV, vi, 106–7). In both of these examples we have what appear to be confirmations of the persistence of identity, expressed in the singular or peculiar nature (the 'trick') of a person's voice. But in each of these exchanges we are also presented with a kind of strangeness as well: in the context of Eliot's novel, for example, we may reflect on the irony of the fact that what the mother recognizes in her children, what it is in their voice that confirms the persistence of their identity, is something that cannot be heard, a lisp perceived only by the mother. Moreover, there is something strange in the idea that an adult's speech should be, in a dream like or hallucinatory fashion, haunted by the past in this way. In the example from Shakespeare, on the other hand, it is difficult for us not to be aware of the terrible precariousness of recognition and, by implication, of identity: Gloucester may believe that he recognizes, and may indeed recognize, the trick of the king's voice, but we are all too aware of the fact that he can never again *see* the king, never confirm the king's identity by sight. And ironically, Gloucester is only reunited with Lear thanks to help from his son Edgar, whose voice (disguised as Tom o' Bedlam) Gloucester *fails* to recognize.

The examples from Eliot and Shakespeare appear, at least initially, to be about the familiarity and individuality of voice. But like literary texts more generally, they are also concerned with the ways in which a voice may be strange and disturbing. We may enjoy a novel like Raymond Chandler's

The Little Sister (1949) partly on account of the distinctive, gritty, cinemato-graphic voice-over of Marlowe the narrator, but one of the things that makes this novel haunting and powerful, as well as comical, is its sensitivity to the strangeness of voices. Thus, for example, we have Miss Mavis Weld, apparently concerned about her brother: 'She clutched her bag to her bosom with tight little fingers. "You mean something has happened to him?" Her voice faded off into a sort of sad whisper, like a mortician asking for a down payment' (39). Or we have Marlowe recounting a phone call: 'The phone rang before I had quite started to worry about Mr Lester B. Clausen. I reached for it absently. The voice I heard was an abrupt voice, but thick and clogged, as if it was being strained through a curtain or somebody's long white beard' (41).

The power of a voice is made dramatically clear by the British govern-ment's censorship of the Sinn Fein leader, Gerry Adams: for a number of years (until September 1994) his voice was, in effect, illegal. His words, when broadcast, had to be spoken by an actor. Few voices could be said to have haunted the British media at that time as forcefully as Gerry Adams's. But a concern with what is powerful, haunting and strange about voices is hardly a recent phenomenon. One need only think of the importance of oracles, and the intimate links between voice and prophecy in the Bible and other clas-sical texts. Consider, for instance, the voice that announces in I Corinthians 13: 'Though I speak with the tongues of men and of angels, and have not charity, I am become as sounding brass, or a tinkling cymbal. / And though I have the gift of prophecy, and understand all mysteries, and all knowledge; and though I have all faith, so that I could remove mountains, and have not charity, I am nothing' (1–2). Or think of the apocalyptic voices at the end of the Bible, in the Book of Revelation – for example of the angel who comes down from heaven, whose 'face was as it were the sun, and his feet as pillars of fire' and who

> cried with a loud voice, as when a lion roareth: and when he had cried, seven thunders uttered their voices.
> And when the seven thunders had uttered their voices, I was about to write: and I heard a voice from heaven saying unto me, Seal up those things which the seven thunders uttered, and write them not. (Rev. 10: 3–4)

In both of these biblical quotations voice is described in terms that identify it with the non-human – with musical instruments (sounding brass or tinkling cymbal), with the sound of a lion or with the sound of thunder. It is also pre-sented in terms of multiplicity (speaking in tongues, the voices of the seven thunders) and of uncanniness (the voice that has the gift of prophecy and is apparently omniscient; the voice that is forbidden, that must be sealed up). All of these characteristics are important for thinking about literary texts more generally. Literature, in fact, might be defined as being the space in which, more than anywhere else, the power, beauty and strangeness of the voice is both evoked or bodied forth *and* described, talked about, analysed. In this respect, reading literary texts involves attending to extraordinary voices.

One of the most obvious extremes of voice in literature is in relation to music – in other words, the idea that voice becomes pure sound, turns into music. Here we may recall Walter Pater's proposition that '*all art constantly aspires towards the condition of music*' (Pater, 111): this is as much true of the 'smoky kind of voice' (202) whose singing transfixes and transforms the life of the narrator in Jean Rhys's story 'Let Them Call It Jazz' (1962) as it is of the glozing, serpentine voice that seduces Eve in Milton's *Paradise Lost* (Book IX, 532ff.), or of the song of the skylark or of the nightingale to which Shelley and Keats respectively aspire in their great song-like odes. At the same time, however, we are all perfectly aware that literary texts are *not* (simply) music or song. Part of what makes texts literary is indeed their peculiar, paradoxical relation to music (not least in lyric poems and ballads, originally performed with or as music). That is to say, poems or short stories or other texts may aspire towards the condition of music, but they are necessarily stuck in their so-called linguistic predicament. Thus Coleridge's 'Kubla Khan' (1798) is concerned with the demonic power of music played by 'A damsel with a dulcimer' and with the paradoxical desire to 'build' the very things that the poem has described (a pleasure-dome and caves of ice) 'with music':

> A damsel with a dulcimer
> In a vision once I saw:
> It was an Abyssinian maid,
> And on her dulcimer she played,
> Singing of Mount Abora.
> Could I revive within me
> Her symphony and song,
> To such a deep delight 'twould win me,
> That with music loud and long,
> I would build that dome in air,
> That sunny dome! those caves of ice!

In Shelley's ode 'To a Sky-Lark' (1820), on the other hand, the speaker ends by implying that he is unteachable:

> Teach me half the gladness
> That thy brain must know,
> Such harmonious madness
> From my lips would flow
> The world should listen then – as I am listening now.

Shelley's ode thus aspires to the 'harmonious madness' it can never voice. Similarly, Keats's ode of 1819 can acknowledge the 'ecstasy' of the nightingale's 'voice', but the speaker also recognizes that he can never triumph in the desire to 'dissolve' his identity with that voice. Being stuck, in this respect, is no doubt a fundamental *condition* of literature. Not surprisingly then, literary texts call to be thought about not only in terms of how they *body forth* voices but also in terms of how they reflect, comment on and analyse what 'voice' *means*. As Eve's temptation by the snaky sibilants of Satan suggests, in Milton's *Paradise Lost*, a voice can be astonishingly seductive. Interestingly, a voice can become even *more* seductive by referring to the fact that it is being seductive. (The contemporary commercial success of phone-sex may also testify to this.) Voice seduces: as the etymology of seduction may suggest (*se-*, aside, *ducere*, to lead), it leads us aside or draws us away.

What does it mean to talk about voice in relation to literary texts? Take the opening of a short story by Raymond Carver, entitled 'Fat' (1963). It begins:

> I am sitting over coffee and cigarettes at my friend Rita's and I am telling her about it.
> Here is what I tell her.
> It is late of a slow Wednesday when Herb seats the fat man at my station.
> This fat man is the fattest person I have ever seen, though he is neat-appearing and well dressed enough. Everything about him is big. But it is the fingers I remember best. When I stop at the table near his to see to the old couple, I first notice the fingers. They look three times the size of a normal person's fingers – long, thick, creamy fingers. (64)

This is, in some ways at least, a descriptively straightforward opening. But once we reflect on it, we find that it is doing many different and quite sophisticated things. The first point to observe is that this is a first person narration with a strong sense of a speaking voice: we are drawn away by what we might call the 'reality effect' of a speaking voice that is produced in part through the conversational language – the lexical items and syntax, the topic, use of the present tense, repetition – and in part through the explicit reference to the fact that the narrator is speaking and 'telling' us something. The opening sentences, in a quite subtle way, put the reader in the position of the narrator's friend Rita

('I am telling her . . . Here is what I tell . . .'). Despite the seductively 'realistic' or 'everyday' quality of voice here, something fairly complex is going on: we are presented with a narrator who, even in the apparently straightforward language of the opening two sentences, makes it clear that this is a self-referential or metafictional story, a story that is at least at some level a story *about* storytelling. The seductiveness of an apparently casual speaking voice tends to distract attention from this dimension of the text. Moreover, without really drawing attention to the fact, we have up till now been referring to the 'I' of the story as the narrator. In other words, we have been making an implicit distinction between narrator and author. This is a first-person narration and the narrator, we quickly learn, is a waitress. What we are being presented with, in other words, is the 'voice' of a girl or young woman. At the same time, however, there is a sort of double-voicing here to the extent that we may recognize this text as being characteristic of Raymond Carver's work. In this respect, we could say, there is also the phantasmatic voice of Carver lurking in these lines. We hear the 'voice' of Carver in a figurative, ghostly sense (like a signature tune).

Rather differently, there is Thomas Hardy's poem, 'The Voice':

> Woman much missed, how you call to me, call to me,
> Saying that now you are not as you were
> When you had changed from the one who was all to me,
> But as at first, when our day was fair.
>
> Can it be you that I hear? Let me view you, then,
> Standing as when I drew near to the town
> Where you would wait for me: yes, as I knew you then,
> Even to the original air-blue gown!
>
> Or is it only the breeze, in its listlessness
> Travelling across the wet mead to me here,
> You being ever dissolved to wan wistlessness,
> Heard no more again far or near?
>
>   Thus I; faltering forward,
>   Leaves around me falling,
> Wind oozing thin through the thorn from norward,
>   And the woman calling.

Written in December 1912, 'The Voice' belongs to the series of so-called '1912–13 poems' that Hardy wrote following his first wife's death. (Emma

Hardy died in the preceding month, November 1912.) It is difficult, in other words, not to read this poem as autobiographical – to understand it as a poem about the poet's experience of mourning following his wife's death. But the poem is more than simply autobiographical: it is about the radical uncertainty of human identity and experience, their faltering. 'The Voice' not only describes the uncanny experience of hearing a dead person's voice but in some sense transfers the call to us in turn. The poem functions as a kind of strange textual switchboard. Again, we can respond to the poem in quite straightforward terms – it is a poem about someone who is out walking in an autumn or early winter landscape and who thinks he hears the voice of a woman whom he once loved (who was 'all' to him) but who is no longer above ground ('heard no more again far or near'). As its title suggests then, it is about 'the voice' he hears. But it is also a poem about voice more generally, and about the relationship between poetry and hearing a woman's call. (This may in turn recall the notion of inspiration in classical Greek and Roman times, in other words, hearing the voice, music or song of a female Muse or Muses.) This is evident, for example, in the opening line: 'Woman much missed, how you call to me, call to me'. What we are presented with here is an affirmation of the spooky actuality of hearing a dead woman's voice – an affirmation which the poem proceeds to question ('Can it be you that I hear?'), but which it concludes by reaffirming ('Thus I; faltering forward . . . And the woman calling'). This opening line, however, is at the same time grammatically ambiguous: 'how' suggests a questioning as well as an exclamation. 'Call to me, call to me', on the other hand, can be read as an echo (as *two* voices, even if the second is a double of the first) or as changing from an exclamation – 'how you call to me' – to a demand or appeal: 'call to me'.

The ending of the poem suggests either that the speaker is off his head, hearing voices, or that the dead really do come back and it is indeed possible to hear voices from beyond the grave. But it also suggests something about literary texts in general. Every one of the writers who has been discussed in this chapter is dead. But as we indicate in our discussion of the 'death of the author' (in Chapter 3), every literary text can be thought of as involving a voice from beyond the grave, since every text is at least potentially capable of outliving the person who originally gives voice to it. The woman in Hardy's poem is in this respect a figure of the poet *par excellence*. Do we hear Hardy's voice in 'The Voice' or not? Or – to reflect on the poem in a quite different way altogether, that is to say in the light of what Harold Bloom calls 'the anxiety of influence' – do we perhaps hear Keats's voice in this poem? Bloom's celebrated theory (Bloom 1973) is that what impels poets to write is not so much the desire to reflect on the world as the desire to respond to and to challenge the voices of the dead. For Bloom, any 'strong' poem will always involve an encounter between the 'living' poet – in this case Hardy – and the dead – in this case perhaps most obviously Keats, whose 'Ode to a Nightingale' is also explicitly concerned with the 'dissolving' qualities of voice and identity. From a Bloomian perspective, Hardy's reference to 'You being ever dissolved to wan wistlessness' might be read not so much as an address to the poet's dead wife (strange enough as that gesture may itself seem) but rather as an eerie and ambivalent 'revisitation' of Keats's lines:

> That I might drink, and leave the world unseen,
>   And with thee fade away into the forest dim:
> Fade far away, dissolve, and quite forget
>   What thou amongst the leaves hast never known . . .

Keats's voice might, in this sense, be said to haunt 'The Voice' as much as it does other Hardy poems, such as 'The Darkling Thrush' (1900) – the very title of which explicitly refers us to Keats's ode ('Darkling I listen . . .'). In poems such as 'The Voice' and 'The Darkling Thrush', in other words, we can recognize the 'trick' of Hardy's voice in terms of an idiomatic tone (lugubrious, plaintive, ironic etc.) and idiomatic rhymes and neologisms ('listlessness', 'wistlessness'). But this is 'voice' in a figurative, ghostly sense. Moreover, it is 'voice' as plural – haunted by, for example, the voice or voices of other poets such as Keats.

The examples of Carver and Hardy are helpful because they highlight a number of important ideas for thinking about voice in relation to literature. First they suggest that the question of voice is never simple, even (or perhaps especially) when it appears to be. Second, and more specifically, they suggest that literary texts not only *present* voices but also have things to say *about* what voices are and how we might or might not hear them. Third, there is invariably more than one voice in a literary text, even if it is a matter of a voice ostensibly just talking or responding to itself.

This final point can be thought about further in at least two ways. On the one hand – and this has been an important feature of recent literary theoretical concerns – there is the importance of seeing literature as a space in which one encounters multiple voices. Literary texts call upon us to think about them in terms of many voices – for instance, in terms of what M.M. Bakhtin calls *heteroglossia* or of what he, Julia Kristeva, Roland Barthes and others refer to as *polyphony*. Literature is, as Salman Rushdie has observed, 'the one place in any society where, within the secrecy of our own heads, we can hear *voices talking about everything in every possible way*' (Rushdie 1990, 16). Saleem, the narrator of Rushdie's novel *Midnight's Children* (1981), is an excellent example: he is telepathic, like every so-called omniscient narrator in a work of fiction, and he is continually hearing multiple voices. As he remarks: 'I was a radio receiver, and could turn the volume down or up; I could select individual voices; I could even, by an effort of will, switch off my newly-discovered inner ear' (164).

On the other hand – and this has been a related and similarly important feature of recent critical and theoretical concerns – literature encourages us to think about the idea that there may in fact be no such thing as *a* voice, a single, unified voice (whether that of an author, a narrator, a reader or anyone else). Rather, there is difference and multiplicity *within* every voice. There is, then, not only the kind of socio-literary polyphony that Bakhtin describes, and which he illustrates for example by looking at the way Dickens orchestrates, inhabits and detaches himself from the role of various speakers in his novel *Little Dorrit* (Bakhtin 1992, 203–5). But in addition to this, and more fundamentally, any one voice is in fact made up of multiple voices. There is difference and polyphony *within* every voice. We have tried to suggest this by looking at some of the ways in which the voice of an author or poet is always a sort of ghostly site for a gathering of voices. We might conclude, then, with a thought proffered in one of the 'Adagia' (or 'aphorisms') of the poet Wallace Stevens: 'When the mind is like a hall in which thought is like a voice speaking, the voice is always that of someone else' (168).

Further reading

For two traditional but in some respects still stimulating accounts of voice and literature, see Yvor Winters, 'The Audible Reading of Poetry' (1957), and Francis Berry, *Poetry and the Physical Voice* (1962). A more recent and theoretically informed account is provided by Furniss and Bath (1996), in their chapter on 'Hearing Voices in Poetic Texts'. Roland Barthes has very engaging, thought-provoking things to say about voice, for example in *S/Z* (Barthes 1990b). On heteroglossia, see M.M. Bakhtin, *The Dialogic Imagination* (1981). For Kristeva and polyphony, see for example the essay 'Word, Dialogue and Novel' (Kristeva 1986). For a challenging but compelling account of the strangeness of the narrator's 'I' in a literary text, see Maurice Blanchot's 'The Narrative Voice' (Blanchot 1981). On voice in relation to print and reading, see Griffiths, *The Printed Voice of Victorian Poetry* (1989). On poetry, voice and hearing, see Geoffrey Hartman's eclectic and stimulating essay, 'Words and Wounds' (Hartman 1981), and, for a more technical, difficult but fascinating study, see Garrett Stewart's *Reading Voices* (1990).

Steven Connor's remarkable study *Dumbstruck – A Cultural History of Ventriloquism* (2000) offers a wide-ranging account of voice especially in relation to spiritualism and teletechnology. The philosopher David Appelbaum's *Voice* (1990) is a brilliant and idiosyncratic study of such dimensions of 'voice' as the cough, laugh, breath and babble. Oliver Sacks's *Seeing Voices* (1991) is a thought-provoking exploration specifically in the context of deafness, while Wesling and Slawek's *Literary Voice* (1995) draws on philosophy, linguistics and other disciplines to defend literary voice against 'modern philosophy's critique of the spoken'. Finally, from a specifically psychoanalytic perspective, see Mladen Dolar's essay 'The Object Voice' (1996).

10. Figures and tropes

I t's not for nothing that some still call Elvis Presley 'The King' and Eric
Clapton 'God'. But the force of these acts of renaming depends on the
assumption that no one takes them literally. We take it that no one ever supposed that the United States had become a monarchy and put Elvis Presley on
the throne. No one, not even the most loyal of fans, even in his heyday, believed
that Eric Clapton created the world in six days and rested on the seventh.
They may have believed that his guitar-playing was transplendent, but even
those whose judgement was blurred by an unholy mixture of illegal substances
and Clapton's heavenly guitar solos are unlikely to have taken him for the
Almighty Himself. These renamings of Presley and Clapton, then, involve the
kind of exaggeration or verbal extravagance known as hyperbole. By the same
token, few are likely to take as gospel the theologically unorthodox if slightly
more credible statement in Pink's 2004 hit single, that 'God is a DJ' ('If God is
a DJ / Life is a dance floor / Love is the rhythm / You are the music'). To refer
to Elvis as 'The King' or Clapton as 'God', or to talk in turn about God as a DJ,
is to use figurative language.

Literary language is sometimes thought about in terms of its deviations
from or distortions of ordinary language. Like many generalizations, this idea
is both useful and misleading. It suggests that literary texts are characterized
by the use of figures of speech or tropes, conceiving these as basically synonymous – in other words, as deviations from 'ordinary' or 'literal' language. Thus
Chambers Dictionary defines a rhetorical figure as 'a deviation from the
ordinary mode of expression', and trope as 'a figure of speech, properly one in
which a word or expression is used in other than its literal sense'. Such figures
include, for example, hyperbole, metaphor, metonymy and anthropomorphism. Metaphor is the general term for the figure of resemblance, whereby

one thing is likened to another. Metonymy is a general term for the figure of association or contiguity, whereby one thing is talked about by referring to something associated with it. Anthropomorphism is the general term used to refer to the non-human as if it were human. So-called 'ordinary' language, by contrast, is thought to use far more literal language, language that calls a spade a spade.

As the examples of Presley, Clapton and Pink suggest, however, the figurative is by no means restricted to literary texts: rather, it saturates all language. Friedrich Nietzsche famously argued that even truth itself is figurative. In his essay 'On Truth and Lie in an Extra-Moral Sense' (1873), Nietzsche asks 'What, then, is truth?' and offers the following answer:

> A mobile army of metaphors, metonyms, and anthropomorphisms – in short, a sum of human relations, which have been enhanced, transposed, and embellished poetically and rhetorically, and which after long use seem firm, canonical, and obligatory to a people: truths are illusions about which one has forgotten that this is what they are; metaphors which are worn out and without sensuous power; coins which have lost their pictures and now matter only as metal, no longer as coins. (Nietzsche 1980, 46–7)

When we think that we speak 'truthfully', without the distortions of figuration, Nietzsche suggests, we only deceive ourselves. The language of truth, language supposedly purified of figures and tropes, is simply language to which we have become so habituated that we no longer recognize it as figurative. This suggests that our world is constituted figuratively, that we relate to ourselves, to other people, to the world, through figures of speech. The manipulation and exploitation of figurative language may therefore be understood to have fundamental implications for the political, social, even economic constitution of our world. The very way that we understand the world may be said to be mediated by the kinds of figures that we use to speak about it. We could think about this in terms of any everyday aspect (aspect is a visual metaphor) of life – for example, the names of newspapers, those 'organs' (a metaphor) that help to *organize* (the same organic metaphor) our world: the *Herald, Guardian, Sun, Mirror, Telegraph, Tribune* and so on. While such discourses as history, philosophy, psychology, economics and so on may, at least in principle, attempt to rid themselves of figurative language, it is precisely figuration which is, unavoidably, at the heart of the discipline of literary studies. This unavoidability is suggested in the passage from Nietzsche, with its concluding figuration of metaphors as coins. Nietzsche explicitly relies on the figurative to demystify language and thus to formulate a definition of the truth. As Paul de Man remarks, tropes are not 'a derived, marginal, or aberrant form of language but the linguistic paradigm par excellence': figurative language 'characterizes language as such' (de Man 1979, 105).

Central to literary criticism and theory, then, are such questions as: What are the effects of rhetorical figures in literary texts? What purpose do they serve? And how do they function? One of the most common misconceptions about literary texts is that their figurative language is simply decorative, something added to the text to make it more readable, more dramatic, or more 'colourful'. It is certainly true that the perceived presence of figurative language often seems to increase at points of emotional and dramatic intensity, like the soaring violins at moments of sexual passion or dramatic tension in a Hollywood film. Thus D.H. Lawrence, for example, is known for his so-called 'purple passages'. But simply to suggest that figures are 'added' to literary language, like the musical soundtrack to a movie, does not get us very far. The soaring violin theory of rhetorical figures is misguided because, as Nietzsche suggests, language is inescapably figurative: the meaning of a text cannot be separated from its expression, its figures.

Figuration is fundamental to our world, to our lives. An alteration in the way we figure the world also involves an alteration in the way that the world works. Take Ralph Ellison's *Invisible Man* (1952), for example. This novel uses invisibility as a figure (both metaphorical and literal) for the marginality, the oppression, effacement and dehumanization of black people in the United States. Here is the opening to the prologue to Ellison's great novel:

> I am an invisible man. No, I am not a spook like those who haunted Edgar Allan Poe; nor am I one of your Hollywood-movie ectoplasms. I am a man of substance, of flesh and bone, fiber and liquids – and I might even be said to possess a mind. I am invisible, understand, simply because people refuse to see me. Like the bodiless heads you see sometimes in circus sideshows, it is as though I have been surrounded by mirrors and hard, distorting glass. When they approach me they see only my surroundings, themselves, or figments of their imagination – indeed, everything and anything except me. (3)

Visibility and invisibility figure the social, political and economic effacement and consequent oppression of blacks in the United States. The man is invisible because he cannot escape the preconceptions that others have concerning him. These preconceptions are produced by a 'perception' of his skin colour. This so-called perception is itself an effect of the kind of rhetorical figure we call synecdoche, whereby a part – here, the skin – stands for the whole – a man. But simply to categorize someone as 'black' (or 'white') is in a sense laughably reductive and inaccurate. Likewise, to say that someone is 'coloured' is in a sense to say nothing at all, because the skin, hair, nails, eyes, teeth of each one of us is a multichromatic assemblage of different hues. The categories of black, white and coloured operate as instances of synecdoche. What people 'see' is a form of metaphor, a figment or figure of imagination – a 'phantom in other people's minds . . . a figure in a nightmare which the sleeper tries with all his strength to destroy' (3). It is in this way that Ellison's narrator is invisible, for while people think that they see – they think they see a black man – in fact they see nothing, they are blinded by metaphor. Ellison's novel suggests that such habitual blindness may be challenged and in turn transformed by acts of language. It presents a metaphor or allegory of the invisible man to counter the worn coin of representation. After all, the effacement of the black man is, in a crucial sense, constituted through acts of language. Without the vocabulary of prejudice and racism, any such effacement would be inconceivable. Racism is an effect of language. In particular, the passage from Ellison cited above suggests that racism is an effect of synecdochic substitution – skin pigment for personal identity, individual for collective or racial identity. The invisible man can be seen again, his invisibility perceived, through alternative metaphors, through rhetorical figures.

The opening of Ellison's novel, then, gives us one answer to the question of how figures and tropes function in literary and other texts: they can make us see what is otherwise invisible, concealed by prejudice, effaced by habit. They seek to change the world. To recall the term used by Viktor Shklovsky and other Russian formalist critics writing in the 1920s, figurative language has the capacity to 'defamiliarize' our world – to refigure, reform, revolutionize.

What kinds of effects can be produced through figuration and how far can a reading of such figures go? Let us consider another example, a poem by the nineteenth-century New England poet Emily Dickinson. In Dickinson's work, figures, like language considered more generally, tremble on the edge of meaning. One reason why her poetry is particularly appropriate in a discussion of figurative language is that it characteristically 'deconstructs' or defamiliarizes its own rhetorical figures: her poetry constitutes a subtle yet decisive assault on figuration itself. This poem (no. 328) was written around 1862:

> A Bird came down the Walk—
> He did not know I saw—
> He bit an Angleworm in halves
> And ate the fellow, raw,
>
> 5   And then he drank a Dew
> From a convenient Grass—

And then hopped sidewise to the Wall
To let a Beetle pass—

He glanced with rapid eyes
10   That hurried all around—
They looked like frightened Beads, I thought—
He stirred his Velvet Head

Like one in danger, Cautious,
I offered him a Crumb
15   And he unrolled his feathers
And rowed him softer home—

Than Oars divide the Ocean,
Too silver for a seam—
Or Butterflies, off Banks of Noon
20   Leap, plashless as they swim.

In language at once direct and elusive, the poem describes a bird eating a worm, taking a drink and flying away. The rhetorical figure which stands out in the opening lines is personification or anthropomorphism. Both the bird ('he') and the worm (the 'fellow') of the first stanza are described as if they were human. But the anthropomorphic insistence of the first half of the poem becomes strangely convoluted as it goes on to explore the specificity of simile (a is like b) as a species of metaphor (a is b, in other words the 'like' is unstated). In line 11 we learn that the bird's eyes 'looked like frightened Beads'. But this simile is not as simple as it looks. It remains unclear whether 'looked like' means that the eyes actively *looked* (they looked, in the way that beads look, assuming that they do), or whether the bird's eyes, to the narrator, looked *like* beads. The simile is itself ambiguous. Moreover, *what* the eyes looked like – the beads – also undergoes an uncanny metamorphosis. To refer to beads as 'frightened' is to employ the rhetorical figure called animism, whereby an inanimate object is given the attributes of life. Far from clarifying the look of the bird's eyes, the simile makes it *less* concrete, less visible or imaginable, by making a comparison with something that cannot possibly be seen. It is entirely incorrect to say that the bird's eyes 'looked like' frightened beads, since *frightened* beads are not available to the gaze at all, and beads cannot look. The simile, a peculiar example of a 'transferred epithet', disturbs the sense of who or what is frightened and confounds the distinction between the figurative and the literal, image and word, the imagined and the visible.

The last two stanzas of the poem increase these uncertainties. In the penultimate stanza, rowing on an ocean is the 'vehicle' for the metaphor, the 'tenor' or 'meaning' of which is flying. But once again the figure is ambiguous: the ocean metaphor is inadequate, the line suggests, to express the softness, the silvery delicacy of the movement of the bird's flight. Where a boat would leave a wake in the water, a kind of seam, the bird leaves none in the air. But while 'Too silver for a seam' may be 'translated' as meaning something like 'too delicate for a wake or track in water', the line may also be understood to be referring to the delicacy of figurative language and its relation to the world. Critics usually distinguish simile within metaphor more generally by pointing out that phrases such as 'like' or 'as' mark simile as explicitly figurative. Through another kind of figure known as paronomasia – produced by the homophone 'seam'/'seem' – the poem reflects silently on figuration itself. Metaphors seem to be unmarked, too silver, too subtle, for a seam, or for the word 'seem' (or 'as' or 'like'), too delicate for the mark of figuration. Just as there is no seam left behind after the bird's flight – it flies as if by magic – metaphor also leaves no mark, no 'seem' and no seam. Or, to put it more paradoxically but more accurately, like the word 'plashless', a word which negates 'plash' but does so only by referring to it, metaphor both does and does not leave a mark.

The extraordinary ending to the poem involves another metaphor for the bird's flight – the flight of a butterfly – but presents this in terms of swimming. The bird is like a butterfly leaping off a bank into the water so delicately that there is no (s)plash. With the phrase 'Banks of Noon', however, Dickinson's poem disturbs the basis of metaphorical transformation itself. 'Banks of Noon' is no more comprehensible than the 'frightened Beads' encountered earlier. The metaphorical transitions are short-circuited, for while it is possible to see that a bird's flight is 'like' rowing a boat, it is unclear how a bank of noon can be 'like' anything physical – are we to believe that 'noon' can be a kind of riverbank, for example? The phrase highlights the deceptiveness of figuration, its potential for linguistic effects of *trompe l'œil* and hallucination. It dramatizes the ease, the inevitability with which language slides away from referential assumptions. On the other hand, 'Banks of Noon' can be considered in terms of another kind of phenomenon – intertextuality – whereby a text is woven out of words and phrases from elsewhere. In this respect, the phrase recalls the Shakespearean 'bank and shoal of time' from Macbeth's murderous speech (*Macbeth* I.vii.6) – giving the sense of the present as a kind of isthmus within the ocean of eternity – and suggests the end or the edge of time, time strangely suspended or delayed. The ending of Dickinson's poem suggests that figurative language entails a series of displacements and substitutions which both produce and withhold the illusion of reference. In these and other ways, Dickinson's poem suggests that figures make and unmake our world, give us meaning and take it away.

In our discussion of Dickinson's poem, we have drawn attention to the self-reflexive possibilities of figuration, to the way that figures can turn reflexively back on themselves, trope themselves, so that the text remarks on its own language. To end our discussion of figures, we shall turn briefly to another text which may also be shown to register the uncanny potential of figurative language. In our chapter on narrative we referred briefly to James Joyce's great long short story 'The Dead'. The story begins with the following sentence: 'Lily, the caretaker's daughter, was literally run off her feet' (199). In fact, Lily is not *literally* run off her feet at all. Strangely, we say 'literally run off her feet' to mean *not* literally but figuratively run off her feet. The use of the word 'literal' here, like the phrase about feet, is metaphorical. In this respect, we can see that the opening sentence to the story produces a play of figuration which refers indirectly both to the subject of the story, death, and to its telling. 'Literally run off her feet' is a dead metaphor, a metaphor which has become so common that its identity as figurative has largely been lost: dead metaphors are Nietzsche's worn coins of language. We can say 'I was literally run off my feet' without recognizing that we are using a metaphor at all, that far from using the phrase literally, we are exploiting a figure of speech. The metaphorical use of the word 'literally' in this phrase is a good example of the evocative possibilities of 'catachresis', the rhetorical term for a misuse or abuse of language. 'The Dead', which is above all about death, is also about dead language, dead metaphors.

Joyce's story ends with the return of a 'figure from the dead' (251), the haunting memory of Gretta's dead boyfriend, Michael Furey. In the final pages, Gretta's husband Gabriel looks out of the window of a hotel as his wife sleeps. The last paragraph of the story is couched in intense, swooning, highly figurative prose:

> A few light taps upon the pane made him turn to the window. It had begun to snow again. He watched sleepily the flakes, silver and dark, falling obliquely against the lamplight. The time had come for him to set out on his journey westward. Yes, the newspapers were right: snow was general all over Ireland. It was falling on every part of the dark central plain, on the treeless hills, falling softly upon the Bog of Allen and, farther westward, softly falling into the dark mutinous Shannon waves. It was falling, too, upon every part of the lonely churchyard on the hill where Michael Furey lay buried. It lay thickly drifted on the crooked crosses and headstones, on the spears of the little grate, on the barren thorns. His soul swooned slowly as he heard the snow falling faintly through the universe and faintly falling, like the descent of their last end, upon all the living and the dead. (255–6)

The most remarkable, the most pressing feature of this paragraph is, perhaps, repetition. In particular, the word 'falling' occurs seven times: falling obliquely, falling, falling softly, softly falling, falling, falling faintly, faintly falling. This verbal repetition produces a mesmeric sense of descent, sleep, fading and death. What Joyce appears to be evoking here, through figurative effects of language – repetition, alliteration, assonance and sibilance, syntactic inversion or chiasmus ('falling faintly, faintly falling') – is a fading out, a falling off, of language itself. 'The Dead' is about the death of (figurative *and* literal) language.

To borrow Joyce's metaphor and reverse it, it is indeed the metaphorical death of language (rather than the death of metaphorical language) that gives the story life. And it is, more generally, the productive tensions of figurative language that give life to literary texts. In this chapter, we have tried to suggest that, like literature itself, literary criticism begins and ends with figuration. In reading we should try to figure out ways in which figures at once generate and disturb literary texts. Like Marvell's lover in his desire to stop the sun (see Chapter 4), if we cannot escape figures, still we can make them run.

Further reading

Two good recent 'introductions' to the idea of metaphor from the perspective of literature and literary theory in the one case and linguistics and stylistics in the other, are David Punter, *Metaphor* (2008) and Murray Knowles and Rosamund Moon, *Introducing Metaphor* (2006). For an engaging and informative further guide to figures and tropes, see Arthur Quinn's little book *Figures of Speech* (1993). See Paul Ricoeur's *The Rule of Metaphor* (1978) for a difficult but comprehensive work on metaphor from the perspective of a philosopher. For a classic literary critical approach, see Brooke-Rose's *A Grammar of Metaphor* (1958). An influential structuralist account of figuration or 'poetic' language is Roman Jakobson's 'Closing Statement: Linguistics and Poetics' (1960). Derrida's 'White Mythology' (1982) is a dense and difficult but by now classic argument against the notion that there could be any simple escape from figurative language. Other useful books are Todorov, *Introduction to Poetics* (1981) and Lakoff and Johnson, *Metaphors We Live By* (1980). 'Silva Rhetoricae' is a very helpful website for figures of speech, at www.humanities.byu.edu/rhetoric/silva.htm.

11. Creative writing

Is this it then? Is this creative writing? What is 'creative writing' anyway, and what is a chapter on creative writing doing in a book on literature, criticism and theory? What is it that writing creates? And what is the difference between 'creative writing' and 'literature'?

In what follows we would like to explore two general propositions: (1) 'creative writing' doesn't appear from nowhere. It has a history and is closely bound up with both the contemporary university and the current state of English (both as a language and as a subject of study). In particular, the recent surge in the popularity of 'creative writing' courses is intricately entwined with the history of the term 'literature' and with recent developments in literary criticism and theory. (2) Despite appearances perhaps, 'creative writing' often serves to delimit the liberating and exhilarating, but also fearful possibilities of language. In this, it shares something with the dictionary, which offers the following definition of 'creative':

> Specifically of literature and art, thus also of a writer or artist: inventive, imaginative; exhibiting imagination as well as intellect, and thus differentiated from the merely critical, 'academic', journalistic, professional, mechanical, etc., in literary or artistic production. So **creative writing**, such writing. (*OED*, sense 1b)

Let us note first of all that the *OED* has no hesitation in identifying 'creative writing' with 'literature' and 'art'. The *OED* definition is predicated on the basis of a firm distinction between 'imagination' and 'intellect'. Thus 'creative' is differentiated from other sorts of writing ('the merely critical, "academic", journalistic, professional, mechanical, etc.'). But how seriously can we take this distinction? Is there nothing 'creative' about other sorts of writing?

Definitions, as we know, are never 'merely academic': they are forms and conduits of power. We might note one further intriguing detail in this dictionary definition, namely the scare quotes around 'academic'. 'Creative writing', this might suggest, is both 'academic' and non-academic. As the deceptive simplicity of the *OED* definition is perhaps beginning to make clear, 'creative writing' has a strange relation to the academy and to the academic. In fact, creative writing appears to have been institutionalized, in more than one sense of that word, since the incorporation of 'creative writing courses' within educational institutions is inevitably a form of appropriation and control. As early as 1958 we find the *Oxford Magazine* (4 December, no. 164/2, cited in *OED*) declaring that 'In America established, or at any rate committed, writers have been absorbed, permanently or temporarily, into the apparatus of creative writing workshops.' This 'apparatus', establishing itself across British universities and elsewhere, has become increasingly powerful. Few practising writers (novelists and poets in particular) today can become commercially successful without becoming a part of this apparatus, however temporarily or unwillingly. But there is also a more radical way of construing this apparatus or 'creative writing machine', namely as the means by which the dangerous and disruptive possibilities of language, and of 'writing' in particular, are (apparently) contained, reduced, locked up. What does it mean that the unpredictable powers of creativity, of creative writing, are being incorporated into and assessed by the university? What is going on in the desire or apparent need to turn creative writing into an 'apparatus', a useful tool or machine?

To begin to respond to such questions, we have first of all to reckon with the ways that the emergence of 'creative writing' is linked to the history of the concept of literature. As the *OED* definition makes clear, 'creative writing' is inseparable from the question of literature. It has been fashionable in recent years, especially in the field of cultural studies, to regard literature as one sort of discourse or cultural product among others, such as philosophical discourse, or a film, or a restaurant menu. But in this context, Bennett and Royle, we like to think, is nothing if not unfashionable. Our concern is with the idea that there is in fact something distinctive about literature and that, in short, literature is not commensurable with other sorts of discourse. One reason for this is quite simple: literature in a sense does not exist. It has no essence. It is not a case of X being a literary text, and Y being non-literary. Literariness is more spectral and elusive. Any text conventionally considered as literary (Geoffrey Chaucer's 'The Wife of Bath's Prologue and Tale', say) can be read as non-literary (for example, as an account of female sexuality in the Middle Ages); and conversely, any text conventionally considered as non-literary (a political speech, say) can be read as literary (for example, in terms of an enactment of the strange ways of language, the workings of metaphor and other rhetorical figures). As Jacques Derrida has put it: 'There is no literature without a *suspended* relation to meaning and reference' (Derrida 1992a, 48). It is not that literature does not refer – for instance, we have to construe 'wife' and 'Bath' in relation to a world of 'meaning and reference', we have to make some sort of sense of these two words. But literature has to do with a certain *suspendedness* of such referring, as well as a *dependence* on what is referred to.

To take another example: how should we read the phrase 'midnight's children', in the title of Salman Rushdie's 1981 novel? We are impelled by a desire to go beyond suspense, for example in order to be able to state categorically and definitively that the words 'midnight's children' refer to the moment on the 14/15 August 1947 when India became independent and to the children who happened to be born just at that time. But the peculiar literariness of the title-phrase consists, *at the same time*, in the fact that it is enigmatic, resistant to any final stable determination. One could not, after all, even hope to exhaust the readings of the title without an exhaustive reading of the text to which that title refers. Strangely suggesting that children are *of* or *belonging to* a time ('midnight' with its connotations of the witching hour, darkness and mystery, the peculiarly decisive yet uncertain, spooky border between day and night), that there could be children of time but perhaps not space and that a book could itself somehow *be* these children, Rushdie's title conjures the bizarre telepathic mass of fictional narrative opened up in its name. *Midnight's Children*, after all, is not – or not only – social or political history: it is a novel, a work of literature or (notice how odd this might sound) creative writing.

As we argue elsewhere in this book (see the chapter entitled 'Mutant'), 'literature' is a comparatively modern invention. The emergence of creative writing in the mid-twentieth century in the USA, and more recent institutional expansions in the UK and elsewhere, are part and parcel of the process whereby the question 'What is literature?' or 'What is literariness?' becomes a central topic in literary texts themselves, as well as in literary criticism and theory. It is in this context that we might situate the proliferation, in the twentieth century, of poems about poetry and novels about novels. We might recall here Wallace Stevens's declaration in his great long poem *The Man with the Blue Guitar* (1938): 'Poetry is the subject of the poem, / From this the poem issues and / To this returns' (Stevens 176); or Samuel Beckett's characterization of the work of James Joyce: 'His writing is not *about* something; *it is that something itself* ' (Beckett 1983, 27). Significantly also, in this context, the last decades of the twentieth century witnessed the appearance of the term 'metafiction', to designate 'fiction about fiction', 'self-conscious' or 'self-reflexive fiction' (a term dating from 1960, according to the *OED*). And the word 'postmodern' is of course bound up with this increasingly explicit attention to the nature of the literary, to the literariness of the literary. But we should not oversimplify this. No doubt literary works have, to greater or lesser extents, always drawn attention to themselves, foregrounding their own strange nature: think of Shakespeare's plays within plays, in *Hamlet* or *A Midsummer Night's Dream*, or Cervantes's *Don Quixote*, or Sterne's *Tristram Shandy*, or Diderot's *Jacques le fataliste*, or Wordsworth's *The Prelude*. Nevertheless it also seems clear that creative writing is itself a new and different kind of foregrounding. It is as if 'Creative Writing' were calling out: 'Look at me, come and write literature here, come and experience the literary, it'll be fun! This way to the creative writing class!' This particular institutionalized flagging of literature could also be regarded as a flagging in the sense of 'becoming exhausted' – and here we might think of Gilles Deleuze's marvellous essay on 'the exhausted' (in Deleuze 1998) as a way of understanding contemporary literature (especially in the wake of Samuel Beckett). In all sorts of ways, in fact, we might see literature (and therefore creative writing) as coming to an end, its very existence increasingly threatened for example by the ubiquities of visual, digital and text cultures (film, TV, video, DVD, texting, email, the Internet, gaming). It is not without reason that J. Hillis Miller opens his book *On Literature* (2002) with the words: 'The end of literature is at hand. Literature's time is almost up' (Miller 2002, 1).

But we do not necessarily want to link the rise of creative writing with the 'end of literature'. (As Hillis Miller's book goes on to make clear, things are in fact more complex than his initial apocalyptic pronouncement might suggest.) Instead, we would like to conclude by proposing six ways in which creative writing offers new challenges and insights in relation to thinking about literature and literary studies.

1. 'Creative writing' is not simply opposed to 'critical writing'. We might most readily understand this in terms of the notion of metalanguage. Metalanguage is language about language, a discourse that takes another discourse as its object. Literature might thus be viewed as the 'object-discourse' for which literary criticism or theory functions as a metalanguage. But the logic of metalanguage is everywhere. It was already operating in our title phrase: 'Creative writing', this chapter, is not in any simple or conventional sense an *example of* creative writing. 'Creative writing' signifies rather that this is a chapter *about* creative writing. Wherever we encounter talking about talking, stories about stories, poems about poetry, statements (like this one) that refer to themselves, we are engaged in effects of metalanguage. But there is something odd about metalanguage,

something that makes it a double-bind, that is to say at once necessary and impossible. A metalinguistic or metadiscursive text (for example, a work of literary criticism or theory) cannot proceed to take another text (a work of literature or creative writing) as its object without that 'object' being at the same time, in this very gesture, part of the 'meta-text'. Metalanguage is never pure, it always entails a logic of being apart from *and* dependent on in its object-language. The acknowledgement that you cannot write about another text without either doing something to it or its doing something to your 'own' writing (if only by virtue of your quoting it, and therefore quoting it out of context, in a new and different context) led Roland Barthes to his celebrated declaration: '*Let the commentary be itself a text*' (Barthes 1981, 44). Is Barthes a creative writer? The difficulty of responding to this question has to do, at least in part, with the ways in which his work unsettles, plays with and over the putative borders and distinctions between creative and critical writing. His texts (like those of Maurice Blanchot, Jacques Derrida and Hélène Cixous) call for new forms, styles and inventions both in literary criticism or theory *and* in literature or creative writing. This is not to suggest, however, that creative and critical writing are really just the same thing. Such is the other side of the double-bind: metalanguage is *necessary*, as well as impossible. Critical writing does not involve 'a suspended relation to meaning and reference' in the way that literary or creative writing does.

2. One does not know, as one writes or as the writing comes, one cannot know if it is creative or not, if it will have been creative or not. Who will have been the judge of whether such and such a piece of writing is or is not 'creative'? Isn't 'creative writing' necessarily predicated on an experience of reading that is to come, like a promise? 'I promise to be creative,' you might say. But unlike other kinds of promises, it may not be in your own power to determine whether or not you will be 'creative'. Following Cixous, we could say that the only 'creative writing' worthy of the name entails the experience of what is beyond us, beyond our capabilities, impossible. She declares: 'The only book that is worth writing is the one we don't have the courage or strength to write. The book that hurts us (we who are writing), that makes us tremble, redden, bleed' (Cixous 1993, 32).

3. Creative writing, if there is any, entails what Timothy Clark (in his study of the idea of inspiration) calls 'a crisis of subjectivity' (Clark 1997). He suggests we might think about this in terms of the blank page facing the would-be writer. This 'blank page' has been conceived in various ways. The seventeenth-century poet Thomas Traherne, for example, described it metaphorically, in terms of infancy: 'An empty book is like an infant's

soul, in which anything may be written. It is capable of all things, but containeth nothing' (Traherne 1991, 187). Clark, on the other hand, describes the blank page as a 'virtual space' that is 'neither in the psyche of the writer nor . . . outside it': this 'space of composition', as he calls it, 'skews distinctions of inner and outer', of 'self and other' (Clark 1997, 22, 27). Writing, creative writing, is transformative, performative in ways that cannot be calculated or foreseen. The writer does not simply precede the writing. The figure of 'the writer' is in crucial respects always 'phantasmatic', never simply 'empirical' or given (see Clark 1997, 24–6). As Blanchot puts it: 'Writing is nothing if it does not involve the writer in a movement full of risks that will change him [or her] in one way or another' (Blanchot 1995, 244). One of the things that makes creative writing, in the context of the university, so distinctive and potentially troublesome is that it entails an explicit engagement with these forms of the transformative and performative, the risky and incalculable.

4. If creative writing involves an openness to otherness, to what has traditionally been called 'inspiration' or 'the muse' or 'God', it nevertheless also involves something singular, apparently unique, like a signature. It is something 'akin to style', as Raymond Carver remarks in his brief but powerful essay 'On Writing', 'but it isn't style alone. It is the writer's particular and unmistakable signature on everything he [or she] writes. It is his [or her] world and no other . . . [The writer] has some special way of looking at things and . . . gives expression to that way of looking' (Carver 1986, 22). It is thus possible to read a phrase or sentence or two by, say, William Blake (the Argument to 'The Marriage of Heaven and Hell') or Emily Dickinson (Poem 214) or Franz Kafka (Aphorism 43 in *The Collected Aphorisms*), and recognize in this the sort of style or signature to which Carver is referring:

> Rintrah roars and shakes his fires in the burdened air;
> Hungry clouds swag on the deep.

> I taste a liquor never brewed—
> From Tankards scooped in Pearl—

> As yet the hounds are still playing in the courtyard, but their prey will not escape, however fast it may already be charging through the forest.

In each case it is a question of these lines, these phrases marking the distinctive 'style' of a writer. No one but Blake could talk about Rintrah roaring or hungry clouds *swagging* on the deep; no one but Dickinson could achieve quite this combination of the wondrous, the visceral and the abstract; no one but Kafka offers quite this sense of inescapable claustrophobia and doom. We might here recall what Coleridge said of first encountering two lines from Wordsworth's 'Winander Boy': 'had I met these lines running wild in the deserts of Arabia, I should have instantly screamed out "Wordsworth!"' (Coleridge 1956–71, 1: 453).

In an extraordinary essay entitled 'He Stuttered', Gilles Deleuze describes this sort of signature or singularity in terms of the invention of a new kind of language, a kind of foreign language within a language. He writes:

> a great writer is always like a foreigner in the language in which he expresses himself, even if this is his native tongue. At the limit, he draws his strength from a mute and unknown minority that belongs only to him. He is a foreigner in his own language: he does not mix another language with his own language, he carves out a nonpreexistent foreign language *within* his own language. He makes the language itself scream, stutter, stammer, or murmur. (Deleuze 1998, 109–10)

This foreign language is never purely the writer's own, of course: it is always made up of words from elsewhere and might always turn out to have been the wrong language. Such is the anguish and uncertainty evoked by Roland Barthes when he writes, of himself, as if he were a character in a novel: 'Writing a certain text, he experiences a guilty emotion of jargon, as if he could not escape from a mad discourse no matter how individual he made his utterance: and what if all his life *he had chosen the wrong language!*' (Barthes 1977c, 114–15).

5. Creative writing happens, if it happens, in a strange nursery. This is another way in which, as a course or subject, 'creative writing' inhabits a quite disturbing and peculiar place within the university: the university is perhaps no longer to be understood as an adult venue, or even as a place in which you mature or 'grow up'. As Sigmund Freud remarks in 'Creative Writers and Day-Dreaming' (1907): 'every child at play behaves like a creative writer' (Freud 1985f, 131). The greater the creative artist, in Freud's view, the more he (or she) remains childlike. As he declares in another essay, on Leonardo da Vinci: 'all great [artists] are bound to retain some infantile part. Even as an adult [Leonardo] continued to play, and this was another reason why he often appeared uncanny and incomprehensible to his contemporaries' (Freud 1985g, 220).

6. Creative writing, if there is any, is urgent despatch, with radically uncertain address. Paul Celan's description of a poem as 'a message in a bottle' (Celan 1986, 34; quoted in Clark 1997, 272) is apt here. A work of creative

writing would be a sort of letter, perhaps a letter-bomb. Elizabeth Bowen says of her first experience of reading Rider Haggard's strange novel *She*: 'After *She* . . . I was prepared to handle any book like a bomb' (Bowen 1986, 250). If you are thinking of writing a novel, it is 'Not a bad plan to think [it's] going to be a letter' (Forster 1976, 162), suggests E.M. Forster – but a letter being read, we might add, after you're dead. Creative writing: keep it compact, think of that iceberg Ernest Hemingway talked about (seven-eighths of the text should be invisible: see Hemingway 2000, 1694), hurry up, it's a matter of life and death, write now. As the Jewish proverb has it: 'Sleep faster! We need the pillows' (quoted in Bloom 1994, 448).

Further reading

The Station Hill Blanchot Reader (1999) brings together an excellent selection of Maurice Blanchot's fiction as well as of his remarkable meditations on the nature of writing, critical and creative. For two of Barthes's most influential and provocative essays on the unstable or dissolving boundaries between literature, criticism and theory, see Barthes 1977c, 1981. For two fine collections of Hélène Cixous's extraordinary essays on writing, see *Three Steps on the Ladder of Writing* (1993) and *Stigmata: Escaping Texts* (1998); for an excellent collection of interviews with her, on and around the subject of writing, see *White Ink* (2008). Gilles Deleuze's *Essays Critical and Clinical* (Deleuze 1998) contains numerous fascinating pieces, including 'Literature and Life', 'He Stuttered' and 'The Exhausted'. Timothy Clark's *The Theory of Inspiration* (Clark 1997) offers a rich and stimulating historical and theoretical account of the nature of inspiration and literary composition, especially from the eighteenth century to the present. For an important broader account of creativity, especially engaging with more scientific perspectives, see Margaret A. Boden's *The Creative Mind* (Boden 2004). On the concept and practice of metafiction, there is a good collection of essays entitled *Metafiction*, edited by Mark Currie (1995). On issues relating to literature, politics and the university, see Derrida's brilliant essay on 'The University without Condition' (Derrida 2002a). Finally, on the relationship between creative writing and psychoanalysis, see Freud's 'Creative Writers and Day-Dreaming' (Freud 1985f); on Freud himself as a writer, see Mahony 1987, Edmundson 1990 and Young 1999; and for a particularly 'wild' but fascinating exploration of the implications and effects of psychoanalysis for creativity, see Chasseguet-Smirget 1984.

12. Laughter

'We are very sorry, indeed, to learn what happened,' said a BBC spokesman on hearing about the *death of a Goodies fan while watching the show.* 'He just laughed heartily and too long,' said his wife. 'After 25 minutes of laughing he gave a tremendous belly laugh, slumped on the settee, and died. (He) loved the Goodies, and it was one of the best for a long time' . . . (*Guardian*, 26 March 1975)

The man's death was, no doubt, a great misfortune. But, as the response of his wife might suggest, there was also something quite funny, and even appropriate about it. The word 'funny' here is oddly ambiguous: how funny it is, after all, that a word ('funny') should mean both 'amusing' and 'strange'. The peculiar appropriateness of the death of this Goodies fan consists not only in the fact that it was a particularly *good* episode of the comedy programme ('one of the best for a long time'), but also in the way in which it is suggestive of a more general and perhaps more intimate link between laughter and death. When we say that someone 'died laughing' or 'laughed themselves to death' we are, in most circumstances, speaking metaphorically. What is funny (in both senses) about the case of the Goodies fan is that it involves a literalization of this metaphor. To take a metaphor literally (which can also be called 'catachresis' or 'misapplication of a word') is an example of a rhetorical device that is often very effective as a means of generating laughter. In this respect it would seem that the man's death conforms to the conventions of comedy. But, of course, there is also a darker side to this, the side that involves 'funny' in the sense of 'funny peculiar'. In other words, what this newspaper report also prompts us to ask is: why do we talk about 'dying with laughter' or 'laughing oneself to death'? Why do we talk about actors 'corpsing', in other words, of being unable to speak their lines because of a sudden fit of hysterical laughter? Are all these instances *simply* metaphorical? Is there something about laughter that, in a profound if ticklish way, puts it in touch with death? Let us leave these questions in suspense for a little while.

What about laughter and literature? We often think of literature as very (or, dare one say, 'deadly') serious, especially if we are studying it. In part this is because (as we suggest in greater detail in Chapter 19) literature is linked to notions of the sacred, to a sense of hushed respect. But literature is also about pleasure, play and laughter. In this chapter we shall attempt to provide an account of some of the ways in which laughter has been theorized, down the centuries, and attempt to illustrate these theories in relation to particular literary texts. Finally, we shall focus on the idea of literature as a space in which the notion of seriousness itself, and the distinctions between the 'serious' and 'non-serious', are fundamentally unsettled, thrown into question, discombobulated.

There are few things worse than the prospect of trying to talk about laughter, or trying to define what is humorous. It is something of a lost cause from the start. It automatically seems to put us – if we dare risk a slightly risible analogy at this point – in the position of the frog, in the joke about the frog, the chicken and the librarian. A chicken walks into the local town library, goes up to the librarian's desk and says: 'Bok!' So the librarian gives the chicken a book. The chicken goes away, but comes back the next day, goes up to the librarian's desk and says: 'Bok, bok!' So the librarian gives the chicken two books, the chicken goes away, comes back the next day: 'Bok, bok, bok!' So the librarian provides the chicken with three more books. And the next day 'Bok, bok, bok, bok!' and so on until the fifth day, when the chicken comes in and says to the librarian, 'Bok, bok, bok, bok, bok!' The librarian hands over five books but then decides to follow the chicken, at a surreptitious distance, out of the library. The librarian follows as the chicken goes down the street, across the road and down a smaller street, then through an unbolted wooden door, down a passageway, into a garden, across the garden to a small lake, across a narrow bridge to an island in the middle, where the chicken puts the books down in front of a frog who says: 'Reddit, reddit . . .'

If there is laughter here it would be the result of a number of things. First, there is the ridiculous anthropomorphism: chickens do not go to libraries, librarians do not respond to chickens as if they were simply 'members of the public', frogs do not read books. Second, there is the pleasure of recognition as we realize that the 'bok, bok' of a chicken could after all be heard as a request for a book, or for two books, and that the croaking of a frog might indeed be construed as 'read it, read it'. Third, there is the sense of a so-called shaggy dog story, the feeling that the story could go on indefinitely, that the chicken could, at least in principle, order up the entire holdings of the British Library. Bok, bok, bok . . . Here laughter would be linked to suspense, and more specifically perhaps to the hysterical effect of a potentially permanent post-ponement of a resolution. It is this which in part at least constitutes the comic force of a play such as Beckett's *Waiting for Godot* (1953). But by the same token it would also be what haunts or menaces every tragedy: comedy in this sense could be defined as the overturning of the tragic. But there is perhaps also, by contrast, something comical about the very corniness (so to speak) of the joke, its 'cheepness' and groan-making quality. In this respect the joke relies on a certain surprise – the surprise of the punchline – *and* a certain recognition: you know that a punchline is going to come and what sort of punchline it will be, but you cannot tell exactly what it will be. There is a child-like pleasure involved in laughing at something at once surprising and familiar. Perhaps indeed, as Freud argues in his fascinating book *Jokes and Their Relation to the Unconscious* (1905), 'everything comic is based fundamentally on degradation [or "stepping down"] to being a child' (Freud 1976, 292). Finally, this ridiculous story about the frog, the chicken and the librarian sug-gests something about the relations between laughter, reading and mystery. For perhaps what is also funny about the story is the implicit hyperbole whereby anyone (let alone a frog) could be expected to have read *everything*. In this respect we can never be in the position of the frog or – to put it more specifically in terms of our argument in this chapter – there is never a truly froglike position from which to provide a serious account of laughter. Any theory of laughter, we would like to suggest, is necessarily infected, under-mined, displaced by the experience of laughter itself.

Let us consider a couple of the basic theories of laughter. The first is the 'superiority theory'. It is succinctly and memorably formulated by the seventeenth-century English philosopher Thomas Hobbes: 'The passion of laughter is nothing else but *sudden glory* arising from some sudden *conception* of some *eminency* in ourselves, by *comparison* with the *infirmity* of others, or with our own formerly' (Hobbes 1840, 46). We laugh, according to this argument, out of a sense of superiority – the 'sudden glory' or 'conception of eminency' in relation to the stupidity or weakness of others, or of ourselves at some point in the past. Thus, for example, we may laugh at the man who slips over on the banana skin, or we may laugh at Bottom, in *A Midsummer Night's Dream*, because he is such an ass, or we may laugh with Swift at the small-mindedness of other human beings, for example in Book I of *Gulliver's Travels* (1726).

The second theory is what we could call the 'nothing theory' or the 'no theory' theory. This may be illustrated by way of the Monty Python sketch in which a woman called Miss Anne Elk (John Cleese in drag) is interviewed because she is supposed to have a new theory about the brontosaurus. Miss Elk will not disclose her theory but seems instead concerned simply to say over and over again that she *has* a theory and that the theory is hers: 'my theory that I have, that is to say, which is mine, is mine'. Chris, the interviewer (Graham Chapman), becoming exasperated, says: 'Yes, I know it's yours, what is it?' Looking rather nervously around the studio, Anne Elk replies: 'Where?' (*Monty Python's Flying Circus* 1989, 119) When Miss Elk does finally enunciate her theory it is truly bathetic – in fact, no theory at all:

Miss Elk   Ready?
Presenter   Yes.
Miss Elk   My theory by A. Elk. Brackets Miss, brackets. This theory goes as follows and begins now. All brontosauruses are thin at one end, much much thicker in the middle and then thin again at the far end. That is my theory, it is mine, and belongs to me and I own it, and what it is too.
Presenter   That's *it*, is it?
Miss Elk   Spot on, Chris. (119)

In more sombre and philosophical terms, the 'nothing theory' or 'no theory' theory is suggested, for instance, by Immanuel Kant's proposition that '*Laughter is an affection arising from a strained expectation being suddenly reduced to nothing*' (Kant 1988, 199). Laughter is nothing more than the bursting of a bubble. When we laugh, according to this argument, we are laughing in a sort of 'absurd' vacuum: 'merely' laughing, with nothing to support us. In a fascinating essay entitled 'The Laughter of Being', Mikkel Borch-Jacobsen suggests a radicalization of this Kantian formulation. Following the work of the French writer Georges Bataille in particular, he argues that 'There is no theory of laughter, only an experience' (Borch-Jacobsen 1987, 742). Moreover, this experience is of a decidedly 'funny' sort – for it is an experience of, precisely, *nothing*. As Bataille puts it: '[when I laugh,] I am in fact nothing more than the laughter which takes hold of me' (Bataille 1973, 364, cited by Borch-Jacobsen, 744).

Let us turn from 'theory' to consider some literary examples. Laughter can be dependent on the visual – and literature is full of instances of visual comedy. But laughter, at least in literature, is perhaps more fundamentally a matter of language. One of the greatest eighteenth-century English comedies is Richard Brinsley Sheridan's play *The School for Scandal* (first performed in 1777).

It contains numerous classic moments of visual comedy (characters in disguise, hiding themselves behind screens, being thrust hastily into closets and so on), but the comic power of Sheridan's play consists above all in its language. This starts from the very title of the play – with its satirical implication that scandalmongering is something to be taught – and from the names of its characters – a woman called Lady Sneerwell, her servant, Snake, a gentleman called Sir Benjamin Backbite, and so forth. We could consider a brief exchange between Lady Sneerwell and Mr Snake on the subject of her 'superiority' over other slanderers and scandalmongers such as Mrs Clackitt:

> *Lady Sneerwell*   Why truly Mrs Clackitt has a very pretty talent – and a great deal of industry.
> *Snake*   True, madam, and has been tolerably successful in her day. To my knowledge she has been the cause of six matches being broken off and three sons disinherited, of four forced elopements, and as many close confinements, nine separate maintenances, and two divorces. Nay, I have more than once traced her causing a *tête-à-tête* in the *Town and Country Magazine*, when the parties perhaps had never seen each other's face before in the course of their lives.
> *Lady Sneerwell*   She certainly has talents, but her *manner* is gross.
> *Snake*   'Tis very true. She generally designs well, has a free tongue, and a bold invention; but her colouring is too dark and her outlines often extravagant. She wants that delicacy of hint and mellowness of sneer which distinguishes your ladyship's scandal.
> *Lady Sneerwell*   You are partial, Snake. (I, i, 10–26)

We can imagine the comic possibilities of the characters' gestures and appearance, but what is most comic is in the language itself – in the satirical observation on what it means to be 'tolerably successful', in the incongruity or absurdity of evaluating who has the more beautiful 'sneer', in the snaking sibilance of Snake's last sentence, in the playful truth of Lady Sneerwell's final remark.

The play called *The School for Scandal* is, then, fundamentally wordplay. Indeed, we could say, literature in general has to do with wordplay or – to use a more technical-sounding term – with paronomasia. This is in part what makes it potentially so subversive and disturbing. Could there really be a character called Snake? Or a woman called Lady Sneerwell? What kind of world do they belong to? Literature is a matter of linguistic as well as social scandal. It poses a constant challenge to the realms of so-called 'good sense' and represents an affront to what could be called the ideology of seriousness. Paronomasia is indeed so originary a dimension of literary works that one is tempted to agree with the narrator of Samuel Beckett's *Murphy* (1938) and say: 'In the beginning was the pun' (41). Even Shakespeare becomes open to criticism on this front. Literary critics may not have much of a reputation for being amusing – but critical indignation at Shakespeare's soft spot for the 'quibble' (or 'pun') gives rise to what we think is one of the funniest paragraphs in the history of literary criticism. Here is Samuel Johnson's fascinating and irresistible paragraph from his Preface to Shakespeare (1765):

> A quibble is to Shakespeare what luminous vapours are to the traveller; he follows it at all adventures; it is sure to lead him out of his way and sure to engulf him in the mire. It has some malignant power over his mind, and its fascinations are irresistible. Whatever be the dignity or profundity of his disquisition, whether he be enlarging knowledge or exalting affection, whether he be amusing attention with incidents or enchaining it in suspense, let but a quibble spring up before him, and he leaves his work unfinished. A quibble is the golden apple for which he will always turn aside from his career or stoop from his elevation. A quibble, poor and barren as it is, gave him such delight that he was content to purchase it by the sacrifice of reason, propriety, and truth. A quibble was to him the fatal Cleopatra for which he lost the world and was content to lose it. (Johnson 1969, 68)

It is perhaps difficult not to find the 'dignity' and 'profundity' of Johnson's 'disquisition' amusing: he quibbles about quibbling in terms as extravagant as any in Shakespeare. In the process he also delightfully intimates what is often so compelling about such wordplay, namely its playful mixing of sex and death: the quibble is the apple of Shakespeare's I, the obscure object of desire, at once 'barren' and 'the fatal Cleopatra'.

We will now consider another, rather different kind of literary work, Geoffrey Chaucer's 'The Miller's Tale'. This is the story, set in Oxford, about the superstitious old carpenter John, his beautiful young wife Alisoun, and their handsome lodger, Nicholas. Along with a rather absurd rival called Absolon, Nicholas is after the young wife. Chaucer's tale recounts, with superb comic concision, how Nicholas persuades John that the end of the world is coming, in order to distract him so that he can get into bed with the old man's wife. John ends up with a broken arm, but Nicholas finally fares worse. That same night, Alisoun has already humiliated Absolon: he craves a kiss from her and she agrees, but in the dark Absolon finds himself kissing her arse, not her mouth. When Nicholas tries to repeat this jape, and indeed embellish it with a thundering fart, he receives a burning hot poker up his bum. In order to try to convey what makes Chaucer's 'The Miller's Tale' one of the greatest comic poems ever written we could point to the visual comedy of John the Carpenter up in the rooftop cutting the cable and crashing down, convinced that the flood is coming and that he'll be safe in the 'kneeding-tubbe' that will be his mini Noah's ark. This fall might be seen as a literaliza-tion and structural equivalent of the fall of the tragic hero. In this respect comedy is not the *opposite* of tragedy but the same, viewed from a different perspective. While we identify with the tragic hero or heroine, we stand apart from or above the comic victim. Chaucer's poem, then, offers a clear example of the Hobbesian motif: we laugh because we are not stupid like John the Carpenter. The carpenter falls. We remain where we are, superior, riding high.

But we must at the same time acknowledge that all of this is in a sense only happening *in language*, as something being narrated. And indeed the comic force of 'The Miller's Tale' is very specifically linguistic. It is not only a matter of the brutally eloquent account of John's cuckolding, or the satirical portrayal of Absolon's fashion-conscious, prancing character, or the bawdy language of pissing and 'letting flee' monumental farts. It is also, and most crucially, that the whole story seems to be structured like a joke condensed from or into the single word, 'water'. The whole text turns on the double signification of 'water': for Nicholas it's a screamed request for an anodyne to salve his sizzling arse, for John it signifies that the flood is upon them. The two parts of the story are explosively assembled in the wordplay or paronomasia around this single word:

> The hote culter brende so his toute,
> And for the smert he wende for to dye.
> As he were wood, for wo he gan to crye—
> 'Help! water! water! help, for Goddes herte!'
> This carpenter out of his slomber sterte,
> And herde oon cryen 'water!' as he were wood,
> And thoghte, 'Allas, now comth Nowelis flood!'
> He sit him up withouten wordes mo,
> And with his ax he smoot the corde atwo,
> And doun goth al . . .
> (lines 709–18)
> [The hot poker burnt his bum so badly he thought he was going to die of the pain. Like a lunatic he cried out in woe: 'Help! Water! Water! Help, for God's sake!' Hearing someone madly cry 'Water!' the carpenter started out of his sleep and thought 'Oh no! It's Noah's flood!' He sits up like a shot and cuts the rope with his axe, and every-thing gives way . . .]

The visual comedy of the fall (whether from the roof in Chaucer, or on a banana skin in *The Simpsons*), and the accompanying emphasis on high and low, seems to have a 'funny' counterpart in the terms of rhetorical figures and tropes. Thus what creates laughter in a text is often either hyperbole (exaggeration) or litotes (understatement). Some examples of hyperbole would be the sorts of comparative metaphor for which Raymond Chandler's work is celebrated. In *The Little Sister* (1949), for instance, we encounter the gorgeous Miss Gonzales who, Marlowe tells us, 'smelled the way the Taj Mahal looked by moonlight' (70), had a 'mouth as red as a new fire engine' (158) and who proceeds to make 'a couple of drinks in a couple of glasses you could almost have stood umbrellas in' (70). Correspondingly we are told of a man wearing 'sky-blue gaberdine slacks . . . and a two-tone leisure jacket which would have been revolting on a zebra' (84) and a police lieutenant called Maglachan who 'had a jaw like a park bench' (167). Litotes, on the other hand, is a pervasive trope in Jonathan Swift's *A Modest Proposal* (1729), a text which also illustrates the fundamental, if in many ways disturbing, power of irony as a comic dimension of literary texts. *A Modest Proposal* works by understatement and irony. It modestly (or litotically) proposes that a solution to poverty and population management in Ireland might be the killing of small children, then selling and eating them.

Outside of literature, we might say, it is possible to entertain perfectly serious ideas about laughter, about jokes, comedy and humour. Thus Freud's *Jokes and their Relation to the Unconscious* (Freud 1976) is a fascinating work, not only for the similarities it reveals between the structure of jokes and dreams (and by implication, therefore, the structure of works of literature as well), but also for the basic and in some ways disturbing truth it offers as regards the nature of most jokes. Freud argues that jokes tend to be sexist, 'dirty', violent, racist: they transgress social taboos and (momentarily) 'lift' repression. But literature, conversely, might be defined as the space in which the seriousness of Freud's or anyone else's claims are ironized, satirized, parodied or otherwise put into question. For literature is the discourse that is, perhaps more than any other, concerned with questioning and unsettling assumptions about what is serious and what is not serious. Such a questioning and unsettling is often associated with 'the postmodern'. Postmodern works such as the plays of Samuel Beckett, the poetry of John Ashbery or the fiction of David Foster Wallace present a disquieting, irresolvable mixture of the serious and non-serious, tragic and comic, macabre and laughable. This uncomfortable mixture, however, might also be seen to be at play in Shakespeare's tragedies, for example, or indeed in Chaucer's 'The Miller's Tale', which ends with a scene in which everyone is laughing but where it is no longer clear what kind of laughter it is or who is laughing at what or who. As we have suggested, the study of literature is in various ways policed by a kind of ideology of seriousness. There is a strong tendency to accept the rules, to adhere to boundaries and categories, to say: the study of literature is a serious affair. Or to say: X is a serious text or a serious moment in a text, whereas Y is not serious. No doubt in the context of the novel, 'realism' has been and in many ways continues to be the very embodiment of a certain 'seriousness'. But the postmodern prompts us to ask various questions in this respect: how seriously, for example, should we take 'realism' or 'reality effects' in literature? What does seriousness imply or assume? Who are the police and what is the nature of their authority?

Laughter can both liberate and mystify. It can be diabolical. It can be at once offensive (laughing at sexist or racist jokes, for instance) and inoffensive (it was 'only a joke'). It can be cruel, a means of exclusion or of exerting power over people ('then she just laughed in my face'). But it can also be joyous, a means of sharing and of confirming one's sense of 'social community'. As Freud observes of jokes: 'Every joke calls for a public of its own and laughing at the same jokes is evidence of far-reaching psychical conformity' (Freud 1976, 203–4). Laughter can be undecidably 'real' and 'unreal', 'genuine' and 'false'. It can be tiring, it can have you on your hands and knees. It can be uncontrollable, as if with a life of its own. In the engulfment of uncontrollable laughter we lose a sense of who or what we are. We can feel ourselves reduced to nothing. Every pretension to mastery or superiority collapses and dissolves. Laughter becomes the obliteration of identity. It is this obliteration – when one is truly engulfed in laughter, when one is nothing *but* this laughter – that perhaps gives laughter its strange intimacy with death.

Further reading

For two classic accounts of laughter and the comic, see Henri Bergson, *Laughter: An Essay on the Meaning of the Comic* (1921) and Sigmund Freud, *Jokes and their Relation to the Unconscious* (1976). Freud also has a short but extremely interesting essay on the nature of humour (in Freud 1985d). Bergson's essay is reprinted in Sypher, ed., *Comedy* (1956) which also reprints George Meredith's eloquent 'An Essay on Comedy' (1877). Barry Saunders's *Sudden Glory: Laughter as Subversive History* (1996) is an accessible and thought-provoking account of the anti-authoritarian powers of laughter. Glen Cavaliero's *The Alchemy of Laughter* (2005) is an engaging exploration of laughter in literature from Henry Fielding to Samuel Beckett, while *A History of English Laughter: Laughter from Beowulf to Beckett and Beyond*, ed. Manfred Pfister (2002) comprises an enjoyably eccentric gathering of essays, on writers including Chaucer, Milton, Sterne and Joyce. Simon Critchley's *On Humour* (2002) is an informative and entertaining little book, dealing in further detail with many of the topics discussed in the present chapter. Arthur Koestler's *The Act of Creation* (1964) contains some engaging and thoughtful material on 'the jester' and the nature of laughter. On quibbling in Shakespeare, see M.M. Mahood's *Shakespeare's Wordplay* (1957) and, especially in a sexual context, Eric Partridge's classic *Shakespeare's Bawdy* (2001, first published in 1947). For an account of Chaucer in a similar vein, see Thomas W. Ross (1972). For a wide-ranging and challenging collection of essays on puns and wordplay, see Jonathan Culler, ed., *On Puns* (1988a). For a varied collection of essays on comedy from a historical perspective, see Cordner, Holland and Kerrigan, eds, *English Comedy* (1994). Borch-Jacobsen's complex but excellent account of theories of laughter, 'The Laughter of Being', appears in a 'Laughter' special issue of *Modern Language Notes* (1987). Of particular interest in the same issue are Samuel Weber's 'Laughing in the Meanwhile' (1987) and Jean-Luc Nancy's 'Wild Laughter in the Throat of Death' (1987); see also Nancy's interrogation of his own question 'Is it possible to be in the presence of laughter?' in 'Laughter, Presence' (1993). From a feminist perspective, see Gray, *Women and Laughter* (1994).

13. The tragic

Tragedy tears us apart, it shatters our sense of ourselves and the world. The terrifying power of tragedy is suggested by Sir Philip Sidney when he speaks, in *An Apology for Poetry* (1595), of

> high and excellent Tragedy, that openeth the greatest wounds, and showeth forth the ulcers that are covered with tissue; that maketh kings fear to be tyrants, and tyrants manifest their tyrannical humours; that, with stirring the affects of admiration and commiseration, teacheth the uncertainty of this world, and upon how weak foundations gilden roofs are builded . . . (98)

Tragedy has to do with strangeness. It involves an overwhelming sense of what Sidney calls 'the uncertainty of this world'. It involves – as Aristotle suggested, more than 2,300 years ago – a paradoxical combination of emotions, at once pity and fear or (as Sidney says) 'admiration and commiseration'. Tragedy involves an encounter not only with the death of a character on stage (or in the pages of a book) but also with the idea of our own deaths. Tragedy resists simple explanations. As A.C. Bradley observed, in 1904: 'tragedy would not be tragedy if it were not a painful mystery' (38). In this chapter we propose to elucidate this sense of 'painful mystery' and to consider some examples of tragic literature, ranging from Shakespeare to the present.

When we think of tragedy in the context of literature in English, no doubt we think first of Shakespeare and especially of the 'great tragedies', *Hamlet* (1600–1), *Othello* (1604), *King Lear* (1605) and *Macbeth* (1606). With such plays in mind, and adapting Aristotle's definition in the *Poetics*, we could suggest that tragedy comprises four basic elements. The first is that there is a central character (the protagonist), someone who is 'noble' and with whom we are able to sympathize or identify. The second is that this character should suffer and (preferably) die, and that his or her downfall or death should roughly coincide with the end of the play. The third is that the downfall or death of the central character should be felt by the spectator or reader to be both inevitable and 'right' but at the same time in some sense unjustifiable and unacceptable. The fourth element can be referred to as apocalypticism. As we have already indicated, it is not just the death of the protagonist that we are presented with in a tragedy: in identifying with the protagonist who dies, we are also drawn into thinking about our own death. And because the protagonist's death is invariably shattering to other characters, tragedy always engages with a broader sense of death and destruction, a shattering of society or the world as a whole.

Without these four elements there cannot be a tragedy. From an Aristotelian perspective we might want to propose additional elements, in particular the notions of *peripeteia* ('reversal'), *anagnorisis* ('revelation' or 'coming to self-knowledge') and *hamartia* ('tragic flaw' or 'error'). *Peripeteia* is a useful term for referring to the reversals or sudden changes in fortune that a character or characters may experience – Lear's being made homeless, for instance, or Othello's being transformed by 'the green-ey'd monster' (III, iii, 166) of jealousy. Aristotle introduced the term in the context of tragedy, though it is also apposite in other contexts, including comedy (where a character may experience a reversal or sudden change for the good). *Anagnorisis* refers to the idea of a moment of revelation or recognition, especially the moment when a protagonist experiences a sudden awakening to the truth or to self-knowledge. A tragic work may contain more than one such moment: Hamlet's life, for instance, might be described as a sort of *anagnorisis* 'block', a ghostly series of apparent but ineffective *anagnorises* starting with his exclamation 'O my prophetic soul!' (I, v, 40) on discovering the murderous truth about his father's death and realizing that this is what he had imagined, deep in his 'prophetic soul'. Classically, though, a tragedy tends to be construed as having one crucial or climactic moment of *anagnorisis*. In Sophocles's *Oedipus the King*, for example, this can be very specifically located in lines 1306–08, as Oedipus finally realizes that he is himself the criminal he has been seeking:

> O god—
> all come true, all burst to light!
> O light—now let me look my last on you!
> I stand revealed at last.

Finally, *hamartia* refers to the idea of tragic characters having a particular flaw or weakness, or making an error of judgement which leads to their downfall or death. Thus, for example, each of the male protagonists of Shakespeare's 'great tragedies' could be considered in terms of a fundamental moral or psychological weakness. Hamlet's irresolution, Othello's jealousy, Lear's pride and Macbeth's ambition might then be seen as a key element in each of these works. A primary aim in this chapter, however, is to stress the ways in which the tragic entails a fundamental sense of what remains painful, mysterious or uncertain. That is to say, to focus on a character's 'tragic flaw' or 'error' tends to suggest something straightforwardly *causal*: Hamlet's irresoluteness is the cause of his tragedy and so on. This is not to say that Hamlet's irresolution or Othello's jealousy are unimportant. These 'flaws' or 'weaknesses' are crucial – they are integral to what we think and feel about Hamlet and Othello as characters and therefore to what we think and feel about their tragic fates. But what constitutes the tragic is always stranger and more painful than is suggested by the inevitably moralistic and reductive claim that, for instance, Othello should not have allowed himself to get so jealous and worked up. His jealousy has a crucial but partial and perhaps finally uncertain significance in terms of the tragic power of the play. About to murder his beloved wife, Othello begins what is one of the most anguished and intolerable soliloquies in Shakespeare's work: 'It is the cause, it is the cause, my soul; / Let me not name it to you, you chaste stars, / It is the cause' (V, ii, 1–3). 'Cause' here may mean 'crime', 'legal or other case' or 'reason'. What is conveyed in these lines is a sense of what *cannot be named*, a profound strangeness and uncertainty regarding the very sense of this repeated and equivocal word, 'cause'. Tragedy, we want to suggest, and as *Othello* pointedly demonstrates, is not only about the sense of particular causes or explanations but also, and more importantly, about a painful absence or uncertainty of cause.

Tragedy (and here we use the word to embrace both Shakespearean and more recent forms) is not only inimical to the pleasure-button-pushing mentality of Hollywood or Broadway, but also at odds with the very idea of identity and meaning. As Howard Barker puts it, in a series of aphoristic statements entitled 'Asides for a Tragic Theatre' (1986, later published 1989):

> In tragedy, the audience is disunited . . . Tragedy is not about reconciliation . . . Tragedy offends the sensibilities. It drags the unconscious into the public place . . . After the carnival, after the removal of the masks, you are precisely who you were before. After the tragedy, you are not certain who you are. (Barker 1989, 13)

Tragedy is offensive, it generates disunity and exposes disharmony. Like psychoanalytic theory (itself of course crucially indebted to Sophocles's *Oedipus the King*), tragedy makes the unconscious public. It leaves us uncertain about our very identities, uncertain about how we feel, about what has happened to us.

Finally, there is something apocalyptic about the tragic, not only in the sense that it consistently entails an experience of unmanageable disorder but also in that this experience of disorder is linked to a more general kind of *revelation* (the meaning of the original Greek word 'apocalypsis'). The apocalyptic revelation at the heart of the tragic has to do with a sense that no God or gods are looking down on the world to see that justice is done, or that, if there are gods, they are profoundly careless, indifferent, even sadistic. The heavens may be occupied or vacant, but the world is terrible and *makes no sense*. To illustrate this idea in relation to *King Lear*, for example, we could look to a few lines spoken by Albany – addressed to his wife Goneril and concerned with the 'vile' behaviour of herself and her sister Regan towards their father, the King:

> If that the heavens do not their visible spirits
> Send quickly down to tame these vile offenses,
> It will come.
> Humanity must perforce prey on itself
> Like monsters of the deep. (IV, ii, 46–50)

The tragic revelation of *King Lear* concerns the sense that humanity is indeed monstrous and that there are no 'visible spirits' or any other sort of spirits that might properly or profitably be called down from the heavens. One of the shortest, yet perhaps most powerful lines in Shakespeare – 'It will come' – is apocalyptic both in terms of the dark revelation of the idea that there are no gods or divine justice and in terms of the sense of an impending or accumulating cataclysm of general destruction and death. The word 'come' is crucial here – as indeed it is in the final passages of several of Shakespeare's tragedies – in part because it resonates with the apocalypticism of the end of the Bible: 'He which testifieth these things saith, Surely I come quickly. Amen. Even so, come, Lord Jesus' (Revelation 22:20). Tragedy says 'come' in a double sense: it summons us, it engages our feelings of sympathy and identification, it demands that our emotions be involved in what is happening. But at the same time tragedy says: we have to suffer, we are going to die, there is no justice and there is no afterlife. It, death and cataclysm, will come. In this way, tragedy engages with the limits of sense, verges on the senseless. Because what tragedy is about *is* senseless, meaningless – the unjust and yet unavoidable shattering of life. This would be another way of trying to highlight the mysterious and paradoxical nature of the tragic. When Ludovico says, of the bed displaying the corpses of Othello and Desdemona, 'Let it be hid' (*Othello*, V, ii, 365), Shakespeare's play paradoxically conceals or encrypts this intolerable sight that tragedy calls us to witness. Correspondingly, in *King Lear*, the death of Cordelia and Lear's madness of grief are figured in apocalyptic terms – Kent asks, 'Is this the promis'd end?' and Edgar retorts, 'Or image of that horror?' (V, iii, 264–5) – but what the tragedy finally and paradoxically reveals is perhaps rather the ethical and spiritual horror of a world in which violence, torture and terror recur unendingly. What is revealed in *King Lear*, in other words, is the sense that there is no image of the end except as this unendingness.

With these rather dark thoughts in mind, let us try to say a little more about the first three elements of a tragedy. First of all, there is the idea of the central character with whom one strongly sympathizes or identifies. 'Sympathy' here entails primarily the idea of 'entering into another's feelings or mind' (*Chambers*). It carries clear connotations of the original Greek terms 'syn', *with*, and 'pathos', *suffering* – that is to say, 'sympathy' as 'suffering with'. It is important to distinguish this from 'feeling sorry for'. In tragedy, sympathy with a character is indistinguishable from a logic of identification, of identifying with that character and experiencing and suffering with her or him. The tragic has to do with a sense of *loss* of identity – the sense that (in Barker's words) 'you are not certain who you are'. We might try to clarify this a little more by remarking on the paradoxical nature of sympathy specifically in relation to drama. Sympathy involves going out of ourselves, and sharing or identifying with the position of another. Putting it slightly differently, it involves a sense of going out of ourselves but, at the same time, *putting our- selves on stage*. In this respect we have an intriguing example of *chiasmus*, which can be formulated as follows: there is no drama without sympathy, but there is no sympathy without drama. This proposition may also help us to appreciate why, in historical terms, tragedy has so consistently been associ- ated with the dramatic. More than any other genre, tragedy explores the limits of the experience of sympathy, as it broaches self-obliteration and death. In a manner especially suited to the stage, tragedy is exposure to death – to that extreme of sympathy or identification where, putting oneself on stage, one loses a sense of oneself *in the scene*, in the figure of the one who dies.

It is only on the basis of this first element (sympathy) that the second (the suffering and death of a character) can be described as tragic. This may seem logical enough, but the third element of a tragedy is distinctly paradoxical: the death that occurs at the end of a tragedy is experienced as being at once unavoidable and unjust. This is sometimes talked about as tragic inevitability. Every tragic work will generate a sense of the inevitable or (to use a term that is perhaps too easily loaded with religious connotations) the *fated*. The tragic invariably concerns a sense of what is *foreseeable* but *unavoidable*. But what is unavoidable (Desdemona in *Othello* must die, Tess in Hardy's novel must die, Ikem and Chris in Achebe's *Anthills of the Savannah* must die) is also unacceptable: the tragic seems to involve a peculiar contradiction whereby death is inevitable and therefore (however painfully) appropriate *but at the same time* unjust, unacceptable and therefore inappropriate. Consider, for example, the moment in the final scene of *Hamlet* when Hamlet confides to Horatio: 'If it be now, 'tis not to come; if it be not to come, it will be now; if it be not now, yet it will come – the readiness is all' (V, ii, 220–2). At this moment we, like Horatio, may not *want* Hamlet to die, but at the same time it is hard to imagine that there could be any other outcome to this dark 'coming' to 'readiness' about which Hamlet is speaking here.

The paradoxical nature of this third element of the tragic is analogous to the Aristotelian notion of cartharsis. 'Catharsis' is generally understood to refer to the 'cleansing' effect of watching (or reading) a tragedy and to involve the combination of two kinds of emotion (pity and fear). The cathartic effects of watching (or reading) are linked to the peculiar fact that tragedy can give pleasure. Likewise, as we noted earlier, the combination of pity and fear seems contradictory. After all, how can one feel pity and fear at the same time? If there were a simple answer to this question we would no longer be thinking within the terms of the tragic, since the tragic comprises precisely this kind of contradictoriness of feeling. Pity (*pathos* in ancient Greek) is understood by Aristotle in terms of a movement towards the spectacle of destruction and death on stage (or page), while fear or terror (*phobos* in ancient Greek) is a movement away from it. In this way, the spectator or reader is torn apart. And it is in this sense that we can say that the tragic is not rationalizable, rather it is an *affront* to our desires for meaning and coherence.

In thinking about a particular drama or other work in terms of the tragic, then, perhaps the most obvious thing to do in the first instance is to consider the question of sympathy and/or identification. One could for example think about such questions as the following: how does a tragic text generate sympathy? Which character or characters elicit our sympathy? What is it that *happens* in the text that produces a feeling of sympathy or identification on our part? It is not only a question of character (what is he or she *like* as an individual?) and plot (what happens to him or her, the poor sod?) but also, and more fundamentally, a matter of how character and plot are created *in language*. In short, it is worth trying to think about which particular passages,

speeches, and even phrases or words help to generate sympathy in the spectator or reader. To get a clearer sense of this it may be useful to give an example
in which one might reasonably suppose that sympathy is at work, and to offer
a paraphrase. Take Lady Macbeth's words of murderous guilt as overheard
by the Doctor and Gentlewoman. (It is, of course, an illustration of the disturbing power of this tragedy that Shakespeare is able to make us sympathize
or identify with a psychopathic murderer.) Lady Macbeth says: 'Here's the
smell of the blood still. All the perfumes of Arabia will not sweeten this little
hand. O, O, O!' (V, i, 50–2). Lady Macbeth does *not* say: 'Oh what a bore, this
smelly blood. Not even industrial cleansing fluid will get this off my hands.
Hell, what am I supposed to do?' There are numerous observations one might
make regarding the extraordinary *pathos* of Lady Macbeth's language – in
its Shakespearean form, that is. The first word she says, 'Here', is significant
precisely because it draws us into absolute proximity with her. 'There' would
have a quite different effect. The deictic 'Here' suggests how a play such as
Macbeth establishes and maintains sympathy or identification through the
presentation or indication of psychological interiority, in other words the
inside perspective of a given character's thoughts and feelings. The 'smell
of the blood' and the felt persistency of the word 'still' may be mere somnam-
bulistic hallucination, but the spectator or reader is here being presented
with intimate, indeed appalling, knowledge of Lady Macbeth's thoughts and
sense-impressions. Through the strangeness of soliloquy (the theatrical
device that most explicitly facilitates our access to the interior world of a character's thoughts and feelings), we feel in turn the pouring out of guilt in 'All the
perfumes of Arabia . . .' and the stammering nullity of 'O, O, O!' We cannot
claim to truly understand or identify with Lady Macbeth (that would be sleepwalking madness), but her language, pitifully overheard by other characters
and by spectators or readers alike, generates sympathy. Sympathy, in short, is
something that calls to be described and analysed not only at the macro-level
of character and plot but also, and more importantly, at the micro-level of individual words, phrases, sentences.

Finally, we could consider the question of the tragic in some of its more
contemporary forms. One can think of many sorts of literary works that are
tragedies of one kind or another – and often showing obvious conformities
with the model we have outlined. But it is also evident that tragedy has undergone certain changes in the past century or so. There are various reasons for
this. One reason has to do with the notion of 'the death of God'. Tragedy, that
is to say, is bound to be different if it is considered, at the outset, from a secular
perspective. Shakespearean tragedy might be said to be modern to the extent
that it seems to dramatize the terrible revelation of a secular and arbitrary

world, a purposeless universe of suffering and death (countered only by the quasi-miraculous tenacity of notions of goodness, dignity and justice – with or without religion). Thomas Hardy's novels – *The Mayor of Casterbridge* (1886), *The Woodlanders* (1887), *Tess of the d'Urbervilles* (1891) and *Jude the Obscure* (1895), for example – might be regarded as limit-texts in this respect: they are remarkably close to the sort of model of tragedy that we have outlined in this chapter but their tragic force consists less in a dramatic revelation that there is no God or ultimate justice and more in an ironic toying with the very grounds of such a revelation. If, as Paul Fussell has argued, irony is the 'dominating form of modern understanding' (Fussell 1975, 35), this is especially clear in the sort of ironization of tragedy evident in Thomas Hardy's work. The fact that these novels incorporate allusions to what Hardy calls the Immanent Will, the 'intangible Cause' or 'Unfulfilled Intention', as well as to more familiar classical deities, is simply part of this ironization. In terms of drama itself, there have been quite traditional examples of the tragic – one might think of Arthur Miller's great allegorical work, *The Crucible* (1953), for example – but more characteristic of the past century have been the kind of secular tragicomedies of Chekhov or Beckett.

A second reason why tragedy is not what it used to be concerns the transformations that have taken place over the past two hundred years or so regarding notions of the individual and society. If modern tragedies tend to be about ordinary people rather than kings or queens, they also show how far the lives of such 'ordinary people' are bound up, determined and constrained by broader social, economic and political realities. One of the first modern tragedies in European drama, Henrik Ibsen's *A Doll's House* (1879), for example, is not simply about the break-up of the 'doll' Nora's marriage: it is about the ways in which the patriarchal institution and conventions of marriage effectively *programme* this tragic break-up. Particularly in the wake of Ibsen's work, in other words, there is a fundamental shift from a classical idea of tragedy as inevitable and beyond human control to the modern idea of a tragedy as something humanly engineered and happening in a world in which something could and should be done, for instance about sexual inequality, racism and so on. In his autobiography, Bertrand Russell remarks that 'One of the things that makes literature so consoling, is that its tragedies are all in the past, and have the completeness and repose that comes of being beyond the reach of our endeavours' (Russell 1968, 169). Russell's observation may be appropriate for thinking about tragedy in its classical modes; but it is quite inadequate and misleading for thinking about modern tragedy. New historicist and poststructuralist critics, in particular, have been concerned to underline what many of the more recent examples of tragic works of literature make clear, namely that what Russell comfortably refers to as 'the past' is precisely what is in question. And if the past is in question, so is the present. Whose past are we talking about? From whose perspective? With whose interests at stake?

We could illustrate this by referring briefly to a couple of contemporary works of tragic literature. The first example is a novel about the United States. Toni Morrison's *The Bluest Eye* (1970) contains the basic elements of tragedy – even if this includes a modification of Shakespearean 'suffering and death' into Morrisonian 'suffering and terrible abuse'. It is set in Ohio, and the narrative begins in 1941. It recounts the story of a young black girl called Pecola and how she comes to be sexually abused by her grimly named father, Cholly Breedlove. Morrison's novel may be set in the past but its power as a tragic text consists partly in the fact that it is making an explicit political statement not only about racism in contemporary US society but also about the perception of history itself. The novel involves a lucid but terrible elaboration of *why* this man called Breedlove should have abused his daughter. By stressing the ways in which Breedlove himself had in the past been racially and physically abused in turn, Morrison's novel provides a complex historical account of racism and violence. *The Bluest Eye* is tragic but the villain is paradoxically part of the tragedy. Morrison's novel broaches a despairing realism quite foreign to Shakespearean tragedy. *King Lear* concludes with Edgar's words:

> The weight of this sad time we must obey,
> Speak what we feel, not what we ought to say:
> The oldest hath borne most; we that are young
> Shall never see so much, nor live so long. (V, ii, 324–7)

His words may sound like a hollow formality or formalism – even as they ironically refer to the importance of saying 'what we feel, not what we ought to say' – but there is at least an implicit affirmation here of some kind of future. Toni Morrison's novel concludes more blankly: 'It's too late. At least on the edge of my town, among the garbage and the sunflowers of my town, it's much, much, much too late' (190).

The second example is Chinua Achebe's *Anthills of the Savannah* (1987). Achebe's novel is at once more and less than a tragedy in a classical or Shakespearean sense. It is set in a semi-fictional present-day African state and recounts the process by which one of the protagonists, a newspaper editor called Ikem Osodi, is 'fatally wounded' (169) by the military authorities, and the other male protagonist, the Commissioner for Information, Chris Oriko, gets shot by a policeman who is apparently about to rape a schoolgirl. The narrator adopts the perspective of Chris's lover, the mourning Beatrice:

The explanation of the tragedy of Chris and Ikem in terms of petty human calculation or personal accident had begun to give way in her throbbing mind to an altogether more terrifying but more plausible theory of premeditation. The image of Chris as just another stranger who chanced upon death on the Great North Road or Ikem as an early victim of a waxing police state was no longer satisfactory. Were they not in fact trailed travellers whose journeys from start to finish had been carefully programmed in advance by an alienated history? If so, how many more doomed voyagers were already in transit or just setting out, faces fresh with illusions of duty-free travel and happy landings ahead of them? (220)

Though in many respects tragic, *Anthills of the Savannah* suggests a powerful circumscription and questioning of classical notions of tragedy – not least in the light of what Achebe calls 'an alienated history'. Like Morrison's *The Bluest Eye*, it is an explicitly political novel, directly focusing on the contemporary while exploring ways of rethinking the past. Both novels suggest, in their different ways, the extent to which tragedy is – humanly and unacceptably – 'carefully programmed'. In its broadest implications, the 'alienated history' to which Achebe's novel refers is perhaps alien to the very forms of Western thought, prompting us to reflect on the ways in which 'history' and 'tragedy' are themselves Western concepts.

Further reading

Aristotle's *Poetics* is the single most important account of tragedy in Western history. For a rich and stimulating elaboration of Aristotelian notions, see Elizabeth S. Belfiore's *Tragic Pleasures: Aristotle on Plot and Emotion* (1992). Also on the peculiar relations between the tragic and pleasurable, see A.D. Nuttall's *Why Does Tragedy Give Pleasure?* (1996) and Terry Eagleton's *Sweet Violence* (2003). John Drakakis and Naomi Liebler's *Tragedy* (1998) has a very useful introduction and provides an excellent range of critical material, from Hegel to Derrida. For a psychoanalytic understanding of tragedy, see André Green's now classic *The Tragic Effect* (1979). Of related interest, Heinz Politzer's *Freud and Tragedy* (2006) explores Freud's work on and in terms of the tragic, from Oedipus to *Macbeth*. For an influential account of how the sense of the tragic in the modern world has all but disappeared, see George Steiner's *The Death of Tragedy* (1961). And by way of equally influential riposte, see Raymond Williams's *Modern Tragedy* (1969), which vigorously demonstrates how tragedy has changed and will continue to do so. K.M. Newton's *Modern Literature and the Tragic* (2008) focuses on tragic drama from Ibsen through to the Theatre of the Absurd and beyond. *Rethinking*

Tragedy, ed. Rita Felski (2008) collects a range of essays on topics from Euripides to Sebald. Specifically on Shakespeare, *Shakespearean Tragedy* (1992), ed. John Drakakis, contains a good deal of valuable critical material, while Jonathan Dollimore's *Radical Tragedy: Religion, Ideology and Power in the Drama of Shakespeare and His Contemporaries* (3rd edn, 2004) is a fascinating, now classic study.

14. History

What is the relationship between a literary text and history? Broadly speaking critics have produced four answers to this question:

1. Literary texts belong to no particular time, they are universal and transcend history: the historical context of their production and reception has no bearing on the literary work which is aesthetically autonomous, having its own laws, being a world unto itself.
2. The historical context of a literary work – the circumstances surrounding its production – is integral to a proper understanding of it: the text is produced within a specific historical context but in its literariness it remains separate from that context.
3. Literary works can help us to understand the time in which they are set: realist texts in particular provide imaginative representations of specific historical moments, events or periods.
4. Literary texts are bound up with other discourses and rhetorical structures: they are part of a history that is still in the process of being written.

These four models of literature and history characterize various schools of criticism. The first model is often associated with new criticism or more generally with formalism, especially influential in literary studies in the middle decades of the twentieth century. New critics are concerned with literary texts as artifacts which transcend the contingencies of any particular time or place and which resist what they see as a reduction of the aesthetic whole to a specific historical context. Thus, for example, R.S. Crane argues in an essay first published in 1935 that literary history is essentially part of 'the general history of culture' (Crane 1967, 20), while a 'program of literary studies based on criticism' would focus on 'imaginative works considered with respect to those qualities which can truly be said to be timeless . . . in the sense that they can be adequately discerned and evaluated in the light of general principles quite apart from any knowledge of their origin or historical filiation' (18). The second model is the kind of approach favoured by philological or what we might call 'background' critics. Such critics are concerned to describe and analyse literary texts through a consideration of their historical 'background', whether biographical, linguistic, cultural or political. The titles of Basil Willey's two classic studies from 1934 and 1940 respectively indicate this approach: *The Seventeenth Century Background: Studies in the Thought of the Age in Relation to Poetry and Religion* and *The Eighteenth Century Background: Studies on the Idea of Nature in the Thought of the Period.* For such critics, knowledge of a literary text's historical circumstances forms the basis for an understanding of that text. The third model tends to be associated more with traditional historical scholarship than with literary criticism, as it assumes that literary texts are in some respect subordinate to their historical context. It also tends to assume that literary texts provide undistorted 'reflections' of their time. Thus, for example, in his book *Religion and the Decline of Magic* (1971), Keith Thomas appeals to Shakespeare's works on a number of occasions to justify his arguments. Discussing the practice of cursing, Thomas points out that 'In Shakespeare's plays, the curses pronounced by the characters invariably work', and argues that this is 'not just for dramatic effect' but that 'it was a moral necessity that the poor and the injured should be believed to have this power of retaliation when all else failed' (Thomas 1971, 507). We might call this model the 'reflective' approach. The last model is associated with a new kind of concern with the historical dimensions of literary studies particularly since the early 1980s. This model is specifically associated with new historicist critics in the United States and with cultural materialist critics in Britain (for convenience, we shall use the term 'new historicist' in this chapter to cover both varieties). In both cases, this new interest in history has been refracted through the concerns of both Marxism and post-structuralism to produce a complex model of the literary. In this chapter we shall focus on strategies of reading developed by new historicism in order to consider ways in which literary texts may be thought about in historical terms.

New historicists argue that to ask about the relationship between literature and history is the wrong question. The form of the question presupposes that there is literature on the one side and history on the other. Despite their differences, 'new critics', 'background critics' and 'reflectionists' tend to rely on precisely such a polarity: they assume that the categories of 'literature' and 'history' are intrinsically separate. They distinguish, more or less explicitly, between the need for the interpretation of literary texts on the one hand, and the transparency of history on the other. In an essay entitled 'Literary Theory, Criticism, and History' (1961), for example, René Wellek argues that 'Literary study differs from historical study in having to deal not with documents but with monuments' and that the literary critic 'has direct access to his [*sic*] object', while the historian 'has to reconstruct a long-past event on the basis of eye-witness accounts' (Wellek 1963, 14–15). For old-historicist critics, history is not so much textual as more simply a series of empirically verifiable events. And they also assume that it is possible for our knowledge of both historical events and literary texts to be detached and objective, outside the forces of history.

New historicism may be understood as a reaction against such presuppositions: put briefly, it may be defined as a recognition of the extent to which history is textual, as a rejection of the autonomy of the literary text and as an attempted displacement of the objectivity of interpretation in general. Stephen Greenblatt, the critic who is often seen as the instigator of new historicism, remarks in an essay entitled 'Toward a Poetics of Culture' that 'methodological self-consciousness is one of the distinguishing marks of the new historicism in cultural studies as opposed to a historicism based upon faith in the transparency of signs and interpretive procedures' (Greenblatt 1990a, 158). In the first place, then, new historicism involves a questioning of the critics' own position and interpretative procedures. New historicists argue that the production of literary texts is a cultural practice different only in its specific mode or formulation from other practices – from furniture-making to teaching to warfare to printing. According to this reasoning, no absolute distinction can be made between literary and other cultural practices. As Stephen Greenblatt puts it, art is 'made up along with other products, practices, discourses of a given culture' (Greenblatt 1988, 13). Literary texts are embedded within the social and economic circumstances in which they are produced and consumed. But what is important for new historicists is that these circumstances are not stable in themselves and are susceptible to being rewritten and transformed. From this perspective, literary texts are part of a larger circulation of social energies, both products of and influences on a particular culture or ideology. What is new about new historicism in particular is its recognition that history is the 'history of the present' (to borrow a phrase from the godfather of new historicism, Michel Foucault), history is in the making rather than being monumental and closed, history is radically open to transformation and rewriting.

New historicists argue that any 'knowledge' of the past is necessarily mediated by *texts* or, to put it differently, that history is in many respects textual.

In this, at least, they are in agreement with Jacques Derrida who declared in *Of Grammatology* in 1967 that 'The age already in the *past* is in fact constituted in every respect as a *text*' (Derrida 1976, lxxxix). A number of major consequences follow from such an assertion. In the first place, there can be no knowledge of the past without interpretation. (This is also one of the ways in which new historicism is specifically Nietzschean: as Nietzsche declared in *The Will to Power* (1901), 'facts is precisely what there is not, only interpretations' (Nietzsche 1968, section 481).) Just as literary texts need to be read, so do the 'facts' of history. Thus, theorists such as Hayden White suggest that our knowledge of the past is determined by particular narrative configurations – that in talking about the past we tell stories. 'Properly understood', White remarks,

> histories ought never to be read as unambiguous signs of the events they report, but rather as symbolic structures, extended metaphors, that 'liken' the events reported in them to some form with which we have already become familiar in our literary culture . . . By the very constitution of a set of events in such a way as to make a comprehensible story out of them, the historian charges those events with the symbolic significance of a comprehensible plot structure. (White 1978, 91–2)

In this respect, the strategies and tools of critical analysis – the consideration of figures and tropes, a critical awareness of the rhetorical elements of language and so on – are as appropriate to a critical study of history as they are to literary studies.

From a new historicist perspective, any reading of a literary text is a question of negotiation, a negotiation between text and reader within the context of a history or histories that cannot be closed or finalized. Indeed, Stephen Greenblatt argues that literary works themselves should be understood in terms of negotiation, rather than in the conventional (Romantic) sense of a 'pure act of untrammeled creation' – negotiations which are 'a subtle, elusive set of exchanges, a network of trades and trade-offs, a jostling of competing representations' (Greenblatt 1988, 7). 'The work of art', declares Greenblatt, 'is the product of a negotiation between a creator or class of creators, equipped with a complex, communally shared repertoire of conventions, and the institutions and practices of society' (Greenblatt 1990a, 158). Greenblatt and other new historicist critics reject any attempt to produce a 'whole' or final reading and argue for readings which are apparently disjunctive or fragmented. Similarly, questioning the boundaries of text and world, of art and society, such critics work 'at the margins of the text' in order to gain 'insight into the half-hidden cultural transactions through which great works of art are empowered' (Greenblatt 1988, 4). A critic might study legal documents, for example, or arguments concerning the politics of kingship, or handbooks on the education of children, or accounts of exotic travels and exploration and so on, in order to get a purchase on a particular work of literature. But such texts are not to be construed as either the background or the essential key to understanding the literary text. Rather, like plays, poems and novels, they are to be understood as texts through which questions of politics and power can be negotiated.

Such negotiation concerns, not least, our reading. If 'history' necessarily entails interpretation, then such acts of reading will themselves be embedded within a particular social and cultural situation. There is no escape from history even if this history is regarded as multiple and in a process of unceasing transformation. New historicism argues that we are inescapably implicated – even in the fantasy of academic objectivity and detachment – in structures and strategies of power. Power is produced and reproduced in research, teaching and learning as it is in any other practice or discourse. As Michel Foucault remarked in his 1976 *Introduction* to *The History of Sexuality*, power is 'omnipresent'. It is as 'the moving substrate of force relations which, by virtue of their inequality, constantly engender states of power', states of power which are, however, 'always local and unstable'. 'Power', Foucault goes on, 'is everywhere' (Foucault 1981, 93).

In order to consider how such an approach might work in practice, we propose to discuss a poem by the English Romantic poet William Wordsworth entitled 'Alice Fell, or Poverty'. The poem was written on the 12th and 13th March 1802, and first published in 1807. It is a seemingly uncomplicated account of an incident that was recounted to Wordsworth by his friend Robert Grahame. As the subtitle indicates, the poem presents itself as an allegory concerning poverty:

> The Post-boy drove with fierce career,
> For threat'ning clouds the moon had drowned;
> When suddenly I seemed to hear
> A moan, a lamentable sound.
>
> 5 As if the wind blew many ways
> I heard the sound, and more and more:
> It seemed to follow with the Chaise,
> And still I heard it as before.
>
> At length I to the Boy called out,
> 10 He stopped his horses at the word;

But neither cry, nor voice, nor shout,
Nor aught else like it could be heard.

The Boy then smacked his whip, and fast
The horses scampered through the rain;
15   And soon I heard upon the blast
The voice, and bade him halt again.

Said I, alighting on the ground,
'What can it be, this piteous moan?'
And there a little Girl I found,
20   Sitting behind the Chaise, alone.

'My Cloak!' the word was last and first,
And loud and bitterly she wept,
As if her very heart would burst;
And down from off the Chaise she leapt.

25   'What ails you, Child?' She sobbed, 'Look here!'
I saw it in the wheel entangled,
A weather beaten Rag as e'er
From any garden scare-crow dangled.

'Twas twisted betwixt nave and spoke;
30   Her help she lent, and with good heed
Together we released the Cloak;
A wretched, wretched rag indeed!

'And wither are you going, Child,
Tonight along these lonesome ways?'
35   'To Durham' answered she half wild –
'Then come with me into the chaise.'

She sate like one past all relief;
Sob after sob she forth did send
In wretchedness, as if her grief
40   Could never, never, have an end.

'My child, in Durham do you dwell?'
She checked herself in her distress,
And said, 'My name is Alice Fell;
I'm fatherless and motherless.

45   And I to Durham, Sir, belong.'
      And then, as if the thought would choke
      Her very heart, her grief grew strong;
      And all was for her tattered Cloak.

      The chaise drove on; our journey's end
50   Was nigh; and, sitting by my side,
      As if she'd lost her only friend
      She wept, nor would be pacified.

      Up to the Tavern-door we post;
      Of Alice and her grief I told;
55   And I gave money to the Host,
      To buy a new Cloak for the old.

      'And let it be a duffil grey,
      As warm a cloak as man can sell!'
      Proud Creature was she the next day,
60   The little Orphan, Alice Fell!

From a new historicist perspective we might try to situate this poem in relation to other contemporary discourses which deal with poverty, charity and property. We could, for example, investigate the rhetorical strategies and discursive conventions of debates surrounding the Poor Law, economics, poverty and charity at the turn of the nineteenth century. One such text is Adam Smith's *The Wealth of Nations*, first published in 1776 and perhaps the most influential work of political economy of the time. In this book, Smith twice refers to beggars, once when he argues that 'Before the invention of the art of printing, a scholar and a beggar seem to have been terms very nearly synonymous' (Smith 1986, 237), and once when he considers beggars as the only people who do not take part in the circulation of exchange and barter. In this latter passage, from the second chapter of his multi-volume work, Smith argues that there is 'a certain propensity in human nature' which is 'to truck, barter, and exchange one thing for another' (117). It is this 'propensity' which distinguishes humans from animals: 'When an animal wants to obtain something either of a man or of another animal, it has no other means of persuasion but to gain the favour of those whose service it requires' (118). But humans – unlike animals, consistently dependent on others – cannot constantly expect others' benevolence. Instead, a man must 'interest [another person's] self-love in his favour': 'Nobody but a beggar chooses to depend chiefly upon the benevolence of his fellow-citizens' (118–19). Although Smith goes on to say that even beggars take part in the circulation of monetary exchange by buying goods with the money that they are given, in this extraordinary passage he has managed to dehumanize beggars, to put them outside of humanity, on the level of the animal. By arguing that human relations are relations of exchange, based on the principle of 'self-love', however, Smith suggests an apparent paradox in the discourse of charity: he claims that 'the charity of well-disposed people' supplies the beggar with 'the whole fund of his subsistence' (119), but does not explain *why* such people should give to beggars. According to his own arguments, people would only give to beggars if they were to gain something in return. There is, in this sense, no pure gift, no possibility of a gift. A number of significant rhetorical manoeuvres, then, may be seen to be at work in Smith's discourse of charity and begging. In the first place, beggars are dehumanized. Secondly, charity becomes a paradoxical or perverse, even an impossible act. Thirdly, by saying 'a beggar *chooses* to depend', Smith implies freedom of choice where economic necessity may be at stake. Finally, and most generally, Smith makes it clear that questions of charity and begging are part of a larger discourse of property and the exchange of property, indeed, part of a specific ideology of free-market liberalism.

We might think about these points in relation to Wordsworth's poem for, although Alice Fell does not actually beg and is not referred to as a beggar, the poem puts her in the position of a beggar and is specifically concerned with that particular kind of exchange of property named 'charity'. What we might then seek to do is not to produce a thematic reading of the poem: rather, we might consider how the rhetorical strategies at work in Smith's account of beggars, property and charity are reproduced and transformed in those of the poem.

We might start by thinking about ways in which the poem articulates questions of property. Property in 'Alice Fell' is not simply a question of the cloak, but of poetry itself as property. The very origins of the narrative are bound up with questions of ownership in that the story originated with Wordsworth's friend Robert Grahame. Moreover, Dorothy Wordsworth, the poet's sister, wrote an account of the same incident in her journal before Wordsworth wrote his poem. Dorothy's account goes as follows:

> Mr. Graham said he wished Wm had been with him the other day – he was riding in a post chaise and he heard a strange cry that he could not understand, the sound continued and he called to the chaise driver to stop. It was a little girl that was crying as if her heart would burst. She had got up behind the chaise and her cloak had been caught by the wheel and was jammed in and it hung there. She was crying after it. Poor thing. Mr. Graham took her

into the chaise and the cloak was released from the wheel but the child's
misery did not cease for her cloak was torn to rags; it had been a miserable
cloak before, but she had no other and it was the greatest sorrow that could
befal her. Her name was Alice Fell. She had no parents, and belonged to
the next Town. At the next Town Mr. G. left money with some respectable
people in the town to buy her a new cloak. (Wordsworth 1984, 702)

As with a number of William's most famous lyrics, 'Alice Fell' resembles
Dorothy's journalistic account in many ways: both poem and journal entry
are concerned with the strangeness of the girl's cry, with the girl's continuing
misery, with the ragged state of her cloak. More specifically, there are numerous verbal echoes of the journal entry in William's poem, most strikingly,
the poem's 'she wept, / As if her heart would burst' and the journal's 'crying as
if her heart would burst'. In this respect, William may be said to have appropriated the story from his friend and from his sister. This leads us to the question of what property it is that constitutes this text as a poem. Is it *properly*
a poem? How is it different from Grahame's oral account or from Dorothy's
journal entry? And where does the poem originate, who owns it and author-
izes it? We might want to follow these questions through to an investigation of
the institution of literature itself. How is the canon produced, for example,
what factors are at work in canon-formation in England such that women's
diaries have tended to be excluded, canonically marginalized? Can it be said
that in choosing the form of the journal-entry to record the story Dorothy is
excluding herself from the public discourse of literature? How is Dorothy's
account both reproduced and effaced in William's poem and in the critical
tradition, and why? Rather differently, we could argue that Dorothy's diary
entry is not simply supplementary to the poem but is an essential part of it.
Indeed, it becomes difficult to distinguish property as regards the cloak and
property as regards the Wordsworths. In these respects, questions of property
cannot be considered to be simply the context or the thematic focus of the
poem: the poem originates in certain problematic exchanges, transfers or
gifts of narrative property.
   The poem is also 'about' an exchange of property. The girl loses her cloak
in the wheel of the carriage, and the speaker gives her enough money to buy a
new one. But along with this exchange go a series of property disturbances.
The girl's proper name, Alice Fell, for example, is curious. It is not a name
Wordsworth invented, it seems. But is it 'historical' or 'literary'? The poem,
indeed, exacerbates the sense of uncertainty regarding the strange properties
of this proper name. Not only is it transferred from the title to the main body of
the poem, or from the girl to the poem, but it also has a curious grammatical

status in itself: it is suspended between a name and a minimal sentence, a kind of mini-narrative in itself – Alice fell. The poem is not only called 'Alice Fell', but is also about the fall of Alice. And once we recognize that there is something strange about the girl's name, we might also notice that 'Alice Fell' is haunted by the figure of a 'fallen woman', a woman outside 'respectable' society. Dorothy's text seems to pick up on this in its use of the verb 'befal', just prior to naming the girl herself. Conversely, we may recall that 'fell' also means the skin or hide of an animal, so that Alice might be like her cloak, a kind of rag, caught up and torn apart by the moving carriage. Finally, 'fell' as 'wild', as 'fierce, savage, cruel, ruthless, dreadful, terrible' or 'intensely painful' and even (of poison) 'deadly', or 'shrewd, clever, cunning' (*OED*) gives us a sense of the outcast, inhuman, dangerous, improper nature of this figure, and perhaps partly explains her – and the poem's – haunting power: she is, as the narrator himself declares, 'half wild' (l.35). The dehumanization at work in Adam Smith's account of beggars is also wildly at work in Wordsworth's poem.

If the poem is about the exchange of property, it is also about the question of charity. Every act of charity may be understood as an implicit assertion that the end of suffering is possible. Dorothy's account of the incident recognizes that, after the girl's cloak was released, her 'misery did not cease'. One of the key stanzas of Wordsworth's poem in this respect is stanza 10:

> She sate like one past all relief;
> Sob after sob she forth did send
> In wretchedness, as if her grief
> Could never, never, have an end.

The phrases 'like' and 'as if' seem to deny the unspeakable possibility that the girl really is 'past all relief', and that her 'grief / Could never, never, have an end'. But much of the force of the poem may be said to reside precisely in this terrifying possibility – that nothing can be done, that charity cannot finally help. In this respect, it is significant that unlike Dorothy's account, the poem ends in a blustering statement of self-satisfaction: in the final stanza, the girl is said to be 'proud' on account of her new cloak. But the girl's poverty and orphanhood remain and the pride appears to be as much a projection of the speaker's emotions as the girl's. The *speaker* apparently does have reason to be proud – he can feel proud of his charitable action. Attributing pride to the girl simply increases the speaker's own reasons to be proud. It might be argued that the poem works against itself, implicitly exposing the self-deceptive nature of the charitable act. Given this logic of projection, the poem clearly suggests that self-deception is necessary to charity or that, in Adam Smith's terms, there is no pure gift, that in giving the cloak, the speaker receives the satisfaction of pride. Moreover, the poem's triumphant ending implies that charity can end suffering. But this sense of triumph and of an ending are simultaneously undone: we must give and to do so we must believe that our gift will help to end suffering, but suffering is never-ending. The hardly audible, ghostly historical counter-voice of the poem cries that, as an orphan, Alice Fell cannot but suffer (etymologically, 'orphan' means 'one who has lost'). Her suffering is never-ending because it cannot be ended. Unlike the speaker, who is on a journey that will end (see line 49, 'our journey's end'), the suffering of Alice Fell has no end. Just as the speaker is haunted by a strange voice at the beginning of the poem, so he is haunted by the uncanny disembodied voice of suffering, haunted by what he knows but cannot know – that suffering and the improper or 'fell' (wild, inhuman, fallen) disturbances of property are never-ending.

Stephen Greenblatt argues that culture 'is a particular network of negotiations for the exchange of material goods, ideas, and – through institutions like enslavement, adoption, or marriage – people'. Greenblatt also contends that 'Great writers are precisely masters of these codes, specialists in cultural exchange' (Greenblatt 1990b, 229–30). Our account has sought to locate Wordsworth's poem in relation to the discourses of property and charity as articulated in one particular text. Wordsworth, we might say, is a master of – and is mastered by – the codes of property and charity. New historicism seeks to explore such mastery, while remaining alert to ways in which such codes continue to play themselves out in the discourses of the present – including, not least, the discourses of history and criticism.

Further reading

For eloquent and readable accounts of a historicized theory of culture, see Stephen Greenblatt's essays 'Towards a Poetics of Culture' (1990a) and 'Culture' (1990b). See his *Shakespearean Negotiations* (1988) and *Marvelous Possessions* (1991) for witty and penetrating readings of various Renaissance texts, and for overviews of his work, see Mark Robson, *Stephen Greenblatt* (2008), and Michael Payne, ed., *The Greenblatt Reader* (2005). Useful collections of new historicist and cultural materialist essays include Catherine Gallagher and Greenblatt's *Practising New Historicism* (2000), Dollimore and Sinfield, eds, *Political Shakespeare* (1994), Wilson and Dutton, eds, *New Historicism and Renaissance Drama* (1992), Veeser, ed., *The New Historicism* (1989) and *The New Historicism Reader* (1994), Ryan, ed.,

New Historicism and Culture Materialism (1996), and Tamsin Spargo, ed., *Reading the Past* (2000). For a good but demanding overview of historicisms old and new, see Paul Hamilton's *Historicism* (1996). For a sharp and engaging account of new historicism and cultural materialism, see Brannigan, *New Historicism and Cultural Materialism* (1998); and see Scott Wilson, *Cultural Materialism* (1995). Todd, *Feminist Literary History* (1988) provides a valuable feminist account of literary history. On Foucault, see Sara Mills, *Michel Foucault* (2003) and Gary Gutting, *Foucault* (2005).

15. Me

Who are we? What am I? What is an 'I'? What does it mean to say 'me'? What is the relationship between an 'I' in a literary text and an 'I' outside it? One of the central ideas of this book is literature's capacity to question, defamiliarize and even transform the sense of who or what we are. In the next few pages we would like to elaborate further on this, by trying to look at the nature of personal identity or 'me' both in broadly historical and theoretical terms and more specifically in terms of what literary texts themselves suggest.

In Flannery O'Connor's story 'Revelation' (1961) a woman called Mrs Turpin has a traumatic and bizarre reaction when a strange girl sitting in a doctor's waiting room tells her: 'Go back to hell where you came from, you old wart hog' (217). Mrs Turpin is scandalized by this statement and that same evening, back at the farm, by herself, hosing down the pigs, she demands an explanation. Being Christian and superstitious (as well as grotesquely racist and class-prejudiced), Mrs Turpin regards the girl's words as a message from God:

> 'What do you send me a message like that for?' she said in a low fierce voice, barely above a whisper but with the force of a shout in its concentrated fury. 'How am I a hog and me both?' (222)

What is striking here is not only the woman's confusion and indignation at the apparently contradictory idea that she might be a human being and an old wart hog at the same time, but also the fact that her 'fury' is expressed in a direct, personal address to God. Mrs Turpin's sense of outrage becomes outrageous in turn, as her questions addressed to God culminate in a questioning *of* God: 'A final surge of fury shook her and she roared, "Who do you think you are?" '

(223) The strangeness of putting this question to God comes from the fact that it is a question that should properly, perhaps, only be asked of another human. Only humans are supposed to be able to reflect on who they are and at the same time be obliged to take seriously a questioning of their own identity. If the question 'Who do you think you are?' is one that cannot or should not be asked of God, nor is it a question one would normally ask of a wart hog. In this respect it would seem that there is something characteristically human about the question. 'Who do you think you are?' is the question that humans ask of others and try to answer about themselves. As Socrates said, 'The unexamined life is not worth living' (Plato 1961, (*Apology*, 38a)). And the definition of being human must remain in the form of a questioning: Mrs Turpin's 'concentrated fury' is, in this respect, pitifully, comically human.

At the same time, it could be said that this question ('Who do you think you are?') is most clearly raised and most fully explored in works of literature. This might in fact allow us to formulate another general definition: literature is the space in which questions about the nature of personal identity are most provocatively articulated. For many decades literary critics have talked about 'the person' and 'the individual'. In more recent years, however, there has been a tendency to refer to 'the human subject' or just 'the subject'. This may sound jargonistic but there are good reasons, in fact, for talking about 'the subject' rather than, say, 'the person' or 'the individual'. The French poststructuralist Michel Foucault has written: 'There are two meanings of the word "subject": subject to someone else by control and dependence, and tied to one's own identity by a conscience or self-knowledge' (Foucault 1983, 212, cited by During 1992, 153). The word 'person', by contrast, perhaps too easily retains connotations of the 'I' or 'me' as detached from everything, a *free agent*. Likewise, the term 'individual' (etymologically from the Latin *individuus*, 'undivided' or 'not divisible') suggests a sense of the 'I' as simply free, as being at one with itself and autonomous or self-ruling. It is this idea of the sovereignty of the 'I' that Freud gestures towards and ironizes when he speaks of 'His Majesty the Ego' (Freud 1985f, 138).

The term 'subject' is useful, then, in that it encourages a more critical attentiveness to the ways in which the 'I' is *not* autonomous, to the fact that it does not exist in a sort of vacuum. Rather an 'I' or 'me' is always *subject* to forces and effects both outside itself (environmental, social, cultural, economic, educational, etc.) and 'within' itself (in particular in terms of what is called the unconscious or, in more recent philosophical terms, otherness). We are subjects in the sense of being 'subject to' others 'by control or dependence' (in Foucault's phrase) right from birth and even before: not only are we radically dependent on the father who sires us and the mother who bears us (or on their various surrogates), but also on the environment (ecological, economic, familial, social, etc.) into which we are born, as well as on the multiple forms of authority and government which condition our upbringing. A 'me' born to a single mother in Soweto is not the same kind of 'me' as a 'me' born to a duchess in Kensington, but they are both in their different ways *subjects*. Of course if the Kensington 'me' had been in line for the throne, things would have looked slightly different: in Britain, at least, one is subject not only to the authority of one's parent or parents, one's local authorities, the police and central government, but also – at least on paper – to the Queen (thus one is 'a British subject') and, beyond her, to the Christian God. That, then, is one way in which every 'I' is necessarily and fundamentally a *subject*. Rather differently, being a subject has specifically to do with language. You cannot be an 'I' without having a proper name, and in English-speaking countries you usually acquire a proper name around the time of birth or even before. We are born into language, we are born – more precisely – into patriarchal language, into being identified by a patronym, by a paternal proper name. (Even the mother's maiden name is, of course, a patronym.) We are also endowed with a forename and again this is not something *we* choose, it is something to which we are *subject* – even if, in Britain for example, people do legally have the right to change their names at the age of 18. Juliet's complaint is haunting and even tragic precisely because it highlights the way in which we are *subject to* names, even if we wish to ignore or disown them:

> Oh Romeo, Romeo, wherefore art thou Romeo?
> Deny thy father and refuse thy name;
> Or, if thou wilt not, be but sworn my love,
> And I'll no longer be a Capulet.
> (*Romeo and Juliet*, II, ii, 33–6)

More broadly, questions of personal or individual identity are indissociably bound up with language. We may like to suppose that there is some 'me' outside language or that there is some way of thinking about ourselves which involves a non-linguistic 'me'. But the *idea* of this non-linguistic 'me' must found itself in language – beginning with the name itself, or with the words 'I', 'me', 'mine', 'myself' and so on. We cannot, in any *meaningful* way, escape the fact that we are *subject to* language. As Jacques Derrida has put it: 'From the moment that there is meaning there are nothing but signs. We *think only in signs*' (Derrida 1976, 50).

We can also consider this topic from a more explicitly historical perspective. The idea of the 'I' or 'me', in other words, is not unchanging and unchangeable. It is in many respects historically and ideologically determined. The way we think about 'I' today is inevitably different from the way in which 'I' was thought about and defined in, say, seventeenth-century France by René Descartes. The principle of the Cartesian *cogito* ('I think therefore I am') – that is to say, the model of the *rational subject* which Descartes theorizes in his *Discourse on Method* (1637; 1977) – in many respects continues to govern Western thinking. But there are other ways of thinking, and other ways of thinking about thinking. In the mid-twentieth century, for example, the German philosopher Martin Heidegger declared: 'Thinking begins only when we have come to know that reason, glorified for centuries, is the most stiffnecked adversary of thought' (Heidegger 1977, 112, cited by Judovitz 1988, 186). Likewise, and more recently, Jacques Derrida has been consistently concerned to demonstrate that, as he puts it: 'reason is only one species of thought – which does not mean that thought is "irrational"' (Derrida 1983, 16).

But perhaps the most obvious way of illustrating the changes over the past century in thinking about thinking, and in thinking about the model of the rational subject, is in terms of psychoanalysis. Psychoanalysis has changed the way in which we are obliged to think about 'the subject'. In the light of the psychoanalytic theory of the unconscious, the proposition '*cogito, ergo sum*' ('I think, therefore I am') becomes manifestly problematic. I do not, and perhaps strictly speaking never can, know precisely *why* or *how* I think what I think, if only because of the extent to which what I think is necessarily determined by forces and effects of which I am (in many ways thankfully) unaware. In a short essay written as an encyclopedia entry on 'Psychoanalysis' first published in 1923, Freud suggests that the unconscious is evident not only in dreams but in

> such events as the temporary forgetting of familiar words and names, forgetting to carry out prescribed tasks, everyday slips of the tongue and of the pen, misreadings, losses and mislayings of objects, certain errors, instances of apparently accidental self-injury, and finally habitual movements carried out seemingly without intention or in play, tunes hummed 'thoughtlessly', and so on. (Freud 1986, 136–7)

The significance of Freud's theory of the unconscious thus consists in the demonstration that the subject who thinks (the subject of 'I think') is composed of forces and effects which are at least in part unconscious. 'I', let us remind ourselves, is not 'God' – even if it may be *subject to* fantasies of being so.

Psychoanalysis, then, has been a particularly disturbing but valuable discourse because it has promoted an awareness of the extent to which any 'I' or human subject is *decentred*: I, in other words, can never be simply or precisely who or what I think. What makes this idea disturbing and at the same time valuable is that it involves a dislocation of notions of human mastery and autonomy of self. It introduces instead the humility of recognizing that the human subject is not centred in itself, let alone centred in relation to the surrounding world or solar system. In an essay on 'The Resistances to Psychoanalysis' (1925), Freud talks about the 'emotional' difficulties people have in accepting the ideas of psychoanalysis and draws analogies between this and the theories of Darwin and Copernicus. In the case of psychoanalysis, he says, 'powerful human feelings are hurt by the subject-matter of the theory. Darwin's theory of descent met with the same fate, since it tore down the barrier that had been arrogantly set up between men and beasts.' Freud goes on to suggest that 'the psychoanalytic view of the relation of the conscious ego to an overpowering unconscious was a severe blow to human self-love', and that, 'as the *psychological* blow to men's narcissism', it compares 'with the *biological* blow delivered by the theory of descent and the earlier *cosmological* blow aimed at it by the discovery of Copernicus' (Freud 1986, 272–3). In this sense, psychoanalysis complements the Copernican revolution and nineteenth-century evolutionary theory in providing a powerful critique of anthropocentric or humanist values and ideas. Psychoanalysis demonstrates in uncomfortably clear terms how the 'arrogance' or narcissism of anthropocentrism – that is to say, every kind of thinking, including every kind of philosophy and politics, which puts the human at the centre of the earth and solar system, if not of the universe – is both unwarranted and unsustainable.

The Cartesian 'I think, therefore I am' can be further considered specifically in relation to language. Language determines the 'I' and the 'I think'. This can be illustrated simply by reflecting on the idea that Descartes's formulation was first published in Latin ('*cogito, ergo sum*'). We anglophone subjects are already adrift in effects of language and translation, but so too was Descartes himself: after all, his works appeared not in some form of seventeenth-century French but in a foreign, 'dead' language. He was subject to the scholarly protocols of his own time and the requirement to write (and in some sense presumably think) in Latin. What is at stake in this logic of being *subject to language* is a conception of language as not simply *instrumental*: language is not simply something that we *use*. Language governs what we (can) say as much as we govern or *use* language. Language is not simply an instrument: we are, unavoidably, *agents* of language. Moreover we are, more precisely perhaps, secret or double agents of language: we do not necessarily know, from one moment to the next, *how* we are being used by language or where it might be leading us. As in the most compelling kind of espionage story, however, this is not a situation we can get out of. As the narrator neatly puts it, in Margaret Atwood's short story 'Giving Birth' (1977): 'These are the only words I have, I'm stuck with them, stuck in them' (225–6). The 'in' is, no doubt, more difficult to reflect on than the 'with', but it is no less important.

How do these various questions and ideas relate to literary works more generally? First of all, let us emphasize that, if literature is concerned with exploring and reflecting on the nature of personal identity, it is also a space of exhilarating, even anarchic openness and imaginative or transformational possibility. Literature can be thought of as being, in Derrida's words, 'the institution which allows one to *say everything*, in *every way*' (Derrida 1992a, 36). In particular, there is this astonishing, anarchic freedom in literature: at least in principle, the author of a literary work can be any 'I' he or she wishes to. To put it like this is to imply that the author is an 'I' before or outside the literary work. But who is to say that there is an 'I' anywhere that is not in part *literary*? This rather strange question is a focus of one of the greatest comical literary or philosophical works in the twentieth century, Samuel Beckett's *The Unnamable* (first published in English in 1959). This text is preoccupied with the idea that it is the 'I' itself that is in a sense the unnamable: the 'I' that speaks, or that seems to speak, is never true, never precisely itself, never the same, for example, as the 'I' who has spoken or the 'I' that writes 'I'. *The Unnamable*, then, starts off from the apparently simple but perhaps unfathomable remark, 'I, say I', and from the paradox that 'I seem to speak, it is not I, about me, it is not about me' (293). Nearly 50 pages later the narrator is still impelled to observe that 'on the subject of me properly so called . . . so far as I know I have received no information up to date' (338). In Beckett's wonderfully funny, but also dark and unnerving text, the Cartesian-rationalistic 'I think' becomes: 'I only think, if that is the name for this vertiginous panic as of hornets smoked out of their nest, once a certain degree of terror has been exceeded' (353). As with so much of Beckett's writing, this sentence is at once quite straight-forward and semantically dense, unsettling, surprisingly resistant to a single interpretation. We might note, for example, the explicit attention to the uncertainties of language ('if that is the name') and of the relationship between terror and thinking. To think about this sentence can induce vertiginous panic and become terrifying. It succinctly illustrates literature's complex and unsettling effects when it comes to thinking about thinking – when it comes to thinking about identity and about the 'I' that claims to think.

We could conclude by trying to say a little more about the ways in which, as we suggested earlier, the 'I' or 'me' is in fact historically determined. One very broad but decisive example of this would be the question of the 'I' or 'me' in relation to romantic and post-romantic literature. In *Of Grammatology* (1967), Derrida argues that the importance of Jean-Jacques Rousseau's work consists in the fact that he 'starts from a new model of presence: the subject's self-presence within *consciousness* or *feeling*' (Derrida 1976, 98). European Romanticism in general might be characterized in terms of this kind of 'new model of presence', and in particular in terms of a new emphasis on the centrality and importance of the 'I' as a subject who both thinks and feels. This could be exemplified by a celebrated stanza written by George Gordon Byron on the back of a manuscript-page of canto 1 of *Don Juan* (1819–24):

> I would to heaven that I were so much clay,
>   As I am blood, bone, marrow, passion, feeling –
> Because at least the past were pass'd away –
>   And for the future – (but I write this reeling,
> Having got drunk exceedingly to-day,
>   So that I seem to stand upon the ceiling)
> I say – the future is a serious matter –
> And so – for God's sake – hock and soda-water!

The poet situates himself and the very act of writing in the comical immediacy of being drunk and feeling as if he is upside-down, standing on the ceiling.

The new emphasis on the 'I' in romantic culture is consistently articulated in terms of the polarity or gulf between a subject ('I feel') and an object (the clouds, a skylark, a nightingale). The (impossible) desire for a fusion between subject and object (the idea for example of being, in Matthew Arnold's words, 'in harmony with nature') is one of the most striking characteristics of the work of the English romantic poets. It is clear, for instance, in Keats's 'Ode to a Nightingale', in which the speaker is eventually compelled to admit defeat in his attempt to fuse or dissolve into the nightingale's song: the word 'forlorn' is 'like a bell / To toll me back from thee to my sole self'. This emphasis on the 'sole self' broaches the notion of solipsism – that is to say the refusal or inability to believe in the reality of anything outside or beyond the self. The idea of such an isolation of the self has its representatives in classical philosophy and literature, but it is particularly pervasive in nineteenth- and twentieth-century European culture. It is evoked by the pathos, or bathos, of the opening lines of Matthew Arnold's poem, 'To Marguerite – Continued' (1849):

> Yes! in the sea of life enisled,
> With echoing straits between us thrown,

> Dotting the shoreless watery wild,
> We mortal millions live *alone*.

It is also implicit in the work of Freud, to the extent that psychoanalysis suggests that everything comes down to the power and significance of *projection*, of the qualities, moods or emotions which we *project on to* people and things. Wallace Stevens sums this up when he says:

> few people realize on that occasion, which comes to all of us, when we look at the blue sky for the first time, that is to say: not merely see it, but look at it and experience it . . . – few people realize that they are looking at the world of their own thoughts and the world of their own feelings. (Stevens 1951, 65–6)

But as we hope will by now be clear, solipsism is a myth, a delusion or mirage. Solipsism presupposes the idea of something like what Wittgenstein calls a private language (Wittgenstein 1984). There is no such thing as a private language: the phrase 'private language' is an oxymoron. Language is social or, at least, language comes from elsewhere, from others and from otherness in general. Even to say, as a self-avowed solipsist might, 'I do not believe in the reality of anything apart from myself', is to demonstrate a dependence on what is not 'me', not oneself. It is to demonstrate that one is *subject to* language. As the voice, or one of the voices, in *The Unnamable* puts it: 'I'm in words, made of words, others' words . . .' (390).

Literature, like art more generally, has always been concerned with aspects of what can be called the unconscious or 'not me' or other: it is and has always been centrally concerned with dreams and fantasy, hallucinations and visions, madness, trance, and other kinds of impersonality or absences of self. But we could say that romantic and post-romantic literature has been increasingly sensitive to the role of otherness and increasingly aware of what might be described as our *responsibilities* in relation to otherness. Beckett's writing is perhaps only the most philosophically refined recent example of post-Romantic literature which is concerned to explore, deflate and transform our understanding of the question, 'Who do you think you are?' In this respect his work might be seen to anticipate and encapsulate much of what is called poststructuralism. Poststructuralism demonstrates that the 'I' or human subject is necessarily decentred. It argues against the reductiveness (and even the possibility) of rationalism, in particular through its attention to what is other (though not simply 'irrational') as regards Western 'rational' thinking. And it persistently shows up the presumptuousness of the model of an autonomous, supposedly masterful human being, and thus points beyond 'merely' literary questions, exposing the barbarities of anthropocentrism in general. Some of this may be felt in a faltering, haunting few words from *The Unnamable*:

> if only I knew if I've lived, if I live, if I'll live, that would simplify everything, impossible to find out, that's where you're buggered, I haven't stirred, that's all I know, no, I know something else, it's not I, I always forget that, I resume, you must resume . . . (417)

Further reading

For some very clear and stimulating introductory accounts of psychoanalysis and its implications for 'me', see Freud 1986; for a complex and challenging analysis of Freudian thinking on the idea of the subject, see Borch-Jacobsen, *The Freudian Subject* (1988). For a careful and thought-provoking discussion of the human subject from the perspective of the social sciences, see Paul Hirst and Penny Woolley, *Social Relations and Human Attributes* (1982). A highly influential account of romanticism stressing the importance of conflicts and disjunctions between subject and object, me and the world, etc., is M.H. Abram's classic study, *The Mirror and the Lamp* (1953). Another influential discussion of these issues, this time from the perspective of the history of philosophy (particularly from Descartes to the Romantic period) is Charles Taylor's wide-ranging and informative *Sources of the Self* (1989). For two very good general accounts of poststructuralism, see Robert Young's Introduction to *Untying the Text* (1981) and Josué Harari's Introduction to *Textual Strategies* (1979); and see Joel Fineman's *The Subjectivity Effect in Western Literary Tradition* (1991) for a theoretically and critically astute exploration of such issues in a number of literary (especially Shakespearean) texts. For a challenging but compelling recent work that explores the nature of the self in the context of psychoanalysis, violence and the value of what they call 'impersonal narcissism', see Leo Bersani and Adam Phillips's *Intimacies* (2008).

16. Eco

Why in the world would we destroy the world in which we live, our own world, our only world? What drives that destruction? Why can't we stop it?

William Wordsworth's 'Nutting' (1800) cannot answer these questions; perhaps no poem could. But this 54-line poem might help us to begin to think about them, and about questions of human-environmental interaction and ecological destruction and the ways in which literary study in recent years has started to be transformed by such concerns. In 'Nutting', the speaker recalls an occasion when, as a boy, he 'sallied' from his home to gather hazelnuts with 'A nutting crook in hand'. He remembers 'forcing' his way through the uncultivated countryside, through woods and 'pathless rocks', until he comes to 'one dear nook / Unvisited'. It is, he recalls, 'A virgin scene' and he stands there awhile, 'Breathing with such suppression of the heart / As joy delights in'. This bower is, he thinks, a place where the seasons pass, year after year, 'unseen by any human eye'. He sits down in the bower enjoying the murmuring of a brook, his heart 'luxuriat[ing] with indifferent things' (ll.3–39); but after a while he gets up:

> Then up I rose,
> And dragg'd to earth both branch and bough, with crash
> And merciless ravage, and the shady nook
> Of hazels, and the green and mossy bower,
> Deform'd and sullied, patiently gave up
> Their quiet being; and unless I now
> Confound my present feelings with the past,
> Even then, when from the bower I turn'd away,
> Exulting, rich beyond the wealth of kings—

I felt a sense of pain when I beheld
The silent trees and the intruding sky.— (ll.41–51)

The poem ends with what might appear to be a rather weak 'moral': we should adopt a 'gentleness of heart' in relation to nature, 'for there is a Spirit in the woods' (ll.53–4), the speaker declares. More powerful, alarming and provocative is the shock of this sudden, unmotivated and violent destruction. In Western literary and other culture, 'nature' is often fundamentally distinguished from the human and, at the same time, gendered as female and even as maternal (as in the phrase 'Mother Nature'). There certainly seem to be indications of femininity and motherhood in Wordsworth's description of the womb-like bower before it is defiled: it is a (feminized) 'virgin scene' but it also features hazels hung with (maternal-sounding) 'milk-white clusters' (l.18). The poem has consequently been read from the perspective of psychoanalysis as an expression of a child's rage (his rage and love, his rage because of his love, or need) for his mother, in terms of the desire to destroy what gives him physical, emotional, spiritual nurture. And it has been read in terms of sexual violence, as a kind of 'rape' of a feminized nature. It should also be said that, in keeping with the sexual suggestiveness of Wordsworth's language, there is also a case for seeing the bowers and the hazels as phallic and virile: 'not a broken bough / Droop'd with its wither'd leaves . . . / . . . but the hazels rose/ Tall and erect' (ll.15–18).

But these are not the only ways of reading Wordsworth's poem. What is most striking about 'Nutting' is the way that the destruction of nature seems *not* to be motivated, the way that it is unexplained, seemingly inexplicable. So that we are left with the question with which we started: what drives us, or what drives Wordsworth's speaker, to destroy the world? This, in a sense, is the core ecological question, perhaps finally the only question (along with the related question: how do we prevent this destruction?). In recent years, there has been what amounts to an 'ecological turn' in thinking about literature, a turn that, as we shall argue, has the potential fundamentally to transform the way that we think about literature and about reading. Critics have begun to analyse ways in which literature engages with the destruction of nature, and with the relationship between humanity and the biosphere (of which, of course, humanity is ambiguously a part – both part of nature and not part of nature). In focusing on this interaction, ecocritical thinking complicates and adds to the more conventional idea that literature is concerned with questions of gender, race, class, economics, history, sexuality, and so on. It is for this reason that Timothy Clark calls ecocriticism 'a provocative misfit amidst . . . literary and cultural debate' (Clark, forthcoming). It may be the case that writers and critics, *as* writers and critics, can do little or nothing to prevent or resolve problems of global warming, over-fishing, widespread pollution, the destruction on epic scale of animal and plant habitats, mass extinction of species along with human-engineered ecological disasters in all forms – to prevent what Martin Amis starkly sums up as the 'toiletization of the planet' (quoted in Deitering 1996, 196). Writers and critics are, however, well placed to analyse the ways in which this wasting of our world is not simply material or physical, but also rhetorical – the ways in which it is defined, conditioned and even, in certain respects, controlled by language itself.

Rather than focusing on the question of the subjectivity of the speaker in Wordsworth's poem and drawing on Oedipal models of development, an eco-inflected approach would register the larger contexts with which the speaker struggles in this poem. An ecocritical reading might notice, for example, the way in which Wordsworth's poem seems to be structured around a series of oppositions: before/after; nature/human; wilderness/cultivation; and most explicitly, 'virgin' nature and its destruction and desecration by the boy. But it might also reckon with the way in which the destruction of the bower is in fact prefigured in the description of nature before the attack: in a sense, nature has already been desecrated, even in its representation as wilderness. Nature is always already contaminated by the human and by language. Death, after all, is present in the opening lines: 'It seems a day', the poem begins, 'One of those heavenly days which cannot die / When forth I sallied from our cottage-door' (ll.1–3). It *seems* that it cannot die, yet it is already in the past tense ('I sallied'): thus there is already an intimation of mortality hanging over the day in question. It is indeed as if in Wordsworth's 'sallied', 'sullied' might also be heard, so sallying forth would already be a sullying. And, after all, there is something slightly nutty about 'Nutting'. The boy himself seems a little crazed. (Later in life Wordsworth declared of the poem 'I was an impassioned nutter' (Wordsworth 1992, 391).) The speaker describes his younger self as being 'Trick'd out in proud disguise of Beggar's weeds' (l.7), as if his whole bearing and 'Motley' appearance (l.10) is a kind of 'trick'. It is as if his clothes are the socially and culturally constituted other of fruitful, productive, desirable nature, as if they are 'weeds'; and as if humanity is as a beggar to nature. These and other traces of deception, violence, cruelty, insanity, jesting, clowning and impoverishment are strangely at work within Wordsworth's pastoral opening, his apparently 'innocent' description of a country walk. So that rather than a strict opposition between a boy's harmony with nature and his despoliation of it, the language of the poem (also) presents us with the idea that that relationship is always mediated, compromised, violent. It leads us to reflect, indeed, on the idea that, as Jacques Derrida puts it, 'there is no natural violence, an earthquake is not violent, it is only violent insofar as it damages human interests' (Derrida and Ferraris 2001, 92). Violence has to do with the human, starting with the violence of language itself, in its representations and appropriations of 'nature'.

Despite the 'ism' in its name, ecocriticism is not in fact constituted as yet another 'ism': it does not offer a distinctive *methodology* of reading, but draws on feminist or Marxist or historical or postcolonial or psychoanalytic or deconstructive approaches, in order to attend to a world of environmental questions. The term 'ecocriticism' is perhaps useful as a means of referring to a relatively new dimension and emphasis in literary studies and beyond, but in many respects it makes no sense. It is not a matter of choosing to be or not to be an ecocritic. We are all eco-critters, so to speak, some less responsible and thoughtful than others. Ecocritical thinking in this respect involves a change of scale and vision: rather than an obsession with human-sized objects, it attends both to the miniature realm of a blade of grass, an ant, amoeba, or pathogen, and to the mega-scale of the ocean, the mountain, or even the earth itself (as well as everything in between). An ecocritical reading might foreground those strange lines towards the end of Wordsworth's poem about the boy 'Exulting, rich beyond the wealth of kings' while also feeling 'a sense of pain' when he sees what he has done; and it might consider the lines as a reflection on the way that both public and private wealth are dependent on the exploitation and ultimately the destruction of nature. From this perspective, the poem would seem to encapsulate a pattern that the environmental sociologist Franz Broswimmer analyses in his compelling study of the destructive effects of human communities throughout history, *Ecocide: A Short History of Mass Extinction of Species* (2002), in which successful societies accumulate wealth through ecological destruction to the point at which their very existence is undermined as a result of that wasting of the environment, in an eco-unfriendly cycle of boom-and-bust.

The pattern of destruction that Broswimmer describes has, of course, accelerated in the 200 years since Wordsworth was writing. While early societies produced their own localized form of unintended 'ecocide' and their own subsequent demise (Broswimmer examines the cases of temporarily 'successful' societies such as the Mesopotamians, the Romans, the Mayans, and others), twenty-first century global capitalism is currently facing the possibility that within the lifetime of many of us living today, our rapacious, land-grabbing, polluting rage for road- and air-travel, consumables and other material possessions will lead inexorably, unstoppably to the effective destruction of more or less all life on the planet. Such a future is imagined in Cormac McCarthy's Pulitzer-Prize winning novel *The Road* (2006), a book that has been hailed by the British journalist and environmental activist George Monbiot as 'the most important environmental book ever written', one that will 'change the way you see the world' (Monbiot 2007). Since for some people, such praise might make the novel sound like a worthy but dull attack on global capitalism, we would like to affirm that *The Road* is also a compelling narrative written in brilliant but restrained, almost biblical prose, and that, despite its bleak attenuations of verbal texture, it presents a richly moving and highly readable narrative of a post-apocalyptic future. For Monbiot, the importance of McCarthy's novel lies in its vivid imagining of the devastating reality of life for a few survivors after an apocalyptic event which has left the world dimmed, grey with floating ash, and in which almost all animal and plant life is dead. Nights in this world are 'beyond darkness', while days are 'more grey each one than what had gone before' (1). McCarthy imagines a desperate, barren end for a world in which language itself is dying out:

> The world shrinking down about a raw core of parsible entities. The names of things slowly following those things into oblivion. Colors. The names of birds. Things to eat. More fragile than he would have thought. How much of it was gone already? The sacred idiom shorn of its referents and so of its reality. Drawing down like something trying to preserve heat. In time to wink out forever. (93)

There are scattered, mostly murderous human survivors, but the only other living animal and plant life encountered are a few mushrooms, at one point, which are quickly eaten, and at another point the distant bark of a dog – which, if its ominous silencing is anything to go by, also quickly becomes someone's dinner. The narrative concerns an unnamed man and his young son who are travelling south through a devastated America in search of the ocean and life-saving warmth – and the possibility, the tenuous and almost entirely unwarranted hope, of some community with which to settle, of some possible future. The pair walk slowly through a scorched and blackened landscape almost entirely denuded of life, scavenging for sustenance amongst the detritus left after an apocalyptic event several years earlier (a nuclear war? an impact with a large asteroid? – the text does not disclose). Since the catastrophe and the almost complete destruction of animal and plant life, survival has depended on scavenging for residual products of lost modernity such as canned food. But such products have become more and more scarce and the savagery with which the few survivors treat each other has consequently become more extreme: everyone is now starving and other people are therefore seen as rivals for food or even *as* food. The most shocking scenes in this often harrowing novel involve cannibalism: the man opens a locked cellar to see a group of prisoners whose limbs are to be harvested for their captors' nourishment even while they are still alive; later, the man and the boy come across a fire, recently abandoned in panic, over which is the blackened, gutted torso of a baby on a spit. In this new world, order, morality, humanity itself has almost entirely broken down and remains only in the father's love for his son, his determination to protect him, and in the refusal of the man and the boy to exploit others to save themselves. The importance of McCarthy's novel lies in its bleak, almost affectless world of its prose, and its starkly conceived, terrifying vision of a post-apocalyptic future, with its warning against our current profligate existence.

Wordsworth's poem and McCarthy's novel might help us to think about the kinds of ideas, and the ways of reading, that ecocritical thinking opens up. The following might be considered as some of the most important terms whereby literature can be reconceived and literary texts reread:

Externality

'Externality' is the idea that there is an environment elsewhere, outside of our immediate habitat available for exploitation – another village, town or region, another country or, best of all, another continent or even another planet. The concept of externality links with questions of colonialism and postcolonialism in particular since this 'elsewhere' is typically a colony whose natural resources can be exploited for the economic benefit of the colonisers regardless of the effect on the indigenous population (whether human or not). It is everything that is at issue in the idea of the *exotic*. But a properly ecological thinking figures externality as a dangerous myth, bringing us up against the fact that there is only one world, in which everything is connected to everything else. It has been estimated that for all of the six billion people now alive to have a standard of living equivalent to that of the average American citizen there would need to be two or three extra Earth-sized planets. But there are no such planets, and the idea that we could colonize, say, the atmosphere-thin wastes of the moon or the arctic desert of Mars seems little more than a consoling but dangerous fantasy (like ideas of heaven or any other after-life Nirvana in which the failings of this life are imagined to be magically redeemed in another, alternative 'world'): outside of science-fiction or the wilder speculations of scientists, there is effectively no other space, no externality, apart from the Earth, no other world but this one. Externality in Wordsworth's poem is the compromised, sullied wilderness into which the boy sallies. In McCarthy's novel, there is a sense in which the external, the other of American global colonialism, has become internal, a sense that this externality has finally been destroyed, that there is finally no elsewhere, no place to go that is not already a devastated, alien, dead, waste land.

Ethics of the future

While ecology is concerned with the suffering of millions of people on the planet today whose lives are compromised or indeed wasted by environmental destruction and mismanagement, it is also necessarily future-oriented. Ecocriticism therefore demands a rethinking of ethics, extending the notion of our responsibility for others unpredictably into the future, since those others include people yet to be born, as well as those who will live after our death. While the consequences of our communal addiction to road use and to cheap foreign holidays may not seem to involve significant human suffering, ecological thinking would stress that your cheap flight to a destination of sunshine and inexpensive booze is directly correlated to the unknown suffering of future generations. McCarthy's *The Road* is concerned with a man's commitment to preserving the life of his son, and in this sense with the father's sense of responsibility for future generations. At the same time, this dystopian novel has to do with a thinking of an unbearable future – and the *lack* of a future – that we may be preparing for generations to come (or those generations that might in consequence *not* come) thanks to the choices that we make today.

Nature

Raymond Williams, one of the first modern ecocritical thinkers, famously refers to 'nature' as 'perhaps the most complex word in the language' (Williams 1983, 219). Nature has itself come under renewed attention, has been rethought and redefined, in recent ecocritical writing. One of the key questions regarding 'nature' concerns its relationship with the human. Is 'nature' that which is outside of, other to, the human, as is suggested by certain forms of religion, for example those that deny the naturalism of Darwinian evolution? Or are humans *part of* nature, as is suggested by Darwinism and more generally by the Western scientific paradigm? While ecocritical thinking would tend to align itself with the 'scientific' paradigm, with the idea of the human as animal, it also pays attention to ways in which this ambiguity or uncertainty operates in literary texts and in cultural production more generally. Wordsworth's presentation of nature in 'Nutting' is, as we have seen, ambiguous: 'nature' is where the boy is not; but for the poet to register nature he must have experienced it, nature must be humanized (and in being humanized it is contaminated, destroyed). In a sense, there is no such thing as nature, no such thing as the unmediated, unsullied, non-human nature that Wordsworth's poem might seem to suggest. 'There is no nature', Alan Liu has famously remarked in a monumental tome on Wordsworth and history, 'except as it is constituted by acts of political definition' (Liu 1989, 104).

Environmental criticism

'Environmental criticism' is the term that one of its leading proponents, Laurence Buell, uses to describe a certain engagement with 'nature writing'. Environmental criticism can be distinguished from what has come to be called ecocriticism in that a critic like Buell is primarily concerned with the kind of writing that has as its focus the environment and its relationship with humanity – so-called 'nature writing' – while ecocriticism is also concerned with teasing out the ecological questions, implications and challenges of *any* writing, whether or not that writing might involve a conscious and explicit engagement with nature. For ecocriticism, Jane Austen's studies of upper-middle class manners and customs in a novel like *Pride and Prejudice* (1813) are as valid a source of ecological speculation and analysis as Henry David Thoreau's philosophical musings on his pond in *Walden: Or, Life in the Woods* (1854). For the ecocritic, the famous sentence that opens Austen's novel ('It is a truth universally acknowledged, that a single man in possession of a good fortune must be in want of a wife') is profoundly ecological: 'universally' raises the question of which 'universe' we are speaking of and of whether in fact this very restrictive Anglo- or at least Euro-centric late eighteenth- or early-nineteenth century social formation can be exported to other parts of the world and to other times; a 'good fortune' is necessarily premised on ecological exploitation (whether in the form of private ownership of land, the privatization of the commons in the eighteenth- and nineteenth-century enclosures movement, the slavery-based economy of Caribbean plantations, or the newly industrialized exploitation of mineral and other resources); and the fact that marriage is premised on reproduction, on the propagation of the species, means that it is necessarily linked to the questions of population and overpopulation that, in his controversial book *An Essay on the Principle of Population* (1798), Thomas Malthus was beginning to bring to the attention of the English-speaking world at about the time that Austen was writing. An ecocritical reading of the first sentence of Austen's novel would be alert to all of these and other 'environmental' factors in her famous novel; it would reread the novel, indeed, according to the terms dictated by such questions, just as much as it would focus on the more obviously 'ecological' questions raised by Wordsworth's poem or McCarthy's novel.

Deep ecology

Deep ecology is an environmental movement that rejects the notion of 'sustainable development' and suggests that capitalism, progress, even Western liberalism itself is responsible for the current ecological crisis that afflicts the world. Deep ecology might be compared to the literary and philosophical work of deconstruction in its call for a radical critique and transformation of conventional ways of conceiving of 'human' values, of humanism, even of science itself. For deep ecologists, it is a matter of new ways of thinking about our relationship with the world, a new ethics and politics that will challenge the instrumentalist view that the world is and should be available for human exploitation. Both Wordsworth's poem and McCarthy's novel allow for the possibility of a rethinking of the relationship between humans and the biosphere: it would be possible to read Wordsworth's poem as a radical critique of the colonizing tendency of humans; McCarthy's novel is, among other things, a polemic that calls for a fundamental revaluation of environmental ethics and of the way we live now.

Ecofeminism

As we have suggested in relation to Wordsworth's poem, ecofeminism attends in particular to the figurative language in which women and nature are presented and it responds to ways in which nature and the feminine are often linked in a gesture that denigrates both. In a landmark essay from 1984, for example, Annette Kolodny comments on 'how bound we still are by the vocabulary of a feminine landscape and the psychological patterns of regression and violation that it implies' (Kolodny 1996, 176). Thus, ecofeminist critics such as Kolodny, Louise Westling, Patrick Murphy, Greta Gaard, Donna Haraway and others have highlighted and questioned the gendering of 'nature' in literary and other discourse. From this perspective, patriarchy is itself understood to be responsible for the exploitation of both nature and women. Such exploitation is produced partly by way of an identification of one with the other (women are said to be less rational than men, thus 'closer to nature', and therefore in need of civilizing, through masculine control and order). Non- or anti-patriarchal thinking, according to this analysis, would allow for a relationship with the ecosystem that is not exploitative and would demand, indeed, an ethics and politics that is no longer driven by patriarchal codes of bourgeois individualism and what Marx calls 'primitive accumula-tion', by colonization, the violent and rapacious drive for mastery, and, neces-sarily, ecological destruction. Gender, like nature itself, is written into *The Road* just by the fact that there are virtually no female characters in the novel: it's a man's world, as the chilling saying goes. Nature – in the sense of living things – has been almost completely destroyed, and there are almost no women in this new, brutally savage world. But in the novel's denoucment the boy finds a family – a substitute father *and* mother – in a scene which at least offers the hope of new life, of women and of nature.

Anthropomorphic, anthropocentric

To borrow a distinction that Don Scheese makes, ecocritical thinking is eco- rather than ego-centred (Scheese 1996, 307). As such, it draws our atten-tion to the multiple ways in which literary texts figure the non-human as human – to anthropomorphism – in what is often a sentimental appropriation of the non-human for human ends. Anthropomorphism includes the casual use of what John Ruskin calls the 'affective fallacy' (*Modern Painters* (1860) Part 4, Chapter 12). For example, the lightning that strikes the old oak tree in Chapter 23 of *Jane Eyre* somehow articulates the double threat and temptation that Rochester's proposal of marriage represents to Jane; the storm in Chapter 83 of *Middlemarch* similarly reflects the 'stormy' passions of Dorothea and Will Ladislaw; and so on. The ruses and delusions of anthro-pomorphism are also at work in the celebration of natural sublimity in a poem like Percy Bysshe Shelley's 'Mont Blanc' (1816), in which the mountain is figured as (or as resembling) 'My own, my human mind' (l.37), as well as in the famous presentation of Egdon Heath as one of the main 'characters', even the protagonist, of Thomas Hardy's *The Return of the Native* (1878). Anthropomorphism also concerns the way in which animals are regularly treated as having human motivations, emotions, language, consciousness, even morality – from countless examples of fables, children's literature and fairy tales to more subtle anthropomorphisms such as the whale in Herman Melville's *Moby-Dick* (1851), bees in some of Sylvia Plath's *Ariel* poems (1965), ants in Derek Walcott's 'The Bounty' (1997), or the crow in Philip Roth's *The Human Stain* (2000) that is presented as part of an attack on late-twentieth century conceptions of the 'human'. Ecocritical thinking ana-lyzes the ways in which such figurations of the apparently non-human lead inexorably to anthropocentrism, to the configuration of the world in human terms – which in turn leads to the exploitation of the non-human (however that category is defined) for human benefit. The world is conceived of as human-centred and therefore endlessly available as a resource for human comfort, wealth and well-being. The ecologist Michael Robins offers a striking suggestion for rethinking anthropocentrism when he comments on human armpits (yours as well as ours, we fear): 'From the biosphere's perspective, the whole point of Homo sapiens is their armpits, aswarm with 24.1 billion bacteria' (quoted in Campbell 1996, 133).

So where does this leave us (apart from worrying about our underarms and deodorants)? As well as praising *The Road*, George Monbiot has expressed his enthusiasm for the first Hollywood global-warming disaster movie, *The Day After Tomorrow* (2004), declaring it a 'great movie' and, despite its 'lousy science', 'one of the best movies ever released' (Monbiot 2004). But we think that Monbiot should get out more (at least to the movies). In our judgment, *The Day After Tomorrow* stinks. The science is not just lousy, it's preposterous, matched only by the blockbuster's toxic combination of melodrama and sentimentality (served up in alternating chunks at regular 10-minute intervals), by its frankly cruddy special effects, characterization and dialogue, and by the absurdity of its plot. We can hardly bring ourselves to sketch the story: a maverick climatologist, having personally briefed the US President in Washington on the coming global disaster and advised evacuation of the population of the southern US states to Mexico – it is too late to save the inhabitants of the northern states; the population of Canada doesn't get a look in – nevertheless sets out, amidst the mother of all snap ice-ages, to drive and then walk to New York in order to save his son, who is sheltering in the famous public library with a handful of other refugees. (All those who foolishly left the library have perished in the −150°C freeze along with most other New Yorkers.) *The Day After Tomorrow* shares with *The Road* a cataclysmic scenario and a recuperative father–son narrative, and despite the radical nature of McCarthy's dystopian novel, its truly inventive evocation of a post-apocalyptic world, an ecocritical reading might finally see both novel and movie as embedded in a troubling anthropocentrism that undermines the ability of either to fully confront ecological questions. In both, father and son encapsulate the liberal-humanist idea that individual human life (rather than populations, rather than the biosphere or ecosystem) is the ultimate and finally the only value. Both are characterized by the familiar Hollywood ethical calculus (the basis of *all* 'disaster movies', indeed) which asserts that the survival of a single unique individual allows redemptive closure (and a happy ending) regardless of how many others get wiped out along the way. And both affirm the values of the so-called 'nuclear' family: at the end of McCarthy's novel, although the father dies, the boy finds another family with whom he might survive and even thrive; the movie ends with the father finding and rescuing his son, and with the son's romantic attachment to the attractive young woman with whom he has shared his life-threatening library experience. Life goes on, at least for these few people, for these individual families.

So while we share Monbiot's enthusiasm for narratives that might indeed shake up people's indifference to environmental degradation and disaster, we would stress that ecocritical readings of such texts should be alert to the complexities both of their environmental contexts and their linguistic and indissociably linked aesthetic values. To put it simply, the failures of *The Day After Tomorrow* as a movie are bound up with its failures of ecological analysis; and the weaknesses of *The Road*, such as they are, have to do with a certain redemptive sentiment that recoils at the full implications of its own radical vision of an ecologically bereft future. It is increasingly possible, and indeed urgent and necessary, therefore, to develop forceful and compelling ecocritical readings across the entire range of literary and other writings, readings that go beyond the business-as-usual anthropocentrism of conventional liberal humanism, and that take as their focus the ecosystem itself – that place, that home (*eco-* is from Greek *oikos*, house, dwelling) in which we have no choice but to live and, like other animals, die.

Further reading

Two essential and reasonably accessible texts to start with are Greg Garrard's lucid and intelligent introduction to the field, *Ecocriticism* (2004), and Laurence Coupe's valuable collection of fairly brief extracts from influential essays from the Romantic period to the present, *The Green Studies Reader* (2000). In writing this chapter we have been helped by seeing a draft of Timothy Clark's excellent *Cambridge Introduction to Literature and the Environment* (forthcoming), which we recommend as a readable and highly informative primer. Raymond Williams's *The Country and the City* (1973) is an important and influential precursor of ecocriticism, and Jonathan Bate's' *Romantic Ecology* (1991) is another influential early intervention in the field, mainly focused on Wordsworth (see also Bate's more recent and wider-ranging *The Song of the Earth* (2000)). Much more demanding is Timothy Morton's *Ecology Without Nature* (2007), a sophisticated study which, like Clark's book, stresses the importance of engaging ecocriticism with deconstructive literary and cultural theory. There is some interesting recent work on ecology and early-modern literature, including Mary Floyd-Wilson and Garrett A. Sullivan, Jr, *Environment and Embodiment in Early Modern England* (2007), Gabriel Egan, *Green Shakespeare* (2006), and Robert N.

Watson, *Back to Nature* (2006). Three useful collections of essays that also offer helpful introductions are Glotefelty and Fromm, ed., *The Ecocriticism Reader* (1996), Armbruster and Wallace, eds, *Beyond Nature Writing* (2001), and Kerridge and Sammells, eds, *Writing the Environment* (1998). The journal *Interdisciplinary Studies in Literature and the Environment* (*ISLE*) publishes essays on ecocriticism and topics around literary ecology (see www.unr.edu/cla/engl/isle/).

17 Animals

Here are four animals:

1.
His small Umbrella quaintly halved
Describing in the Air
An Arc alike inscrutable
Elate Philosopher.

2.
This animal which, like a ship's anchor,
first casts off in the void,
In order to – even upside down – maintain
itself there suddenly

3.
Spacefarers past living planetfall
on our ever-dive in bloom crystal:
when about our self kin selves appear,
slowing, rubber to pulp, we slack from spear . . .

4.
Queer, with your thin wings and streaming legs,
How you sail like a heron, or a dull clot of air,
A nothingness.

All of these poems concern animals, whether mammal, insect or fish. Some of them may be easier to identify than others. The first is a bat, by Emily Dickinson; the second a spider, by Francis Ponge; the third, cuttlefish, by Les

Murray; and last but not least, a mosquito, by D.H. Lawrence. Everything we hope to explore here, apropos the question of animals and literature, might be illustrated on the basis of these four brief extracts. We say 'literature' but we need in fact to be wary: all of these examples are poems. Indeed there is, we want to suggest, something special about the relationship between poetry and animals, something that takes us, perhaps, to the very heart of what we mean by terms such as the 'poetic', 'poetic language' and even 'poem'. And this can in turn, we will argue, illuminate in a more general way what we call literature.

This might sound like a merely aesthetic exercise confined to looking at how a few poets write about little creatures, furry or otherwise, but our topic is of course far larger. The world is currently challenged, not only by terrible poverty, injustice and inequality, and by environmental degradation and climate change, but also by the widespread and massive destruction of so-called 'wildlife' habitats, the rapid disappearance of countless different animal species and the threat of many more extinctions to come. These challenges are all interrelated in different and highly complex ways, but at their core is the violence of what is called anthropocentrism. Anthropocentrism has to do with how humans think and act as if 'man' (in Heidegger's phrase) were 'the lord of the earth', going around 'everywhere and always encounter[ing] only himself' (Heidegger 1977, 27). As we try to argue elsewhere in this book (in 'Me', 'Laughter' and 'Eco', in particular), the human is not at the centre of the world, however much we might imagine or behave otherwise. In many ways, no doubt, the implications and consequences of Darwin's *On the Origin of Species* (1859) and *The Descent of Man* (1871) are still sinking in. So too, perhaps, is the gender-biased presumptuousness of referring to humanity as 'man'. The crisis here is obviously not just one of language and naming – though that, as we shall see, is perhaps more significant than might be supposed. Nor is it only of concern to those who regard themselves as 'green' or 'feminist'. Like the question of environmentalism that we discuss in 'Eco', the question of animals and animality watches over us all, every moment. The latter indeed may be still watching, literally, after the end of humanity.

In calling this chapter 'Animals' and opening with a few brief examples of poems about animals, we have perhaps already managed to give the impression that there are animals (bats, spiders, cuttlefish and mosquitoes) on the one hand, and humans (poets) on the other. Humans *are* animals, after all: an 'animal' is fundamentally simply 'a living creature' (*OED*, sense 1a), a word deriving from the Latin *anima*, 'breath'. So what happens when humans write about other animals? We know that Dickinson's poem is about a bat because it opens with the words, 'The Bat is dun, with wrinkled Wings –' (Poem 1575).

But the four-line stanza we have quoted is in fact extraordinarily difficult to pin down, on account of its imaginative and syntactic complexity. The verse in question seems to evoke the bat's wings and the movement they trace in the air. The lines appear to constitute a sentence, but there is no main verb. We are compelled to take the present participle 'describing' as the main verb, but we are still left with the conundrum of 'alike' and the strangeness of 'elate' as an adjective (meaning lifted, raised, exalted, inspired). The four-line sentence notably lacks all punctuation: it is as if the words and phrases themselves were batting about, this way and that, unpredictable and, indeed, like an animal, *inscrutable*. A provoking rapport emerges here between the poem and the bat. You cannot pin down the lines anymore than you could the creature described. It is perhaps no coincidence that in a famous essay in which he tries to pin down consciousness, the philosopher Thomas Nagel should choose to reflect on the question of what it is like to be a bat (Nagel 1974). Inscrutability is a feature of these lines of poetry as it is of the line or lines of the 'Arc' that 'the Bat' itself describes. For Dickinson's bat, after all, is himself a sort of poet or writer: 'Describing in the Air / An Arc alike inscrutable / Elate Philosopher.'

Dickinson's has a strikingly self-reflexive dimension: it can be read, among other things, as a poem about the poetic, about writing, and more particularly about writing (itself) as act or event, doing or making. (We might helpfully recall here the etymology of 'poetry', from the ancient Greek *poiein*, to do or make.) The lines from Ponge's poem 'The New Spider' are up to something similar: the very syntax, slipping and interconnectedness of the lines seems to cast forth the impression of a spider weaving: 'In order to – even upside down – maintain / itself there suddenly'. (Another etymology comes to mind here: the word 'text' derives from the Latin *textere*, to weave.) Likewise, Murray's strangely beautiful, ghostlike poem 'Cuttlefish' concludes with an image of writing in the ink of cuttlefish culture: 'leaving, of our culture, an ectoplasm of ink'. (Murray is here alluding to 'sepia', another name for cuttlefish. The sepia of sepia photography and water-colour paint is indeed, literally, a product of cuttlefish. The earliest photographs were writings not just in light but in cuttlefish ink.)

Lawrence's 'The Mosquito' is in some ways the most surreptitious in its self-reflexivity. It differs from the other poems discussed here in that it addresses the animal itself. It is characterized by a sort of bantering, questioning, conversational tone, opening with the words: 'When did you start your tricks, / Monsieur?' Everyone knows that mosquitoes are not French: the poem's opening address is at once comical and indicative of the tricksiness of Lawrence's language. Likewise the 'clot': 'dull clot of air' is marvellously suggestive of the almost imperceptible, ghostly character of the creature addressed. At the same time it evokes the image of a blood-clot. 'Clot', in other words, is self-reflexive, a subtle projection *on to* this blood-sucking creature of precisely what, later in the poem, it *does* to the speaker. It sucks 'live blood, / My blood', the poet reports. It becomes a 'winged blood-drop'. Already, from the beginning, the play in the sounds of 'monsieur' and 'mosquito' intimates that this is a poem working explicitly at the level of the signifier, with the arbitrariness of language. 'Monsieur' has no more natural or logical a relation to the creature in question than does 'mosquito' itself. Lawrence's poem is a wonderfully funny account of the sort of enraged anthropomorphic telepathy a mosquito can indeed inspire: 'I hate the way you lurch off sideways into air / Having read my thoughts against you'. The poem, it transpires, is about the poet becoming a mosquito in turn: 'Am I not mosquito enough to out-mosquito you?' And it concludes, perhaps not entirely surprisingly, with the death of the addressee, the mosquito squished: 'Queer, what a dim dark smudge you have disappeared into!'

In a sense, then, each poem is not only *about* an animal, but also aspires to be a sort of animal. Each *would be* an 'animal poem'. In a certain imaginative register (*as if*), the poem inscribes itself in the world of the creature described. It *would* be a true 'animal poem': it would *like to be*, but of course it cannot. It would like to be telepathic, it would like not only to communicate with but to speak on behalf of the animal, as an animal, from the animal's point of view. But this would be a kind of anthropomorphism, in other words a fantasy or projection. In truth, what all of the poems sharply convey is a sense of the *impossibility* of finding the right words, of adequately describing, of putting in language what a specific animal is like, what is entailed in an encounter with this particular creature (bat, spider, cuttlefish, mosquito). For how on earth do you, should you describe a non-human animal? How can you say what it is like to be one? The English language is stuffed (as a taxidermist might say) with figurative references to animals. Just spinning off a few examples can make us sound faintly poetic: quiet as a mouse, sweating like a pig, slow as a tortoise, a bear hug, a dog's breakfast, sick as a parrot, crow's feet, pigeon-toed, the elephant in the room, rabbit in headlights, dead as a dodo, going the whole hog, can of worms, dark horse, lion's share, crocodile tears, snake in the grass, wolf in sheep's clothing, sly as a fox, happy as a clam, bullish, lousy, waspish, hare-brained, headless chicken, water off a duck's back, eyes like a hawk, frog in your throat, you can lead a horse to water, whale of a time, loan sharks, lying toad, swansong, running around like a blue-arsed fly, being badgered, beavering away, bee in your bonnet, cat got your tongue, completely batty . . . The list is as long as the queue for Noah's ark. We are forever *comparing ourselves* to other animals. These idioms seem to affirm the implicit violence of our relations with other animals: many of the examples just given involve a negative figuration of the animal and all seem to involve a kind of easy anthropomorphism. But in the very gesture of such appropriation these idioms also register the *otherness* of these creatures.

It is striking, for example, that when Lawrence is trying to describe a mosquito, he resorts to a simile involving *another animal* ('like a heron'), then to a kind of oxymoron ('clot of air'), and finally to a blank absence of all image or resemblance ('A nothingness'). Correspondingly, Ponge turns to a nautical metaphor to evoke the spider as it casts off 'like a ship's anchor' into the air. In the case of the lines from Dickinson and Murray, the explicit marker of figurative language, the 'like' (or 'as'), is tacit or omitted: the bat's wings are (like) a 'small Umbrella quaintly halved', the bat is (like) a 'philosopher'; the cuttlefish are (like) 'spacefarers', their bodies are (like) 'rubber', 'pulp' and 'spear'. The elision of such markers, however, merely accentuates the extravagance or fancifulness of the descriptions. Dickinson's language is anthropomorphic, but in a quirky, defamiliarizing way. The figuration of the bat as a sort of neat and pleasant gentleman ('His small Umbrella quaintly halved') entails unsettling undersides. Murray's poem on the other hand crucially depends on its title. Without the word 'Cuttlefish' at the top of the page we could hardly be expected to surmise who or what is the subject of the fantastical, science-fictional phrases: 'Spacefarers past living planetfall / on our ever-dive in bloom crystal'. ('Planetfall', as the *OED* informs us, is originally a mid-twentieth-century word for 'A landing on a planet after a journey through space'.) We are so immersed in a language of strange compounds and juxtapositions ('ever-dive', 'bloom crystal'), in a fluid syntax that seems to let odd phrases float by ('past living', 'in bloom') while unsettling any easy identification of parts of speech (is 'bloom' an adjective, 'pulp' a verb, 'spear' a noun?), that we may not even notice on first reading that these are rhyming couplets. These opening lines are rendered even more bizarre, perhaps, by the poet's anthropomorphic strategy of speaking in a cuttlefish royal we ('our ever-dive', 'our self', 'we slack'). Perplexed (but also delighted) we may well find ourselves asking: 'we'? what is this? what is this poem or poet *like*? The most powerful poems about animals are those that disorient us, leave the reader stranded, up in the air, underground or underwater, breathtaken. Murray's 'Cuttlefish' appears in a volume that is suggestively entitled *Translations from the Natural World*: all animal poems are 'translations', we might say, but *without access to an original*. In a sense they are all works of science fiction or strangely 'elate' philosophy.

There is a growing body of critical and theoretical work (sometimes referred to as 'animal studies') concerned with 'the question of the animal' as the basis for what Matthew Calarco, in his book *Zoographies*, has called 'new social movements that are seeking to develop a postliberal, posthumanist approach to politics' (Calarco 2008, 6). Debate concerning 'the question of the animal' is, so to speak, a real hornet's nest. Do animals have rights, as Peter Singer (1990) and Tom Regan (1983), among others, have argued? Don't lots of species of animal exhibit characteristics that are often said to define the human, such as use of tools, language, altruism, play, inventiveness, suffering, mourning and so on? Is it true, as Aristotle suggested, that 'no animal laughs save Man' (Aristotle 2001, 69)? Is it the case that animals don't die but merely 'perish', as Heidegger suggested (see Heidegger 1962, 291; Heidegger 2001, 176)? Or, conversely, should we not suppose that, as Gilles Deleuze puts it, 'contrary to the spiritualist prejudice, it is the animal who knows how to die, who has a sense or premonition of death' (Deleuze 1998, 2)? Should we feel OK about eating other animals? Can battery-farming be justified? What about some of the other barbaric ways in which non-human animals are treated and killed? What gives us the right to make these decisions? Calarco himself is one of many who argue emphatically that '*the human-animal distinction can no longer and ought no longer to be maintained*' (3). There are, however, good reasons for being cautious about such an assertion. A woman is not a spider (despite her appearance in Marvel Comics), any more than a man is a bat (despite numerous impersonations, from Bram Stoker to Christian Bale's 'dark knight'). Questioning and indeed seeking to dismantle or deconstruct anthropocentrism, in philosophy as in everyday life, is one thing; but dropping or claiming to drop distinctions altogether is something else.

Rather than blurring the line between 'animal' and 'human' we should attend to differences. In his remarkable work *The Animal That Therefore I Am*, Jacques Derrida explores the idea that, perhaps more effectively than anything else in the world, the 'question of the animal' prompts us to think about 'the wholly other' (Derrida 2008, 11). In a startling moment the eminent French philosopher recalls being naked in the bathroom with his cat. (We say 'his cat' in order to simplify matters. In fact, like every cat-lover, Derrida knows argues that no one can truly own a cat because, as he says, 'A pussycat never belongs' [7].) He is talking about that 'strange moment' when, 'before even wanting it or knowing it myself, I am passively presented to it as naked, I am seen and seen naked, before even seeing *myself* seen by a cat', seen by that '*wholly other they call "animal", for example "cat"*' (11). Entirely at odds with any sentimental or anthropomorphic appropriation of the cat, Derrida, naked before it, summarizes: 'Thinking perhaps begins there' (29). In this way Derrida seeks to elaborate on the notion that every living creature constitutes what he calls an 'unsubstitutable singularity' (9). It is a question of *this* cat, in

Derrida's bathroom, not just any old cat. Indeed, in his terms, there is no such thing as 'any old cat'. Every cat is other, and every other is wholly other. This sense of the unsubstitutable singularity of any and every animal, he contends, is especially evident in poetry. And this is one of the ways of distinguishing poetry from philosophy. As Derrida puts it: 'thinking concerning the animal, if there is such a thing, derives from poetry. . . . [This] is what philosophy has, essentially, had to deprive itself of' (7).

Walt Whitman writes, in 'Song of Myself': 'I think I could turn and live with animals, they are so placid and self-contain'd, / I stand and look at them long and long' ('Song of Myself', section 32). But these lines tell only half the story: it is also and perhaps more significantly a question about what happens when the animal looks back, or just looks, *at us*, in plain day or (imperceptibly perhaps) at night. Poetry, we have suggested, is especially *in sympathy with* the otherness of animals and with the notion of unsubstitutable singularity. As Ted Hughes puts it, in the context of a discussion of the experience of composing a poem: 'the poem is a new species of creature, a new specimen of the life outside your own' (Hughes 1967, 17). Every poem would be a different creature, looking at its author and each of its readers in a unique way, bespeaking a being unlike any other poem or any other kind of text. This is perhaps what poetic originality or genius entails (no pun intended).

The association that Derrida makes between poetry and animals might lead us to the supposition that the more poetic a novel, short story or play is, the more likely we are to find animals pervading and haunting it. We could consider, for example, Shakespeare (for whose animals a supplementary volume of the *Introduction to Literature, Criticism and Theory* would be required), Herman Melville (author of that whale of a book, *Moby-Dick*), Franz Kafka or Elizabeth Bowen. Let us just briefly recall one or two instances from the last two of these writers. One of Kafka's greatest short fictions, 'The Burrow' (written in 1923), begins with the following immortal sentence: 'I have completed the construction of my burrow and it seems to be successful' (Kafka 1992, 325). The narrator is, apparently, a burrowing animal: thinking, to recall Derrida's formulation, perhaps begins there. We never discover quite what size or indeed what species this burrowing creature is, but we are drawn nonetheless into the fascination and strangeness of a kind of poetic, imperceptible place. As Deleuze and Guattari nicely observe in *Kafka: Toward a Minor Literature* (1986): 'Kafka is fascinated by everything that is small. If he doesn't seem to like children that is because they are caught in an irreversible becoming-big; the animal kingdom, in contrast, involves smallness and imperceptibility' (Deleuze and Guattari 1986, 37). Elizabeth Bowen, on the other hand, does not so much write from the point of view of animals, as let animals roam, flap around, animate and haunt her writing. Just two of very many instances from her novel *Friends and Relations* (1931) may suffice. A car departs from a country railway station with avian effects: 'Then his Aunt Janet drove off rapidly; water went up in wings from some deep puddles' (65). And, a little later, a hot summer day in a local market town is evoked through a sort of soundless feline music: 'A cat's yawn gave the note of the afternoon. Pavements sleepily glared; over the butcher's a piano played in its sleep' (80). (That last example leaves us not only with the subtle enchantment of a cat's yawn, but also the easily missed rawness of 'the butcher's'.)

Despite the pervasive or recurrent presence of animals in such works, it is as if, to borrow a formulation from Akira Mizuta Lippit, they 'exist in a state of *perpetual vanishing*' (Lippit 2000, 1). They haunt these texts. It's like the White Rabbit, or the Cheshire Cat, or so many other animals in Lewis Carroll's *Alice* books. It's like the Ghost in *Hamlet*, momentarily evoked as a mole under the earth, or beneath the stage. 'Well said, old mole!' exclaims Hamlet, but it has already shifted away: as he goes on to ask, 'Canst work i' th' earth so fast?' (1.5.170). Focusing attention on the appearances and disappearances of such animals (metaphorical or literal, fabulous or recognizable) can perhaps enable us to think differently not only about poetry but also about the 'poetic' in literature more generally.

We conclude with another creature that has made ghostly appearances in literature across the ages, from Homer's *Iliad* to Shakespeare's *Richard III* (I, ii, 100) to Beckett's *Company*, namely the hedgehog. Perhaps the best-known correlation between the hedgehog and a work of art is the one made by the German philosopher and poet Friedrich von Schlegel, who wrote, in 1798, regarding the literary or philosophical fragment: 'Like a little work of art, a fragment must be totally detached from the surrounding world and closed on itself like a hedgehog' (quoted in Derrida 1995b, 302). In a wonderful little text called 'Che c'osè la poesia?' (in English, 'What is poetry?' or 'What is the thing called poetry?'), Derrida obliquely explores this and other figures, transforming these into a new way of thinking about the poetic in relation to the 'humble' hedgehog (see Derrida 1995b, 288–99, 301–3). Derrida's hedgehog is a figure for what it is that makes us love language, what makes us want to remember a poem or a phrase or even a feeling or experience, what makes us want to 'learn by heart'. A poem, he proposes, is 'that very thing that teaches the heart' and even 'invents the heart' (Derrida 1995b, 295). It's a kind of ghostly hedgehog that has nothing to do with 'literary poetry' (297), with self-enclosed fragments or sonnets or epic poems. The hedgehog cannot be owned. It is a creature that attests to otherness, and above all perhaps to mortality and to the otherness of death that affects human and non-human animals alike. It is difficult to say whether Derrida's little text is a work of philosophy or literary theory or poetry. Correspondingly, the poetic nature of this hedgehog cannot, he suggests, be confined to any genre, poetic, literary or otherwise.

Further reading

In accord with the logic of what we have argued in this chapter, perhaps the best place to pursue further reading is in the work of poets rather than critics or theorists: D.H. Lawrence, William Blake, Shakespeare, Elizabeth Bishop, Ted Hughes, Les Murray, Francis Ponge and so many others. And Kafka's stories tell us as much about animals and literature, animals in literature, or animal literature, as any critical or theoretical writings. Literary works such as those we have been discussing in this chapter point towards a sense of the text as (in Hélène Cixous's phrase) a 'poetic-animal machine' (Cixous 1998) and towards a thinking in terms of what Deleuze and Guattari have called 'becoming animal' (Deleuze and Guattari 1986). Among the burgeoning growth of critical and theoretical material, there are in addition several especially stimulating books. For a short introductory account, Greg Garrard has a useful chapter on 'Animals' in his book *Ecocriticism* (2004). Of a more demanding nature, *Zoontologies: The Question of the Animal* (2003), ed. Cary Wolfe, is an excellent collection of poststructuralist, posthumanist interdisciplinary essays. So, too, is *Knowing Animals*, ed. Lawrence Simmons and Philip Armstrong (2007). Cary Wolfe has also written a fine study with a more specifically American focus, *Animal Rites: American Culture, the Discourse of Species, and Posthumanism* (2003), while Philip Armstrong's *What Animals Mean in the Fiction of Modernity* (2008) looks at literary works from Daniel Defoe and Jonathan Swift to Will Self and J.M. Coetzee. For a very helpful study focusing on the early modern period, see Erica Fudge's *Perceiving Animals: Humans and Beasts in Early Modern English Culture* (2002). For work in a more predominantly philosophical vein, see *Animal Others: On Ethics, Ontology, and Animal Life* (1999), ed. Peter H. Steeves, and Matthew Calarco's *Zoographies: The Question of the Animal from Heidegger to Derrida* (2008). Akira Mazuta Lippit's *Electric Animal: Toward a Rhetoric of Wildlife* (2000) is a compelling but challenging work that brilliantly explores the 'question of the animal' across philosophy, science and psychoanalysis, as well as literature and cinema. Derrida's *The Animal That Therefore I Am* (2008) is an extremely rich and complex set of essays that forms a crucial point of reference in many of the aforementioned secondary works. For two collections of essays especially concerned with the elaboration of Derrida's work in this area, see *Derridanimals*, a special issue of the *Oxford Literary Review* (2007), ed. Neil Badmington, and *Demenageries* (2009), ed. Anne Berger and Marta Segarra.

18. Ghosts

What has literature to do with ghosts? The word 'ghost' is related to and originates in the German *Geist*, a word that *Chambers Dictionary* defines as 'spirit, any inspiring or dominating principle'. The *OED* gives, as its first and fourth definitions of 'ghost', the 'soul or spirit, as the principle of life' and 'A person'. In these respects, the ghost is fundamental to our thinking about the human: to be human is to have a spirit, a soul, a *Geist* or ghost. But the more common modern sense of 'ghost' (albeit only listed seventh in the *OED*) involves the idea of a spectre, an apparition of the dead, a revenant, the dead returned to a kind of spectral existence – an entity not alive but also not quite, not finally, dead. Ghosts disturb our sense of the separation of the living from the dead – which is why they can be so frightening, so uncanny. These conflicting senses of the word 'ghost' suggest that ghosts are both exterior and central to our sense of the human. Ghosts are paradoxical since they are both fundamental to the human, fundamentally human, and a denial or disturbance of the human, the very being of the inhuman. We propose to devote this chapter, to dedicate it, to the living-dead, to the ghost(s) of literature. And we propose that this scandal of the ghost, its paradox, is embedded in the very thing that we call literature, inscribed in multiple and haunting ways, in novels, poems and plays.

Ghosts have a history. They are not what they used to be. Ghosts, in a sense, *are* history. They do not, after all, come from nowhere, even if they may appear to do just that. They are always inscribed *in a context*: they at once belong to and haunt the idea of a place (hence 'spirit of place' or *genius loci*), and belong to and haunt the idea of a time (what we could call a 'spirit of time' or rather differently what is called the 'spirit of the age' or *Zeitgeist*). In other words, it is possible to trace a history of ghosts, as well as to think about history itself as ghostly, as what can in some form or other always come back. We might, for example, pursue a history of ghosts in terms of what J. Hillis Miller calls 'the disappearance of God' (Miller 1963) in the nineteenth century. If the Christian God is, as Karl Marx claimed, 'Spectre No. 1' (Marx 1976, 157), it is fair to suppose that this 'disappearance' has altered the conception of ghosts, holy or otherwise. Correspondingly, we might pursue a history of ghosts in terms of the nineteenth-century emergence of psychology and, in particular, psychoanalysis. Ghosts, that is to say, move into one's head. In the course of the nineteenth century the ghost is internalized: it becomes a psychological symptom, and no longer an entity issuing commandments on a mountain-top or a thing that goes bump in the night.

In particular, psychoanalytic accounts of ghosts have revolutionized literary studies. We might illustrate this in terms of what is arguably the greatest 'ghost work' in English literature, Shakespeare's *Hamlet* (1600–01). The play itself is cryptic and elusive about the apparition and truthfulness of the figure of the ghost of Hamlet's father: why is it, for instance, that when the ghost appears in Act III, scene iv, it is only seen by Hamlet and not by his mother? But it is also clear that the play's representation of the ghost is grounded in the Christian mythology of Shakespeare's time – hence Hamlet's fear that 'The spirit that I have seen / May be a devil' who 'Abuses me to damn me' (II, ii, 598–9, 603). In twentieth-century psychoanalytic readings such as those advanced by Jacques Lacan or Nicolas Abraham, however, the ghost has become something very different. Lacan develops the ghostly or phantasmatic dimensions of the basic Freudian reading of the play as Oedipal drama: Hamlet cannot take revenge on his murderous uncle Claudius because he is haunted by the sense that what Claudius has done is what he would have wanted to do – kill his father and go to bed with his mother. In Lacan's scandalous and brilliant development of this reading of *Hamlet* (in a seminar in 1959), the ghost has to do with the phallus. As 'an imaginary object which the child comes to accept as being in the father's possession' (Wright 1992, 318), the phallus is in a sense the very symbol of paternity. For Lacan, the reason for Hamlet's inability to kill Claudius (until, at least, the moment of 'complete sacrifice', i.e. of his own death) is that 'one cannot strike the phallus, because the phallus, even the real phallus, is a *ghost*' (Lacan 1977b, 50–1). In this way, Lacan makes *Hamlet* an allegory of phallocentric culture: phallocentrism (everything in a culture that serves to equate the symbolic power of the father, the phallus, with authority, the proper, presence, truth itself) becomes a sort of farcical but terrible ghost story. In Lacan's reading, Hamlet's being haunted by his father is an allegory of the nature of the ego. In an appalling pun, he calls Hamlet an 'hommelette', a little man, a son, who is both dependent on his namesake King Hamlet and has his 'ego' scrambled – like an egg – by this haunting. As Maud Ellmann neatly summarizes it: 'the ego is a ghost' (Ellmann 1994, 17). There are problems with what Lacan does with a literary work like *Hamlet*, in particular in seeming to appropriate it simply as an allegorical means of presenting the 'truth' of psychoanalysis. But his thinking has proved extremely productive and stimulating for critics and theorists concerned to analyse the ghostliness of identity in literary texts and to question the nature and terms of the phallocentric ghost story in which we continue to have our being.

In the work of Nicolas Abraham, on the other hand, *Hamlet* is a central text for his theory that ghosts have to do with unspeakable secrets. The only reason why people think they see ghosts is because the dead take secrets with them when they die. In his essay 'Notes on the Phantom: A Complement to Freud's Metapsychology' (1975), Abraham observes that 'the theme of the dead – who, having suffered repression by their family or society, cannot enjoy, even in death, a state of authenticity – appears to be omnipresent (whether overtly expressed or disguised) on the fringes of religions and, failing that, in rational systems' (Abraham 1994, 171). Ghosts are everywhere, a painful fact of life. Abraham contends that 'the "phantom" [or "ghost"], whatever its form, is nothing but an invention of the living'. People see ghosts because 'the dead were shamed during their lifetime or . . . took unspeakable secrets to the grave'. These secrets remain, like a crypt, a gap, in the unconscious of the living. The ghost or phantom thus embodies 'the gap produced in us by the concealment of some part of a loved object's life . . . what haunts are not the dead, but the gaps left within us by the secrets of others' (171).

Abraham's account is helpful in illuminating the strangeness of Shakespeare's *Hamlet*, its obscure but persisting sense of secrets taken to the grave, of what the ghost calls the untellable 'secrets of my prison-house' (I, v, 14). But his 'Notes on the Phantom' also opens up new ways of thinking about ghosts in literature more generally: in effect, it inaugurates a theory of literature as a theory of ghosts. We can think of this ghostliness, first, in the relatively straightforward sense described by a character called Stella Rodney in Elizabeth Bowen's *The Heat of the Day* (1948): ' "What's unfinished haunts one; what's unhealed haunts one" ' (322). From the great fourteenth-century Middle English dream-elegy *Pearl* to Don DeLillo's very different dream-elegy *The Body Artist* (2001), literature is a place of ghosts, of what's unfinished, unhealed and even untellable. But more precisely, and perhaps more eerily, Abraham's work alerts us to a ghostliness about which characters, and even authors themselves, are unaware. Here we encounter the strangeness of the ghostly secret as, in Esther Rashkin's words, 'a situation or drama that is transmitted without being stated and without the sender's or receiver's awareness of its transmission' (Rashkin 1992, 4).

If psychoanalysis has been important in providing new ways of thinking about ghosts, however, this has not happened in a vacuum. As we suggested earlier, it is in fact part of a more general shift in how ghosts have been figured, theorized and experienced since the end of the nineteenth century. The emergence of psychology and psychoanalysis has its ghostly counterpart in literature, especially in the emergence of psychological realism and the psychological novel. Nowhere is this clearer than in the fiction of Henry James (1843–1916). In an essay on his ghost stories, published in 1921, Virginia Woolf writes:

> Henry James's ghosts have nothing in common with the violent old ghosts – the blood-stained sea captains, the white horses, the headless ladies of dark lanes and windy commons. They have their origin within us. They are present whenever the significant overflows our powers of expressing it; whenever the ordinary appears ringed by the strange. (Woolf 1988, 324)

Stories such as *The Turn of the Screw* (1898), 'The Beast in the Jungle' (1903) and 'The Jolly Corner' (1908) conjure and explore the ghostliness of experience in profoundly unsettling ways. All of these stories bear witness to the ungovernable, overflowing strangeness which Woolf evokes. More particularly, they also illustrate the sense of ghostly secrets, of what Abraham called the 'gaps left within us by the secrets of others', together with a sense of the ghostliness of the ego (or 'I') itself.

The last of these stories, 'The Jolly Corner', is especially forceful in its evocation of the idea of the 'I' as ghost. As in a number of other ghost stories – for example, Emily Brontë's *Wuthering Heights* (1848), Nathaniel Hawthorne's *The House of the Seven Gables* (1851) and George Douglas Brown's *The House with the Green Shutters* (1901) – 'The Jolly Corner' is both the name of a house and the name of the text itself. The literary work is a haunted house. 'The Jolly Corner' recounts how a 56-year-old, wealthy New Yorker called Spencer Brydon, long settled in Europe, makes a 'strangely belated return to America' (190), having been absent for 33 years. He goes back to his childhood home, 'his house on the jolly corner, as he usually, and quite fondly, described it' (191). Rented out and a source of income for decades, the house is now, ostensibly, empty. Brydon becomes obsessed with the place, with visiting and wandering around it, increasingly caught up by the sense that it contains some ghostly secret of the past. Following a dense but queerly captivating third-person so-called omniscient narration, we are drawn into a hunt, in which the protagonist turns out to be both hunter and hunted, haunter and haunted. As the narrator asks, with the bizarre tone of detachment characteristic of the text as a whole: 'People enough, first and last, had been in terror of apparitions, but who had ever before become himself, in the apparitional world, an incalculable terror?' (202). Of course – and this is where fiction is itself most manifestly a *haunt* – this 'apparitional world' to which James refers only appears through writing. The very strangeness of fiction may be said to consist in this idea of a 'medium', a text, in which the apparitional and non-apparitional are made of the same stuff, indistinguishable. As E.M. Forster put it, in *Aspects of the Novel* (1927): 'Once in the realm of the fictitious, what difference is there between an apparition and a mortgage?' (Forster 1976, 103).

Despite appearances, then, we don't want to limit our talk about ghost stories just to ghost stories. Indeed, we would like to suggest that the greater the literary work, the more ghostly it is. This might be one way of understanding what Derrida is getting at when he proclaims, in his book *Spectres of Marx*, that 'A masterpiece always moves, by definition, in the manner of a ghost' (Derrida 1994, 18). Playing on the earlier Latin sense of 'genius' as 'spirit', he says that a masterpiece is 'a work of *genius*, a *thing* of the *spirit* which precisely seems to *engineer itself* [*s'ingénier*]' (18). Masterpieces, such as *Beowulf* or *Hamlet* (which is the example Derrida is discussing) or James's 'The Jolly Corner' or Beckett's *Molloy*, are *works* that give a sense of having been spirited up, of working by themselves. Great works call to be read and reread while never ceasing to be strange, to resist reading, interpretation and translation. This is one basis for thinking about canonicity in Harold Bloom's terms: the canon is always a spectral affair. As he declares, in *The Western Canon*: 'One ancient test for the canonical remains fiercely valid: unless it demands rereading, the work does not qualify' (Bloom 1994, 30). A great work will always seem uncanny, at once strange and familiar; a surprising, unique addition to the canon and yet somehow foreseen, programmed by the canon; at once readable and defiant, elusive, baffling. For Bloom, writing itself is essentially about a relationship (always one of anxiety, according to him) with the dead, with earlier great writers. The point is most succinctly made by Bloom's precursor, T.S. Eliot, when he says in his essay 'Tradition and the Individual Talent' (1919) that the 'best', 'most individual' parts of a literary work are 'those in which the dead poets . . . assert their immortality most vigorously' (Eliot 1975b, 38). It is a relationship eerily evoked in Eliot's 'Little Gidding' (1943), where the speaker describes an encounter in which he 'caught the sudden look of some dead master / . . . The eyes of a familiar compound ghost

/ Both intimate and unidentifiable' (Eliot 1975a, 193). For Bloom, as for Eliot, poetry is also a ghostly discourse in a more general sense. This is hauntingly exemplified by Wallace Stevens's 'Large Red Man Reading' (1948), in which the subject of the poem, the reader himself, evokes ghosts: 'There were ghosts that returned to earth to hear his phrases, / As he sat there reading, aloud, the great blue tabulae. / They were those from the wilderness of stars that had expected more' (423). We are all haunted: experience itself is never enough; and it is the ghostly discourse of literature which most sharply testifies to this.

One problem with talking about the canon in the way Bloom does is that it appears to be ahistorical: in other words, literature seems to belong to a time-less realm, the canon seems to be impervious to the material effects of social, political, economic and cultural history. Our argument in the present chapter, however, is that while literature is indeed 'ghost work', its haunt is historical. The ghosts of the twentieth century are not the same as those of the nine-teenth, and so on. We might, for example, reflect on the links between ghosts and technology. In the context of Western culture in the third millennium, and from the point of view of so-called common sense, we may like to believe that we do not believe in ghosts any more; but in important respects the world has become and is continuing to become increasingly ghostly. As Jacques Derrida has observed:

> Contrary to what we might believe, the experience of ghosts is not tied to a bygone historical period, like the landscape of Scottish manors, etc., but . . . is accentuated, accelerated by modern technologies like film, tele-vision, the telephone. These technologies inhabit, as it were, a phantom structure . . . When the very *first* perception of an image is linked to a structure of reproduction, then we are dealing with the realm of phantoms. (Derrida 1989, 61)

This recalls, or calls up, the image of Derrida in Ken McMullen's film *Ghost Dance* (1989) being asked if he believes in ghosts and replying: 'That's a hard question because, you see, I am a ghost.' In a film, everyone is a ghost. If the ghost is the revenant, that which uncannily returns without ever being prop-erly present in the first place, it becomes clear that, more than ever, we live in the midst of ghosts: the voice on the telephone is only ever the reproduction of a voice, the image on television or movie-screen only ever a reproduction. Freud conveys his amazement at the surreal nature of telephones when he remarks in *Civilization and Its Discontents* (1930) that 'With the help of the telephone [one] can hear at distances which would be [regarded] as unattain-able even in a fairytale' (1985e, 279). But since Freud's day, we have witnessed the new ghostly arrivals of the space age, the answer phone, video recorder, camcorder, personal computer, email, the Internet and World Wide Web, virtual reality, genetic engineering, nanotechnology, the mobile or cell phone and so forth.

Whether in literature, psychoanalysis or philosophy, contemporary thought is irrevocably hooked up to developments in technology and telecommunications. Contemporary literature faces new kinds of challenge in terms of how to represent, assimilate or think the increasing ghostliness of culture. The question of literature today is inseparable from an increasingly prevalent, indeed unavoidable encounter with a technics of the ghost. DeLillo's *The Body Artist*, for example, with its haunting evocations of ghost-voices and ghost-images in telephones, answering machines, voice-recorders, webcams and video projections, suggests that calling up ghosts in the twenty-first century is inseparable from such new technologies.

We would like to conclude by trying to explore some of these ideas in relation to Toni Morrison's novel *Beloved*. This novel, first published in 1987, is set in America, in the years leading up to and following the abolition of slavery. It is about the unspeakable reality of slavery, about ghosts and the way in which US culture continues to be haunted by the atrocities of its past. The narrative of the novel rests on the dynamic of ghostly secrets and the untellable. 'Beloved' is a baby murdered by her mother, Sethe, because the mother sees death for her daughter as preferable to slavery; 'Beloved' is also a beautiful 'shining' ghost of a woman who, years later, haunts the lives of Sethe and her other daughter, Denver, and Sethe's drifting partner Paul D. The novel, in its very title, is a ghost, or gathering of ghosts. *Beloved* is about

> what it took to drag the teeth of that saw under the little chin; to feel the baby blood pump like oil in [Sethe's] hands; to hold her face so her head would stay on; to squeeze her so she could absorb, still, the death spasms that shot through that adored body, plump and sweet with life. (251)

This, 250 pages into the text, is the most 'graphic' description we are given of what nevertheless haunts the book from the title onwards. The haunting is inscribed in the passage just quoted, for example, in the eerie double sense of 'still' (as adverb 'yet' and verb 'stop'): this gross moment is a still, stilled moment, caught in time, which still haunts, is still to be absorbed. On the final page of the novel we encounter the statement that 'This is not a story to pass on' (275). This statement suggests that the story should not or cannot be told, but also that it is not one we can pass by. The history of the United States is an untellable ghost story that must not, however, be forgotten. Every house in the USA is a haunted house. As Baby Suggs says in grimly comic response to her daughter-in-law Sethe's suggestion that they vacate the baby-haunted house known only by its number (124): ' "Not a house in the country ain't packed to its rafters with some dead Negro's grief. We lucky this ghost is a baby. My husband's spirit was to come back in here? or yours? Don't talk to me" ' (5).

Beloved is set in the nineteenth century and is faithful to the modes of ghost-liness, spirits, tele-culture and telecommunications available at that time: the text opens with an attempted exorcism and an instance of apparent telekinesis ('The sideboard took a step forward but nothing else did': 4); there are allusions to telegraphy and the recently invented Morse code (110), to 'long-distance love' (95) and even to photography (275). But in other ways *Beloved* is a profoundly contemporary novel, a work of the late twentieth century not only in style and form but also in terms of its conception and implacable analysis of ghosts. In particular, it is written out of or through a psycho-analytically inflected understanding of deferred meaning, a sense of trauma as ghostly, as that which comes back again and again, which continues, haunt-ingly. Morrison's novel is about the unspeakable not only now but in the future, slavery as a legacy *still*, not as something belonging to what we call the history books.

Marx in 1848 saw communism as 'a spectre . . . haunting Europe' (the famous opening words of *The Communist Manifesto*). One hundred and fifty years later, Derrida too sees communism as spectral. Hence its rapport with deconstruction. Deconstruction, as Derrida describes it, is concerned to think about the sense that 'everyone reads, acts, writes with *his or her* ghosts' (Derrida 1994, 139), to think about presence (and absence) as necessarily haunted, about meaning as spectralized. In these respects, deconstruction offers perhaps the most important contemporary theory of ghosts. Commun-ism is like democracy itself: 'it has always been and will remain spectral: it is always still to come' (Derrida 1994, 99).

Further reading

For two helpful and wide-ranging accounts of the ghostly in literature from a 'gothic' perspective, see David Punter, *The Literature of Terror*, 2nd edition (1996), and Fred Botting, *Gothic* (1997). Terry Castle (1995) has a good chapter on eighteenth- and nineteenth-century conceptions of ghosts, entitled 'Spectral Politics: Apparition Belief and the Romantic Imagination'. For a lucid and helpful exposition of Lacan's notoriously difficult essay on *Hamlet*, see Bruce Fink (1996). More generally, for some very good, clear and access-ible readings of literature-with-Lacan, see Linda Ruth Williams (1995). More complex Lacanian accounts of the literary may be found in the brilliant work of Shoshana Felman (1987) and Jacqueline Rose (1996). Nicolas Abraham's 'Notes on the Phantom: A Complement to Freud's Metapsychology' and 'The Phantom of Hamlet *or* The Sixth Act, *preceded by* The Intermission of "Truth"' are collected in *The Shell and the Kernel* (1994). For a difficult but thought-provoking elaboration of Abraham's work on ghosts, see Esther Rashkin, *Family Secrets and the Psychoanalysis of Narrative* (1992). For a very rich, demanding but now classic account of spectrality and politics, focusing on *Hamlet* and the writings of Karl Marx, see Jacques Derrida, *Spectres of Marx* (1994). For the links between psychoanalysis, technology and telecommunications, see Derrida's challenging but fascinating *Archive Fever* (1995a); for an account of the cultural and philosophical importance of the telephone, see Avital Ronell's *The Telephone Book* (1989). Peter Nicholls's essay, 'The Belated Postmodern: History, Phantoms and Toni Morrison' (1996), offers a subtle and stimulating reading of *Beloved* by way of many of the notions of the ghostly discussed in this chapter. For more on American ghosts (from the Salem witchcraft trials to contemporary film and politics), see *Spectral America: Phantoms and the National Imagination*, ed. Weinstock (2004); for ghosts and Victorian literature, see Julian Wolfreys's *Victorian Hauntings* (2002); for ghosts and modernism, see Jean-Michel Rabaté's *The Ghosts of Modernity* (1996) and Helen Sword's *Ghostwriting Modernism* (2002); and for a good collection of essays on ghosts in relation to deconstruction, psychoanalysis and history, see Buse and Stott (1999).

19. Moving pictures

What do movies tell us about literature? Over recent decades cinema has increasingly come to be incorporated into university literature courses and literature professors have been pronouncing on films, as well as on novels, poems and plays. But what do we learn about literature when we watch and talk about film? And what do we learn about moving pictures when we study literature? We are all familiar (if not bored to tears) with talk of 'the film of the book' and even 'the book of the film', with discussion of how the film version is or is not faithful to the 'original' book version, of whether the film is as good as the book or vice versa. We want to get away from such talk: to put it simply, the film of the book is a film, it's not a book. We need a different vocabulary and different critical perspectives. Film is, nevertheless, inextricably tied in with the study of literature. Thinking about film provides innovative ways of thinking about literature, and vice versa. While the study of one informs, stimulates and provokes the study of the other, however, we do not want to suggest that the specificity of literature can or should be done away with. Our purpose in this chapter is, above all, to elucidate and explore the nature of the literary through thinking about film.

Sadly, there is no DVD or YouTube clip featuring a rendition of Wordsworth's great nineteenth-century autobiographical epic, *The Prelude* (although YouTube does offer some pretty funny Wordsworthiana). Nevertheless, in talking about moving pictures, we would like to focus on this poem. First published after the poet's death in 1850, *The Prelude* was written and revised between 1798 and 1839. Wordsworth began writing it, in other words, almost a hundred years before the first film (shown by the Lumière brothers in 1895). Not only has *The Prelude* not been turned into a movie, then, but it would be unreasonable to expect Wordsworth to be interested in the technologies of film production. Except for the fact that the word 'cinema' derives from the Greek *kinema*, 'motion', and that such precursors of the cinema as the panorama, the 'eidophusikon' and the 'diorama' were invented and became popular during Wordsworth's lifetime, the idea might seem quite deranged. But, as we hope to make clear, things are not as simple as this. In particular, we want to suggest that *The Prelude* is composed or organized around a series of 'stills', moments taken from the moving picture of the poet's own mind, the cinema of his life. Wordsworth's poem is often regarded as the first great autobiographical narrative in English, an account of 'the growth of a poet's mind' that – in the 1805 version we will concentrate on here – stretches over 13 books and roughly nine thousand lines of blank verse. Vital to an understanding and appreciation of *The Prelude* are Wordsworth's 'spots of time', which are concerned with the effects of childhood memories on later life.

At a key moment in Book 11 of *The Prelude*, Wordsworth arrests the movement of his narrative, to speculate on its workings:

> There are in our existence spots of time,
> Which with distinct preeminence retain
> A renovating virtue, whence, depressed
> By false opinion and contentious thought,
> Or aught of heavier or more deadly weight
> In trivial occupations and the round
> Of ordinary intercourse, our minds
> Are nourished and invisibly repaired . . .
>   Life with me,
> As far as memory can look back, is full
> Of this beneficent influence.
>   (*The Prelude* 1805, Book 11: 257–78)

There are certain memories, especially from early childhood, which stay with us, and have a capacity to renew, to 'nourish' and 'invisibly repair' our minds. 'As far as memory can look back': Wordsworth presents his autobiography and indeed his life in visual terms, and evokes these 'spots of time' as a kind of montage of moving pictures. 'Spots of time' are intensely visual and emphatically moving. They are arresting and affecting, moving in their stillness.

Wordsworth's 'spots of time' can be related to moving pictures in at least three ways. A spot of time is mobile, a matter of motion, a shifting scene. Second, it entails a moving or agitation of the mind and feelings. (The word 'emotion', we may recall, is from the Latin *movēre*, to stir up, to create motion.)

Finally, in a way that is not only or not simply anachronistic, we might suggest that a spot of time resembles a movie or movie clip in terms of its apparently closed-off or framed quality (it's a 'spot'), and in terms more generally of what it allows us to think about the nature and experience of time itself. Above all perhaps, Wordsworth's 'spots of time' prefigure modern cinema in terms of what Gilles Deleuze calls 'the time-image' (Deleuze 1989). We will try to elucidate this idea in greater detail shortly.

Wordsworth famously declares in the Preface to *Lyrical Ballads* (1800) that poetry 'takes its origin from emotion recollected in tranquillity' (Wordsworth 1984, 611), suggesting that it involves at once a stilling and a revision or re-gathering of what has been moving. The phrase 'spots of time' likewise suggests something paradoxical, a strange fixing of time in place, *as* place. What, we may ask, is the 'time' of a 'spot of time'? In order to start thinking about this we need to reckon with the ways in which Wordsworth exploits the sheer slipperiness of poetic language. Even the brief 'spots of time' passage quoted a moment ago was written and revised over a period of years. In the earliest version, in 1799, the spots of time are said to have 'a fructifying virtue', a little later 'a vivifying virtue', and in a third version 'a renovating virtue' (see *The Prelude*, 428, n. 2). For all their apparent stillness or tranquillity, these 'spots of time' are in motion, pictured in unstable, altering, moving language.

Let us zoom in on one of these 'spots of time', namely the passage in which Wordsworth recalls the experience, as a young boy, of stealing ravens' eggs:

> Nor less in springtime, when on southern banks
> The shining sun had from her knot of leaves
> 335 Decoyed the primrose flower, and when the vales
> And woods were warm, was I a plunderer then
> In the high places, on the lonesome peaks,
> Where'er among the mountains and the winds
> The mother-bird had built her lodge. Though mean
> 340 My object and inglorious, yet the end
> Was not ignoble. Oh, when I have hung
> Above the raven's nest, by knots of grass
> Or half-inch fissures in the slippery rock
> But ill sustained, and almost, as it seemed,
> 345 Suspended by the blast which blew amain,
> Shouldering the naked crag, oh, at that time
> While on the perilous ridge I hung alone,
> With what strange utterance did the loud dry wind
> Blow through my ears; the sky seemed not a sky
> 350 Of earth, and with what motion moved the clouds!

> The mind of man is framed even like a breath
> And harmony of music . . .
> (*The Prelude* 1805, Book 1: 333–52)

This 'spot of time' apparently ends with the words 'with what motion moved the clouds!' We have quoted the words that follow on from it in order to draw attention to the remarkable, often unfathomable breaks that characteristically splice together Wordsworth's poetry. Having concluded his moving picture of this spot of time, he starts a new verse-paragraph, now in a quite different tone and place: 'The mind of man is framed even like a breath / And harmony of music'. But the boy Wordsworth is literally left hanging, clinging to the tiny fissures in the rock and seeming to be held in place largely by the wind itself. With the extraordinary editing of this moment, with this singular cliffhanger, we are offered a fitting example of what Paul de Man calls Wordsworth's 'sheer language' (de Man 1984, 92). 'Sheer language' means language alone, working by itself, in the sense that our access – and indeed *Wordsworth's* access – to these memories of stealing ravens' eggs is in and through language. But we might also hear in 'sheer language' the sense of something precipitous, vertiginously headlong. The blank on the page immediately following 'with what motion moved the clouds!' figures a sort of abyss.

Wordsworth chooses to stop the spot, leaves himself (a portrait of the poet as a young thief) on a perilous ridge, just about hanging on by 'knots of grass / Or half-inch fissures in the slippery rock'. 'Oh, when I have hung / Above': which way up is he? What is the point of view? This last question actually enfolds three questions, each of them as relevant to film as to literary studies: (1) What is the point of view in a literal sense? From what position or angle is this being seen? (2) What is the narrative point of view? Who is seeing it and who is describing it, and from what perspective or perspectives? (3) What is the temporal perspective? How are issues of past, present and future involved here? From what position in time is this 'spot of time' to be viewed? One of the most important differences between literary narrative and film narrative is that, with the former, the reader is almost always presented with a knowledge of what is going on in the thoughts and feelings of a specific narrator or character. With literary narrative you get 'inside information' as to what is going on in the mind and body of a character. This is particularly the case when the story is told by a so-called omniscient or (perhaps more accurately) telepathic narrator. More generally, however, a fictional exposure of 'secret' interiority is at the very heart of literature and there is something strange and magical about this – about the idea of being able to read the mind of the author, a narrator or character. This interiority is fundamentally alien to film: the 'eye of the camera' is doomed to the visible. The only way that film can provide 'inside information' is through strategies or techniques from literature (the 'telling' voice-over, in particular).

Being John Malkovich (dir. Spike Jonze, 1999) is a witty, at moments hilarious movie that ironically acknowledges and foregrounds these limits. The film involves the discovery and exploitation of a 'portal' through which people are able to enter the head of the 'real-life' actor and have the chance of 'being John Malkovich'. One of the most memorable scenes is when Malkovich himself insists on going through the portal and finds himself (as it were) in a dreamlike restaurant-cum-nightclub surrounded by other John Malkovichs. At a table where a couple of John Malkovichs are dining, he looks over the restaurant menu and sees that it consists entirely of dishes called 'Malkovich'. Everywhere he is confronted by a proliferation of John Malkovichs, all of them saying (or singing) over and over again the single word 'Malkovich', 'Malkovich', 'Malkovich'. In this cinematic hall of mirrors everyone is the same, the name says it all, and interiority is rendered comically non-existent.

Wordsworth's account of stealing ravens' eggs allows us a particularly intimate sense of the poet's interior world. While Spike Jonze's film seems at once to celebrate and ridicule the mad narcissism of a stammering 'Malkovich, Malkovich, Malkovich', Wordsworth's poetry offers us a rather different experience of what Keats called the 'egotistical sublime' (Keats 1958, 1:387). As William Hazlitt once remarked: Wordsworth 'sees nothing but himself and the universe . . . His egotism is in some respects a madness' (Hazlitt 1930–34, 5:163). This conception of Wordsworth corresponds, perhaps rather unnervingly, to how Hugo Münsterberg described the impact of cinema in his 1916 book, *The Photoplay: A Psychological Study*: 'the massive outer world has lost its weight, it has been freed from space, time, and causality, and has been clothed in the forms of our own consciousness' (Münsterberg 1916, 220, quoted in Armstrong 1998, 240). We might be tempted to think of Wordsworth's account of stealing ravens' eggs as profoundly ego-centred: what else would you expect from that self-regarding genre known as autobiography? But we would argue that the poem also goes far beyond this obsession with self. Besides the strange and disorienting ambiguity of the literal 'point of view' of the 'plunderer' (above or below the sky, upside down or right way up?), for example, there are the temporal disjunctions of the scene. This 'spot of time' is both 'at that time' (l.346), in the past, and at the same time it is in this strange 'here and now' of sheer language, being written or being read, still. It is also, crucially, a moving picture that entails an intimate sense of the unknowable and incalculable. It involves a logic of unforeseeable *becoming*: 'spots of time' work 'invisibly', we are told, and go on working, work on, in the future. The scene shifts inwardly, from the present perfect tense ('when I have hung' [1.341]) to the simple past ('I hung'). The place of the present 'I', the 'I' that recollects, speaks or writes, gives way to an image of alien suspension, an 'I' blown through with 'strange utterance', lost to an alien sky: 'With what strange utterance did the loud dry wind / Blow through my ears; the sky seemed not a sky / Of earth, and with what motion moved the clouds!'

Alfred Hitchcock's *Vertigo* (1958) is also a masterpiece of suspense. In the opening sequence the protagonist Scottie (James Stewart) is seen hanging on for dear life to the ripped guttering of a San Francisco rooftop as a police officer, having tried to help him, plummets to his death. As Susan White puts it: 'we never see (or hear about) Scottie's rescue – in a sense [he] remains hanging over the edge of the precipice throughout the film' (White 1991, 911). Something similar happens in *The Prelude*: in a sense the boy trying to steal ravens' eggs remains hanging there throughout the rest of that epic poem. The moment in *Vertigo* is, we might say, weirdly Wordsworthian. On the one hand it is difficult not to project (the word is as much cinematic as psychoanalytic) back on to the past, on to literary works of the pre-film era, critical ideas and perspectives generated by film. On the other, it is striking how many of our current ways of thinking were in fact already quite firmly established in the nineteenth century.

Had he still been living when cinema began, Wordsworth would have been at once fascinated and appalled. With its intimations of cinematicity, however, *The Prelude* also suggests that he would not have been entirely surprised either. Wordsworth's poem communicates the power of ocularcentrism, of what he calls 'The state . . . / In which the eye was master of the heart . . . The most despotic of our senses' (Book 11: 170–3). The quasi-hypnotic draw of twenty-first-century 'visual culture' (TV, video, cinema, DVD, computer games, and so on) was, we might say, already in play in Wordsworth's day. Thus the poet reminisces, for example, about 'Still craving combinations of new forms, / New pleasure, wider empire for the sight' (Book 11: 191–2). And while, in his amazing account of life in London (in Book 7), he conveys a moral disapproval of such newfangled visual pleasures as panoramas and 'mimic sights that ape / The absolute presence of reality' (Book 7: 248–9), his own depiction of the city and its inhabitants is achieved through a series of moving pictures. In this way he evokes London as 'the quick dance / Of colours, lights and forms, the Babel din, / The endless stream of men and moving things' (Book 7: 156–8). And in one of the most memorable encounters anywhere in his poetry, Wordsworth picks out – or feels uncannily picked out by – a blind beggar 'amid the moving pageant' (Book 7: 610). The 'spectacle' at the centre of this 'moving pageant' is reproduced and interiorized in turn as a moving picture, a kind of monstrous mill in Wordsworth's mind: 'My mind did at this spectacle turn round / As with the might of waters . . . I looked, / As if admonished from another world' (ll.616–23).

In another 'spot of time' in *The Prelude*, Wordsworth recalls when, aged five, he is out riding with a servant (or 'guide') called James, becomes separated from him and stumbles on alone, down to a valley where 'in former times / A murderer had been hung in iron chains' (Book 11: 288–9). Nearby he comes across the eerie graffiti of 'fresh and visible' letters scored in the turf where 'Some unknown hand had carved the murderer's name' (l.293). He quickly quits this 'spot', 'reascending the bare common' (ll.301–2), approaching 'A naked pool that lay beneath the hills' (l.303) overlooked by a summit with a stone beacon on top. Closer at hand, he sees a windblown girl bearing a pitcher on her head. And, all of a sudden, he is halted at this sight:

> It was, in truth,
> An ordinary sight, but I should need
> Colours and words that are unknown to man
> To paint the visionary dreariness
> Which, while I looked all round for my lost guide,
> Did at that time invest the naked pool,
> The beacon on the lonely eminence,
> The woman, and her garments vexed and tossed
> By the strong wind. (Book 11: 307–15)

Wordsworth writes of painting with colours and words that are unknown (not yet, perhaps never to be, invented), as if it were a matter of something fixed, the landscape painting of a visionary dreariness (in effect, a seeing of seeing, a vision of visionariness); and yet, as with the earlier passage we encountered ('with what motion moved the clouds!'), it is at the same time explicitly a question of a moving picture (the girl's 'garments vexed and tossed / By the strong wind'). Wordsworth's 'spots of time' are concerned with senses of movement that have yet to be captured in colours or words.

In this respect his writing offers a singular twist to the classic tradition of *ut pictura poesis*, in which painting and poetry are regarded as 'sister arts', painting being seen as a kind of mute poetry and poetry a speaking picture. In his *Lectures on Rhetoric and Belles Lettres* (1759–83), Hugh Blair echoes this tradition when he argues that 'a true poet makes us imagine that we see [the object or natural landscape] before our eyes; he catches the distinguishing features; he gives it the colours of life and reality; he places it in such a light that a painter could copy it after him' (Blair 1842, 549). Wordsworth's concern is rather with the sense of an impossible word-painting, with a sense of the impossibility of *ekphrasis* (a verbal representation of the visual). He is moved by a vision he can neither paint nor describe, that is not yet realized or realizable. In this way we might suggest that Wordsworth's spots of time are concerned with that sense of 'moving' evoked in the 'Intimations' ode, where the child is described as 'Moving about in worlds not realized'. They are (about) moving pictures, visions in process, still to be realized, as well as sights that move, disturb, exhilarate, stir the emotions.

Finally, our attempt to explore the moving pictures of Wordsworth's 'spots of time' might helpfully be illuminated by brief discussion of the work of the philosopher Gilles Deleuze (1925–95). Deleuze has provided perhaps the most provocative account of cinema in recent decades. His books *Cinema 1: The Movement-Image* (Deleuze 1986) and *Cinema 2: The Time-Image* (Deleuze 1989) are complex and challenging, in particular because he argues that cinema alters the very nature of thinking, writing and philosophy. Elaborating on the work of Henri Bergson, Deleuze contends that the universe becomes 'a cinema in itself, a metacinema' (Deleuze 1986, 59). With cinema, Deleuze argues, we *see* 'seeing'. It is no longer a question of 'point of view', of *someone's* (a character's or a director's) point of view. The eye of the camera is not an 'I'. As Claire Colebrook glosses it: 'What makes the machine-like movement of the cinema so important is that the camera can "see" or "perceive" without imposing concepts. The camera does not organise images from a fixed point but itself moves across movements' (Colebrook 2002, 32). Related to this is what Deleuze calls the 'time-image', that is to say the way in which cinema presents us with a thinking or experience of time cut off from any question of a succession of past-present-future.

The time-image is not an image *of* something, it is what comes about with the effects of 'false continuity and irrational cuts' (Deleuze 1989, xi), for example with a certain disjunctiveness of seeing and hearing. Such disjunctiveness is evident from the very start of Hitchcock's *Vertigo*, as we are presented with the spiralling graphics and seeing of seeing in Kim Novak's eye, Bernard Herrmann's madly melodramatic, 'irrational' soundtrack accompanying us into the opening realization of vertigo in the image of Scottie hanging from the rooftop. The opening of *Vertigo* illustrates the distinctiveness of the cinematic image which, according to Deleuze, involves 'a dissociation of the visual and the sound' (Deleuze 1989, 256). And although it is a poem, something like this vertiginous 'dissociation' might be read back into Wordsworth's juxtaposition of the unearthly sky and moving motion of the clouds and the 'strange utterance' of 'the loud dry wind' as his younger self clings to the 'slippery rock' in *The Prelude*.

Deleuze's work engages with new kinds of thinking, writing and becoming. His books on cinema, along with his writings on literary texts, challenge us with the question: how should we think, read and write about literature *after* cinema, or with what we have learnt from cinema in mind? And, indeed, what new kinds of literary writing might be envisaged? Leo Tolstoy appears to have foreseen such questions when he commented in 1908, a year before he died and almost twenty years before the first talkies:

> [cinema] will make a revolution in our life – in the life of writers . . . We shall have to adapt ourselves to the shadowy screen and to the cold machine. A new form of writing will be necessary . . . This swift change of scene, this blending of emotion and experience – it is much better than the heavy, long-drawn-out kind of writing to which we are accustomed. It is closer to life. In life, too, changes and transitions flash before our eyes, and emotions of the soul are like a hurricane. The cinema has divined the mystery of motion. And that is its greatness. (Tolstoy, quoted in Murphet and Rainford 2003, 1)

As Colin MacCabe remarks, in a recent essay entitled 'On Impurity: the Dialectics of Cinema and Literature', 'it is impossible to give a serious account of any twentieth-century writer without reference to cinema' (MacCabe 2003, 16). This is the case not only with such cinematically self-conscious writers as John Dos Passos, Gabriel García Márquez or Salman Rushdie, but also with writers such as Virginia Woolf, James Joyce and T.S. Eliot. In an interview entitled 'The Brain Is the Screen' (1986), Deleuze uses cinema to make some illuminating remarks about works of art in general. He offers a compelling vision of the nature of literary works, the future of moving pictures and 'new emotions':

> A work of art always entails the creation of new spaces and times (it's not a question of recounting a story in a well-determined space and time; rather, it is the rhythms, the lighting, and the space-times themselves that must become the true characters). A work should bring forth the problems and questions that concern us rather than provide answers. A work of art is a new syntax, one that is much more important than vocabulary and that excavates a foreign language in language. Syntax in cinema amounts to the linkages and relinkages of images, but also to the relation between sound and the visual image. If one had to define culture, one could say that it [consists in] perceiving that works of art are much more concrete, moving, and funny than commercial products. In creative works there is a multiplication of emotion, a liberation of emotion, and even the invention of new emotions. This distinguishes creative works from the prefabricated emotions of commerce. (Deleuze 2000, 370)

If it is impossible to read modernist and postmodern literature without engaging with questions of cinema, it is also the case that we can no longer read Wordsworth without doing so through the kinds of thinking that cinema makes possible. At the same time, it is part of the cryptic and enduring power of Wordsworth's poetry, and of his 'spots of time' in particular, that they can continue to give us new ways of thinking about emotions, liberating and inventing in moving pictures.

Further reading

Literature and Visual Technologies: Writing After Cinema, eds. Murphet and Rainford (2003) is a valuable collection of essays on the comparatively new field of reading film through literature and literature through film. For two valuable recent studies especially concerned with cinema and Modernist literature, see Laura Marcus's *The Tenth Muse: Writing About Cinema in the Modernist Period* (2007) and David Trotter's *Cinema and Modernism* (2007). For two other critical works that, like the present chapter, are concerned with thinking about literature in relation to the history and prehistory of cinema, see Bill Readings's 'Milton at the Movies' (in Readings and Schaber 1993) and Grahame Smith's *Dickens and the Dream of Cinema* (2003). Gilles Deleuze's *Cinema 2: The Time-Image* (1989) is a fascinating and profound study, though certainly not easy on a first encounter. Claire Colebrook's introductory book, *Gilles Deleuze* (2002), is a lucid and invaluable guide to this difficult but important thinker. For a recent collection of essays more specifically focusing on Deleuze and the literary, see Buchanan and Marks (2000). For important more recent work on cinema and time, see Philip Rosen's *Change Mummified* (2001), Mary Ann Doane's *The Emergence of Cinematic Time* (2002) and Laura Mulvey's *Death 24x a Second: Stillness and the Moving Image* (2006). On the power of the eye and vision, see (so to speak) Martin Jay's monumental *The Denigration of Vision in Twentieth-Century French Thought* (1993), and, more generally in relation to textuality, the fine range of essays collected in *Vision and Textuality* (eds Melville and Readings, 1995). For a recent study of feeling, affect and being moved, see Eve Kosofsky Sedgwick's *Touching Feeling* (2003). For excellent accounts of the long-standing literary-critical tradition of interest in the interaction of word and image, see Mitchell, 'Iconology' (1986) and 'Picture Theory' (1994), Krieger, 'Ekphrasis' (1992), and Heffernan, 'Museum of Words' (1993). For a fine account of Romanticism and visuality, see Sophie Thomas's book of that title (2008).

20. Sexual difference

John laughs at me, of course, but one expects that in marriage.

John is practical in the extreme. He has no patience with faith, an intense horror of superstition, and he scoffs openly at any talk of things not to be felt and seen and put down in figures.

John is a physician, and *perhaps*—(I would not say it to a living soul, of course, but this is dead paper and a great relief to my mind)—*perhaps* that is one reason I do not get well faster.

You see he does not believe I am sick! (9–10)

This passage from Charlotte Perkins Gilman's short story *The Yellow Wallpaper* (1892) presents a number of important issues concerning sexual difference. In particular, it dramatizes conventional presuppositions about the differences between men and women. The phrase 'of course' may signal that the first sentence is satirical and ironic, but the implication remains: a woman is subordinate to her husband and cannot expect to be taken seriously. The differences between men and women, in this passage, are primarily a matter of recognizing certain kinds of gender stereotypes. Such stereotypes depend to a considerable extent on a conceptual opposition: man versus woman. And, like other binary oppositions, this involves a hierarchy. John, the man, is active, 'practical', dominant, unemotional. The narrator, the woman, appears to be passive, non-practical, subordinate, emotional. The opposition between the man and the woman is underscored by the insistent stress on the man's actions, qualities and characteristics (John does this, John is such-and-such) and the corresponding *absence* of information regarding the woman. Gilman is exposing a hierarchy, in other words, involving the dominance of the man and the subordination of the woman. *The Yellow Wallpaper* has become something of a modern classic as regards the literary representation of women and the idea of what Elaine Showalter has called, in a book of that name, 'A Literature of Their Own'.

The Yellow Wallpaper is a first-person narrative which tells the story of a woman whose husband insists that, because she is ill, she must remain confined in a room with revolting yellow wallpaper in a large old house where the couple and their baby are staying for the summer. The woman narrates the frightening process whereby she comes to believe that there is some *other* woman in the room, a woman behind or inside the wallpaper. The text culminates with the demonic turn by which she has *become* the woman behind the wallpaper but has got out. The husband comes into the room to discover his wife creeping around the walls: 'Now why should that man have fainted? But he did, and right across my path by the wall, so that I had to creep over him every time!' (36)

The Yellow Wallpaper offers a particularly striking example of what Sandra Gilbert and Susan Gubar talk about as 'the madwoman in the attic' (Gilbert and Gubar 1979). The story is a dramatic and powerfully ironic account of how a woman is repressed, confined and ultimately driven crazy, specifically by her husband, but more generally by the violence of patriarchy. It is no coincidence, therefore, that *The Yellow Wallpaper* should have been written by a woman known in her own lifetime for her contribution to the women's movement in the United States and, in particular, for her work of non-fiction, *Women and Economics* (1898). *The Yellow Wallpaper* can be read as a powerful satire on patriarchal society and values. In particular it emphasizes the ways in which violence against women need not be physical in a literal sense, but can nevertheless be all-pervading. It is what we could call the soft face of oppression that is satirically presented, for example, when the narrator notes: '[John] is very careful and loving, and hardly lets me stir without special direction' (12). Or when she says: 'It is so hard to talk with John about my case, because he is so wise, and because he loves me so' (23). As these remarks indicate, the text is also about the woman's collusion in her confinement and in her oppressed state. The text explores the ways in which the problem of patriarchy has not only to do with the behaviour of men but also, just as urgently, with that of women.

All literary texts can be thought about in terms of how they represent gender difference and how far they may be said to reinforce or question gender-role stereotypes. Take, for example, an early sixteenth-century sonnet, such as Thomas Wyatt's 'Whoso List to Hunt':

Whoso list to hunt, I know where is an hind,
But as for me, alas, I may no more.
The vain travail hath wearied me so sore
I am of them that farthest cometh behind.
Yet may I, by no means, my wearied mind
Draw from the deer, but as she fleeth afore,
Fainting I follow. I leave off therefore,
Since in a net I seek to hold the wind.
Who list her hunt, I put him out of doubt,
As well as I, may spend his time in vain.
And graven with diamonds in letters plain
There is written, her fair neck round about,
'*Noli me tangere*, for Caesar's I am,
And wild for to hold, though I seem tame.'

Wyatt's sonnet figures men and women in a number of gender-stereotypical ways. Man is the hunter, woman is the hunted. Man is the subject, active, full of 'travail', whereas woman is the object; indeed she is not even figured as human but instead as 'an hind', a female deer. Moreover Wyatt's poem integrates this gender-stereotyping within its very structure of address. The poem, that is to say, is addressed to men (to those who wish, or 'list', to hunt), not to women: in this way it appears to offer a classic example of the construction or assumption of the reader as male. Gilman's short story and Wyatt's sonnet are radically different kinds of text, written at completely different periods and from within almost unimaginably heterogeneous cultures (England in the early sixteenth century, the United States in the late nineteenth century). Yet they do offer significant parallels. Both in their quite different ways invite us to reflect critically on the question of gender and more particularly on the power of gender-stereotypes. In both texts, we encounter such stereotypes (I am a woman and therefore subordinate, passive, hysterical, an object, etc.), but we are also provoked to a questioning of the very idea of gender opposition as such.

On one level, then, there is a valuable and perhaps unavoidable reading of literary texts in terms of essentialism: there is essentially one form of sexual difference and that is the difference between male and female, boys and girls, men and women. The notion of essentialism here consists primarily in anatomical or biological difference: the man has a penis, whereas the woman does not, or the woman has a pudendum, breasts and a childbearing capacity whereas the man has none of these. Various kinds of gender-stereotypes are then articulated, as it were, on to this essentialism: the male is strong, active, rational, the female is weak, passive, irrational and so forth. Within the logic of this description – which has dominated the history of Western culture – having a penis seems to have been so important that it becomes appropriate to speak of its *symbolic* significance, in other words, to speak of the *phallus*. Texts or particular aspects of texts can then be described not only in terms of the patriarchal but also in terms of the phallocentric or phallogocentric. Patriarchy involves upholding the supposed priority of the male. In Gilman's text, for example, John is the head (or patriarch) of the family, he makes the decisions and rules the household. The notion of phallocentrism, on the other hand, involves some of the more subtle, more symbolic and perhaps more fundamental ways in which the phallus can be equated with power, authority, presence, and the right to possession. The 'logo' of 'phallogocentrism' points us towards the argument (promoted by theorists such as Jacques Derrida, Hélène Cixous and Luce Irigaray) that the very notions of truth, reason, rationality, the proper, meaning, etc. are phallocentric. Jonathan Culler has summarized this as follows:

> Numerous aspects of criticism, including the preference for metaphor over metonymy, the conception of the author, and the concern to distinguish legitimate from illegitimate meanings, can be seen as part of the promotion of the paternal. Phallogocentrism unites an interest in patriarchal authority, unity of meaning, and certainty of origin. (Culler 1983, 61)

It is in this context, then, that the French theorist Irigaray speculates on the possibilities of kinds of language that would somehow break with the masculine. As she remarks:

> a feminine language would undo the unique meaning, the proper meaning of words, of nouns: which still regulates all discourse. In order for there to be a proper meaning, there must indeed be a unity somewhere. But if feminine language cannot be brought back to any unity, it cannot be simply described or defined. (Irigaray 1977, 65)

As may already be clear from these very brief accounts of phallocentrism and phallogocentrism, reading literary texts in terms of sexual difference can be more complex and demanding than simply recognizing the gender oppositions and hierarchies to be found at work in a text. As feminist criticism has established, such kinds of recognition are crucial. Inevitably perhaps, we tend to start from an essentialist position and our reading of literary texts is guided by this. But what is most important about literary representations of gender is not merely that a particular text can be shown to be sexist or phallocentric, or even feminist. Rather it is that literary texts call into question many of our essentialist ideas about gender.

In other words, it could be argued that there is no such thing as a feminist, or a masculinist or a sexist, literary work *in itself*: it all depends on how it is read. An obvious example here would be the work of D.H. Lawrence. Kate Millett's *Sexual Politics* (1969) was a groundbreaking book because of the acuity and passion with which it attacked Lawrence's (and other male writers') work for its 'phallic consciousness' (238) and degradation of women. Millett's account still makes powerful reading, but it is also in important respects reductive – especially in its author-centred representations of the novels it discusses. For Millett, that is to say, the aim of literary criticism is to criticize the male author – a figure whose male voice, male presence and male ideas are unequivocally clear, for Millett, in everything Lawrence wrote. More recently, however, critics have tended to focus more on the tensions and paradoxes within Lawrence's writings in themselves, rather than on the author-figure thought to be looming behind them. Critics such as Leo Bersani (1978) and Jonathan Dollimore (1991) have thus emphasized the idea of Lawrence's texts as in many ways working *against themselves* and as unsettling various assumptions that we may have (or Lawrence may have had) about gender as such. Thus Dollimore, for example, focuses on the fact that 'so much [in Lawrence's work] is fantasized from the position of the woman . . . and in a voice that is at once *blindingly heterosexist and desperately homoerotic*' (Dollimore 1991, 275).

We can consider these points by looking again at the Gilman and Wyatt texts. As we have suggested, *The Yellow Wallpaper* reads, on one level at least, as a literary case-study in the oppression and repression of a middle-class white woman in the United States in the late nineteenth century. It may be read as a dynamic feminist demand for liberation from the maddening claustrophobia of patriarchy. But the text is at the same time powerfully equivocal. For instance, simply in terms of the narrative and its conclusion, we must ask ourselves: how much of an affirmation is it, if the only possible liberation for a woman is madness? Is it possible to speak on behalf of women from the position of madness? If, as the narrative of Gilman's text implies, the only way out of patriarchy is to fall, or creep, into madness, is there in fact any way out at all? Isn't *The Yellow Wallpaper* as much caught up in the net of the patriarchal as, say, Henry Miller's *Sexus* (1949)? Such questions are not meant as a way of *closing down* the Gilman text by reducing it to the transmission of a merely negative message about the position of women in relation to patriarchy. Rather they are questions which the text itself can be said to pose:

to read *The Yellow Wallpaper* critically is to engage with its equivocality, with its ironic and complex refigurations of essentialist notions of gender.

In this context it is not surprising that some of the most provocative feminist criticism since the mid-1970s has been closely bound up with what is referred to as deconstruction. Deconstruction could be defined as a strategy of disruption and transformation with regard to every and any kind of essentialism. 'Essentialism' here would include, for example, the assumption that everyone is irreversibly either male or female, that the literal is inescapably different from the figurative, that speech is fundamentally different from writing and so on. In particular, deconstruction involves the desedimentation of those conceptual oppositions through which essentialism operates. In the first place this has meant inverting the hierarchy of male and female, masculine and feminine, father and mother, phallic and (for example) clitoral, along with related couplings such as strong and weak, active and passive, rational and irrational, practical and impractical, presence and absence. Deconstruction, however, is about recognizing that philosophical oppositions are never in 'peaceful coexistence': it is always a matter, as Derrida says, of 'a violent hierarchy' (Derrida 1981, 41). Deconstruction entails not only the inversion or overturning of hierarchies but also the transformation of the basis on which they have operated. This might be thought about in relation to the passage from *The Yellow Wallpaper* with which we began this chapter. The narrator tells us: 'John is practical in the extreme. He has no patience with faith, an intense horror of superstition, and he scoffs openly at any talk of things not to be felt and seen and put down in figures' (9). What we have here is an apparently straightforward assertion of the physician husband's practicality and rationalism, implicitly contrasted with the narrator's own lack of these qualities. But on another level the passage might be said to disturb and even transform the very basis on which we presume to talk about the practical and impractical, the rational and irrational. After all, as George Eliot's great novel *Daniel Deronda* (1876) rhetorically asks: 'Who supposes that it is an impossible contradiction to be superstitious and rationalising at the same time?' (48). Indeed, as Gilman's text here intimates, rationalism can be construed as in turn a kind of superstition. To 'scoff openly', as John does, suggests exaggeration and defensiveness. To have 'an intense horror of superstition' is itself perhaps a mark of superstitiousness. There is, in short, an unsettling of the grounds of reason (here and elsewhere) in Gilman's text: this is deconstructive in the sense that it is specifically concerned with a questioning and dislocation of the logic of non-contradiction. It is interested in disturbing what is perhaps the founding claim of Western philosophy, namely Aristotle's proposal that 'it is impossible for anything at the same time to be and not to be' (Aristotle 1941,

737). This 'law of contradiction' is, as Paul de Man puts it, 'the most certain of all principles' (de Man 1979, 120). Deconstructive feminism puts this founding claim into question. It is rather like the Freudian argument that the unconscious knows no contradictions: one can dream of a compound figure, for example, someone who is (say) both your mother and not your mother but someone else at the same time. Feminism in its deconstructive mode, then, undermines the very basis on which identity and non-identity are constructed. A deconstructive reading of *The Yellow Wallpaper*, for example, might elaborate on the logic whereby the narrator is both mad and not mad at the same time. The narrator both is and is not the woman behind the wallpaper. The narrator both is and is not herself.

Since the late 1960s, feminism has revolutionized literary and cultural studies. But, as recent critical work such as Judith Butler's suggests, the political force of feminism remains limited so long as it promotes itself as an 'identity politics' (politics based on identifying oneself with a particular, usually marginalized and oppressed, group). The problem with the essentialism or (in Butler's terms) the *foundationalism* of 'identity politics' is that 'it presumes, fixes, and constrains the very "subjects" that it hopes to represent and liberate' (Butler 1990, 148). The subjects who empower themselves through 'identity politics' are in some sense disempowered by their very subjection to it. This, in part, is why we have titled this chapter 'Sexual difference' rather than, say, 'Gender and identity'. What the term 'sexual difference' may usefully gesture towards, then, is the idea that identity itself is perhaps most productively and critically seen as fissured, haunted, at odds with itself. As Derrida has remarked, 'an identity is never given, received, or attained': the assertion of identity always betrays a '*disorder of identity*' (Derrida 1998, 28, 14). 'Sexual difference' involves not only difference *between* but difference *within*. In this context, we should perhaps try to think in terms of sexual difference*s* (plural), rather than any simply oppositional sexual difference (singular). We are, in Julia Kristeva's resonant phrase, 'strangers to ourselves' (Kristeva 1991). *The Yellow Wallpaper* could be seen to enact or allegorize this notion of difference *within*. That is to say, it subverts the idea of identity itself, in its presentation of a woman who is, in a sense, uncannily double, always already inhabited by another, in this case the woman behind the wallpaper. The text thus prompts us to ask: what is a woman (and conversely, what is a man) if she is double within herself?

This sort of disruption or subversion of identity is further suggested at the level of *writing* itself. The narrator of *The Yellow Wallpaper* presents herself as a writer. This is indicated in the passage we cited at the beginning of this chapter: 'I would not say it to a living soul, of course, but this is dead paper and a great relief to my mind.' The narrator attests to her own 'imaginative power and habit of story-making' (15). With this in mind we could suggest the following hypothesis: wherever there is writing, sexual or gender identity becomes equivocal, questionable, open to transformation. The hypothesis might be considered in relation to Thomas Wyatt's 'Whoso list to hunt'. We have suggested earlier how clearly this poem seems to categorize and distinguish between men and women, even to the extent of postulating its very addressee as a male. A conventional response to this poem is, in the first instance at least, firmly guided by essentialist and oppositional thinking: man vs. woman, hunter vs. hunted, etc. Originally, of course, Wyatt's poem would have circulated privately among a small group of aristocratic men. And indeed, as Marguerite Waller has remarked in her reading of this poem, even in the twentieth century the critical tendency has been to deny 'the position of any reader who is not male, heterosexual, and politically privileged' (Waller 1987, 6). But there are other ways in which to think about this poem and to appreciate that, like other literary works, it can be seen to call into question various essentialist ideas and assumptions. For example, through its implicit elision of a female reader it provokes the questions: How should a woman read this poem? Is it possible that the apparent *absence* of women as addressees might be construed as a testament to the idea that a woman reader is precisely what the poem calls for but cannot have, and that this strange absence is figured in the rhetoric of the poem itself, for instance in the image of trying to hold the wind in a net? Is the wind that is woman more or less powerful than the net? Is the net of patriarchy that we mentioned earlier only so much wind in turn?

Or to put these questions in a somewhat different form: To whom does writing belong? The idea that writing (and therefore literature in general) is a site of questioning and possible transformation of sexual or gender identity applies to both the Wyatt sonnet as a whole and to its final couplet in particular:

> '*Noli me tangere*, for Caesar's I am,
> And wild for to hold, though I seem tame.'

Whose words are these? To whom are they addressed? Such writing, 'graven with diamonds in letters plain', renders paradoxical the distinctions between man and woman, man and man (the speaker and Caesar), the touchable and untouchable, wild and tame, addressor and addressee.

Literary texts at once encourage *and* exceed essentialist or identity-oriented readings. By rendering the nature of sexual identity fundamentally questionable they provide a particularly disturbing as well as exhilarating space in which to reflect on the question that Foucault asks in the context of the memoirs of Herculine Barbin, a nineteenth-century French hermaphrodite: 'Do we truly need a true sex?' (Foucault 1980b, 3).

Further reading

Joseph Bristow's *Sexuality* (1997) provides a very clear and helpful account of contemporary theories of sexual desire and how these frame issues of identity and difference; see also Claire Colebrook's *Gender* (2004) and Glover and Kaplan, *Genders* (2000). Specifically on literature, sexuality and modernism, see Joseph Allen Boone's *Libidinal Currents: Sexuality and the Shaping of Modernism* (1998). For accessible and clear accounts of contemporary feminist criticism and theory, see Toril Moi, *Sexual/Textual Politics* (1985) and Rita Felski, *Literature After Feminism* (2003). For more challenging and radical views, see Judith Butler's *Gender Trouble* (1990) and *Bodies that Matter* (1993), and Anne-Emmanuelle Berger's 'Sexing Differences' (2005). *Speaking of Gender* (Showalter, ed., 1989) is a good collection of essays on gender, and Warhol and Herndl, eds, *Feminisms* (1997) is a comprehensive collection of over seventy classic and more recent essays on different aspects of feminist literary criticism and theory. Another good collection, oriented towards rethinking gender from within, is *Sexual Sameness* (Bristow 1992b). See, too, in this context, Jonathan Dollimore's wide-ranging and provocative study, *Sexual Dissidence* (1991). Finally, for an important historical account of 'woman', see Denise Riley, *Am I That Name?* (1988).

21. God

John Lennon, playing his celestially white piano, begins the song entitled 'God' (1970) by singing: 'God is a concept / by which we measure / our pain'. What kind of concept is God? In this chapter we propose to explore this question and its relation to literature. In doing this we shall try to emphasize not only that literature is pervasively concerned with religious themes but also that the ways in which we think, read and write about literature are likewise pervaded by religious – and particularly Judaeo-Christian – ideas. The concept of God, in other words, has as much to do with the practice of literary criticism as with the nature of literature. Let us give three very brief instances. The most famous atheist in the history of English poetry, Percy Bysshe Shelley, asserts that 'A poem is the very image of life expressed in its eternal truth' (Shelley 1977, 485): in the phrase 'eternal truth', Shelley is being religious. In his Preface to *Poems* (1853), Matthew Arnold writes of the name 'Shakespeare' that it is 'a name the greatest perhaps of all poetical names; a name never to be mentioned without reverence' (Arnold 1965, 599): with the word 'reverence', Arnold is being religious. Finally, in his essay 'Tradition and the Individual Talent' (1919), T.S. Eliot declares that 'The progress of an artist is a continual self-sacrifice, a continual extinction of personality' (Eliot 1975, 40): by appealing to 'self-sacrifice', Eliot is being religious.

We would like to try to approach the question of 'God' and literary studies by presenting, in a gesture familiar from religious discourse, a series of six edicts. As we hope will become clear, these edicts are not cut in stone. Nor do they add up to a list of systematic principles or rules. Although we write in the rhetorical form of the edict, we wish to make clear that, with respect to God at least, we have absolutely no authority whatsoever to proclaim anything at all. Our aim, as elsewhere in this book, is to provoke questions and further discussion, not to close them off or close them down.

First edict: God is an anthropomorphism

As we have noted elsewhere (for instance in Chapter 5), anthropomorphism is the rhetorical term by which something that is *not* human is attributed with the form or shape (Greek, *morphe*) of the human (*anthropos*). More specifically, as Nietzsche, Freud and others have argued, God is a projection of the human ego on to the surrounding universe. And it comes as no surprise to find that this ego or 'me' writ extremely large is, almost invariably, male. It is in this context that Freud suggests that God (here primarily the Judaeo-Christian God) is a kind of hyperbolic father-figure. He proposes that God is 'a father-substitute; or, more correctly . . . he is an exalted father . . . he is a copy of the father as he is seen and experienced in childhood' (Freud 1985c, 399). God is the figure of authority, the great progenitor, the Big Daddy who is sometimes angry (Old Testament), sometimes loving (New Testament). If one thinks for a moment about the idea of God as 'she', one might quickly sense the whole edifice of traditional Christianity tremble. This is no doubt the reason for the frisson of amusement that may accompany the reading of this car-sticker: 'When God made men-drivers she was only joking!' God, then, is not it: God is 'he' or, if you want to get people's backs up, 'she'. Either way, God would seem to be inconceivable without anthropomorphism.

Second edict: God is dead

This proposition is linked most often with the philosophy of Nietzsche, but it can be understood more generally in relation to the impact on European culture of biblical (especially German) scholarship and of (mainly British and German) fossil discoveries and subsequent developments in the theory of evolution in the nineteenth century. By the mid-nineteenth century it had become clear, at least to a significant number of educated European people, that the Bible was a tendentious collection of writings, many of which simply could no longer be trusted in terms of their historical fact and accuracy. The study of fossils made it impossible to suppose that the earth could be, as the Bible propounds, only a few thousand years old. Most famously, Charles Darwin's *On the Origin of Species* (1859) offered a far more empirically and historically convincing account of how human beings came about and, at the same time, served to cut God out of the equation. Poets and novelists of all sorts were obliged to reckon with what J. Hillis Miller (in a book of that title) refers to as 'the disappearance of God'. It is this sense of disappearance that Matthew Arnold evokes in 'Dover Beach' (written around 1851), when he describes the retreating 'sea of faith':

> The Sea of Faith
> Was once, too, at the full, and round earth's shore
> Lay like the folds of a bright girdle furled.
> But now I only hear
> Its melancholy, long, withdrawing roar,
> Retreating, to the breath
> Of the night wind, down the vast edges drear
> And naked shingles of the world.

European culture, at least according to this story, has become increasingly secularized.

Of course things are inevitably more complex than this. Even to acknowledge, for example, that 'God is dead' is to think in anthropomorphic terms, and to imply that 'He' was once alive rather than that 'He' never existed. The notion of the death of God runs into difficulties in many ways similar to those regarding the notion of the death of the author (see Chapter 3, above). As Virginia Woolf notes, in a somewhat different context: 'It is far harder to kill a phantom than a reality' (Woolf 1942, 151).

Third edict: to acknowledge the idea that God is an anthropomorphism or that he is dead is not the same as getting rid of him

As Roland Barthes makes clear, the idea of God is inescapably linked to ideas of truth, presence, revelation and meaning in general. In this respect, the issue of God is liable to creep into the discussion of literary texts, wherever questions of meaning, truth and so on are at stake. Barthes sees the notion of the author as interdependent with that of God. And he presses for a theory and practice of literature that would no longer be theological, declaring:

> The space of writing is to be ranged over, not pierced; writing ceaselessly posits meaning ceaselessly to evaporate it, carrying out a systematic exemption of meaning. In precisely this way literature (it would be better from now on to say *writing*), by refusing to assign a 'secret', an ultimate meaning, to the text (and to the world as text), liberates what may be called an anti-theological activity, an activity that is truly revolutionary since to refuse to fix meaning is, in the end, to refuse God and his hypostases – reason, science, law. (Barthes 1977a, 147)

The intimate linkage between 'God' and 'meaning' is implicit in the Bible, in the opening sentence of the Gospel according to St John: 'In the beginning was the Word, and the Word was with God, and the Word was God' (John

1: 1). The original Greek for 'Word' here is 'logos', which means not only 'word' but also 'sense' or 'meaning'. It is in this context that we might consider the notion of what Jacques Derrida has called logocentrism, in other words, the entire system (of Western thought, culture and philosophy) that is implicitly or explicitly governed by notions of essential and stable meaning and ultimately by what Derrida refers to as a transcendental signified (God, for example). To put this more specifically in terms of literary texts, we could say that perhaps our greatest desire in reading a poem or a novel is to know what it 'means'. Knowing what the text 'means' has often been seen as synonymous, for example, with knowing what the author (who here becomes a sort of substitute for God) meant by writing it. No doubt a crucial part of reading and doing criticism concerns precisely such a 'theological' activity. What Barthes helps us to see, however, is that this activity is *theological* in the sense that it presupposes a single, stable and authoritative centre.

Barthes's account is appealing – for instance in its associating literature, or *writing*, with the 'truly revolutionary' – but it is also in certain respects problematic. While he is doubtless right to link literature with notions of revolution, anarchy, transgression and liberation, his own phraseology remains, at least to some extent, complicit with what it claims to be rejecting or refusing. Just as an atheist could be said to be complying with a kind of theistic thinking through the very gesture of denial (you cannot say, for example, that God does not exist without presupposing a kind of ultimate knowledge of the universe), so the idea of 'an *anti*-theological activity' inevitably remains bound up with an understanding of the 'theological' to which it is being opposed. Similarly Barthes's use of the word 'truly' ('truly revolutionary') could be said to reinstate the notions of 'reason, science, law' precisely at the moment that he is claiming to denounce or refuse them. This is not to say that the general value and significance of his observations can be discounted. Rather it is to suggest that non-theological thinking is perhaps more difficult than one might imagine. It is in this respect that we could recall Nietzsche's supposition that we shall not get rid of God so long as 'we still believe in grammar' (Nietzsche 2003, 48). Like many of Nietzsche's more disturbing aphoristic remarks, this assertion borders on the unthinkable: What could one say about anything if there were no rules governing how to speak or what to say?

Fourth edict: religion is everywhere

It perhaps becomes clearer how deeply Western culture is theologically embedded if we reflect on the way we structure time. In the most fundamental way, the year is based on the Christian religion. Every year (1789 or 2010, for example) is *anno Domini*, 'in the year of our Lord'. Things in, say, Europe and the United States would look very different without a Christian framework: imagine, to begin with, a concept of the year that does not involve Christmas or Easter, or a concept of the week that does not have a Sunday. Christianity, in short, is more pervasive and insidious than many people, including non-practising Christians, agnostics or indeed atheists, might suppose.

How should we think about this in relation to reading and writing about literary texts? In many ways, searching for religious and particularly Christian ideas and motifs in the field of literary studies is like being the Edgar Allan Poe character in 'The Purloined Letter' who is faced with a map and cannot see the name of the country he is looking at because the letters of the name are so big. Being critical of religion is also more unusual than one might think. As Jonathan Culler points out, in an essay entitled 'Political Criticism: Confronting Religion': 'literature departments these days contain people with all manner of views – Marxists, Lacanians, deconstructionists, feminists – but seldom anyone who seriously attacks religion' (Culler 1988b, 78). Culler goes on to provide a forceful summary of the responsibilities of the teacher and critic in this context:

> The essential step is to take up the relation of our teaching and writing to religious discourse and to maintain a critical attitude when discussing religious themes – that is, not to assume that theistic beliefs deserve respect, any more than we would assume that sexist or racist beliefs deserve respect. This might involve us in comparing Christianity with other mythologies when we teach works imbued with religion, or making the sadism and sexism of religious discourse an explicit object of discussion, as we now tend to do when teaching works containing overtly racist language. (Culler 1988b, 80)

Culler's exhortation remains as challenging as ever. Especially since the early 1990s, and even more markedly in the wake of the events of 11 September 2001 and the commencement of the so-called 'war on terror', there has been a 'return of the religious'. More than ever before, perhaps, we find ourselves in the midst of religious conflicts. The US and British response to 'September 11' has entailed, in various ways, a reassertion of Christian structures, traditions and beliefs: the 'war on terror' has been insidiously enmeshed within an oppositional structure 'Islam vs. Christianity'. In the early twenty-first century Western leaders (Bush and Blair in particular) have appeared catastrophically blind or indifferent to that uncanny logic outlined by René Girard in an essay on the power-play of Shakespeare's *Hamlet*, namely that opponents become more and more similar the more they perceive themselves to be different from one another. 'Retaliation and reprisals are a form of imitation' (Girard 1986, 282), as he points out. Moreover, as 'September 11' dramatically showed, 'Islam' is not merely *outside* the US: multi-ethnic Western democracies need to reckon with Islamic as well as Christian religions *at home*. One important consequence of this is that, as Alex Thomson has argued, thinking seriously about contemporary democracy entails 'tak[ing] seriously the prospect that the future of "the West" might come from "the East"' (Thomson 2007, 77).

Fifth edict: literature has an evil streak

Rather than naively assume that literature in its creativity and *joie de vivre* is somehow innately *good*, or innocently claim, as did critics such as Matthew Arnold (in the nineteenth century) and F.R. Leavis (in the twentieth), that reading and studying literature in some 'natural' way make you a 'better' person, we should recognize instead that literary creativity has at least as much to do with evil as with good. In his influential and characteristically religious essay 'The Function of Criticism at the Present Time' (1864), Matthew Arnold described literature as 'the promised land' that contains 'the best that is known and thought in the world' (Arnold 1964, 34, 33). Very much within this Christian-spiritualistic critical tradition, F.R. Leavis propounded a theory of literature as the embodiment of 'our spiritual tradition . . . the "picked experience of ages"' (Leavis and Thompson 1964, 82). Such conceptions epitomize the sorts of spurious claims traditionally made of what Leo Bersani has described (and incisively criticized) as 'the authoritative, even redemptive virtues of literature' (Bersani 1990, 1). Indeed, it may be said that there is something diabolical about the literary. As Elizabeth Bowen once remarked, the novelist is a kind of fiend: the novelist exposes his (or her) characters to 'a relentless daylight in which nothing is hid. No human being, other than a fiend, would treat his [or her] fellow humans, in daily life, in so ruthless, uncompromising a manner' (Bowen 1970, 22). As Georges Bataille makes clear in his pathbreaking study, *Literature and Evil* (1953), a collusion between creation, imagination and evil is characteristic of literary works in general. 'Literature is not innocent', writes Bataille: 'Literature, like the infringement of moral laws, is dangerous' (Bataille 1985, x, 25).

We can illustrate this by considering the example of John Milton's *Paradise Lost* (1667). In the following lines from Book I, Milton describes the unsettling ability that devils have of being able to change instantaneously from the size of giants to the size of pygmies or to the size of 'fairy elves':

> . . . they but now who seemed
> In bigness to surpass Earth's giant sons
> Now less than smallest dwarfs, in narrow room
> Throng numberless, like that Pygmean race
> Beyond the Indian mount, or fairy elves,
> Whose midnight revels, by a forest side
> Or fountain some belated peasant sees,
> Or dreams he sees, while overhead the moon
> Sits arbitress, and nearer to the earth
> Wheels her pale course: they on their mirth and dance
> Intent, with jocund music charm his ear;
> At once with joy and fear his heart rebounds. (ll.777–88)

Unfolding the comparison of devils with 'fairy elves', these lines have to do with seduction and uncertainty, the charming power of music (or, by extension, poetry) – to which even the moon seems drawn – and the rebounding undecidability of 'joy and fear', the moment in which one does not know what one sees (or dreams one sees). Is one charmed by this vision or not? Milton leaves the comparison there, on the point of the rebound. And in a sense the whole of *Paradise Lost* is inscribed in the moment of this rebounding heart.

The passage from *Paradise Lost* demonstrates the workings of a powerful ambivalence and what we might call an aesthetic tribute to the devilish. This may help to explain William Blake's famous remark about *Paradise Lost*, in 'The Marriage of Heaven and Hell' (1790–3), that 'The reason Milton wrote in fetters when he wrote of Angels & God, and at liberty when of Devils & Hell, is because he was a true Poet and of the Devil's party without knowing it.' One of the most controversial literary critics of the past fifty years, Harold Bloom, has elaborated an entire theory of poetry (Bloom 1973) in accordance with this Blakean insight: for Bloom, Milton's Satan is the very epitome of the strong modern (i.e. Miltonic and post-Miltonic) poet. In any case it seems clear that Milton's great epic poem, and Blake's poetry in turn, is profoundly indebted to a kind of aesthetic of evil. As Bataille shows, evil and the literary imagination are in cahoots. We could illustrate this quite succinctly in terms of Shakespeare's *Othello*, by supposing that this play were retitled *Iago*: Iago may indeed be abominable, but he is clearly the imaginative focus of Shakespeare's play, the embodiment of its creativity and dramatic energy. A similar case could be made for the ways Shakespeare draws us into the interior worlds of Richard III, or Edmund in *King Lear*, or the Macbeths. A corresponding sense of the literary aesthetic of evil is suggested by Henry James when he offers an explanation of the power of *The Turn of the Screw* (1898), in his comments on that short but enthralling horror novel in a preface to *The Aspern Papers*: 'Only make the reader's general vision of evil intense enough', James says, '. . . Make him [*sic*] *think* the evil, make him think it for himself . . .' (James 1986, 343).

Putting our fifth edict in slightly different terms, we could say that literature tends towards the demonic: it is about entrancement, possession, being invaded or taken over. The word 'demonic' here is deliberately ambiguous: a demon is 'an evil spirit' or 'devil', but can also be 'a friendly spirit or good genius' (*Chambers*). It is in this respect that we might understand Jacques Derrida's contention that a love of poetry is inseparable from the experience of a kind of 'demon of the heart', a demon in one's heart (Derrida 1995b, 288–99). To argue that literature has an evil streak is not to imply a moral denunciation of literary works any more than it is to provide support for the liberalist notion that reading literature makes you a better person. At the very least, reading a literary work (or watching a play) entails an encounter with the unforeseeable: for better or worse, poems, stories and plays can alter our sense of the world, our selves. They can shake our thoughts and beliefs and trigger new ones, previously unentertained. Literary texts can be dangerous. No one is perhaps more palpably aware of this than the author of *The Satanic Verses* (1988) who, following the novel's publication, notoriously became subject to a *fatwa* (a death sentence pronounced by a Muslim judicial authority). Reading literary texts engages us, in a disturbing but creative and singular way, in the obligation to 'think the evil for oneself'. The paradoxically creative force of evil in literary texts is what makes them in turn the exemplary space for experiencing the undecidable and for thinking about ethics. Far from being immoral or even amoral, literature involves us in what Bataille calls a 'hypermorality' (Bataille 1985, ix). It confronts us with questions which call for different kinds of decision-making and critical responsibilities. Is *The Satanic Verses* an evil work? Is it any more evil than *Paradise Lost*, say, or Mary Shelley's *Frankenstein* (1818) or Elizabeth Bowen's *The House in Paris* (1935)? To rush to decisions in response to such questions is to turn a blind eye to the enigmatic powers of the literary and to ignore what could be called its peculiar ethical imperatives.

Sixth edict: literature is sacred

This would be another side to what is paradoxical about the literary. Salman Rushdie's Herbert Read Memorial Lecture, 'Is Nothing Sacred?' was given in his absence by Harold Pinter, at the Institute for Contemporary Arts in London, on 6 February 1990: Rushdie himself was at that time in enforced hiding as a result of the *fatwa* and unable to appear in public for the occasion. Rushdie's lecture starts off by stating that nothing is sacred:

> nothing is sacred in and of itself. . . . Ideas, texts, even people can be made sacred – the word is from the Latin *sacrare*, 'to set apart as holy' – but . . . the act of making sacred is in truth an event in history. It is the product of the many and complex pressures of the time in which the act occurs. And events in history must always be subject to questioning, deconstruction, even to declaration of their obsolescence. (Rushdie 1990, 3)

But the lecture then moves on to cast doubt on this idea that nothing is sacred. Rushdie suggests that he may be obliged 'to set aside as holy the idea of the absolute freedom of the imagination and alongside it [his] own notions of the World, the Text and the Good' (5). He goes on to speculate on the idea that art can and must offer us something like 'a secular definition of transcendence' where transcendence is defined as 'that flight of the human spirit outside the confines of its material, physical existence which all of us, secular or religious, experience on at least a few occasions' (7). Finally, Rushdie withdraws and appears to want to retract these earlier claims about art and, in particular, literature. He declares: 'now I find myself backing away from the idea of sacralizing literature with which I flirted at the beginning of this text; I cannot bear the idea of the writer as secular prophet' (14).

The shifts in Rushdie's position, the different kinds of flirtation going on in this brief text, 'Is Nothing Sacred?' are neatly illustrative of the seemingly paradoxical, contradictory nature of the concept of literature. We may, as readers or students or teachers, be powerfully motivated by a sense of the secular (and even, to phrase it more provocatively, by a sense that religion has been the greatest evil in human history, that it is nothing more than what Don Cupitt calls a 'hatred machine' (Cuppit 1997, 98)). But so long as we are concerned with the question of literature we are concerned with what is sacred. The murder in 1991 of Hitoshi Igarashi, the Japanese translator of Rushdie's novel *The Satanic Verses*, may allow us to reflect sombrely on the terrible blindness by which certain people have arrived at the belief that *The Satanic Verses* is an evil work, a blasphemous book which cannot or should not be read as fictional (or in that sense '*literary*') at all. But it also tragically gestures towards what may after all be the *something* that is sacred about literature, namely its untranslatability. Jacques Derrida has spoken of this, in the context of the German writer and philosopher Walter Benjamin, as follows:

> if there is something untranslatable in literature (and, in a certain way, literature is the untranslatable), then it is sacred. If there is any literature,

it is sacred; it entails sacralization. This is surely the relation we have to literature, in spite of all our denegations in this regard. The process of sacralization is underway whenever one says to oneself in dealing with a text: Basically, I can't transpose this text such as it is into another language; there is an idiom here; it is a work; all the efforts at translation that I might make, that it itself calls forth and demands, will remain, in a certain way and at a given moment, vain or limited. This text, then, is a sacred text. (Derrida 1985b, 148)

The sacred nature of literature has to do with this logic of untranslatable singularity. As critics such as Terry Eagleton (1996) have stressed, literary studies in Britain and the USA, for example, in many ways arose out of the desire or need to find a substitute for religion. As soon as we set it apart (*sacrare*) and recognize the singularity or uniqueness of a work, its demand that it be translated and its insistence on being untranslatable, we are engaging with the sacred.

> To be, or not to be, that is the question . . .

> Season of mists and mellow fruitfulness,
>   Close bosom-friend of the maturing sun . . .

> Sexual intercourse began
> In nineteen sixty-three . . .

Further reading

Salman Rushdie's 'Is Nothing Sacred?' (1990) is an accessible and very stimulating essay on literature and the sacred. Jonathan Culler's 'Political Criticism: Confronting Religion' (1988b) is clear and provocative, as is the book on which his discussion is centrally focused, William Empson's *Milton's God* (1965). On religion and the historical emergence of English Studies in Britain, see Eagleton 1996. Amardeep Singh's *Literary Secularism: Religion and Modernity in Twentieth-Century Fiction* (2006), explores the continuing, if oblique, importance of religion in the novelistic practice of ostensibly secular twentieth-century writers. For a very challenging reading of Nietzsche's 'God is dead', see Heidegger's 'The Word of Nietzsche' (1977). For a collection of complex but fascinating essays on God and language, religion, law, philosophy and politics, see Jacques Derrida's *Acts of Religion* (Derrida 2002b). For two excellent studies that consider the Bible itself from a literary critical perspective, see Robert Alter, *The Art of Biblical Narrative* (1981) and

The Art of Biblical Poetry (1985). For a useful collection of texts concerned with historical perspectives on the question of evil, see Rorty (2001). A helpful general survey of theology in relation to the work of various contemporary theorists and philosophers can be found in Graham Ward (1996). For a few challenging and thought-provoking books on some of the paradoxes of religion today, see Don Cupitt, *After God* (1997), Hent de Vries, *Philosophy and the Turn to Religion* (1999), Derrida and Vattimo, eds, *Religion* (1998), and John D. Caputo and Gianni Vattimo's *After the Death of God* (2007).

22. Ideology

The way you think, what you think – about society, ethics, politics, justice, about poverty and wealth, about education and the health and welfare systems, about crime and punishment, about human rights, race, religion and ethnicity, unemployment and the minimum wage, sexuality and gender, the environment, the ecosystem and global warming, about war and revolution, about terrorists and freedom fighters – is a matter of language. You make up your mind about these and a host of other questions in and through the words you and others use to describe them. Politicians know this, of course, not least because the politician's job is almost exclusively concerned with talking (and to a lesser extent writing) – in parliament, on TV and radio (if she gets the chance), on the streets and in election campaigns, in her weekly 'surgery', on the telephone or on weblogs, in newspapers, in committees and other meetings. The politician's job is to talk, to manipulate language in order to influence the way others think about and see the world. Her job is all about 'ideology': ideology, the way that people think about their world, is produced and altered in and through language. Language changes, and even creates the social and political world in which we live. Ideology in that sense *is* language. Some readers might even feel that our decision to speak of the politician here as female is itself an instance of ideology – for example, as 'politically correct' language. To have called her a 'him' could likewise, of course, be called 'ideological'.

We could illustrate some of these issues through a brief consideration of a few of the political slogans that have washed over us in the last 75 years or so – since radio, TV and more recently the Internet have established themselves as the dominant ways by which political communication happens, and since politicians have developed the knack of producing phrases (political slogans or 'sound bites') that can be extracted, quoted and re-quoted, in and out of context, in order to sum up a policy, a political position, a world view. The following snippets of language may be said to have influenced people's mentalities, their 'ideology', and consequently their social, political and economic world: 'the only thing we have to fear is fear itself' (Franklin D. Roosevelt, 1933); 'We will fight on the beaches' (Winston Churchill, 1940); people have 'never had it so good' (Harold Macmillan, 1957); 'ask not what your country can do for you; ask what you can do for your country' (John F. Kennedy, 1961); the 'white heat' of the technological revolution (Harold Wilson, 1963); 'I have a dream' (Martin Luther King, 1963); get the government 'off the backs of the people' (Ronald Reagan, 1981); there is 'no such thing' as society (Margaret Thatcher, 1987); 'back to basics' (John Major, 1993); 'tough on crime, tough on the causes of crime' (Tony Blair, 1992); the 'war on terror' (George W. Bush, 2001); 'change we can believe in' (Barack Obama, 2008). In fact, of course, political slogans or sound bites are nothing new: pre-TV and radio, the US presidential candidate Abraham Lincoln, for example, used a memorable metaphor from cowboy culture to influence the way people voted: 'Don't swap horses in the middle of the stream' (1864). And the US constitution is itself partly founded on the series of sound bites making up Benjamin Franklin's preamble to the Declaration of Independence of 1776: 'We hold these truths to be self-evident . . . all men are created equal . . . certain unalienable Rights . . . Life, Liberty and the pursuit of happiness'. But the growth of democracy and of the propagation and dissemination of ideas through new communication technologies in recent years has significantly increased the importance and power of the isolated sound bite.

What do these isolated pieces of language have to do with literature? And what can they tell us about the relationship between literature and ideology? The literary critic and theorist Paul de Man suggests one answer in a statement that has itself become a sound bite, in his 1982 essay 'The Resistance to Theory': 'What we call ideology is precisely the confusion of linguistic with natural reality' (de Man 1986, 11). What de Man seems to be alluding to is the way that, for example, by designating the man with a gun and a balaclava as a 'terrorist' you understand his actions in one way and thereby 'confuse' that naming with the 'reality' of his actions and purpose; but by naming him a 'freedom fighter', you understand him differently, and 'confuse' your phrase with another sense of his 'reality'. 'Ideology' has to do with the attempt to establish one of these ways of talking about the man in the balaclava as the dominant discourse, as the 'hegemony'. De Man's remark places literature, the art of language, at the centre of political or 'ideological' debate: as de Man himself asserts, it means that, 'more than any other mode of inquiry', literary criticism and theory (what de Man calls 'the linguistics of literariness') is itself 'a powerful and indispensable tool in the unmasking of ideological aberrations' (de Man 1986, 11).

The word 'ideology' has something of a bad name: the 'crude' Marxist notion of ideology is of 'false consciousness', 'the system of ideas and representations which dominate the mind of a man [*sic*] or a social group' (Althusser 1977, 149), as contrasted with the underlying reality of economic and class relations. The influential theorist Louis Althusser summarizes Marx's notion of ideology by contrasting it with 'the concrete history of concrete material individuals': ideology, instead, is a 'pure dream', it is 'empty and vain' and 'an imaginary assemblage'. 'Ideology', Althusser continues, 'represents the imaginary relationship of individuals to their real conditions of existence' (Althusser 1977, 151, 153). In classical Marxism – which, as we shall see, Althusser radically develops – ideology is an imagined representation of reality: it is false, distorted by definition. Ideology is not, Terry Eagleton remarks, 'a set of doctrines': rather, it 'signifies the way men [*sic*] live out their roles in class-society, the values, ideas and images which tie them by their social functions and so prevent them from a true knowledge of society as a whole' (Eagleton 1976, 16–17).

From a poststructuralist perspective, the notion of ideology is fundamentally suspect, since it relies on a questionable opposition of true and false, of reality and false consciousness. By this view, ideology appears too easily as a master term for totalizing readings of literary texts. In this chapter, however, we shall attempt to suggest ways in which the work of the neo-Marxist critic Louis Althusser has effectively produced a poststructuralist Marxism by substantially modifying the 'crude' opposition of disguised or distorted representations on the one hand and an underlying political and material reality on the other.

In a famous essay entitled 'Ideology and Ideological State Apparatuses' (1969), Louis Althusser seeks to describe ways in which the state exerts its power outside such institutions as the army, the courts, the police, etc. – that is to say, in culture and society generally. The central insight of this essay is that ideology is bound up with the constitution of the subject, that 'man is an ideological animal by nature' – meaning that people constitute or define themselves *as humans* through ideology. Althusser argues that

> the category of the subject is constitutive of all ideology, but at the same time . . . the category of the subject is only constitutive of all ideology insofar as all ideology has the function (which defines it) of 'constituting' concrete individuals as subjects. (Althusser 1977, 160)

To put it simply: subjects – people – make their own ideology at the same time as ideology makes them subjects. The implications of this idea are enormous because it means that 'ideology' goes to the heart of personal identity, of how we conceive ourselves as subjects in the world and all that this involves. Althusser avoids a reductive opposition of ideology and reality by suggesting that ideology *makes* our reality in constituting us as subjects. Ideology, Althusser argues, 'hails or interpellates concrete individuals as concrete subjects' (162): it calls us or calls to us as subjects and we recognize ourselves as subjects in our response to this call. To become human, to identify oneself as a subject, then, is an effect of ideology. For Althusser, the function of Art generally is, as he remarks in 'A Letter on Art', 'to make us see', and what it allows us to see, what it forces us to see, is 'the ideology from which it is born' (Althusser 1977, 204). What is most terrifying and compelling about this is the fact that being a subject feels so real, so natural – and yet, as Althusser remarks, this very 'reality' or 'naturalness' of being a subject is itself an 'ideological effect'.

This is heady stuff, and rather abstract – if also, as Althusser suggests, terribly real. How can we begin to think about the workings of ideology in literary texts? Etienne Balibar and Pierre Macherey take us some way towards an understanding of the question in their important essay 'On Literature as an Ideological Form' (1981). They argue that literary texts produce the illusion of 'unity'. Such writing is, for them, itself ideological. For Balibar and Macherey a 'material analysis' needs to look for 'signs of contradictions' which appear 'as unevenly resolved conflicts in the text' (87). For these critics, indeed, literature *begins* with 'the imaginary solution of implacable ideological contradictions': literature is there because 'such a solution is impossible' (88). In capitalist society, literature itself is an 'ideological form', both produced by and producing ideology. The task of the critic would be to look beyond the unity that the literary text strives to present, and forcefully to explore the contradictions embedded within it. The strange case of detective fiction illustrates this point very well. The genre produces its own consoling fictions, its own ideology. While we may think of crime as eternally recurring, for example, as an unavoidable function of any sociopolitical context, detective fiction allows us to perceive it as both solvable and the result of the actions of specific, isolated and morally culpable individuals.

The cultural theorist Tony Bennett has argued that a thoroughgoing Althusserian criticism would not simply restore or reveal the contradictions that are already in texts: rather, it would 'read contradictions into the text' in such a way that it would 'effect a work of transformation on those forms of signification which are said to be ideological' (Bennett 1979, 146–7). In this respect, an 'ideological criticism' is not one that understands the reality of a text better. Rather it is criticism that changes the text. Such a reading of, say, an Agatha Christie detective novel would not simply seek to expose ways in which such writing conforms to and reinforces the status quo of bourgeois capitalism. Instead, it would recognize reading as an intervention in and transformation of that text itself. Bennett argues that there can be no notion of '*the* text' underlying any reading: texts have 'historically specific functions and effects' (Bennett 1979, 148), they change in time, and what changes them is reading.

In order to think about some of these points and questions, we shall briefly consider Edgar Allan Poe's story 'The Purloined Letter' (1845). This story, and Poe's earlier 'The Murders in the Rue Morgue' (1841) and 'The Mystery of Marie Roget' (1842–3), are often considered to be the first examples of modern detective fiction. Set in Paris, the narrative concerns a detective named Auguste C. Dupin, who is asked to solve a mystery concerning the theft of a letter from the 'royal apartments' belonging to 'a personage of the most exalted station' (495), that is to say, presumably, the Queen of France. The contents of the letter have the potential to compromise the Queen and leave her open to blackmail. As she is reading the letter she is interrupted by her husband, from whom the letter must be concealed. She does not have time to hide the letter so she lays it on the table as she talks to her husband, relying on the fact that it is *not* concealed to hide the fact that it *must* be concealed. While they are talking, another person, 'Minister D.', enters the room, notices the letter and manages to exchange it for a worthless letter that he happens to be holding. The Queen sees this exchange but can do nothing to stop it without drawing attention to the secret letter. She is now open to blackmail and her letter must be discreetly retrieved by the head of the police service. The police have surreptitiously searched Minister D.'s house but have been unable to find the letter. Dupin is asked to help. He goes to the minister's house and manages to spot the letter, turned inside out, but revealed for all to see, hanging from the minister's mantelpiece. Later, by returning to the house with a copy of the letter and arranging for the minister to be distracted while he is there, Dupin manages to substitute his copy for the genuine article and retrieve the now doubly purloined letter.

Detective fiction may be understood to have a conservative ideological form because of its generic investment in the restoration of the status quo. A detective story typically involves a disturbance of order in the wake of an originary event of physical violence or theft of property, followed by the re-establishment of order by the discovery of the criminal – after which the jewels are returned or the murderer is punished (or both). Moreover, the genre conventionally relies on the idea of the criminal as an autonomous individual: he or she must be morally responsible for his or her actions and must not be insane (or at least be sane enough to be morally culpable). This is because the genre depends, on the one hand, on an outcome in which society's and the reader's desire for moral restitution is fulfilled and, on the other hand, on the detective's ability rationally to deduce the criminal's motives. If the criminal is mad, he or she cannot be punished (he or she must be cured), and his or her motives and actions cannot be rationally deduced because they will be, by definition, irrational. Similarly, any critique of society or social institutions is likely to be counterproductive in a work of detective fiction because of the danger that 'society', rather than a particular individual, will itself come to be seen as the culprit. This is a dilemma which is particularly acute in, for example, contemporary feminist detective fiction: the novels of such writers as Sara Paretsky, Amanda Cross and Gillian Slovo are concerned as much with exposing the gross injustices of patriarchal society as with finding a specific criminal. In such cases there is a sense in which the criminal cannot finally be punished and the status quo restored because it is that very status quo which is responsible for the crime. Encoded within classic detective fiction, then, is a reactionary political agenda. This ideological form of the genre might be said to be an unspoken but necessary part of any conventional detective story. From this point of view, one could say that 'The Purloined Letter' involves the re-establishment of power relations, the assertion of the culprit as autonomous and independent, and the implementation of reason to restore the status quo.

But what is particularly interesting about Poe's story from this perspective is not so much the way in which it institutes and reinforces the ideological for-mation of a certain literary genre, as it is the fact that this formation also entails a number of paradoxes, sites of disturbance and displacement. One of the key elements of the story is the identification of the detective with the criminal. Dupin explains that he was able to discover the letter by identifying himself with Minister D. and, in particular, by identifying the minister's mode of thinking as both rational and poetic (like Dupin, he is both mathematician and poet). The story establishes what we might call 'inspired reasoning' – as con-trasted with the rational approach of the regular police – as the characteristic technique for both detective and criminal in detective fiction. But the story also initiates a central paradox of the genre whereby the detective not only identifies with but is in some ways identical to the criminal. In this sense, it is no accident that the letter is, in fact, 'purloined' twice – once by the minister and once by Dupin. The detective in this story, and in detective fiction more generally, must obey the double bind of identity with, but difference from, the criminal. This intrinsic generic paradox suggests ways in which the ideological conservativism of the genre, its investment in a restoration of the status quo and reinforcement of an absolute distinction between criminal and non-criminal, may be undermined. Similarly, in establishing 'inspired reasoning' as the modus operandi for both detective and criminal, Poe's story opens the way for its own deconstruction. While detective and criminal, author and reader all need to employ reason to attain their ends, such reason is continually disturbed by its 'other', inspiration or unreason. It comes as no surprise, therefore, that Poe was also obsessed with occultism, spiritualism and the uncanny. Nor is it any surprise to discover that the inventor of Sherlock Holmes, Arthur Conan Doyle, was on the one hand a trained physician and, on the other, a keen amateur in the study of telepathy and the afterlife. The detective in this context combines a doctor's empirical and scientific acumen with a telepath's ability to read the criminal's mind. More generally, detective fiction seems to be continually threatened with its generic other – the gothic, tales of psychic phenomena, spiritualism – as is suggested by such gothic tales as Doyle's *The Hound of the Baskervilles* (1902), for example, or such apparently supernatural tales as his 'The Parasite' (1893). Finally, the genre of detective fiction is organized through a precarious relation with social critique. As we have pointed out, classic detective fiction must distance itself from an ideological critique of society which, however, can never be finally erased. Detective fiction can only exist if there are crimes to detect, and if there are crimes to detect society cannot be perfect. Some of the most interesting exponents of detective fiction – Dashiel Hammett, Raymond Chandler, Elmore Leonard, or more recently Paul Auster, William McIlvanney, Sara Paretsky, Philip Kerr, Walter Mosley, Ian Rankin, Henning Mankell – gain much of their narrative energy from precisely such a tension – the possibility that the constitution of their narratives as detective fiction will be dissolved by their unavoidable engagement in social and political critique.

Our final point concerning Poe's story and its relation to ideology concerns the way in which it is based on the idea that what is most open or revealed, most 'obvious', may itself be the most deceptive or most concealing. The fact that Minister D. conceals the purloined letter precisely by *not* hiding it, by leaving it where all can see it (the place where no one – except Dupin – will look, because it is too exposed), makes 'The Purloined Letter' an allegory of ideological formation. Ideology may be defined in terms of the obvious, in terms of common sense. It is, in the West, 'common sense' that a 'normal' subject or person is autonomous, for example, that crime is the result of individual actions, or that such an individual operates through rational motivation. But at the same time each of these obvious, self-evident or commonsensical points disguises a very specific concept of the self, an ideology.

Rather than offering an escape from ideology, then, literary texts may be considered as places where the structures and fractures of ideology are both produced and reproduced. Literary texts do not simply or passively 'express' or reflect the ideology of their particular time and place. Rather, they are sites of conflict and difference, places where values and preconceptions, beliefs and prejudices, knowledge and social structures are represented and, in the process, opened to transformation.

Further reading

A good brief account of ideology is the entry in Williams, *Keywords* (1976). More recent, more detailed and exhaustive is Terry Eagleton's *The Ideology of the Aesthetic* (1990). Good short introductions to the subject include Terry Eagleton, *Ideology: An Introduction* (1991), David Hawkes, *Ideology* (1996), James Decker, *Ideology* (2004), and Michael Freeden, *Ideology* (2003). For useful collections of essays, see Eagleton, ed., *Ideology* (1994) and Mulhern, ed., *Contemporary Marxist Literary Criticism* (1992). Althusser's 'Ideology and the Ideological State Apparatuses' (1977) is a basic text for a considera- tion of the fundamental importance of ideology in the constitution of the human subject. The classic Althusserian account of literature is Macherey's astute and highly readable *A Theory of Literary Production* (1978); see also Balibar and Macherey, 'On Literature as an Ideological Form' (1981). For a more up-to-date account, drawing on numerous Althusser texts posthu- mously published in French, see Warren Montag, *Louis Althusser* (2003). A valuable work on the ideology of detective fiction in particular is Stephen Knight's *Form and Ideology in Detective Fiction* (1980); for a more recent study of the genre, see John Scaggs's *Crime Fiction* (2005). Poe's 'The Purloined Letter' has itself become a site of intense ideological conflict and theoretical speculation following important essays by Lacan and Derrida: see Muller and Richardson, eds, *The Purloined Poe* (1988).

23. Desire

In 1954 Alan Turing, the inventor of one of the first modern electronic computers (the 'Turing Machine'), killed himself. Two years earlier, he had been prosecuted for 'gross indecency' – that is, for having sex with another man. His crime had been to desire the wrong person, to have the wrong desire. The man who, with others, has transformed our world by the manipulation of a binary system (on/off), was prosecuted and persecuted thanks to another binary system – right/wrong, good/evil, moral/immoral, legal/illegal, heterosexual/homosexual, normal/perverse. There is a terrible irony here. Turing's machine and its descendants exploit a simple polarity to develop the most complex patterns imaginable (and those beyond imagination). Society's programme of ethics and legality, by contrast, can often seem to be based on rigid and unforgiving binary oppositions. Desire: right or wrong.

Is it possible that desire is more complex? The most influential philosopher of desire in the twentieth century has been Sigmund Freud. For Freud, all desire goes back to the child's original desire for the mother, for the mother's breast. This desire is so strong that it produces an absolute identification: ' "I am the breast",' wrote Freud, ventriloquizing the unspoken words of the infant (Freud 1975b, 299). Beyond this originary desire, however, Freud tends to see the precise structure of desire as determined by socialization, by the way in which the child is brought up. In such texts as *On Sexuality: Three Essays on the Theory of Sexuality* (1905/1977), Freud argues that desire is 'essentially' mobile – it has no essence, no proper object, beyond the child's hallucinatory desire for the breast. Most justifications for the proscription of desire – against homosexual acts, for example – rely on assertions about what is 'natural'. But if we accept Freud's arguments, we find that the appeal to the natural is highly questionable.

The mobility of desire is demonstrated by a text such as Shakespeare's comedy *Twelfth Night* (*c.* 1601). While his *Romeo and Juliet* (*c.* 1595) may seem to reproduce the myth of an absolute and eternal love between one man and one woman, *Twelfth Night* is concerned rather with the contingency and mobility of desire. Duke Orsino sees himself as a true lover, a man overwhelmed by love and constant only in his desire:

> For such as I am, all true lovers are,
> Unstaid and skittish in all motions else,
> Save in the constant image of the creature
> That is belov'd. (II, iv, 17–20)

In love with an image of the woman he claims to love, Orsino is at the same time in love with the image of himself in love. A philosopher of love – most of his speeches meditate, often absurdly, on the nature of love and the lover – Orsino is unaware that 'true love', including his own, is ultimately love of love, that desire is desire for its own image. In spite of himself, Orsino illustrates the accuracy of Nietzsche's aphorism: 'In the end one loves one's desire and not what is desired' (Nietzsche 1989, 93). In fact, by the end of the play it has become clear that Orsino's desire is radically mobile and contingent. Orsino uses his servant Cesario as a messenger between himself and Lady Olivia, the woman he desires. Cesario is really a woman called Viola, dressed as a man, and is herself in love with the Duke. At the end of the play, Olivia marries Viola's twin brother and Viola reveals that she is really a woman. At this point, unabashed by the ease with which his desire can move from one object to another, Orsino proposes marriage to Viola. The 'true lover' in Shakespeare's play turns out to have mobile and vicarious desires, and even gender seems to be more a comedy of convention than a matter of nature. Does Orsino finally desire Viola or Cesario?

In the context of literature more generally, we can begin to think about the importance of desire in two fundamental ways. In the first place, we would suggest that every literary text is in some way *about* desire. To say this, however, is not to suggest that it is everywhere and always the same desire. As Michel Foucault's influential three-volume *The History of Sexuality* (1976–84) makes particularly clear, desire is bound up with all sorts of social and institutional practices and discourses – with questions of law, gender and sexuality, with the discourses of medicine, theology, economics and so on. Thinking about desire in literary texts – about representations of desire – inevitably opens on to questions of historical context. For example, nowadays we may take for granted the term 'homosexual' and the notion of homosexual desire.

But as we show in more detail in Chapter 24, below, the term and indeed the concept is relatively recent. The first entry for 'homosexual' in the *OED* is from 1892. Critics such as Joseph Bristow have demonstrated that a critical appreciation of a play such as Oscar Wilde's *The Importance of Being Earnest* (1895) is crucially dependent on an understanding of the historical emergence of a homosexual lifestyle at the end of the nineteenth century (Bristow 1992a). While the term 'homosexual' can refer to both men and women, its entry into the English language in the late nineteenth century did not result in a sudden visibility for lesbians, however. Indeed, the most striking aspect of lesbianism in 'straight' culture generally has been the denial of its existence. There's a well-known story that in 1885 Queen Victoria reacted to the suggestion that there should be a law for women corresponding to the new law against 'gross indecency' between men by remarking that 'no woman could ever do that' (quoted in Castle 1992, 128). The story is probably apocryphal, but it does register something important about the historical denial of sex between women. A similar denial is recorded in Leonard Woolf's mother's response to Radclyffe Hall's lesbian novel *The Well of Loneliness* (1928): 'I am seventy-six – but until I read this book I did not know that such things went on at all. I do not think they do' (quoted in Knopp 1992, 118). And, in literary criticism, it is only since the 1980s, despite pioneering studies such as Jeannette Foster's *Sex Variant Women in Literature* from 1958, that a critical vocabulary for talking about lesbian writing has begun to emerge. As far as 'straight' culture goes, critics such as Joseph Allan Boone, for example, have shown how the very *form* of conventional nineteenth-century narrative is bound up with the Victorian social dynamics of courtship and marriage (Boone 1987). According to Boone, the traditional marriage plot 'owes much of its idealizing appeal to its manipulation of form to evoke an illusion of order and resolution': this 'illusory' sense of order, he suggests, itself 'glosses over the contradictions, the inequalities, concealed in the institution of marriage' (Boone 1987, 9).

But literary texts are not only about how and why characters desire each other and what happens to those desires. Literary texts also produce or solicit desire. They make us desire, in reading. Literary texts, we might say, are (in Deleuze and Guattari's phrase) 'machines of desire'. Not only do they generate desire (such as the desire to read on), but they are generated by it (by the desire, for example, to tell). In this respect it might be useful to turn Freud's famous question of female desire, 'what does a woman want?' (quoted in Jones 1953–7, 2: 468) – and Gayatri Spivak's reformulation of it as 'what does a man want?' – into a question about literary texts: What does a text want? Does it want to tell us something or conceal something? Does it want to make us want it? How? And so on. But if texts can be thought to desire, readers desire, too: we desire solutions, we desire to get to the end of the story, we desire insight or wisdom, pleasure or sadness, laughter or anger. The fundamental paradox of reading, however, is that we always desire an end (a resolution, an explanation, the triumph of good), but that this end is not the end of desire. As Boone has shown, classic nineteenth-century narratives tend to end with the apparent satisfaction of desire (the reader's, the character's or preferably both). But as Freud has taught us, this end of desire is not the end of the story: as he speculates in 'Civilization and Its Discontents', there is something in the very nature of sexual life which 'denies us full satisfaction' (Freud 1985e, 295).

Perhaps the most important post-Freudian theorist of desire, especially in the context of literary studies, is the French psychoanalyst Jacques Lacan. His particular concern is with what he terms the 'paradoxical, deviant, erratic, eccentric, even scandalous character' of desire (Lacan 1977a, 286, quoted in Bowie 1991, 134). Lacan's texts are notoriously difficult to read, in part because they claim to (or are condemned to) speak on behalf of this strange figure of desire. Any attempt to summarize or explain what he has to say about desire is bound to be misguided – precisely to the extent that it will appear to be putting this scandalous figure in a conceptual straitjacket. With that proviso in mind, however, we could be a bit scandalous in our own fashion and summarize Lacan's characterization of desire as follows: Lacan elaborates on Freud's contention that there is something about the nature of desire that is incompatible with satisfaction. His account of desire is more radical than Freud's, however. Freud emphasizes the ways in which we can never get what we want: we may think we have got it (downloading a new tune to our iPod, paying for a new car), but actually desire will always have moved on again (to the next tune to download, to the chance to get on the road and drive and so on). This, after all, is how capitalism works, what it desires – or needs, indeed – in order to function at all. Waiting for a final fulfilment of desire is like waiting for Godot in Samuel Beckett's play. For Freud, this endlessly deferred complete satisfaction is seen simply as an unavoidable, if rather poignant aspect of what it is to be human. For Lacan, on the other hand, the nature of desire is at once more alien and more subversive. This can be illustrated in two ways. First, for Lacan, the alien or alienating character of desire is not something that happens to come along and make life difficult for people. Instead, people have become alienated before they even become people (or 'subjects' in psychoanalytic terms). The human subject is always already 'split' – divided within itself by the scandalous nature of desire. Second, Lacan gives much greater emphasis than Freud to the role of language in relation to desire. One of Lacan's most famous dicta is that 'the unconscious is structured like a language' (see, for example, Lacan 1977a). For Lacan, language is not something that we can use in order to try to make ourselves more comfortable with the alien nature of desire: desire speaks through language and it speaks us. We are, in a way, the senseless puppets of desire as much when we speak or write as when we fall in love.

The interdependence of desire and language in turn is an overt concern of many literary texts. In such texts, there is a recognition that language or meaning can never finally be closed or completed and that desire can never be fulfilled. Robert Browning's poem 'Two in the Campagna', from 1855, is one such text:

1

I wonder do you feel today
   As I have felt since, hand in hand,
We sat down on the grass, to stray
   In spirit better through the land,
5   This morn of Rome and May?

2

For me, I touched a thought, I know,
   Has tantalized me many times,
(Like turns of thread the spiders throw
   Mocking across our path) for rhymes
10   To catch at and let go.

3

Help me to hold it! First it left
   The yellowing fennel, run to seed
There, branching from the brickwork's cleft,
   Some old tomb's ruin: yonder weed
15   Took up the floating weft,

4

Where one small orange cup amassed
   Five beetles,—blind and green they grope
Among the honey-meal: and last,
   Everywhere on the grassy slope
20   I traced it. Hold it fast!

5

The champaign with its endless fleece
   Of feathery grasses everywhere!
Silence and passion, joy and peace,
   An everlasting wash of air—
25   Rome's ghost since her decease.

6

Such life here, through such lengths of hours,
   Such miracles performed in play,

Such primal naked forms of flowers,
Such letting nature have her way
30   While heaven looks from its towers!
                7
How say you? Let us, O my dove,
Let us be unashamed of soul,
As earth lies bare to heaven above!
How is it under our control
35   To love or not to love?
                8
I would that you were all to me,
You that are just so much, no more.
Nor yours nor mine, nor slave nor free!
Where does the fault lie? What the core
40   O' the wound, since wound must be?
                9
I would I could adopt your will,
See with your eyes, and set my heart
Beating by yours, and drink my fill
At your soul's springs,—your part my part
45   In life, for good and ill.
                10
No. I yearn upward, touch you close,
Then stand away. I kiss your cheek,
Catch your soul's warmth,—I pluck the rose
And love it more than tongue can speak—
50   Then the good minute goes.
                11
Already how am I so far
Out of that minute? Must I go
Still like the thistle-ball, no bar,
Onward, whenever light winds blow,
55   Fixed by no friendly star?
                12
Just when I seemed about to learn!
Where is the thread now? Off again!
The old trick! Only I discern—
Infinite passion, and the pain
60   Of finite hearts that yearn.

The poem is about the impossibility of capturing the moment of desire, of capturing or 'holding' desire, of fulfilling and so ending it. The speaker desires the 'good minute' – analogous to what James Joyce later calls 'epiphany' and

Virginia Woolf 'moments of being' – but recognizes its inevitable escape. The second stanza makes it clear that this is also a poem about language, about the tantalizing nature of a moment which poetry attempts to but cannot capture. In stanza 10, the speaker 'pluck[s] the rose / And love[s] it more than tongue can speak'; but the moment passes immediately and he asks 'Already how am I so far / Out of that minute?' Exploring the central trope of romantic love – the loss of identity in a merging with the other, the desire evoked in stanza nine in particular – Browning's poem suggests the impossibility and inevitable failure of this desire. The poem traces the paradoxes of romantic love while discerning the impossibility of expressing in language the flux of life, the fluidity and fragility of experience.

If literature and theory alike demonstrate that desire is mobile, endlessly displaced, they also suggest that it is 'mediated', produced through imitation and simulation. Particularly influential in this context has been the recent work of Eve Kosofsky Sedgwick. Developing the ideas of the French post-structuralist critic René Girard, Sedgwick has argued that desire is everywhere mediated, that desire is structured by a triangular relation of rivalry. Take three people: A, B and C. A, let us say, desires B. Why? Normally, we would assume that A desires B because B is desirable (at least to A). For Girard and Sedgwick, however, things are rather different. For them, A desires B because B is desired by C. We learn to desire, Girard and Sedgwick argue, by copying others' desires, and our desire is produced, fundamentally, in response to the desire of another. 'The great novelists', Girard claims, 'reveal the imitative nature of desire' and expose what he terms 'the lie of spontaneous desire' (Girard 1965, 14, 16). Now, Sedgwick further points out that most of the examples in Girard's book, *Deceit, Desire, and the Novel* (1965), involve a specific relation of gender, wherein B is a woman and A and C men: the woman is the object of desire, while the two men are rivals. Love stories often concern the rivalry of two men for a woman, in which the rivalry itself indeed becomes more important than the desire for the woman. For Sedgwick, in fact, Western culture in general is structured by a 'crisis of homo/heterosexual definition': 'an understanding of virtually any aspect of modern Western culture must be, not merely incomplete, but damaged in its central substance to the degree that it does not incorporate a critical analysis of modern homo/heterosexual definition' (Sedgwick 1991, 1). She develops these insights to suggest that, in Western discourse, in stories, novels, films and so on, relationships are most commonly structured in terms of what she calls 'homosocial desire'. Homosocial desire is not the same as homosexual desire. It does not need to be explicitly expressed as desire, and it is not necessarily physical. In fact, homosocial desire is often concerned rigorously to exclude the possibility of homosexual relations. The traditional male preserves of locker room, board-room and clubroom are sites of homosocial bonding which, at the same time, may be virulently homophobic. But in a male-dominated society, such relations are fundamental: in all such societies, Sedgwick claims, 'there is a special relationship between male homosocial (*including* homosexual) desire and the structures for maintaining and transmitting patriarchal power' (Sedgwick 1985, 25). Sedgwick argues that a large proportion of the stories, films, songs and other narratives by which Western society imaginatively structures desire can be read as narratives of homosocial desire: while such narratives take as their overt subject the desire of a man for a woman, again and again the really important relationship is that between two men, either as rivals or as colleagues, friends, or associates. Developing the idea first proposed by the French structuralist anthropologist Claude Lévi-Strauss that in many societies women tend to be tokens of exchange, Sedgwick argues that women are effaced in this triangular structure, as mere objects for barter. At some level, then, patriarchal society excludes women even from relations of desire. Homosocial desire in our society, Sedgwick suggests, is both the most required and the most carefully regimented desire.

Sedgwick offers a highly provocative model for thinking about desire in narrative. According to this model, the workings of desire are inextricably linked to the homophobic, homosocial and patriarchal structures of society. Many canonical works of literature might be reread in these terms. This is not to suggest that the Great Tradition is full of closet homosexuality, for example, just waiting to be 'outed' (although we make some suggestions in this regard in our 'Queer' chapter, below). Rather, it is to suggest that homosocial desire in all its forms is central to the workings of what we might like to think of simply as 'heterosexual' writing. The notions of heterosexual and homosexual need to be rethought. Shakespeare's *Hamlet* (*c.* 1601), for example, concerns not only the murder of Hamlet's father and its revenge, but also a relation of rivalry between Prince Hamlet (as a surrogate for his father, King Hamlet) and Hamlet's uncle, Claudius (the dead King's brother), over the Queen. Emily Brontë's *Wuthering Heights* (1847) may gain much of its power from the barely hidden conflicts of homosocial desire between Heathcliff and other men, resulting in rivalry and extraordinary violence. In its focus on the triangle of two men (Eugene Wrayburn and Bradley Headstone) and one woman (Lizzie Hexam), Charles Dickens's *Our Mutual Friend* (1865) is a superb, if disturbing, example of the potentially murderous erotic dynamic that exists between men. Thomas Hardy's *Tess of the D'Urbevilles* (1891), a novel that appears to focus on the eponymous and tragic heroine, is also structured by rivalry between two men who desire her, Angel Clare and Alec D'Urbeville. D.H. Lawrence's *Women in Love* (1921), while overtly about two men and their love for two women, is also, and perhaps more importantly, about the relationship between the two men, Gerald and Birkin.

Desire, then, is both a fundamental topic of literary texts and fundamental to reading. But one of the things that literary texts consistently suggest is that desire is paradoxical, mobile, mediated. And perhaps the homophobia that may have ultimately resulted in the death of Alan Turing can itself be understood in terms of a distortion or displacement of desire – a fear of homosexuality, a fear of the other, which is bound up in society's anxieties about such mobilities and mediations. One of the responsibilities of contemporary literary criticism and theory lies in the exposure, questioning and transformation of the rigid oppositions that result in such fear and oppression.

Further reading

Foucault's *The History of Sexuality: An Introduction* (1981) is a crucial starting point for thinking about desire. Similarly influential is Deleuze and Guattari's difficult but compelling *Anti-Oedipus* (1983). Peter Brooks offers fascinating accounts of the reader's desire in *Reading for the Plot* (1984) and *Body Work* (1993), while Catherine Belsey presents a readable poststructuralist account of a number of literary texts of desire in her *Desire: Love Stories in Western Culture* (1994). William Irvine's *On Desire* (2005) presents a philosopher's wide-ranging meditation on the question of desire. Leo Bersani's *A Future for Astyanax: Character and Desire in Literature* (1976) remains a brilliant and thought-provoking point of reference for exploring the representation and effects of desire in literary texts. For three excellent brief accounts of the work of Lacan, see the introductory books by Bowie (1991), Weber (1992) and Rabaté (2001). On the discourse of homosexual desire and homophobia, see Jonathan Dollimore's influential book *Sexual Dissidence* (1991), and for a collection of essays on lesbian criticism and theory, see Munt, ed., *New Lesbian Criticism* (1992). On the importance of heterosexual desire for the development of the novel in the nineteenth century, see Joseph Allen Boone, *Tradition and Counter Tradition* (1987). For historically wide-ranging discussions of issues of desire, see Dollimore's *Death, Desire and Loss in Western Culture* (1998) and *Sex, Literature and Censorship* (2001).

24. Queer

Queer's a queer word.

The entry of the word 'queer' into the English language is itself a study in the queer ways of words. *Chambers Dictionary* defines the adjective as follows: 'odd, singular, quaint: open to suspicion: counterfeit: slightly mad: having a sensation of coming sickness: sick, ill (*dialect*): homosexual (*slang*)'. What's queer about this synonymatic definition is the way in which it includes three apparently unrelated senses for the 'same' word – clustering around ideas of strangeness, sickness and homosexuality. One question immediately arises: how do you get from 'queer' as 'singular' or 'quaint' or 'slightly mad' or 'ill' to 'queer' as 'homosexual'? While the answer may to some seem to be self-evident, the process is worth examining in greater detail. The *Oxford English Dictionary* shows the slippage from one sense to the other in action: its extensive historical account of the word reveals that in fact there was a delay of more than four hundred years between the introduction of the 'odd' or 'singular' sense of the word into English and the introduction of its 'homosexual' sense. The first entry for 'queer' in the *OED* comes from the early sixteenth century (Dunbar's 'Heir cumis awin quir Clerk', from 1508), while the first entry for the word in its homosexual sense is from 1922 in a publication by the Children's Bureau of the US Department of Labor. The latter comes from the straight (but also rather queer) language of a report entitled *The Practical Value of the Scientific Study of Juvenile Delinquents*, which refers to the idea that 'A young man, easily ascertainable to be unusually fine in other characteristics, is probably "queer" in sex tendency'. The sentence, immortalized as an entry in the *OED* simply by virtue of its priority as the first recorded usage of the word, is intriguing for a number of reasons. It makes stereotypical assumptions about certain 'characteristics', it expresses the idea that queerness is written on the body and implicitly identifies it with delinquency or illness. But it also holds the word at arm's length – with so-called 'scare-quotes' – as if the term is not fully accepted or acceptable, or as if the word is still in process, moving from a sense of oddness to a (related) sense of homosexuality. Homosexuality is 'queer', then, because of the perceived queerness of queers, their difference from 'us' (scientists, US Department of Labor officials, sociologists, and so on): queers are a category apart, a self-defining and identifiable group determined precisely by the queer difference of its members from the regime of the normal – from what Adrienne Rich, the contemporary lesbian poet and critic, calls 'compulsory hetero-sexuality' (Rich 1986).

But the story of 'queer' is not over yet. For the next 70 years or so, 'queer' gained currency in the English language in the United States and elsewhere as (usually) a derogatory term for (usually male) homosexual; it was combined with 'coot' to form the dismissive phrase 'queer as a coot'; and, in the 1960s and 1970s, was combined with 'bashing' to denote (and doubtless to help legitimize) verbal and physical violence against those who were, or who were perceived to be, homosexual. In the late 1980s and early 1990s, however, partly in response to the spread of AIDS among gay men, the word took a queer turn: homosexuals themselves began to 'reclaim' the word, to use it in place of the gender-specific and arguably effete term 'gay' or the clinical and cheerless 'homosexual' or the polite and even mythological-sounding 'lesbian'. 'Queer' becomes a term of pride and celebratory self-assertion, of difference affirmed and affirmative difference. The very reason for the use of 'queer' to denote homosexuality in the first place – the sense that homo-sexuality is associated with singularity and difference – is also inherited in this act of linguistic reappropriation, but the values afforded such strangeness are reversed. The fact that queers are different from 'straight' people is seen as a source of power and pride – and 'straight' now becomes a term with poten-tially negative connotations (conventional, dull, unadventurous). 'Queer' also has the advantage of being an inclusive term which gains in prestige and power just in so much as it shakes up our codes and codings of male and female, or masculinity and femininity, or bi-, hetero- and homo-. As Eve Kosofsky Sedgwick comments, 'queer' can refer to 'the open mesh of possibilities, gaps, overlaps, dissonances and resonances, lapses and excesses of meaning when the constituent elements of anyone's gender, of anyone's sexuality aren't made (or *can't be* made) to signify monolithically' (Sedgwick 1994, 8). Essentially, then, 'queer' challenges all gender and sexual essentialisms.

In homage to this brilliant queering of 'queer', its (re)appropriation as a device for the social and political empowerment of certain more or less defined, more or less discrete, more or less oppressed sexual identities, and linking up with our comments elsewhere on the association of literary texts with the uncanny or the strange, we would like to suggest that literature is itself a little (and sometimes more than a little) queer. By this we mean two things. Firstly, we want to suggest that there is an eminent tradition of queer writing in English, writing by men and women who are more or less permanently, more or less openly, more or less explicitly, queer and writing about queerness. For reasons that will become clear, this tradition is all but invisible before the late nineteenth century, although it arguably includes Marlowe, Shakespeare, the debauchee Lord Rochester, the eighteenth-century poet Katherine Philips, Henry Mackenzie (author of the novel of exquisite sensitivity *The Man of Feeling* [1771]), Matthew Lewis (author of the Gothic high-camp novel *The Monk* [1796]), Lord Byron, Walt Whitman and Herman Melville. But the literary canon from the late nineteenth century onwards is full of authors who are queer, who write homoerotic poetry or write about the experience of homosexual desire – including Gerard Manley Hopkins, Algernon Swinburne, Oscar Wilde, A.E. Housman, Virginia Woolf, Vita Sackville-West, Djuna Barnes, D.H. Lawrence, Dorothy Richardson, Charlotte Mew, H.D., Katherine Mansfield, Rosamund Lehmann, Radclyffe Hall, T.E. Lawrence, E.M. Forster, Elizabeth Bowen, W.H. Auden, Christopher Isherwood, Compton Mackenzie, Tennessee Williams, Allen Ginsberg, Gore Vidal, Truman Capote, James Baldwin, Patrick White, William Burroughs, Edmund White, Thom Gunn, Adrienne Rich, Joe Orton, Alice Walker, Jeanette Winterson, John Ashbery, Hanif Kureishi, Alan Hollinghurst and innumerable others. We might say that there is a canon of queer writers in modern literature, except that the 'straight' canon is itself everywhere inhabited by queers (many of the writers listed above, that is to say, are central to the canon of literature in English, whether they are read as queer or straight).

Our second reason for talking about literature as 'a little (and sometimes more than a little) queer' is to suggest that literary texts in general might be open to what has been called 'queer reading'. Some of the strangeness or uncanniness, some of the power and fascination of literary texts, that is to say, has to do with the singular space which they offer for thinking (differently) about gender and sexuality. This point is illustrated by the work of Eve Sedgwick, one of the most influential queer theorists of recent years, whose notion of 'homosocial desire' we discuss, above, in our chapter on 'Desire'. In an essay entitled 'The Beast in the Closet' (first published in 1986), Sedgwick discusses Henry James's short story 'The Beast in the Jungle' (1903). James's story is an apparently 'straight' story about John Marcher, a confirmed bachelor, who has a terrible and overwhelming secret (the 'beast' of the title), a secret which never is, never could be, articulated, but which is nevertheless understood by his friend May Bartram, a woman who supports him and who, it is clear, could – or should – have been his lover or wife. In a stunning reading of the story, Sedgwick examines a number of aspects of the story and its discursive contexts. She discusses the figure of the bachelor in the late nineteenth century, for example, as a role that allowed certain men to avoid the rigorous demands of the compulsorily heterosexual society in which they lived. (James himself, Sedgwick argues, was a bachelor whose complex sexuality seems to have been notable as much for the obstinacy of its heterosexuality as for anything else.) Sedgwick considers the dynamics of 'male homosexual panic' as the unmanageable fear of homosexuality among heterosexuals, a fear that would also appear to be based on the heterosexual male's fear of his own desire for other men. Sedgwick then examines certain linguistic and rhetorical aspects of the apparently heterosexual story and shows how, viewed in this light, the story turns queer. Thus Sedgwick notes that the story uses the word 'queer' on a number of occasions to denote John Marcher's condition: while it is clear that the primary sense of the word denotes a certain 'strangeness' (after all, the homosexual sense of 'queer' was not an explicit part of its official meaning in 1903), nevertheless, as we have seen, the move within 'queer' from 'strange' to 'homosexual' is never far away – and is not as queer as it might seem. In this respect, James's use of the word may be seen to be haunted by its semantic developments a few years later and to raise the spectre of an unacknowledged difficulty concerning Marcher's sexual identity. Sedgwick also notes a number of less specific 'lexical pointers', all of which are 'highly equivocal' but which add up to a queering of the whole story. Phrases such as Marcher's 'singularity', 'the thing [May Bartram] knew, which grew to be at last . . . never mentioned between them save as "the real truth" about him', 'his queer consciousness', 'dreadful things . . . I couldn't name', 'his unhappy perversion', and so on (quoted in Sedgwick 1994, 203), convey a strong sense of specifically *sexual* disturbance in Marcher's character. In a complex and enthralling piece of literary critical detective-work, Sedgwick develops a reading of the text which compellingly suggests the 'cataclysm' of Marcher's condition to be that of (in Oscar Wilde's poignant formulation) the 'love that dare not speak its name', the unacknowledged and unacknowledgeable homosexuality of his queerness. As far as the normative values of straight society are concerned, queerness is devastatingly and catastrophically *queer*: the 'straight' Marcher's problem is his inability to deal with the problem of (his) queerness.

In her reading of the story, however, Sedgwick is not attempting to argue, definitively, that Marcher (or James, for that matter) is in any simple sense homosexual. Instead, she is queering the narrative by thinking through its linguistic and conceptual slippages and their engagements with the discourse that emerges out of and indeed energizes the otherwise bland, monolithic certainties of heterosexuality. Sedgwick attempts to bring out (from the closet, so to speak) the extent to which the discourse of homosexuality – the heterosexual discourse of homosexuality, that is to say, the way that homosexuality is conceived and expressed by so-called 'heterosexuals' – may be read in a text that is apparently concerned with very different matters. And Sedgwick's reading powerfully demonstrates that the discourse of heterosexuality is itself dependent upon that of homosexuality, governed, even defined, by that which it excludes. There is something rather queer, in other words, about being straight.

As well as opening up new ways of reading 'straight' literary texts, then, queer theory – such as recent work by Michel Foucault, Eve Sedgwick, Judith Butler, Leo Bersani, Alan Sinfield, Jonathan Dollimore, Joseph Bristow and others – has begun to challenge our ideas about gender and sexuality by querying (or queerying) the very basis of the categories we use to talk about ourselves, us queers and us straights. Queer theory, that is to say, queers the pitch as far as sexuality is concerned. As a number of theorists have commented, there is something rather curious, rather queer, about the way in which we divide our human and social worlds into two supposedly discrete (if not always discreet) categories. Of all the possible categories that are available to us to define ourselves and others – our wealth (or lack of it), class, height, hair colour, dietary preferences, shoe size, baldness or otherwise, political or religious beliefs, aesthetic preferences, choice of holiday destination or MP3 player – the one that our culture has fixed upon to define us most profoundly, in some respects perhaps even beyond that of ethnic origin, race or skin colour, is that of sexual preference, the sex of the person whom we desire. This is the case not least because, as Leo Bersani remarks, 'Unlike racism, homophobia is entirely a response to an internal possibility' (Bersani 1995, 27).

In his history of homosexuality, David Halperin observes that 'it is not immediately evident that differences in sexual preference are by their very nature more revealing about the temperament of individual human beings, more significant determinants of personal identity, than, for example, differences in dietary preference' (Halperin 1990, 26). The comment invites us to imagine a world, or a society, in which one's identity would be defined by one's choice of food, a world in which, say, vegetarians would regularly be discriminated against in terms of their careers (they would not be allowed to join the army, for example, for fear that they might seduce others into vegetarianism); would be subject to physical and verbal abuse while walking quietly in the streets of our cities (veggie-bashing, it would be called, and would be caused by veggiephobia, the fear of being forced to eat carrots or green beans or even of finding out that one is, deep down, oneself a vegetarian); would be disqualified from adopting children because of the fear that such children would lack a balanced diet in the crucial early years of their physical and mental development; would often socialize in special veggie bars and clubs generally avoided by carnivores; and would be, or would be thought to be, immediately recognizable by the way they walked and the way they talked, by their clothes, their hairstyles, and their general demeanour. This imagined world might remind us of the pervasiveness and power of sexual preference as a determiner of our everyday lives. Indeed, the absurdity of this fictional scenario brings home how deeply embedded in our thinking is our definition of gender and sexual preference. Michel Foucault makes the point forcefully in an interview when he remarks that 'ever since Christianity, the West has not stopped saying: "To know who you are, find out about your sex." Sex has always been the focal point where, besides the future of our species, our "truth" as human subjects is tied up' (Foucault 1980a, 3). In this context we might think about how odd it is, how queer, that our social worlds and our social prejudices are organized around a choice – the sex of our sexual partners – which in some ways is similar to choices about eating, or not eating, meat.

One of the major projects of queer theory has been to examine the ways in which, in fact, the categories of desire by which we regulate our social and sexual worlds are not as fixed and immutable, not as 'natural' and self-evident, as we might like to think. Indeed, according to the influential argument of Michel Foucault, our ideas about hetero- and homo-sexuality are a function of the 'invention' of homosexuality in the late nineteenth century. While the precise historical configurations of any such 'invention' have been challenged by historians of sexuality, many of whom see the late seventeenth and eighteenth centuries as the crucial period of redefinition and 'crystallization' (see Sedgwick 1985, 83; Glover and Kaplan 2000, 91–3), Foucault's argument has been highly important in the development of queer theory. But it is crucial to understand that when Foucault claims that homosexuality was invented at a particular time in the recent past he is not arguing that men did not love, desire and have sex with other men, or women with women, before that time. Rather, he is suggesting that the apparently unequivocal distinction between *being* homosexual or *being* straight – the sense that you *are* one or the other, and the sense that *who you are* is defined by that distinction – is an aspect of sexual relationships and personal identity which has developed only very recently within certain institutional and discursive practices. According to Foucault, during the nineteenth century a series of shifts in the discourses of medicine, law, religion, politics and social analysis combined to produce the homosexual as a discrete identity. In particular, while medicine began to define a certain type of behaviour and certain desires as characteristic of a certain 'type' of person (the so-called 'invert'), the law redefined sexual acts between men as 'gross indecency' (an offence instituted in the so-called 'Labouchère Amendment' added to a law passed in the United Kingdom in 1885 which was primarily concerned with the regulation of prostitution). The new law criminalized sex between men (it simply ignored sex between women), by contrast with an older law, against 'sodomy', which covered certain forms of sex between men and women as well as various other kinds of 'unspeakable' acts, sexual and otherwise. Thus, for example, Jeffrey Weeks points out that nineteenth-century society imprisoned together atheists, the mute and sodomites, suggesting a strange homology of criminality (Weeks 1998, 693). As a result, the homosexual comes to be seen, within certain legal and medical discourses, as a particular type of person, as having a particular identity. In an eloquent and forceful passage from *The History of Sexuality: An Introduction*, Foucault argues as follows:

> As defined by the ancient civil or canonical codes, sodomy was a category of forbidden acts; their perpetrator was nothing more than the juridical subject of them. The nineteenth-century homosexual became a personage, a past, a case history, and a childhood, in addition to being a type of life, a life form, and a morphology, with an indiscreet anatomy and possibly a mysterious physiology. Nothing that went into his total composition was unaffected by his sexuality. It was everywhere present in him: at the root of all his actions because it was their insidious and indefinitely active principle; written immodestly on his face and body because it was a secret that always gave itself away. It was coinsubstantial with him, less as a habitual sin than as a singular nature . . . Homosexuality appeared as one of the forms of sexuality when it was transposed from the practice of sodomy onto a kind of interior androgyny, a hermaphrodism of the soul. The sodomite had been a temporary aberration; the homosexual was now a species. (Foucault 1981, 43)

Foucault is arguing that within 'the ancient civil or canonical codes' homosexuality as an *identity* is more or less invisible before the mid to late nineteenth century. In other words, in the context of thinking about, say, Shakespeare, asking the question of whether or not he was homosexual is, in effect, an anachronism, inappropriate to the specific ways in which sexuality and sexual identity were constructed, experienced and defined in the late sixteenth and early seventeenth centuries.

The notion of the historically and culturally constructed nature of sexuality, the idea that sexualities are differently defined and differently experienced at different times, is taken one step further by the influential theorist of gender and sexuality Judith Butler. For Butler, gender and sexuality are performative, rather than fixed or determined by biology or 'nature': gender identity 'is performatively constituted by the very "expressions" that are said to be its results' (Butler 1990, 25). 'I'm queer' is not simply a descriptive statement but makes something happen: it not only states but affirms and even creates the identity it refers to. According to this argument, in fact, the more of a man or the more of a woman you are, the more obviously your masculinity or femininity is a performative construct, the more overtly it is acted out. Both gender and sexuality, for Butler, are always kinds of drag acts so that theatrical drag acts play out the implicit logic of sex and gender identity according to which our lives are, more generally, determined. As an example of such a performance of gender and sexuality Butler reminds us of the title of Aretha Franklin's hit 'You Make Me Feel Like a Natural Woman'. Butler remarks that on first sight the line seems to be affirming the notion of the naturalness of gender and sexuality: the singer's love for the man makes her a *natural* woman. Butler comments that the line seems to indicate that 'there is no breakage, no discontinuity between "sex" as biological facticity and essence, or between gender and sexuality' (Butler 1991, 27). But when we think a little more carefully we see that this naturalness is both something that is *learnt* or *produced* ('you *make* me feel . . .'), and something that is *imitated* ('you make me feel *like* . . .'). Playing out and articulating the performative logic of gender and sexuality, Aretha Franklin is singing about it, wittingly or not, as a kind of 'heterosexual drag' (28). This, for Butler, is indicative of the way that all sexualities – homo-, hetero-, bi- and other – are forms of drag, performances of sex and of gender.

'Shakespeare', declares Harold Bloom, 'largely invented us' (Bloom 1994, 40). One way of understanding this claim would be in relation to the cultural construction of gender and sexuality. Reading Shakespeare can help us to think about ways in which sexuality is an unstable site of conflict and transgression, historically contingent, mobile, a performance. Writing at a time before categories of homo- and heterosexual desire had been institutionalized, medicalized, rigidified and policed, Shakespeare's writing questions what it means to be a man or a woman, and what it means, as a man and as a woman, to desire men and to desire women. We might end by thinking about Shakespeare's sonnet 20, a key text in debates surrounding his representations of sexuality and sexual identity: in this sonnet, as Bruce Smith comments, 'for the poet, for his readers, and presumably for the young man', issues of love and sexuality 'reach a crisis' (Smith 1994, 249). Here is a poem that has fascinated (and indeed horrified) readers and critics through the centuries, a poem by a man addressed to a man, his 'master mistress', which thinks about masculinity and femininity and thinks about the different ways in which they inhabit male and female bodies, thinks about how homo- and hetero-eroticism are performed, played out in language. It is a poem that both plays on stereotypes of gender and sexuality (including misogyny) and, at the same time, disorients them, queers them, plays with the idea of a 'natural' gender and sexuality but also with the idea of the constructedness of such identities. This is a natural wo/man: a man who is all man, by nature 'pricked out', but who is at the same time, curiously, queerly, female, his 'woman's face' by 'nature' 'painted':

> A woman's face, with nature's own hand painted,
> Hast thou, the master mistress of my passion –
> A woman's gentle heart, but not acquainted
> With shifting change, as is false women's fashion;
> An eye more bright than theirs, less false in rolling,
> Gilding the object whereupon it gazeth;
> A man in hue all hues in his controlling,
> Which steals men's eyes and women's souls amazeth.
> And for a woman wert thou first created,
> Till nature as she wrought thee fell a-doting,
> And by addition me of thee defeated,
> By adding one thing to my purpose nothing.
> But since she pricked thee out for women's pleasure,
> Mine be thy love, and thy love's use their treasure.

Further reading

Eve Kosofsky Sedgwick's books *Between Men* (1985), *The Epistemology of the Closet* (1991) and *Tendencies* (1994) present inaugural and highly influential accounts of queer theory and homosocial and homosexual desire, focusing on a series of (mainly) nineteenth- and twentieth-century texts. The opening two chapters of the groundbreaking *Between Men* offer a good starting point. Alan Sinfield's brisk, polemical and entertaining books *Cultural Politics – Queer Reading* (1994) and *The Wilde Century: Effeminacy, Oscar Wilde and the Queer Moment* (1994) provide good accounts of many of the ideas encountered in this chapter. Both Nikki Sullivan's *A Critical Introduction to Queer Theory* (2001) and Donald E. Hall's *Queer Theories* (2003) offer good short introductions to the field. A more detailed and scholarly discussion of queer sexuality in Renaissance England is Bruce Smith's *Homosexual Desire in Shakespeare's England* (1994). For a thought-provoking study of nineteenth-century US literature in this context, see Scott S. Derrick, *Monumental Anxieties* (1997). Correspondingly, for a study of 'effeminate England' since 1885, see Joseph Bristow (1995). For a brilliant and often excoriating examination of some of the presuppositions and prejudices surrounding cultural representations of homosexuality (including those of 'queer theorists' themselves), see Leo Bersani's *Homos* (1995). Lee Edelman's *No Future: Queer Theory and the Death Drive* (2004) presents a powerful and provocative analysis of queer ethics, political and culture. For an important recent account of the historicism of queer theory and the history of homosexuality, see Halperin, *How to Do the History of Homosexuality* (2002). Noreen Giffney and Myra Hird, ed., *Queering the Non/Human* (2008), is an impressive and often thought-provoking collection of essays on everything from starfish to nanotechnology. The 'Queer Theory' page at theory.org.uk (www.theory.org.uk/ctr-que1.htm) is also a useful resource.

25. Suspense

In a moment, we shall say something that may be rather shocking. In the meantime, we propose to describe two kinds of suspense, resolved and unresolved. 'Resolved' suspense is usually associated with thrillers, detective stories, Gothic novels, tales of mystery and the supernatural, and romances. The Italian novelist and literary theorist Umberto Eco uses the term 'closed texts' for such narratives, as contrasted with 'open texts' which leave the reader in doubt or uncertainty (Eco 1979). In closed texts, the murderer is found, the mystery resolved, the ghost exposed as a mechanical illusion, or the lovers are able to consummate their love. In these cases, suspense relies for its resolution on the revelation of a secret or secrets. Resolved suspense can also be created by delaying an event that we know will happen. This is especially clear in examples from cinema. We feel certain that the woman behind the shower curtain cannot escape the raised dagger of the psycho-killer, but for a few seemingly endless moments the fulfilment of this expectation is delayed. Similarly, in *Fatal Attraction* (1987) the pet rabbit is never going to avoid the boiling pot, and in *Silence of the Lambs* (1991) it is only a matter of time before Hannibal the cannibal lives up to his name and gets his unjust dessert. Here suspense is not so much created by a hermeneutic gap, by the reader's ignorance, as by our expectation of an event which is delayed: we are pretty sure *what* is going to happen, we just don't know *when*. These are kinds of narrative suspense, then, that can be defined in terms of expectation, delay and resolution.

One of the most notorious instances of literary suspense is Henry James's novella *The Turn of the Screw* (1898). In this story, the reader's expectation of an ending is screwed to an excruciating pitch of tension (the story is about suspense itself, as its title might indicate). The suspense of this haunting story rests largely on whether it is about actual ghosts and real evil, or is simply a psychological case-study of a disturbed mind. Critics have tended to argue for one reading or the other. Recently, however, critics have recognized that the choice of interpretation – the choice, finally, of which story we think we are reading – is irresolvable. As Roslyn Jolly comments, 'critics have become increasingly aware that the irresolvability of the tale's ambiguity puts on trial their own readerly skills and assumptions about meaning in narrative' (Jolly 1993, 102). Indeed, critics have realized that this uncanny and unsettling suspense of interpretation is itself part of what makes the story so terrifying: *The Turn of the Screw* is *suspended* between two mutually exclusive readings. While the tale builds up to an extraordinary pitch of narrative suspense, our sense of what happens at the end of the story may never finally be resolved. James manages to exploit a fundamentally ambivalent narrative structure (the story is told by the governess herself, so there is no one to tell us whether or not she is mad), and to 'end' his story in a kind of *open* suspense, a suspense without end. In particular, James continually provides us with pointers or markers to a final resolution, with suggestions of ghosts, telepathy and evil on the one hand, and of madness on the other, making us wait for a final resolution of ambiguities which never arrives. In Chapter 9, for example, the governess says of the two children, Miles and Flora, that 'There were moments when, by an irresistible impulse, I found myself catching them up and pressing them to my heart' (131). The sentence foreshadows in a suspenseful and undecidable way the extraordinary ending of the story, where the governess does, literally, 'catch' Miles: 'I caught him, yes, I held him – it may be imagined with what a passion' (198). In both cases, however, the *force* of this catching – how forceful it is, and how conscious or rational, what its intention is – is suspended. Is the governess protecting Miles or smothering him? We are left, then, in a state of hermeneutic suspense, of interpretative uncertainty – unable to know, finally, how to read James's story. Suspense, in this case, is open. Critics use various terms to describe suspenseful effects in reading: ambiguity, ambivalence, equivocality, indeterminacy, undecidability, uncertainty, aporia, gap, hiatus. All of these words may be applied to the effects of suspense achieved by James's story.

In addition to such narrative suspense, effects of suspense can be produced on a more local and less melodramatic scale by aspects of syntax and versification, by the very language of the text. James, in fact, is famous for a peculiarly suspenseful sentence structure which complements the intensity of narrative suspense in stories such as *The Turn of the Screw*. The story opens in the form of a 'frame narrative': a group of people get together to tell stories, one of which is that of the governess. Here is the opening sentence of the story:

> The story had held us, round the fire, sufficiently breathless, but except the obvious remark that it was gruesome, as, on Christmas eve in an old house, a strange tale should essentially be, I remember no comment uttered till somebody happened to say that it was the only case he had met in which such a visitation had fallen on a child. (81)

Not only is this sentence *about* suspense – the suspense of being 'held' by a story, the holding of breath and the withholding of comments – but it is also syntactically structured by suspense. The final word, 'child', is the kernel of the sentence, its centre, but the word is withheld until the end. Before that, the sentence develops through multiple subclauses and syntactical digressions. Henry James's prose, then, the syntax of his sentences, is highly suspenseful.

The Turn of the Screw turns on suspense – indeed turns, self-reflexively, on the very idea of 'turns'. Chapter 9, again, is exemplary. The governess is reading Henry Fielding's *Amelia* alone at night: 'I found myself, at the turn of a page and with his spell all scattered, looking straight up . . .' (133). She leaves her room and walks into the hall, where at 'the great turn of the staircase' (134) she sees, for the third time, the ghost of Peter Quint. The chapter ends with a description of this ghost disappearing into 'the silence itself': 'I definitely saw it turn, as I might have seen the low wretch to which it had once belonged turn on receipt of an order' as it disappears 'into the darkness in which the next bend was lost' (135). The 'next bend' may be in the darkness of the staircase, but it is also the next chapter of the story, the dark bend or turn of narrative. It is not only the governess, then, who sees or hallucinates a ghostly presence in the turns: our own reading is suspended on the turns of the narrative.

Verse also relies on turns. The fact that the word 'verse' comes from the Latin *vertere*, 'to turn', might alert us to the way in which verse is wedded to the turns of line endings, suspenseful places of ghostly pausation. In addition to the suspense as we turn from one line to the next, verse produces its own forms of suspense through the exploitation of the possibilities of rhythm. Comparatively rudimentary verse-forms, such as those of nursery rhymes and ballads, for example, are notable for the way in which they generate suspense through rhythmical repetition, by building into the poetry the expectation of a repetition. The opening to the traditional Scottish ballad 'Sir Patrick Spens' is one such example:

> The King sits in Dumferling toune,
>   Drinking the blude-reid wine:
> O whar will I get a guid sailor,
>   To sail this schip of mine?

Much of the force of this powerfully haunting poem (one that, in many ways, anticipates such pseudo-medieval ballads as Coleridge's 'The Ancient Mariner' and Keats's 'La Belle Dame sans Merci') is achieved through the regularity of its metrical arrangement (the regular four-beat first line and three-beat second line, which continues throughout the poem). Together with the regular rhyming of lines two and four of each stanza, the prosody of the poem adds up – in the expectation and fulfilment of rhythmical suspense – to one of the most compelling of its pleasures.

Effects of rhythmical suspense are also explored in more intricate ways by poets such as Thomas Hardy. Hardy's poetry is notable not least for the wide range of its verse-forms. 'Neutral Tones' (written in 1867, first published in 1898) enacts various effects of suspense through rhythm:

> We stood by a pond that winter day,
> And the sun was white, as though chidden of God,
> And a few leaves lay on the starving sod;
>   —They had fallen from an ash, and were gray.
>
> 5 Your eyes on me were as eyes that rove
> Over tedious riddles of years ago;
> And some words played between us to and fro
>   On which lost the more by our love.
>
> The smile on your mouth was the deadest thing
> 10 Alive enough to have strength to die;
> And a grin of bitterness swept thereby
>   Like an ominous bird a-wing . . .
>
> Since then, keen lessons that love deceives,
> And wrings with wrong, have shaped to me
> 15 Your face, and the God-curst sun, and a tree,
>   And a pond edged with grayish leaves.

While not strictly regular, the rhythm of the first three lines of each stanza is more or less regular, consisting of four sets of one or two weak (or 'short') [.] stresses followed by one strong (or long) one [—]: We stōod | bý à pōnd | thàt wīn | tèr dāy. The final line of each stanza, however, lacks one 'foot', having only three combinations of weak and strong stress: Théy hàd fallēn | fròm àn ash, | ànd wère grāy. The regularity of the first three lines of each stanza is disappointed. This gives an effect of blankness, of something missing, of incomplete suspense. This effect is related to the theme of the poem, its sense of blank hopelessness: the poem is concerned with something missing, a lack, a loss, which is inexpressible. This, then, is just one example of the many ways in which poetry is able to create effects of suspense in rhythm such that the *form* of the poem is inseparable from its *content*.

As we have already suggested, poetry can also exploit line endings for effects of suspense. The neoclassical poetry of Alexander Pope, for example, plays on the suspenseful formalities of rhyming couplets. The following lines from Pope's poem 'An Essay on Criticism' (1711) generate suspense through rhyme, rhythm and antithesis:

> *True wit* is *Nature* to Advantage drest,
> What oft was *Thought*, but ne'er so well Exprest . . .
> (lines 297–8)

The fact that the whole of Pope's long poem is in the form of rhyming couplets means that the first line creates the expectation of a second line which will end in the rhyme 'est'. And we are not disappointed. The second line both develops and explains the first, creating an analogy between thought and nature on the one hand, and clothing and expression on the other, to define 'true wit'. Owing to the regularity of the verse-form, the first line creates an expectation of such an answering line and, although the lines are end-stopped (they do not continue syntactically from one line to the next), they produce the expectation of such an answer: the sense of the first line is suspended until its completion in the next.

Writing almost a century later, William Wordsworth also exploits the suspenseful effects of verse, in particular of line endings, but does so very differently. Consider, for example, 'A Slumber did my Spirit Seal' (1800):

> A slumber did my spirit seal;
> I had no human fears:
> She seemed a thing that could not feel
> The touch of earthly years.
>
> 5 No motion has she now, no force;
> She neither hears nor sees,
> Rolled round in earth's diurnal course
> With rocks and stones and trees.

This poem is usually understood to be about a young girl who has died, and critics usually relate it to other poems which were written by Wordsworth at about the same time and which concern a girl named Lucy. The speaker appears to be lamenting not only the girl's death, but also his own ignorance, the fact that he remained unaware that she might die when she was alive. Unlike Pope's poem in almost every other respect, Wordsworth's is similar in that most of its lines are end-stopped. Crucially, however, line three is run on or enjambed: there is no punctuation after the word 'feel', and the next line is required for syntactical completion. In fact, the end of this line exploits not only syntactical but also hermeneutic suspense. After all, it would be possible to read line three as syntactically complete: 'She seemed a thing that could not feel'. But this produces a very different meaning from what we find if we continue to the next line – 'She seemed a thing that could not feel / The touch of earthly years.' There is a significant difference between not being able to feel, and not being able to feel 'the touch of earthly years'. The first possibility gives us the sense that she – like, apparently, the speaker, in line one – is anaes-thetized, closed off, to all sensation and all emotion. The second possibility gives us the sense that this was a young girl who seemed as if she would never grow old or die. What the poem achieves with this line-break, this turn, is to generate and hold both meanings in suspense. While the latter is no doubt the 'correct' reading – we cannot simply ignore line four, once we have read it – the apparent completion offered by line three in isolation remains to haunt this latter sense.

As with our discussion of Henry James, we find that examples of resolved or closed suspense can in fact be read as open – as examples of the unresolved. Wordsworth's poem prompts a number of suspenseful questions. In the very opening line of the poem, for example, it is not clear whether 'my spirit' sealed a slumber or a slumber sealed 'my spirit': in any case it is very difficult to know what the three words ('slumber', 'spirit', 'seal'), either separately or together, are referring to. Likewise, while we have assumed that the referent of 'she' in line three is a girl, Lucy, the word can also be understood to refer back to 'my spirit' in line one. There is, in fact, no final way of determining which reading is 'correct'. While we may want to choose one reading over the other, we have no way to justify such a choice: the point is undecidable or equivocal. And the difference has significant implications for any reading of the poem. In the first place, while the poem appears to be about the relationship between the speaker and a girl, the equivocal reference of 'she' means that we can no longer be sure that the object of the speaker's interest is a person outside of himself, rather than his own 'spirit'. As Paul de Man comments in his reading of this poem in his essay 'The Rhetoric of Temporality', 'Wordsworth is one of the few poets who can write proleptically about their own death and speak, as it were, from beyond their own graves. The "she" in the poem is in fact large enough to encompass Wordsworth as well' (de Man 1983, 225). Rather differ-ently, it may be that this equivocal reference suggests something very import-ant about mourning itself – that in mourning, the object of our grief is neither simply inside nor simply outside the one who mourns. The suspense of reference in this context might be connected to another of the themes of the poem – closure. The speaker talks of his spirit being 'sealed', of 'she' being untouchable in the first stanza, and in the second of 'she' being without motion, force or sensory perception, 'rolled round' with the earth as if sealed in a grave. This sense of closure may even be reinforced by the end-stopped rhymes of each stanza. In all of these ways, the poem is 'about' a sense of closure – being sealed, enclosed, finished, dead. And yet the closure that the poem so intensively suggests is in dynamic tension with the undecidable suspense of reference – with, indeed, the poem's *meaning*. Far from being closed, in fact, the poem is undecidably suspended. Once we recognize the central importance of the tension between what we have called closed and open suspense in the poem, it becomes available as a means with which to map many of the poem's features. In particular, we might recognize that the poem is suspended by the uncanny gap of time between stanza one and stanza two, that moment outside the poem when 'she' dies, the unspoken, perhaps unspeakable event of a death which at once haunts and generates the poem. Wordsworth's poem thus enacts a drama of suspense, an allegory of closure *and* undecidability.

Ambiguity and undecidability have been central to Anglo-American literary criticism and theory in the twentieth century. One of the most influential works has been William Empson's *Seven Types of Ambiguity* (1930; 3rd edn 1953). In the middle decades of the century, partly as a response to Empson's book, the so-called new critics focused on ambiguity as a major concern of literary texts. More recently, poststructuralist critics have emphasized the notion of undecidability. The difference between new critical ambiguity and poststructuralist undecidability, though apparently minimal, is perhaps fundamental. For the new critics, ambiguity produces a complex but organic whole, a unity wherein ambiguity brings together disparate elements. For poststructuralist critics, by contrast, undecidability opens up a gap, a rift in the text which can never be fully sealed. Undecidability opens the text to multiple readings, it destabilizes the reader's sense of the certainty of any particular reading, and ultimately threatens to undermine the very stability of any reading position, the very identity of any reader (as Søren Kierkegaard remarks, 'the moment of decision is madness'). Suspensions of meaning bypass the reductive and constricting determination of what is now recognized to be the illusion of a single, final, determined 'meaning'. To think in terms of undecidability, however, is not to advocate the equal legitimacy of any and every interpretation: to acknowledge and explore aporias or suspensions of meaning involves the responsibilities of the most thoughtful and scrupulous kinds of reading.

Readers tend to want to resolve suspense: like foreplay, suspense carried on beyond a certain point seems to be undesirable, indeed intolerable. We want answers, and we want them soon. And there are all sorts of ways of terminating suspense, of closing it or resolving it. We can appeal to the notion of authorial intention and try to argue that Wordsworth 'meant' this or that, or we can appeal to 'historical evidence' and try to establish whether Lucy 'really is' the referent of this poem, or in line with the dentistry school of literary criticism to which we referred in Chapter 2, we can simply argue for a single extractable molar of meaning for the text. Rather than immediately attempting to resolve suspense, though, we might think about literary texts as themselves sites of suspense, places where suspense can occur without being closed off, without being finished (in this context we might appeal to Jacques Derrida's idea that 'There is no literature without a *suspended* relation to meaning and reference' (Derrida 1992a, 48). We might consider that it is the function of literary texts to go beyond the trite, the comforting, the easy resolution of suspense, to take us to imagined places where suspense cannot be resolved, where questions are more complex and more challenging than can be reduced to a single determined meaning. In this respect, there are reasons to welcome undecidability, this challenge to our desire to master the text.

Further reading

For a brilliant exploration of Wordsworth's line endings, see Christopher Ricks's 'William Wordsworth 1' (1984). For two fine introductory works on rhythm and metre, see Derek Attridge's *Poetic Rhythm* (1992) and Thomas Carper and Derek Attridge's *Meter and Meaning* (2003). An excellent and imaginative exploration of prosody in terms of the sounds of English poetry is John Hollander's *Vision and Resonance* (1985). On suspense in the sense of ambiguity or undecidability, there is, perhaps, no better place to start than William Empson's classic *Seven Types of Ambiguity* (1953), first published in 1930. On the idea of literature as suspended in relation to meaning and reference, see the interview with Jacques Derrida in his *Acts of Literature* (1992a). A classic argument concerning the 'undecidability' of contending meanings in literary texts is J. Hillis Miller's 'The Figure in the Carpet' (1980). For a rather different approach, see D.A. Miller, ' "Cage aux folles": Sensation and Gender in Wilkie Collins's *The Woman in White*' (1989), which offers a fascinating consideration of the physiological effects of suspense fiction on readers.

26. Racial difference

You might reasonably expect a chapter on racial difference to focus on, for example, William Faulkner's great novel of social aspiration and race prejudice *Absalom, Absalom!* (1936) or Toni Morrison's closely related slave narrative, *Beloved* (1987), or perhaps one of Salman Rushdie's narratives of the Indian diaspora, or Derek Walcott's poetry of Caribbean multiculturalism. Our intention here, however, is to argue that questions of race, slavery and racial violence are everywhere, and that they pervade even the most apparently 'innocent' literary works. In this way we will be guided by the provocative and incisive words of the American poet John Ashbery: 'Remnants of the old atrocity subsist, but they are converted into ingenious shifts in scenery, a sort of "English Garden" effect, to give the required air of naturalness, pathos and hope' (Ashbery, *Three Poems* (1956), cited in Wood 2002, 1).

Charlotte Brontë's *Jane Eyre* (1847) is one of the classic nineteenth-century novels in English. It describes a love affair between the eponymous heroine, a governess, and her aristocratic master, Rochester. The novel ends with the marriage of Jane and Rochester after Jane has become both professionally and economically independent. Jane's struggle for independence marks the novel as centrally engaged with the oppression of women in nineteenth-century England and with the possibility of their liberation from constricting roles of subservience to their male 'masters'. Alongside the question of gender, however, *Jane Eyre* raises other questions. These are questions of racial difference and they will form the focal point of this chapter. Jane and Rochester are unable to marry because Rochester is already married to Bertha Mason, a creole woman from the West Indies. This woman, who is mad, is kept locked up in Rochester's attic. Occasionally she escapes, and at one point attempts to set light to Rochester's bed while he is in it. Finally, in a pyromaniacal frenzy, she sets light to the house and dies in the blaze. Her death leaves the way clear for Jane and Rochester to marry, although not before Rochester is blinded and crippled as he tries to save Bertha from the fire.

While the novel has long been recognized as an exploration and critique of the position of women in nineteenth-century society, more recently critics have begun to see questions of racial and ethnic difference as central to the novel. The delayed recognition of the importance of these questions is telling. As in the English literary tradition more generally, such questions have been marginalized or effaced. They have simply not been seen or have been ignored. Such an effacement is, in fact, inscribed in the novel itself. Indeed, representations of race in *Jane Eyre* may be said to constitute a sort of textual unconscious: like the repressed contents of the Freudian unconscious, they repeatedly return in disguised form. In the following passage, for example, racial and ethnic difference becomes part of the flirtatious courtship ritual of Jane and Rochester. At one point, Jane, the narrator, sees Rochester smile: 'I thought his smile was such as a sultan might, in a blissful and fond moment, bestow on a slave his gold and gems had enriched.' This image of sultan and slave then develops into a whole discourse on slavery and racial otherness:

'I would not exchange this one little English girl for the Grand Turk's whole seraglio—gazelle-eyes, houri forms, and all!'
The Eastern allusion bit me again. 'I'll not stand you an inch in the stead of a seraglio', I said; 'so don't consider me an equivalent for one. If you have a fancy for anything in that line, away with you, sir, to the bazaars of Stamboul, without delay, and lay out in extensive slave-purchases some of that spare cash you seem at a loss to spend satisfactorily here.'
'And what will you do, Janet, while I am bargaining for so many tons of flesh and such an assortment of black eyes?'
'I'll be preparing myself to go out as a missionary to preach liberty to them that are enslaved—your harem inmates amongst the rest. I'll get admitted there, and I'll stir up mutiny; and you, three-tailed bashaw as you are, sir, shall in a trice find yourself fettered amongst our hands: nor will I, for one, consent to cut your bonds till you have signed a charter, the most liberal that despot ever yet conferred.' (197–8)

Ironically, Jane is to gain her financial independence and her freedom from what Rochester calls her 'governessing slavery' (298) when she inherits a fortune derived, we can only assume, from the slave-trade of the West Indies. Moreover, although she seriously contemplates it, she does not finally leave England with another man, St John Rivers, who wishes to marry her and take her with him as a missionary to India. Most importantly, however, this passage presents us with the intersection of the discourses of sexual desire and racial otherness. These discourses organize the novel but do so in a way that the novel itself seems to repress. Both Jane and Rochester figure the racially other as sexually active and even passionate, while at the same time being available for purchase, like goods to be bought in a market. By contrast, Jane herself is repeatedly figured in terms of resisting both her own sexual desires and the financial temptations of Rochester's wealth: her sexuality is governed by self-control and she cannot be bought. The passage also brings together questions of sexuality and gender, race and economics, through its references to slavery. Slavery, the buying and selling of the dehumanized and racially other, is central to the novel's plot in that Jane gains her financial and therefore social independence after inheriting a fortune made in the Caribbean, where slavery had been the main source of wealth. Rather differently, the novel repeatedly figures slavery through metaphors of chains and imprisonment. A few paragraphs after the above quotation, for example, Rochester expresses a desire to imprison Jane when he says that ' "when once I have fairly seized you, to have and to hold, I'll just – figuratively speaking – attach you to a chain like this" (touching his watch-guard)' (299). The expression 'figuratively speaking' denies but at the same time exposes the structure of gender and race relations organizing the novel: it exposes the fact that Rochester is *not* only speaking 'figuratively'. Indeed, the phrase marks a textual anxiety concerning the precise status of slavery in the novel – literal or figurative. And this anxiety is compounded by the fact that while Rochester is flirtatiously threatening Jane with enchainment, incarcerated in his attic, imprisoned in chains, is his wife, the racially other Bertha.

A brief reading of a second passage might clarify some of these issues concerning the novel's representations of race. The first time that Jane and the reader see Bertha is a crucial moment. Jane and Rochester are prevented from marrying by the revelation that he is already married. Rochester tells Jane the truth and, in order to excuse his attempted bigamy, takes her into the attic to look at Bertha:

> In the deep shade, at the farther end of the room, a figure ran backwards and forwards. What it was, whether beast or human being, one could not, at first sight tell: it grovelled, seemingly, on all fours; it snatched and growled like some strange wild animal: but it was covered with clothing, and a quantity of dark, grizzled hair, wild as a mane, hid its head and face. (321)

No longer a woman, Bertha is the other of humanity, unrecognizable as human, a beast with a purely animal physiognomy. Almost invisible, Bertha cannot be seen. Invisibility, as this suggests, and as we observe in our reading of the opening to Ralph Ellison's *Invisible Man* in Chapter 10, above, is the condition of racial otherness. As Henry Louis Gates has commented, 'The trope of blackness in Western discourse has signified absence at least since Plato' (Gates 1984, 315). In this novel, Bertha cannot and must not be seen. Despite (or because of) her invisibility as an individual, Bertha embodies the very idea of difference for Rochester and for the novel itself. Rochester explicitly contrasts Bertha with Jane: 'look at the difference! Compare these clear eyes with the red balls yonder – this face with that mask – this form with that bulk' (322). By contrasting the two women, Rochester makes it clear that Bertha should be understood as the other of Jane. But, as we have observed elsewhere, otherness is a tricky business. If you say that one thing is the opposite of another, you are at the same time asserting their mutual dependence, in that it is pointless to contrast two things from different categories. You would not say that a cricket match is the *opposite* of a submarine, for example, if only because there are no obvious points of comparison. What is being asserted in Rochester's comparison, then, is not only difference but also likeness: in particular, they are both women who are, in different ways, imprisoned, and both are partners for Rochester. Bertha is what Jane is not but *could be*. While it is only opposition that is announced, *Jane Eyre* is haunted by the possibility that Bertha is not simply other to but also, in some ways, identical with Jane.

In these respects, then, *Jane Eyre* articulates how racial otherness is constituted – both absolutely other, non-human, bestial, and at the same time an integral element in what defines racial sameness, in this case Englishness and, or as, whiteness. And it is this ambiguous status of the other (racial or otherwise) that makes it so threatening, so disturbing, so dangerous. This dangerous (racial) other, far from being unusual is, in fact, quite common in canonical works of English literature. Figures of the racially other – more or less threatening, more or less destructive – appear as, for example, the Moor in Shakespeare's *Othello* (*c.* 1602), the Jew in *The Merchant of Venice* (*c.* 1596), Caliban in *The Tempest* (1611), Man Friday in Daniel Defoe's *Robinson Crusoe* (1719), some of Lord Byron's dashing, exotic heroes and anti-heroes, the Malay in Thomas De Quincey's *Confessions of an English Opium Eater* (1822), Heathcliff in Emily Brontë's *Wuthering Heights* (1847), Daniel Deronda in George Eliot's novel of that name (1876), and various figures in the colonial stories and novels of Rudyard Kipling (1865–1936), Joseph Conrad (1857–1924), E.M. Forster (1879–1970) and Graham Greene (1904–91), to name only some of the most famous examples. Far from being a marginal concern of English literature, in fact, racial difference is central.

But the internationalizing of contemporary 'English' literature in and as the literatures of the English-speaking 'world' – in the literatures of (for example) Australia, Canada, the Caribbean, Hong Kong, India, New Zealand, Nigeria, Pakistan, South Africa, Sri Lanka, the USA, the West Indies – has also permanently altered our conception of such 'otherness'. The emphatic multiculturalism of the postcolonial canon suggests, indeed, that the racial, linguistic and cultural 'other' may indeed be conceived as the white Anglo-Saxon writer him- or herself. At the same time, the geopolitical, cultural and racial heterogeneity of postcolonial discourses itself provokes a questioning of the apparently stable, established values of canonicity, with its assumptions of paternity and inheritance, its homogenizing linearity of influence, and its cultural exclusivity.

We have tried to suggest elsewhere in the present book that many of the major developments in literary criticism and theory of the past few years have been associated with what is known as a critique of the subject – with a deconstruction of the stable, coherent and autonomous 'self'. This critique investigates the idea that there is nothing *essential* about the nature of any individual or about the human more generally. It is not for nothing that this critique of the subject and of essentialism has been mounted. Our brief reading of the dehumanization of Bertha in *Jane Eyre* has begun to suggest that Western humanism necessarily defines itself through terms of race, by constructing a racial other which then stands in opposition to the humanity of the racially homogeneous. Such essentializing of race is at once philosophically untenable and very dangerous. Racism is, before anything else, the delusion of essentialism. As Robert Young points out, the invention of modern concepts of 'human nature', together with ideas about the universal nature of humanity and the human mind, occurred during the centuries characterized in the West by colonization, 'those particularly violent centuries in the history of the world now known as the era of Western colonization' (Young 1990, 121). Critics such as Frantz Fanon, Edward Said, Gayatri Spivak and Homi Bhabha have argued that the Western discourse of colonialism is constituted by the other subject – by alterities of race, colour or ethnic origin. Western notions of human identity itself as universal or unchanging may be recognized as a historical construct constituted by the exclusion, marginalization and oppression of racial others.

The institution of Literary Studies is far from free of the discursive marginalization of racial and ethnic others. For example, it was long thought possible for writers and critics to appeal to 'universal' values. A notorious instance of this is a series of comments made by the nineteenth-century politician, literary critic and historian Thomas Babington Macaulay in his *Minute on Law and Education* (1835). This minute, presented to the Committee of Public Instruction for Bengal, was destined to have a decisive influence on the education of the indigenous population in colonial India. Macaulay argues for the teaching of English and against the teaching of Arabic and Sanskrit to the Indian population. His argument relies on assertions concerning the aesthetic value of Western culture:

> I have no knowledge of either Sanscrit or Arabic. But I have done what I could to form a correct estimate of their value. I have read translations of the most celebrated Arabic and Sanscrit works. I have conversed, both here and at home, with men distinguished by their proficiency in the Eastern tongues. I am quite ready to take the oriental learning at the valuation of the orientalists themselves. I have never found one among them who could deny that a single shelf of a good European library was worth the whole native literature of India or Arabia. The intrinsic superiority of the Western literature is indeed fully admitted by those members of the committee who support the oriental plan of education. . . . It is, I believe, no exaggeration to say that all the historical information which has been collected in the Sanscrit language is less valuable than what may be found in the paltry abridgements used at preparatory schools in England. In every branch of physical or moral philosophy, the relative position of the two nations is nearly the same. (Quoted in Said 1983, 12)

While expressing appalling prejudice, this passage appeals to standards of objectivity, academic authority and apparently rational statements about 'intrinsic superiority'. The passage is evidence that, as Frantz Fanon remarks, for the native, 'objectivity is always directed against him' (quoted in Said 1993, 196) – that 'objectivity' is ideological. In Macaulay's statement, such objectivity is, in fact, blatantly ideological in its dependence on judgements of aesthetic value. By their very nature, such statements can *only* be culturally, ethnically and historically specific. To judge the aesthetic standards of one culture by those of another is self-evidently problematic. Judged by the standards of Japanese Noh drama, for example, Shakespeare's plays would be absurdly verbose, unstylized and generally incompetent. And yet the history of Western aesthetics is dominated by precisely such notions of the universality of art.

To end this chapter, we would like to suggest two ways of going beyond such ways of reading and writing. Implicit in our discussion has been the idea that there is a connection between the differences of race and of gender. In this respect, Patrick Williams and Laura Chrisman argue that any 'discussion of ethnicity is always also by implication a discussion of gender and sexuality'.

The reason for this is, not least, that 'Women, as the biological "carriers" of the "race", occupy a primary and complex role in representations of ethnicity . . . and it is women's exercise of their sexuality which is an often unacknowledged major concern underlying such representations' (Williams and Chrisman 1993, 17). In Western literature black women have been doubly effaced. As novels such as Alice Walker's *The Color Purple* (1982) and Toni Morrison's *The Bluest Eye* (1970) make clear, black women are silenced both as black and as female. But it is precisely this doubled otherness which might help us begin to move beyond racial essentialism, beyond the repressive politics of identity. In an attempt to get beyond a constricting notion of identity and of a simple and reductive notion of otherness, Mae Gwendolyn Henderson has argued that black women's writing is 'interlocutionary, or dialogic' owing to their position as 'not only the "Other" of the Same, but also as the "other" of the other(s), [which] implies . . . a relationship of difference and identification with the "other(s)" ' (Henderson 1993, 258–9). The value of this analysis is that it allows us to recognize the plurality of identity, to recognize that any identity is constituted by a multiplicity of positions and differences. Black women's writing, in particular, being marginalized twice over, figuring the other of the other, reinforces a sense of the polymorphic nature of identity. In addition, Henry Louis Gates has argued that all black texts are necessarily 'two toned', or 'double-voiced', that they both engage with white canonical discourse and, at the same time, express a black consciousness. This, for Gates, leads to a discourse which is duplicitous, potentially subversive, one that undermines the universalizing and essentializing tendencies of hegemonic white discourse: 'Black people have always been masters of the figurative: saying one thing to mean something quite other has been basic to black survival in oppressive Western cultures' (Gates 1984, 6).

Our second suggestion for displacing the monolithic and oppressive assumptions about racial difference is the possibility of *reading* otherwise – the possibility of what Edward Said calls 'contrapuntal reading' (Said 1993, 78). A number of critics and theorists have suggested different ways of reading, guided by an acceptance of multiplicity, a questioning of binary oppositions and an affirmation of radical otherness. Said suggests that we might read such texts as Brontë's *Jane Eyre* or Jane Austen's *Mansfield Park* 'with an understanding of what is involved when an author shows . . . that a colonial sugar plantation is . . . important to the process of maintaining a particular style of life in England' (78). Such a reading, a contrapuntal reading, two-toned or double-voiced, cannot ignore the economics of slavery through which Jane Eyre's liberation as a woman is effected.

Further reading

Frantz Fanon's impassioned and politically charged *The Wretched of the Earth* (1967) is the classic work on race, nationalism and decolonization. For good recent discussions of race and culture, see David Marriott, *On Black Men* (2000), and Brian Nero, *Race* (2003). For a valuable and thought-provoking account of racism in relation to the emergence and functioning of the modern nation state, see David Theo Goldberg, *The Racial State* (2002). For a wide-ranging and polemical study of the links between race and sexuality, especially in the context of slavery, see Marcus Wood, *Slavery, Empathy and Pornography* (2002). Much of the most interesting work on race and ethnicity in literature has been that associated with studies of postcolonialism: for a useful handbook that clarifies ideas and issues in the field, see Gina Wisker, *Key Concepts in Postcolonial Literature* (2007). Two important collections of essays are Homi Bhabha, ed., *Nation and Narration* (1990) and Williams and Chrisman, eds, *Colonial Discourse and Post-Colonial Theory* (1993). The work of Gayatri Spivak, who comes at the subject of race and ethnicity from a specifically feminist position, has been particularly influential: see her *In Other Worlds* (1987). For another collection of poststructuralist essays, see Henry Louis Gates, ed., *'Race', Writing and Difference* (1986). Gates's *The Signifying Monkey* (1988) is the most sustained elaboration of his theory of writing and racial difference from the perspective of black writing in the United States. From a more specifically feminist perspective, see Toni Morrison's brief and highly readable *Playing in the Dark: Whiteness and the Literary Imagination* (1993). In a British context in particular, see James Procter's *Dwelling Places: Postwar Black British Writing* (2003) and the useful anthology *Writing Black Britain*, ed. Procter (2000).

27. The colony

Colonialism, postcolonialism, neocolonialism: three *isms* that depend upon the figure of the colony. In the preface to this book we remark that theory – particularly when it takes the form of *isms* – can seem intimidating or simply boring. Deeply desiring to be neither, we also have good theoretical reasons for feeling wary of *isms*. As Martin Heidegger put it: 'Every mere *ism* is a misunderstanding and the death of history' (Heidegger 1967, 60–1). This assertion draws attention to the ways in which *isms* inevitably encourage generalization, abstractness, a lack of critical clarity and of historical awareness. But saying this of course does not make *isms* go away. *Isms* are convenient, as well as deadly. Here are three convenient, if deadly, definitions: 'colonialism' is 'the policy or practice of obtaining, or maintaining hold over, colonies, *esp* with the purpose of exploiting them' (*Chambers Dictionary*); 'postcolonialism' is concerned with what 'occur[s] or exist[s] after the end of colonial rule' (*Shorter OED*); 'neocolonialism' is concerned with the *continuing effects* of colonialism after the end of colonial rule, and thus with a questioning of the break implied by the *post-* of 'postcolonial'. Much *ism*-izing energy has been spent on the distinctions or lack of distinctions between these various terms. For example, the authors of *The Empire Writes Back* (1989) argue that the term 'postcolonial' should be seen as covering 'all the culture affected by the imperial process from the moment of colonization to the present day' (Ashcroft, Griffiths and Tiffin 1989, 2). This definition mingles colonialism and 'postcoloniality', and also mixes itself up with the arguably more rigorous and precise conception of 'neocolonialism' as involving 'the half-hidden narratives of colonialism's success in its continuing operations' (Young 1991b, 3). Rather than engage directly with these various *isms*, we propose in this chapter to try to reflect on them indirectly, by focusing on what is common to them all (the colony) and by considering a series of related topics: language, time, point of view, writing, law, justice and drama.

The word 'colony' itself is suggestive: in etymological terms a patriarchal and agricultural metaphor (Latin *colonia* a colony, from *colonus* a husbandsman, from *colere* to till), 'colony' is, according to *Chambers*, 'a name vaguely applied to a state's dependencies overseas or abroad . . . ; a body of persons settled in a foreign country, or forming a separate ethnic, cultural or occupational group; the settlement so formed; the place they inhabit'. One thing is already clear from this definition: the colony, and all the *isms* it colonizes, has to do with the colonizing power and effects of language itself, with language *as* colonization. There is no concept of the colony in the English language that does not depend on the colonization of English by Latin – which is also to say, the colonization of Latin by English. Correspondingly, we might ask, is US English colonized by British English or is it the other way round? Colonization here, as always, works in two directions: to colonize is, however imperceptibly or insidiously, to be colonized. If, as William Burroughs claimed, language is a virus, this is because it is a colonizer. In particular as 'dependency overseas or abroad' or 'settlement in a foreign country', a colony always involves the imposition of a foreign language; and all the colonialist wars in history (there are perhaps no other) are also wars in and over language. Finally, however, we may suppose that there is no way of thinking about any of these matters *in one's own language* without being already *colonized by* language. Colonization is at the origin: we are always already dependants of language, colonized by one or more languages.

To be 'always already' is to be unsure, among other things, about one's sense of time. In this and other respects, the notion of colony has a strange relation to time. As its etymology indicates, 'colony' is fundamentally a spatial term: originally it has to do with tilling the land. When we think about colonies we think, first perhaps, of space, of the appropriation and exploitation of land. But questions of time are just as important in a (post- or neo-) colonialist context. Indeed, as we indicated a few moments ago, the very terms 'post-' and 'neo-' are temporal, concerned with what comes after or continues to haunt the colony. Literary texts offer especially good illustrations of how the colony deranges and disorders the sense not only of place but also of time. We could consider this, for example, in relation to Conrad's *Heart of Darkness* (1902). On the one hand, there is a clear and irrefutable historical context for the narrative: it is a novel about the European (especially Belgian and British) colonial exploitation of Africa (especially the Congo) in the late nineteenth century. On the other hand, however, and *at the same time*, the novel conveys a particularly strong sense of this journey to the colonial heart of darkness as a journey into another time. As Marlow recounts:

> Going up that river was like travelling back to the earliest beginnings of the world . . . The broadening waters flowed through a mob of wooded islands; you lost your way on that river as you would in a desert, and butted all day long against shoals, trying to find the channel, till you thought yourself bewitched and cut off for ever from everything you had once known – somewhere – far away – in another existence perhaps. (48)

Conrad's novel is both historically specific (it illuminates the barbarity of European colonialism in Africa) and pervasively dreamlike (at once timeless and primordial). Jean Rhys's *Wide Sargasso Sea* (1966) also characterizes the colony as unsettling any 'homely' sense of time, in particular by evoking the strange timelessness of dreaming and trance. For the unnamed Mr Rochester (the colonizer who is also colonized by his time in the West Indies) the unnamed Windward Island, where he and Antoinette spend their honeymoon, is 'quite unreal and like a dream' (49). Indeed his colonial experience as a whole may be described as 'all . . . a nightmare' (76). But the strangeness works in two directions. Thus England in turn is repeatedly evoked in terms of the timelessness of a dream for Antoinette (49, 70). Just as *Heart of Darkness* traces a disturbing, circular structure which returns the narrative, finally, to London as the 'heart of darkness', so Rhys's novel complicates our sense of time in more general narrative terms. Its disordering of temporality has to do, above all, with its status as a prequel to Charlotte Brontë's *Jane Eyre*. Post- but also pre-*Jane Eyre*, it exposes the colonialist dimensions of the earlier novel *before the event*.

Finally, we could consider the example of Chinua Achebe's *Things Fall Apart* (1958). Achebe's novel recounts the rise and fall of a man called Okonkwo, and tells how Christian white men come to colonize and largely destroy the culture and identity of the Igbo tribe to which he belongs. Like *Heart of Darkness* and *Wide Sargasso Sea*, *Things Fall Apart* is temporally deranged and deranging: it is impelled by Achebe's own 'decolonizing' mission of seeking to write an alternative version of Conrad's novel, specifically from the perspective of the *colonized*. Yet Achebe's narrator is obliged to occupy a sort of double-time – at once from the late nineteenth-century time of the novel's action (narrating as if from *within* the Igbo tribe) and from the mid-twentieth-century time of its telling (narrating from a position *outside* the tribe and from a considerable distance in time). Achebe's novel is an extraordinary meditation on the difficulty of saying *when* 'things fall apart', of determining when, for example, colonization happens, or when the colonial becomes post-colonial. This difficulty is marked, above all, in the title of the novel, with its haunting suspension in the present tense, and in the fact that it is a quotation. The phrase 'things fall apart' is taken from W.B. Yeats's 'The Second Coming' (1919), a poem that is inseparable from Christian mythology and inseparable in turn from the colonialist context of the First World War and the Irish Troubles. Achebe's novel, from its title onwards, is written (however critically or ironically) in the language of the Christian colonizer.

If from a literary perspective the twentieth century is 'the age of Kafka', as Harold Bloom asserts (Bloom 1994, 448), Kafka's work is perhaps not the most obvious to turn to for thinking about issues of the colony. Let us, how-ever, consider a short story that may help to dislodge this assumption. 'In the Penal Colony' (*In der Strafkolonie*) was written in October 1914 and first pub-lished shortly after the First World War, in 1919. It is one of Kafka's grimmest and least funny stories. Set in an unnamed penal colony, on an unnamed island, it focuses on a number of unnamed characters and is told – primarily from the perspective of an unnamed 'explorer' – by an uncannily knowledge-able or telepathic third-person narrator. The explorer has been invited by the commandant of the colony to witness the execution of a soldier who has been 'condemned to death for disobedience and insulting behaviour to a superior' (140). The story focuses on the gruesome and terrifying machine that is to bring this execution about, and on the 'officer' whose proud, even sacred, responsibility it is to explain the machine to the explorer and ensure that it does its work. By a characteristically eerie Kafkaesque twist, the officer ends up freeing the prisoner and putting himself to death in his place; the story concludes with the explorer leaving the island on a boat with an unnamed ferryman.

The interest of Kafka's narrative in terms of issues of (post- or neo-) colon-ialism has to do with four related ideas: point of view, writing, law and justice. First, it dramatizes the problem and importance of 'point of view', both in a narratological and also in a more broadly cultural and political sense. It offers a basis for thinking about questions such as: From what perspective or point of view can or should one think about, say, Shakespeare's *Othello* (1604), Austen's *Mansfield Park* (1814), Forster's *A Passage to India* (1924), Rushdie's *Midnight's Children* (1981) or indeed any other literary work that engages with colonial differences? And more broadly, from what point of view does one make ethical and other judgements about other people, other societies and cultures? Kafka's story does this by *exploring* (a word in our critical vocabulary that suddenly takes on a new 'colonizing' dimension) the explorer's dilemma from his own point of view: 'The explorer thought to himself: It's always a ticklish matter to intervene decisively in other people's affairs. He was neither a member of the penal colony nor a citizen of the state to which it belonged' (151). The explorer is a foreigner, a stranger, but he is also described as being 'conditioned by European ways of thought' (155). How should the man respond to the seemingly undeniable 'injustice of the procedure and the inhumanity of the execution' (151)? Kafka's text does not offer any simple answer to this question, focusing instead on the increasingly intolerable suspense of withholding judgement. At the same time the story generates an overwhelming sense of the explorer's unique position and responsibility: he is seen as 'an illustrious foreigner' (155) in a privileged position to pass comment and influence events. Indeed, Kafka's story gives a further, more incisive inflection to the dilemma. For while there *is* judgement and decision within the story (the explorer makes clear his strong disapproval of the machine and the punishment; the officer in turn makes a firm decision to free the condemned man and take his place), the reader is left finally with what is in some respects the most 'ticklish matter' of all, namely: who is the narrator of this story, what point of view does he or she have on everything that goes on in the text, and what, in the light of this, is our own point of view? As Gilles Deleuze and Félix Guattari have observed, 'It is by the power of his non-critique that Kafka is so dangerous' (Deleuze and Guattari 1986, 60). 'In the Penal Colony' dramatizes an extraordinary experience of solitude, by posing the question of point of view as a necessary but radically uncertain experience of *responsibility* for each and any reader. To read the story is to be colonized by this dangerous power.

Second, Kafka's text foregrounds the importance of writing itself, of textuality. One of the continuing controversies within the general area of postcolonialist thinking concerns the theoretical complexity of some of its best-known practitioners. Thus postcolonialist theory is perceived as being 'depressingly difficult' (Williams and Chrisman 1993, ix), above all on account of its seemingly abstract, unworldly focus on 'discourse' and 'textuality'. Edward Said, Gayatri Spivak and Homi Bhabha in particular have come to be seen as what Dennis Walder calls 'the three police officers of the postcolonial' (Walder 1998, 4). In his engaging book *Post-Colonial Literatures in English*, Walder seeks to evade the long arm of the law while trying to keep his sights trained on postcolonial literary works themselves. This is a bold but also risky strategy. As Ania Loomba puts it: 'Many writings on colonial or postcolonial discourse may not expressly privilege the textual, but they implicitly do so by interpreting colonial relations through literary texts alone' (Loomba 1998, 95). As Kafka's story suggests, when it comes to thinking about the colony, there is no getting away from the founding complexity of questions of textuality, from the uncanny character of writing, from the limits of the readable. For law itself is inseparable from textuality, writing, inscription. Moreover, Kafka's story is also a disturbing account of law in terms of different, even mutually unintelligible, incommensurable languages or discourses: different characters speak, read and fail to understand different languages. The punishment for the condemned man in Kafka's story involves a harrow which inserts innumerable needles into the prisoner's body and gradually inscribes in his flesh 'whatever commandment [he] has disobeyed' (144). The officer patiently explains:

> 'there are two kinds of needles arranged in multiple patterns. Each long needle has a short one beside it. The long needle does the writing, and the short needle sprays a jet of water to wash away the blood and keep the inscription clear.' (147)

The words being inscribed in this case are 'HONOUR THY SUPERIORS!' (144). For the condemned man the sentence is unreadable, unknown, until it is literally written on his body, by which time he will be at the point of death, beyond all sense of honour, beyond any sense at all.

Finally, Kafka's story provokes the thought that every colony is a penal colony. Every colony entails the imposition of codes of law, justice and punishment from elsewhere, from back 'home' or from a foreign country. This is indeed a central issue in many colonial or postcolonial novels. Forster's *A Passage to India*, for example, turns on the question of justice and the law, culminating in the drama of the trial scene and the attempt to have Dr Aziz found guilty of attempted rape. Likewise in Rhys's *Wide Sargasso Sea*, everything depends on the colonizing power of 'English law' (see 5, 11, 69) and what Christophine calls the 'damn cold lie' of that English word, ' "justice" ' (94). Similarly, we may recall that *Heart of Darkness* concludes with Marlow's meditation on the idea that Kurtz had 'wanted only justice' (111), while *Things Fall Apart* ends with the self-justificatory cogitations of the District Commissioner who is to write a mere paragraph about what we as readers have spent a book experiencing and who has decided, 'after much thought', to entitle his work *The Pacification of the Primitive Tribes of the Lower Niger* (148). 'Be just': these are the key words of Kafka's brief and terrifying text, 'In the Penal Colony'. The dictum appears, according to the officer, among the papers of the former commandant of the colony. But the explorer cannot read it:

> Now the officer began to spell it, letter by letter, and then read out the words. ' "BE JUST!" is what is written there,' he said, 'surely you can read it now.' . . . [T]he explorer made no remark, yet it was clear that he still could not decipher it. (161)

Issues of law and justice are at the heart of all (post- or neo-) colonial literature. On the one hand, as 'In the Penal Colony' suggests, these issues are always context-specific; they can, and perhaps must, call for a dangerous experience of solitude in any and every reader. The reader is judge: Be just! The reader is put in the impossible position of trying to see from the perspective of both the explorer and the narrator at the same time and, alone, to judge accordingly. On the other hand, such texts also remind us of the extent to which ethical and juridical decisions are determined within a context of specific national and state identities. Thus Kafka's text might lead us to think about the need for a revolution in the very concept of international law, beyond the boundaries of any state or colony. As Jacques Derrida has proposed in *Spectres of Marx*: 'international law should extend and diversify its field to include, if at least it is to be consistent with the idea of democracy and of human rights it proclaims, the *worldwide* economic and social field, beyond the sovereignty of States' (Derrida 1994, 84).

In Plato's philosophical colony, his imagined Republic, mimetic art, including poetry and drama, is to be excluded. Such art is dangerous because it 'waters and fosters' false feelings (Plato 1961, 832): it embodies the uncomfortable truth that imitation is formative. This recalls the idea, proposed at the outset of this chapter, that language and colonization are inextricable. To imitate is to be uncertainly colonized *and* colonizing. We could consider this further in relation to the important essay called 'Of Mimicry and Man: The Ambivalence of Colonial Discourse', by Homi Bhabha, one of the 'police officers' mentioned earlier. Bhabha demonstrates how post-Enlightenment English colonialism is dependent on a logic of imitation or mimicry: the colonized other is obliged to mimic the language, and to varying degrees to imitate the customs, gestures and even dress of the colonizers. This mimicry, however, is never pure: mimicry, Bhabha argues, 'is at once resemblance and menace' (Bhabha 1996, 362). There is a fundamental *ambivalence* in the act of colonial appropriation: the colonizer at once desires and fears that the colonized be like him (or, less frequently, her). Colonial mimicry, in other words, is governed by a logic of what Bhabha describes as 'almost the same, *but not quite*' (361). In order to succeed, colonial appropriation must fail. As Angela Smith describes it, in the context of V.S. Naipaul's *The Mimic Men* and Rhys's *Wide Sargasso Sea*: 'The presence of the colonial other imitating the white male colonizer disrupts the authority of the colonizer's language, and [reveals] an inherent absurdity in the colonial enterprise' (Smith 1997, xviii). The appeal and effectiveness of Homi Bhabha's argument is that it undermines the 'authoritative discourse' (362) of colonialism from within: by imitating this discourse, the colonized subject shows it to be different from itself, never at home with its own inner-most desires.

One of the understated effects of Bhabha's essay is to suggest how import-ant the notions of theatre, acting and drama are for thinking about (post- or neo-) colonialism. Indeed, it encourages us to reflect more broadly on the extent to which personal identity is based on imitation, is inherently theatrical. These are hardly new concerns in the context of literature. Work by critics such as Francis Barker and Peter Hulme (1985) and Paul Brown (1994), for example, has emphasized how deeply Shakespeare's *The Tempest* (1611) is a play about these issues. A play about strange derangements in the experience of time as well as place, and pervasively concerned with questions of leg-itimacy, authority and justice, *The Tempest* is also profoundly engaged with the 'colonial' paradoxes of language, acting and identity. It is a play not least about teaching and mimicry. Just as Prospero is Miranda's 'schoolmaster' (I, ii, 172), so she in turn becomes the teacher of Caliban, the 'slave' whom they find when first coming to the island. In a celebrated exchange near the beginning of the play, she reminds Caliban: 'I pitied thee, / Took pains to make thee speak, taught thee each hour / One thing or other' (I, ii, 355–7). Caliban retorts: 'You taught me language; and my profit on 't / Is, I know how to curse. The red plague rid you / For learning me your language!' (I, ii, 365–7). There are a number of paradoxes in play here. This exchange suggests how thor-oughly language determines who or what we are or might become: there is no escape from the colonizing and mimicking power of language as it annexes one subject (Caliban) after another (Miranda). As the quibble on 'red' and 'rid' intimates, one cannot be rid of what is read, what is read cannot readily be unread: language in *The Tempest* is itself a sort of plague. Caliban's capacity to curse, indeed his very capacity to embody any meaning at all, is an effect of linguistic colonization. Yet his cursing at the same time can only ever be based on a reflection or mimicking of the colonizers and, no doubt, of their own 'innermost desires'. Caliban presents Miranda and Prospero with a disturbing and uncertain mirroring of themselves which nothing in the play can finally efface. This is evident in the very syntax and versification of Prospero's final declaration of recognition regarding Caliban: 'this thing of darkness I / Acknowledge mine' (V, i, 275–6). The inverted syntax and the hesitancy of the enjambment underscore this ambivalent sense of Prospero as not merely owning but also, and paradoxically, *being* 'this thing of darkness'.

As Barker and Hulme have emphasized, *The Tempest* is, in various para-doxical and intractable respects, 'a play imbricated within the discourse of colonialism' (204). It is also, as we have tried to make clear, a play about acting, imitation and mimicry. Finally, we would like to suggest that *The Tempest* is also a kind of colony in itself. Indeed in a sense this is just what every dramatic work is. It establishes itself in a strange time and place of its own, linked to but distinct from the rest of the world: the dramatic work is a site of derangement, mimicry, power and transformation. As Captain Phillip, the Governor of New South Wales, observes, in Timberlake Wertenbaker's *Our Country's Good* (1988): 'A play is a world in itself, a tiny colony we could almost say' (Act 2, Scene 2). Engaged in casting a different and complex theatrical light on that penal colony the British called Australia, *Our Country's Good* is also, like any other dramatic work, strangely resistant to being seen merely as a representation or part of the world in which it is set. In its very title, like Shakespeare's *The Tempest* or *A Midsummer Night's Dream*, it establishes a peculiar colony, it 'gives to airy nothing / A local habitation and a name' (*A Midsummer Night's Dream*, V, i, 16–17).

Further reading

For a good introductory book on the literary in particular, see Justin Edwards's *Postcolonial Literature* (2008). On the critical side, Nicholas Harrison's *Postcolonial Criticism* (2003) is original, thought-provoking and extremely good in its expositions. Much valuable material is available in anthologies such as Ashcroft, Griffiths and Tiffin, eds, *The Post-Colonial Studies Reader* (2nd edn, 2006) and Williams and Chrisman, eds, *Colonial Discourse and Post-Colonial Theory* (1993). For two excellent introductory works, see Ania Loomba's *Colonialism/Postcolonialism* (1998) and Robert Young's *Postcolonialism: A History* (2001). Loomba is particularly stimulating for the emphasis she gives to how far issues of gender and sexuality are implicated in (post- or neo-) colonialism. Young provides more detailed coverage of some of these issues in his earlier book *Colonial Desire: Hybridity in Theory, Culture and Race* (1995). Related to issues of gender and sexuality (and indeed apposite in the context of the tacitly homoerotic dimensions of Kafka's 'In the Penal Colony'), increasing critical attention has recently been given to the links between the colony and queerness. On this, see, for example, Christopher Lane's challenging but fascinating *The Ruling Passion: British Colonial Allegory and the Paradox of Homosexual Desire* (1995), Yonatan Touval's playful and thought-provoking essay on *A Passage to India*, 'Colonial Queer Something' (1997) and the very useful collection *Postcolonial Queer*, ed. John C. Hawley (2001). For a couple of important but 'advanced' works in the general field, see Gayatri Chakravorty Spivak's *A Critique of Postcolonial Reason* (1999) and *The Pre-Occupation of Postcolonial Studies*, ed. Afzal-Khan and Seshadri-Crooks (2001). For an excellent general study of deconstructive thinking in relation to 'the colony', see Michael Syrotinski's *Deconstruction and the Postcolonial* (2007). Finally, Edward Said's work on (post- and neo-) colonial issues is both very accessible and highly influential: his most important books are *Orientalism* (1978) and *Culture and Imperialism* (1993).

28. Mutant

We became hominid about five million years ago and 'human' in the sense of *homo erectus* about three million years later. *Homo sapiens*, though, only developed about 30–40,000 years ago. Why it was that our genetic cousins, the Neanderthals, died out just a few thousand years after the arrival of *homo sapiens*, is one of evolution's enigmas. 'Wherever humans advanced,' Henry Gee explains, 'Neanderthals retreated.' In what he calls 'a sudden spasm',

> humanity (the winners) acquired all the external trappings we think of as defining our own tribe. The Neanderthals, in contrast, just pottered around, doing the same kind of timeless nothing-in-particular they'd done for 300,000 years, for all the world like an extended episode of Winnie-the-Pooh (only with real Heffalumps). (Gee 1996, 38)

Just think of it, that could be us: a world of endless honey-pots and Pooh-sticks, with only Heffalumps and Eeyore's chronic depression to worry about, and with just Tigger, Piglet, the god-like Christopher Robin and a few others for company.

Since humans won out, though, things have tended to be a little more complicated, humans being what they are. But what are human beings? What is it like to be human? We don't ask this just because we belong to that species known as academics. Instead it is an inevitable question for anyone who calls herself a human being. In this chapter, we want to look at what it means to be human, but also at what it means to be a mutant or a monster, and to discuss ways in which literature is bound up with these questions. Literature has had a crucial role in configuring the nature and limits of the human. Beginning with Beowulf (*c.* 1000), English literature is a history of monsters. We could think, for example, about the extent to which the literary canon is strewn with dehumanized or otherwise mutated people. Samuel Beckett writes plays that feature disembodied voices, people that spend their time crawling in mud, that live in dustbins or that are just mouths. Wallace Stevens is interested in what he calls the 'inhuman person' (in 'Gigantomachia'), and W.B. Yeats yearns to be a mechanical bird of hammered gold in 'Sailing to Byzantium' (1927). In *Women in Love* (1921) D.H. Lawrence talks repeatedly about his characters 'lapsing out' (for example Lawrence 1960, 48, 199) and all four of the main characters voice a 'grudge against the human being': for Ursula in particular, 'that which the word "human" stood for was despicable and repugnant' (275). Thomas Hardy is impelled to set the human dramas of *The Return of the Native* (1878) against the inhuman geological timescale of Egdon Heath, and the passions and betrayals of *The Woodlanders* (1887) against grotesquely anthropomorphized woodlands. Wordsworth risks scorn by recording the apparently dehumanized, crazed babblings of an idiot boy (in 'The Idiot Boy' (1798)), and becomes strangely fixated by the figure of the leech gatherer, a figure like a 'huge Stone' or a 'Sea-beast', in 'Resolution and Independence' (written 1802). The seventeenth-century poet George Herbert wants to be a tree ('I read, and sigh, and wish I were a tree': 'Affliction I' (1633)). Shakespeare mixes up humans with fairies in *A Midsummer Night's Dream* (1596), spirits and the misshapen monster Caliban in *The Tempest* (1611), and presents us with 'inhuman' characters in plays such as *Richard III* (1592–3), *The Merchant of Venice* (1598) and *Othello* (1604). Western literature as a whole can seem to bulk up like a vast mutation out of the animal, vegetable, astral, bestial, petrific, spirit and parahuman transformations that are recounted in Ovid's *Metamorphoses* (1 BC) and Apuleius's *The Golden Ass* (second century AD).

To study literature is necessarily to engage with the mutant. 'Mutant', from the Latin for 'change', is essentially bound up with inessentiality, with mutability, and with otherness. Contemporary literature in particular is especially concerned with variations on the mutant. But what is it about biotechnology and nanotechnology, about eugenics and genetic engineering, the cyborg and the robot, about monsters and mutants and their interactions with people that is at once so compelling and so terrifying? 'We are all chimeras,' Donna Haraway portentously declares in her influential feminist 'Cyborg Manifesto' (1985). Twentieth-century humans, she asserts, are 'theorised and fabricated hybrids of machine and organism; in short we are cyborgs' (Haraway 2000, 70). What is this fascination with the human as (also) other, this yearning to *be* other, to be unthinking or animal, hybrid or cyborg, mechanical or mutant, virtual, immutable, stony, inhuman, or dead?

In this chapter we would like to explore the workings of such compulsions and terrors in the context of literature and other so-called 'humanities' subjects, and the fascination that the limits of the human seem to hold for humans. Literature is, above all, about the human, about what it means to be human, and therefore about the non-human, about what it might mean not to be human. Literature allows us to think the limits of the human, even to unthink our often unthinking attachment to notions of the human and humanity. Finally, literature itself may be conceived as a monstrous or mutant discourse, a humanism that is also inhuman, alien. In each of the texts mentioned above, there seems to be an engagement with the human that is expressed in terms of a fascination with the inhuman, or with a human becoming non-human, ahuman, abhuman or parahuman. As our reference to biotechnology, nano-technology, genetics and so on suggests, there is a peculiarly millennial, peculiarly topical dimension to these questions. This is perhaps most clearly evident in cinema, with its devotion to mutant, computerized, cyborg or alien beings such as the Terminator (a creature recently mutated into the 'real life' Governor of California, the 'Governator'), ET, Blade Runner or Robocop, those appearing in *Star Trek, Star Wars, Close Encounters, Alien, Men in Black* and *The Matrix* (in all their various mutations), as well as those that have morphed into familiar figures from countless Frankenstein remakes, vampire and horror flicks, and gothic comic books or 'graphic novels'. In all of these movies, Hollywood plays out a cultural desire for and fear of the parahuman and non-human, of the 'invasion of the body snatchers', the invasion of the boundaries of the human: each of the films mentioned presents a battle between the human and the non- or para- or quasi- or post-human. And in each case, human will and imagination, feeling and compassion, is what survives. All of these films attempt, in the end, to confirm the idea that we are each of us unique, sentient and compassionate – that we are 'human'. Despite the state-of-the-art special effects, the hyper-modern and futuristic scenarios, the avant-garde narratives and the balletic digitized violence, films like the *Matrix* series are deeply traditional, deeply concerned with traditional 'human values', with humanity.

But the concern with how humans are made, and with what makes them human rather than mutant or monstrous, is also a preoccupation of contemporary literature. Jeffrey Eugenides's Pulitzer Prize-winning novel *Middlesex* (2002) is a potent and witty example. As if impelled by an attempt to wipe from memory the more sinister reverberations of his eugenic name, Eugenides has produced perhaps the first novel based around Richard Dawkins's theory of the 'selfish gene' (the idea that it's genes that survive, not individuals, or as Eugenides puts it, 'what humans forget, cells remember' (Eugenides 2002,

99)). *Middlesex* tells the story of a genetic mutation – in this case a shared recessive gene, a mutated gene of the fifth chromosome, in the narrator's incestuously married grandparents – which finally results in Calliope's (or Cal's) birth as a hermaphrodite. And the novel is about the genetic, familial, social and political events that lead up to that monstrous birth and the personal and familial consequences that grow out of it. While Eugenides's novel is impressively informed about the biology of genetic mutation, it is also concerned with the social monstering of the mutant, with the different ways in which people respond to those that are different (with rage, desire, disgust, sympathy, rejection, violence, fascination, surgery).

The fascination with the human and the limits of the human in literature is a strange outgrowth of what is called humanism. Humanism involves the belief that human beings have 'unique capacities and abilities, to be cultivated and celebrated for their own sake' (Audi 1999, 397). It entails a resistance to superstitious or religious conceptions of the human on the one hand, and to the reduction of the human to animality or the organic, on the other. 'Man is an invention of recent date', Michel Foucault famously opines in *The Order of Discourse*; but concomitantly it is a 'mutation', he says, that may be 'nearing its end' (Foucault 1970, 386–7). The development of modern humanism, of the idea of 'man' as the ultimate value and as autonomous, individual, self-willing and self-moving, is argued (by Foucault and others) to have occurred between about the sixteenth and the eighteenth centuries. As we have seen (in Chapter 26, above), critics such as Robert Young suggest that the formation of notions of the human and human nature, of 'humanity and the universal qualities of the human mind as the common good of an ethical civilization', coincided with the development of Western colonialism (Young 1990, 121). And it is not by chance that the invention of the human takes place at a time when European imperial expansion makes it necessary to distinguish fundamentally between European colonizers and colonized natives (who can then be appropriated, enslaved, exploited, slaughtered). Indeed, inventions of the human, definitions of 'man' or 'mankind', always seem to be bound up with the exploitation of their others (whether these others are defined in animal, gender, ethnic or racial, class or religious terms). Humanism, the logic of humanity, in other words, is also a dehumanizing discourse. The humanist dimensions of literature are fully manifested only at the end of the eighteenth century when the literary work comes to be associated with an autonomous individual, the 'author', who produces (or 'creates') an 'original' body of 'imaginative' or (as it is now often termed) 'creative' writing. 'Literature was specialized towards *imaginative writing*', Raymond Williams remarks, 'within the basic assumptions of Romanticism', just as the modern sense of 'individual', so central to the new humanism and to the new conception of literature, is linked to the Enlightenment phase of scientific, political and economic thought that finds its full expression in the eighteenth century (Williams 1983, 186, 164). Literary criticism, especially as it has been formulated since the nineteenth century, is often fundamentally humanist in orientation: F.R. Leavis, for example, proclaims that 'there *is* a "human culture" to be aimed at that must be achieved by cultivating a certain autonomy of the human spirit' (quoted in Day 1996, 111). And recent literary theory (including Marxism, psychoanalysis, ecocriticism, structuralism, poststructuralism and deconstruction) has often challenged the anthropocentrism of such criticism precisely with respect to its allegiance to the tenets of humanism.

Literature, like philosophy and religion, is obsessed with what it means to be human – whether it's in the form of Philip Roth's sense of the human as morally stained in *The Human Stain* (2000), or in the form of George Eliot's marvellously intricate meditations on human character and spirit in such novels as *The Mill on the Floss* (1860) and *Daniel Deronda* (1876), or in the form of Jonathan Swift's misanthropic vision of people as bestial, ignorant, irrational Yahoos in *Gulliver's Travels* (1726). But the question of the human is provoked in literary texts above all by means of what is not human, and in post-Romantic literature in particular by the presentation of monsters and mutants. By presenting beings that are specifically and spectacularly *not* human, that are precisely configured as deviations from the human, literary texts allow us to find ourselves, in Wallace Stevens's words, 'more truly and more strange' ('Tea at the Palaz of Hoon' (1921)).

Perhaps the most compelling and most influential of literary monsters is Mary Shelley's creature in her first novel, *Frankenstein* (1818). But *Frankenstein* is also the subject of one of the commonest misapprehensions in English literature, namely that Frankenstein is the name of a monster. This is almost as common as the error of thinking that Wordsworth's poetry is about daffodils, that James Joyce's *Ulysses* is unreadable, or that John Fowles's *The Magus* is a great novel. In fact, though, there are very few daffodils in Wordsworth, *Ulysses* is a wonderful if challenging novel (and a piece of cake compared to *Finnegans Wake*), *The Magus* is verbose, dull, self-regarding and (too often) overrated – and Mary Shelley's Frankenstein is as human as the rest of us. Victor Frankenstein is a young Genovese man of 'distinguished' birth who leaves his family to study at the University of Ingolstadt in Upper Bavaria and there becomes fascinated by the possibility of creating a living being. The monster that Victor Frankenstein creates in fact has no name: this itself is doubtless one reason for the confusion and for the popular idea that Frankenstein is the name of a monster. Naming the monster of Mary Shelley's novel 'Frankenstein', then, is an egregious if understandable mistake.

But it is worth contemplating the error, it is worth thinking about how and why it has been such an important dimension of the novel's reception over the years since its first publication in 1818, why the inventor's name has mutated, morphed, into that of his creature. The error might be seen as valuable and instructive for at least two reasons. In the first place, the idea that 'Frankenstein' is the name of a monster marks an important division between the popular idea of Mary Shelley's novel and the novel itself – the popular idea as disseminated by theatre and film versions, by the appearance of the monster in comic books and cartoons, in advertising and TV comedy sketches, in rock music and on the Internet, rather than any actual reading of Shelley's book. In this popular conception of Shelley's novel, in this common misreading or non-reading of her text, the name 'Frankenstein' often works as shorthand for 'Frankenstein's Monster' or 'Frankenstein's Creature'. In a sense there are two *Frankensteins* – two 'texts' called *Frankenstein* – one being the novel written by Mary Shelley, the other being something like an infection, a virus or outgrowth, a mutant transformation of the novel and its dispersal into popular culture, into popular mythology. The fact that there is a veritable glut of entries (2,666 items are listed) in D.F. Glut's *The Frankenstein Catalogue (Being a Comprehensive History of Novels, Translations, Adaptations, Stories, Critical Works, Popular Articles, Series, Fumetti, Verse, Stage Plays, Films, Cartoons, Puppetry, Radio and Television Programs, Comics, Satire and Humor, Spoken and Musical Recordings, Tapes and Sheet Music featuring Frankenstein's Monster and/or Descended from Mary Shelley's Novel)* (1984) gives an indication of the monstrosity of the novel, its uncontrolled, uncontrollable outgrowth. This leads us to our second point, which is that the misnaming of Shelley's monster nevertheless expresses a truth. It would be true to say that '*Frankenstein* is a monster'. *Frankenstein* – the novel – *is* a kind of mutant or monster, *is*, in a sense, monstrous. Victor refers to his own tale as 'my hideous narration', and it is a tale that Walton, who hears it, describes as one to 'congeal' or 'curdle' the blood (Shelley 1994, 222, 233). One contemporary reviewer even referred to the novel itself as a 'monstrous literary abortion' (quoted in Botting 1995, 5).

The way that the novel is constructed seems in fact to bear an uncanny resemblance to the way that a monster is formed. Both Mary Shelley and Victor Frankenstein are wisely rather unforthcoming about the mechanics of creating a monster (you can find out how to construct a nuclear bomb by surfing the Internet, but you can't find out how to build Frankenstein's monster). All we can gather is that the technique involves the collection of assorted body parts from dead people and their reconstruction and revivification through a (vaguely defined) process of surgery, galvanism and electrification. Victor Frankenstein, we are told, 'pursue[s] nature to her hiding places . . . among the unhallowed damps of the grave'; he 'collect[s] bones from charnel houses' and 'disturb[s], with profane fingers, the tremendous secrets of the human frame'. His laboratory, his 'workshop of filthy creation' is 'a solitary chamber, or rather cell' where he collects materials furnished from the 'dissecting room and the slaughter house' (Shelley 1994, 83). In principle, though less gruesomely, *Frankenstein* is constructed in the same way. In her 1831 Introduction to the novel, Mary Shelley declares that 'everything has a beginning' but that that beginning must necessarily be 'linked to something that went before'. Referring to the Hindu belief that the world is supported by an elephant but that the elephant in turn is supported by a tortoise, Shelley argues that literary 'invention' 'does not consist in creating out of a void, but out of chaos'. Literary creation, in other words, like the creation of a monster or indeed like the theological act of creation, 'can give form to dark, shapeless substances but cannot bring into being the substance itself'. Shelley's comments alert us to the fact that making a literary text is akin to other forms of making, including most pertinently, the making of monsters. In this respect, too, her novel is a kind of monster, mutated or created out of her reading. Shelley draws on contemporary scientific and medical works by Erasmus Darwin, Humphry Davy and others. She alludes to and quotes contemporary poets such as Wordsworth, Coleridge, Goethe, and her lover Percy Bysshe Shelley, as well as Milton and other canonical writers. She engages with works of social, political and moral philosophy by her father William Godwin and her mother Mary Wollstonecraft, and with classical works of historiography by Plutarch and Volney. And before all of these there is the grounding intertext of that great mutant book of creation, the Bible. In other words, just as Frankenstein's creature is constructed out of pieces hewn from dead bodies, the novel is largely constructed – thematically, verbally, conceptually, intellectually – from the huge corpus of Shelley's reading, from the writings of the living and the dead. And the novel comes across, sometimes rather awkwardly, monstrously, like something created out of different genres (the Gothic novel or novels of sensibility, moral or theological disquisitions, novels of ideas), just as it brings together the rational investigation of Enlightenment science with the other of that rationality, the discourse of the superstitious, the monstrous, the Gothic, the uncanny. The Soviet critic M.M. Bakhtin's word for this is 'heteroglossia', the distribution within a text of different discourses or genres or 'voices', while Julia Kristeva, Roland Barthes and others call it 'intertextuality'; our words for it are 'monstrism' and 'mutant'.

This genesis and reception of Shelley's novel, then, offers a dramatic instance of a more general law of literature. Literature, we might say, is a monstrous or mutant form, a mutant discourse. Literary texts don't appear out of nowhere. As we suggest elsewhere in this book, recent literary criticism and theory has been much concerned with intertextuality, with ways in which a poem or novel is constructed out of other cultural and literary discourses, the ways in which texts, ideas and words mutate, ceaselessly evolving and transforming the possibilities of literary forms. This is why literary studies, this unruly, improper discipline, is in fact truly, properly 'interdisciplinary'. The study of literature involves, from the start, a mixing and contamination of disciplines and genres. Literary criticism and theory are themselves mutant, and any significantly 'new' or 'original' critical or theoretical work produces a mutation in the discipline. *Frankenstein* can perhaps also help us to grasp how literary texts are mutated in their reception. Perhaps more virulently than any other nineteenth-century text, the germ of *Frankenstein* has been passed on in endless mutations. Mutation, in this respect, is central to the process that we call canonization: for canonization to occur, a text must be inherited, transformed, responded to, deformed, developed, and imitated – in future texts, in the literary and other traditions to which it gives birth, in being read. Neither Mary Shelley nor Victor Frankenstein is in control of the monsters s/he creates. And this is what is monstrous about the monster in general. It is precisely this fear that we won't be able to control what we create – a fear that Christians project onto God's relationship with his unruly angel, Satan – that defines the contemporary concern with GM products (so-called 'Frankenstein Foods'). And it is a fear expressed in debates surrounding our current crisis of humanity, the development of 'gene therapy' and the suspicion that these technologies will result in the production of genetically modified people (as if we weren't all genetically modified anyway).

Criticism and theory have recently been much taken with mutants and monsters: 'English Studies' sometimes seem to read like an emerging tetralogy, a study or discourse of monsters. But what is a monster? The *OED* – that monster of a book – is, of course, essential reading for students of the monster. The English word 'monster' mutated from the Latin 'monere', to warn, a word related to 'monare', 'to show': the monster is something shown, in other words, as a warning. But the complex of senses in which 'monster' has been used in English, the way in which the word has mutated out of this original sense of warning, is also instructive: the monster is something 'extraordinary, or unnatural; a prodigy, a marvel'; it is 'an animal or plant deviating in one or more of its parts from the normal type . . . a misshapen birth, an abortion'; it is 'an imaginary animal . . . having a form either partly brute and partly human, or compounded of elements from two or more animals'; it is 'a person of inhuman and horrible cruelty or wickedness'; and it is 'an animal of huge size' and by association 'anything of vast and unwieldy proportions'. For Charles Darwin, a 'monstrosity' is 'some considerable deviation of structure, generally injurious to or not useful to the species' (Darwin 1866, 46). All of these senses are useful for a theory of the monster, but what they make clear, finally, is the fact that the monster isn't so much *un*natural as something that comes *out* of nature, something that goes through and beyond nature. The monster is both natural and unnatural, a grotesque development of, an out-growth from or in nature. And it is for this reason that the monster must be abhorred, rejected, abjected, excluded. But let's be clear about this: the monster is excluded, abjected, not because it is entirely other but because it is at least in part *identical* with that by which it is excluded – with, in this case, the human. As Diana Fuss comments in this context, 'sameness, not difference, provokes our greatest anxiety' (Fuss 1996: 3). The monster is both of nature and beyond it: as the *OED* informs us in one citation, 'the vegetable kingdom abounds with monsters'. The monster is, indeed, the most natural thing in the world, and fundamentally allied with birth. Babies are monsters: David Lynch's wonderfully dark *Eraserhead* (1976) knows this, knows what we fear inside (literally) ourselves and in others; the pregnant Desdemona in *Middlesex* knows it too as she 'prepares to meet the creature hidden in her womb' (Eugenides 2002, 123); and 'monstrous birth' is also of course the subject of the play from which the name Desdemona has itself sprouted (see *Othello* 1.3.396).

In the same way, the mutant, the potentially monstrous genetic deforma-tion, is primordially a function of birth. In biology, in the theory of evolution, and in genetics, mutation is a necessary part of the evolution of the species. The word 'mutant' suggests a deformation, transformation, alteration: 'I am fully convinced that species are not immutable,' declares Darwin at the begin-ning of *On the Origin of Species* (Darwin 1866, 6). Without mutation, change, metamorphosis, morphing, no species could develop. Evolution *is*, therefore, mutation, and we are all mutations from our parents, as they were mutations from theirs (children typically have about 100 genetic differences from their parents, 100 mutations (Ridley 1994, 44)). The mutant *is* 'nature', *is* what we all are: you're a mutant, we tell you; and your mother was a mutant before you.

Dictionaries are dangerous books. For the 14-year-old Calliope in *Middlesex* it is the dictionary that finally allows her to begin to understand what she is, to begin to confront everything that she fears about herself and everything that she desires to know. She has heard the gender alignment con-sultant at the clinic use the word 'hypospadias' in relation to her condition as he probes and photographs her, so she checks out the word in Webster's Dictionary. Presenting its definition, the dictionary directs Calliope to look up 'eunuch'. The entry for that word in turn directs her to 'hermaphrodite'. A hermaphrodite has the 'sex organs and many of the secondary characteristics of both male and female', Calliope reads, and the word includes 'anything comprised of a combination of diverse or contradictory elements'. Then the dictionary directs her to 'see synonyms at MONSTER'. 'The synonym was official, authoritative', Calliope thinks:

> it was the verdict that the culture gave on a person like her. *Monster*. That was what she was. That was what Dr. Luce and his colleagues had been saying. It explained so much, really. It explained her mother crying in the next room. It explained the false cheer in Milton's voice. It explained why her parents had brought her to New York, so that the doctors could work in secret. It explained the photographs, too. What did people do when they came upon Bigfoot or the Loch Ness Monster? They tried to get a picture. For a second Callie saw herself that way. As a lumbering, shaggy creature pausing at the edge of the woods. As a humped convolvulus rearing its dragon's head from an icy lake. (Eugenides 2002, 431–2)

Further reading

For three recent collections of essays on the question of the human see Fuss, ed., *Human, All Too Human* (1996), Brewster et al., eds, *Inhuman Reflections* (2000), Neil Badmington, ed., *Posthumanism* (2000), and Marquard Smith and Joanne Morra, eds, *The Prosthetic Impulse* (2006). Tony Davies's *Humanism* (1997) is a good short introduction to the historical development of ideas of humanism, while John Gray's *Straw Dogs: Thoughts on Humans and Other Animals* (2002) is a provocative critique of the fondly held idea of the human and of humanism in Western culture. On monsters, see Clark and Royle, eds, *Monstrism* (2002), and there is a good short chapter on the monster and the Gothic in Punter and Byron, *The Gothic* (2003). On monsters and aliens in popular culture, see Elaine Graham's *Representations of the Post/Human* (2002); on monsters in Shakespeare and the Renaissance, see Mark Thornton Burnett, *Constructing 'Monsters' in Shakespearean Drama and Early Modern Culture* (2002). On the abhuman, see Kelly Hurley's *The Gothic Body* (1996). Tzvetan Todorov's *On Human Diversity* (1993) examines the question of definitions of the human from the Enlightenment onwards, calling for a new and newly enlightened humanism.

29. The performative

'I confess my ignorance': *Chambers Dictionary* gives this as an example of a performative. The word 'performative', declared J.L. Austin in 1956, 'is a new word and an ugly word, and perhaps it does not mean anything very much. But at any rate there is one thing in its favour, it is not a profound word' (Austin 1970, 233). The present chapter is concerned to sort out what this rather odd, perhaps unprofound word does mean. A performative is a statement that not only describes an action but actually performs that action. A performative is, in principle at least, the opposite of a constative statement. A constative statement involves a description of how things seem to be, a statement or assertion of something that can be true or false. 'The teachers are ignorant', for example.

All language can be thought about in terms of the constative and the performative. On the one hand, there is language as *descriptive*, as saying something about something. On the other, there is language as performative, as not only saying something but *doing* or *performing* something at the same time. 'I do' (as words spoken by the prospective wife or husband in answer to a particular question in the marriage service), 'I declare this meeting inquorate', 'I promise to pay the bearer on demand the sum of twenty pounds': these are all examples in which language is clearly supposed to be doing something. If it were not, marriage would be impossible, committee meetings would never end (or, more happily, might never take place at all) and a twenty-pound note would be quite worthless, a mere curiosity. The distinction between constative and performative statements is derived from a particular strand of Anglo-American philosophy known as speech-act theory. Speech-act theory is most famously associated with the work of the Oxford philosopher J.L. Austin and in particular with his book entitled *How to do Things with Words* (1962). It has become an important area of contemporary philosophy and linguistics but has also proved groundbreaking in the field of literary criticism and theory.

At first this idea may seem baffling. Surely, we may tell ourselves, literary texts are simply 'words on a page' and moreover words that relate to fictional or poetic worlds, not to the so-called real world in which marriage ceremonies are genuinely performed, committee meetings truly take place and money is real. But the truth of the matter is a little more complicated than this. Literary texts can indeed be considered from the perspective of the performative. The American poet Wallace Stevens points us in this direction when he writes in a letter, in 1945: 'the power of literature is that in describing the world it creates what it describes . . . You are describing a world and by describing it you are creating it' (Stevens 1966, 495). It is in this respect that we may recall that the very word 'poetry' comes from the Greek verb *poieein*, 'to make', 'to create': this suggests that poetry might in fact be a making or *doing*, as much as a saying or *stating*.

In order to start exploring this idea in more detail, we will look at one or two poems that are particularly illuminating in this context. First of all, John Keats's 'This Living Hand' (written *c.* 1819):

> This living hand, now warm and capable
> Of earnest grasping, would, if it were cold
> And in the icy silence of the tomb,
> So haunt thy days and chill thy dreaming nights
> That thou would wish thine own heart dry of blood
> So in my veins red life might stream again,
> And thou be conscience-calm'd—see here it is—
> I hold it towards you—

These chilling lines, which as it happens were not published until 1892, more than 70 years after Keats's death, are apparently *about* this death. The text functions as a bizarre and complex kind of curse or threat: it suggests that if the writer were dead (if this hand were no longer living but cold and in the grave), 'you' – the reader – would be so haunted that you would be willing to die in order that the writer could live again. The last words then weirdly suggest that this hand really is still living, despite the fact that we know the poet is dead: 'see here it is— / I hold it towards you—'.

Keats's poem may or may not be 'unfinished': we only have the text as recorded in the margin of a manuscript of another poem. Our doubt as to whether it is a fragment or a finished poem is part of a more general sense of uncertainty. 'This Living Hand' promotes a strong sense of the strangeness of writing as such. It testifies on the one hand (as it were) to the fact that a hand, the writer's or anyone else's, is always capable of being outlived by the writing which it produces. Paradoxically, what lives on is the writing and not the hand. On the other hand (so to speak), the poem insists – in a quite threatening and disturbing way – on the power that language has to be *deictic*, to point (like, precisely, a finger) and to say 'this' ('This living hand') and 'here' ('here it is'), now, in a strangely 'icy' present. We may not know how we feel about this poem, we may not know how to understand or earnestly 'grasp' it. But however we may want to think about it, one thing seems clear: the poem is *doing* something to us as readers. It can be related to the notion of the performative in at least two ways: first, in that it is a threat and, second, in that it *enacts* the curious logic of holding out a hand ('This living hand') to us as readers, here and now. Austin notes, in *How to do Things with Words*, that the classic examples of performatives are 'all with verbs in the first person singular present indicative active . . . Examples are "I name", "I do", "I bet", "I give" ' (Austin 1962, 56). Other instances might include 'I promise', 'I swear', 'I bequeath', 'I forgive (you)', 'I love (you)', 'I order (you)', 'I confess', 'I profess', 'I testify', and on on. Austin also adds that another 'useful criterion' for a performative statement is the presence, whether explicit or implicit, of the word 'hereby' (57). Keats's poem, whether considered as finished or unfinished, is clearly saying in some sense: I hereby threaten and haunt you. (To threaten is another sort of performative: indeed, as we hereby promise to show in greater detail below, a promise is itself a sort of threat and a threat a promise.)

Here is another example, a three-line poem by the contemporary English poet Michael Ayres, entitled 'Bittersweet' (1993):

> Survivors again. I never thought we'd make it.
> I never thought I could be forgotten,
> Or that it would be so bittersweet.

There are intriguing similarities between the Keats and Ayres poems. Both are concerned with the idea of survival and both can be read as poems about themselves, in other words as poems that are self-reflexive or self-referential. And like 'This Living Hand', 'Bittersweet' is self-reflexive in a decidedly paradoxical sense. The deployment of the title-word 'bittersweet' at the very end of the poem establishes the self-reflexive or self-referential dimension: it invites us to suppose that what 'would be so bittersweet' would be the poem of that title, the poem we are or have just been reading. The word 'bittersweet' at the end of the poem leads us back to the beginning of the poem, or rather to the very title of the poem, in a way that calls to mind Coleridge's favourite image for a story – that of the ouroboros, or snake with its tail in its mouth. If the sense of time in this poem is paradoxical, so too of course is the very word 'bittersweet'. This word is an oxymoron – an apparent contradiction in terms, comparable to Milton's phrase 'darkness visible' (*Paradise Lost*, I, 63). Finally, Ayres's poem is paradoxical as regards the idea of being forgotten. The 'I' of this poem declares, 'I never thought I could be forgotten'. This can be read as saying 'I never thought I could be forgotten and look, sure enough, I haven't been', but it can also be read as saying the opposite: 'I never thought I could be forgotten but the truth is that I have been.' The more plausible of these interpretations would perhaps be the latter, but if we read the poem in this way we encounter what appears to be its central paradox: being a survivor involves being forgotten. How should we make sense of this? One way would be to say that this is a love poem about the bittersweet experience of surviving some crisis or great difficulty in a relationship: the 'I' of the poem survives but only at the cost of no longer being the 'I' he (or she) used to be. We are left, in this case, with the enigma of an 'I' who has been forgotten, but who never-theless survives in writing, that is to say, in the very words of the poem. If 'I' simply depends on writing, then perhaps so does the 'we' referred to in the first line. This 'we', in turn, could be read not only as referring to the speaker and the speaker's lover, for example, but also as referring to *ourselves*, the poem's readers. In this sense the poem would be doing something to us, turning us into survivors: reading becomes bittersweet.

As if haunted by an aftertaste, we could carry on trying to describe here what 'This Living Hand' and 'Bittersweet' seem to be doing as poems. The basic point, however, is precisely that: they are not poems that are simply descriptive, they are also performative. Keats's text pulls us into its strange and icy grasp, Ayres's poem makes reading bittersweet. Both poems are in fact kinds of riddle. Each is saying, in effect: without your being able fully to understand it, this is a poem about the fact that you have read it. Each of these poems draws particular attention to the fact that it is writing and that it can survive its author, like a monument. In this respect both poems exploit the monumentalizing character of writing in a way similar to that of Shakespeare's sonnet 55:

> Not marble, nor the gilded monuments
> Of princes, shall outlive this pow'rful rime,
> But you shall shine more bright in these contents
> Than unswept stone, besmear'd with sluttish time.
> When wasteful war shall statues overturn,
> And broils root out the work of masonry,
> Nor Mars his sword nor war's quick fire shall burn
> The living record of your memory.

> 'Gainst death and all-oblivious enmity
> Shall you pace forth; your praise shall still find room,
> Even in the eyes of all posterity
> That wear this world out to the ending doom.
>   So till the judgment that yourself arise,
>   You live in this, and dwell in lovers' eyes.

This is a love poem which asserts that it will 'outlive' marble, gilded monuments, masonry and so on. It is thus concerned with the idea that writing – and this text in particular – has a capacity for monumentalization greater than that of anything else that humans might create. Because the poem itself will last until the end of the world ('the ending doom'), so will the memory of the lover who is being addressed. The haunting irony of Shakespeare's poem is that it constitutes not only the 'living record' of the lover's 'memory' but also the very existence of this lover: 'You live in this, and dwell in lovers' eyes.' The poem is not simply a 'record'. Rather, the lover ('you') only exists thanks to these fourteen lines. Poetry, then, in keeping with its etymology, can be performative in the most radical way: it can create 'you'.

The notion of the performative is extremely helpful for thinking about literature, then, because it allows us to appreciate that literary texts not only describe but perform. Literary texts not only say but do things: they do things with words and do things to us. More precisely they do things *by* saying. They create the world they describe (to recall the phrasing from Stevens we cited earlier), but this creation is not a single event, occurring at the time of writing: it happens with every new reading of the literary work. After declaring, in his poem 'In Memory of W.B. Yeats (d. Jan. 1939)', that 'poetry makes nothing happen', the poet W.H. Auden qualifies and even contradicts this by observing that 'it survives', as 'A way of happening, a mouth'. (The mouth and way of happening here would have to do with the reader at least as much as with the writer.) Alongside this we could juxtapose a remark made by Jacques Derrida, who says: 'promising is inevitable as soon as we open our mouths – or rather as soon as there is a text' (Derrida 1986a, 98). A promise is, of course, a classic example of a performative. In this context we might consider looking at poems and other literary texts for examples of the poet, author, narrator or characters literally making promises to the reader or to other characters. Literary texts are more 'promise-cramm'd' (to borrow Shakespeare's phrase: see *Hamlet* III, ii, 88) than one might have supposed. Everywhere in a literary work, for example, that we encounter suspense, deferral of explanation, withholding of facts or truth, hinted at revelation, anticipation, prolepsis or flash-forward, the logic of the promise is at work.

More generally, it is a matter of recognizing that literary texts are, in their very structure, promises. To recall an example that Derrida gives: 'A title is always a promise' (Derrida 1986a, 115). Even (or especially) with its title, a literary text has begun to promise. As soon as there is a text, perhaps before anyone (the poet, author, narrator or character) even opens their mouth, the performativity of a promise is under way. In order to get a sharper sense of the way a title works as a promise, we could consider how a text might be read if it had a different title from the one it has been given. Imagine Shakespeare's *King Lear* if it were retitled *Cordelia*, or Sylvia Plath's 'Daddy' if it were retitled 'Why I Love a Fascist'. Tom Stoppard captures this bizarrerie in his script for *Shakespeare in Love* (1998, dir. John Madden) where the Bard's working title for *Romeo and Juliet* is *Romeo and Ethel the Pirate's Daughter*. And we might wonder how differently we would conceive T.S. Eliot's *The Waste Land* had Ezra Pound not persuaded his friend to alter the title from *He Do the Police in Different Voices*. With a different title, a quite different kind of promise is being made: the work starts doing something quite different to us.

Let us conclude with a few words about one of these examples, Sylvia Plath's poem 'Daddy'. This poem is about the speaker's love and hatred of her father and describes the process by which she comes to exorcise him – by 'killing' him twice and finally driving a stake through his heart. 'Daddy' neatly encapsulates many of the points we have been discussing in this chapter. If 'Daddy' is a particularly crucial word for this poem, starting from its very title, so too is the word 'do'. Plath's text is fundamentally about *doing* and most of all, we can suggest, about doing by saying, about doing things with words. 'You do not do', the poem emphatically opens. 'I do, I do', the speaker exclaims. A powerfully disturbing rhetorical mixture of a marriage and an execution, Plath's poem appears at once to describe *and perform* the process by which the speaker can finally disconnect herself from the addressee ('The black telephone's off at the root') and conclude: 'Daddy, daddy, you bastard, I'm through'. The force of the poem involves the sense that the speaker is exorcising her father *as* she speaks, that these words are what finally get rid of him. The text is like a poetic equivalent of psychoanalysis as 'the talking cure'. Whether or not we construe Plath's poem as autobiographical, 'Daddy' operates in the form of a kind of confession. (It is not by chance that Plath's work is identified with the 'confessional school' of poetry.) It is here, too, that we might note how profoundly the notion of the performative illuminates the intimate depths of psychoanalysis, just as it does the genre of autobiography. At some level all autobiography has a confessional character: it entails an 'I confess' (however implicit this may be) in which the person confessing *makes the truth*.

We have been dealing mainly with poems in this chapter, since they provide an especially clear sense of how the 'I' of the text, or how the text itself, can be seen to create and transform – to perform. But as the example of titles indicates, the idea of the performative is of fundamental importance for all literary texts. In conclusion we would like to suggest another way of approaching this, namely to consider that every literary text is a kind of letter. It is a text addressed privately to each of us, me or you in isolation, at the same time as being a letter that has been made public, published. To read a literary text is to agree to the idea of a possible relationship. The literary text – whether poem, play, short story or novel – is a letter, and by reading it you become its recipient. Pursuing this analogy between a literary text and a letter, J. Hillis Miller argues that what is particularly striking about the performative dimension of literature is that it is in some ways fundamentally unpredictable. Literary texts give an exemplary 'twist' to the conventional, Austinian notion of the performative. Miller writes: 'The "twist" lies in the fact that the performative power of the letter is not foreseen or intended. This is contrary to the strict concept of a performative utterance as defined by Austin' (Miller 1991, 172). We have tried to suggest the workings of such a 'twist' in the paradoxical and 'riddling' effects of the poems we have looked at: poems are performative but not in ways that we can necessarily expect or completely, earnestly grasp. Indeed, the 'twist' may consist in the very failure intimated here. Every performative (a promise or threat or whatever) is haunted by the necessary possibility that it will fail or go astray. The 'twist' of performatives in literature might be illustrated in relation to the final words of Sylvia Plath's poem 'Daddy': 'Daddy, daddy, you bastard, I'm through'. Something appears to be happening here, but what? Is calling daddy 'bastard' a way of renouncing his legitimacy and thus, as it were, excommunicating him? What does 'I'm through' mean? Can the 'I' say this, while still addressing 'daddy'? Does 'I'm through' mean 'I *am* finished' or 'I *have* finished'? Or does it mean, paradoxically, that the 'I' is finally *through to* 'daddy', only now, beyond the last word of the poem, finally able to address him?

Further reading

J. Hillis Miller's work on performatives is particularly accessible. See his excellent studies *Tropes, Parables, Performatives* (1991) and *Speech Acts in Literature* (2001). For an essay specifically focusing on the poetic and the riddle, see his 'Deconstruction and a Poem' (Miller 2000). More difficult but extremely good are the essays of Paul de Man, for instance in his *Allegories of Reading* (1979). De Man gives some startling accounts of literary texts as works of persuasion. From a more psychoanalytically oriented perspective, see also Shoshana Felman's challenging but thought-provoking studies, *The Literary Speech Act* (1983) and (especially of interest regarding the act of promising in relation to literature, philosophy and Lacanian psychoanalysis) *The Scandal of the Speaking Body* (2003). On the performative in the context of British and German Romanticism, see Esterhammer's fine book *The Romantic Performative* (2000). Judith Butler's work, especially *Gender Trouble* (1990), *Bodies That Matter* (1993) and *Excitable Speech* (1997), offers a complex but compelling account of identity, gender and politics in general as 'performative' in ways explicitly indebted to J.L. Austin, even if he would not readily have recognized them. Jonathan Culler has a helpful and stimulating account of Butler and performative language in his *Literary Theory: A Very Short Introduction* (1997).

30. Secrets

Why do we read works of literature? What do we hope to get out of reading a novel, for example? In an essay entitled 'Secrets and Narrative Sequence', Frank Kermode writes: 'To read a novel expecting the satisfactions of closure and the receipt of a message is what most people find enough to do; they are easier with this method because it resembles the one that works for ordinary acts of communication' (Kermode 1983, 138). Most people, according to Kermode, read novels in the hope of reading something that adds up to a complete whole – a story with a clear structure and 'message'. They are looking for a good storyline – something to get their teeth into on a long train journey, for example, something which has a strong sense of what Kermode calls 'narrative sequence'. This is what is implied by the term 'consumer-fiction': to read a novel is to consume it. If a good novel is like a good meal, some novels are no doubt easier to chew and swallow than others. Stephen King's *The Shining* would be fast food in comparison with the feast of Henry James's *The Golden Bowl*. Kermode is working with a very basic model: novels can be compared with 'ordinary acts of communication' (by which he presumably means things like successfully negotiating your order with the person behind the service counter at Burger King) and most novel-reading is as simple and as sequential as abc. There are, however, things which get in the way of narrative sequence, and these are what Kermode calls *secrets*: 'secrets', he argues, 'are at odds with sequence' (138). What he is referring to here is the idea of textual details, specific aspects of the language of a text, particular patterns of images or rhetorical figures that a reader may not even notice on a 'consumerist' reading, but that are nevertheless present and which can provoke a sense of mystery. Thus Kermode focuses on the enigmatic, repeated but apparently superfluous references to black and white in Joseph Conrad's *Under Western Eyes* (1911).

It may be that what draws many people towards the study of literature (the desire not only to consume the novels of, say, James, Conrad or Stephen King, but also to reflect on their cultural, historical and ideological context, on how these novels work and what effects they produce) is a fascination with the possibilities of secrets. As we shall try to show in this chapter, the relationship between literature, secrecy and secrets is fundamental. Indeed, we would like to suggest that in many respects the question, 'What is literature?' can be considered as synonymous with the question, 'What is a secret?'

A secret is what is concealed, deliberately or inadvertently hidden, kept separate and apart. (The word 'secret' comes from the Latin *secernere*, where *se-* signifies 'apart' and *cernere* is 'to separate'.) Even the most rapidly consumed of novels involve secrets, if only because narratives are linear and the contents of a work cannot be presented all at once. Every narrative can be defined as a process of unfolding and revelation. It is precisely because there are things that remain hidden from us, and because we want to know what these things are, that we continue to read. This is the general context in which Roland Barthes elaborates his notion of the 'hermeneutic code'. The hermeneutic code concerns everything in a text that has to do with the creation of an enigma and its possible clarification and explanation. In this respect it is perhaps helpful to recall that etymologically the word 'enigma' is linked to fable and storytelling. It derives from the Greek verb *ainissesthai*, 'to speak allusively or obscurely', from *ainos*, 'a fable'. The most obvious example of enigma in the context of literary narratives is the whodunnit detective story: the question 'whodunnit?' forms the central enigma of the text and the hermeneutic code involves 'the various (formal) terms by which an enigma can be distinguished, suggested, formulated, held in suspense, and finally disclosed' (Barthes 1990b, 19). Why is this character doing this, for instance phoning the police or watching a letter burn on the fire? What is the significance of such and such an object, for instance the concrete-mixer in the cellar? How does this moment in the narrative throw light on the enigma of the crime? What is about to be revealed? All these questions are hermeneutic – they have to do with a work of interpretation and the hope or expectation or desire that the text will provide the answers. The mystery story or whodunnit is a particularly striking example, since (as its name indicates) it is explicitly concerned with drawing the reader into a mystery, and with manipulating her or him into asking questions, becoming watchful for 'clues' and looking for an explanation. In this sense, the pleasure of detective stories involves reading as itself a form of detecting.

But the mystery story or whodunnit is only one example of something that is much more general about the relationship between narratives and secrets. For, in an important sense, Chandler's *The Little Sister* (1949) or William McIlvanney's *Laidlaw* (1977) are no different from, say, D.H. Lawrence's *The Virgin and the Gipsy* (1930) or Toni Morrison's *The Bluest Eye* (1970). All of these novels involve various forms of mystery and concealment: they inevitably hold back a full revelation of what happens, releasing this information only gradually. More importantly perhaps, they generate a sense of mystery and secrecy through the very institution of the so-called omniscient narrator. The idea of such a narrator is basically magical or occult (the word 'occult', it may be noted, literally means 'hidden', 'secret'): such narratives are structured by powers of foresight. For it is invariably part of what is called omniscient narration (including what is known as 'realist fiction') that the narrator 'knows' the future and that this power of foresight is implicitly or explicitly articulated at numerous moments in a given narrative.

The Virgin and the Gipsy, for example, opens as follows:

> When the vicar's wife went off with a young and penniless man the scandal knew no bounds. Her two little girls were only seven and nine years old respectively. And the vicar was such a good husband. True, his hair was grey. But his moustache was dark, he was handsome, and still full of furtive passion for his unrestrained and beautiful wife.
>
> Why did she go? Why did she burst away with such an *éclat* of revulsion, like a touch of madness?
>
> Nobody gave any answer. Only the pious said she was a bad woman. While some of the good women kept silent. They knew.
>
> The two little girls never knew. (167)

This passage not only plays on the idea of secrecy as something related to a particular character (the vicar's 'furtive passion') but, through its apparent omniscient narration, sets up various kinds of secret knowledge. The 'good women kept silent' because they 'knew': 'knew what?' we ask ourselves. 'The two little girls never knew': this, too, the narrator knows though does not, at least for the moment, reveal to us. What is it that the narrator knows? What is it that the two little girls 'never knew'? The 'never', in particular, is a subtle and eerie word, suggesting that the perspective from which the narrator speaks is in fact posthumous as regards the girls themselves. On rereading – that is to say, with the benefits of readerly hindsight – we may find this word 'never' even more peculiar, since the two girls who 'never knew' do not die, in fact, in the course of the narrative. In this context one might want to ask: What planet, or fictional world, does this narrator come from?

Of course, narrators are just linguistic fabrications, textual creatures. Nevertheless, we are drawn into their worlds and a crucial part of the magic, sorcery or 'occultism' of literary narratives has to do with the mysterious but seductive 'reality' of the narrator. An omniscient narrator is a strange figure, by its very nature. The strangeness consists not only in the basic idea of omniscience itself, but also in what is concealed or glossed over within that omniscience. Omniscience is itself a fiction, a strange invention of literary critics drawing on the obviously problematic identification between an author or narrator and the Christian God. (As the *OED* makes clear, the word 'omniscient' originally referred specifically to 'the omniscient Being, the Deity'.) Omniscient narrators may appear to be all-knowing, or at least to know a lot; but they are certainly not all-telling. A narrator is always secretive, in other words, and this secretiveness concerns both the notion of storytelling-as-gradual-revelation and the question of what we do not and perhaps can never know about this narrator. Thus one of the most secretive or enigmatic aspects of a literary narrative may very well concern the character of its narrator (so-called omniscient or not): what, for example, are we to make of the narrator of Henry James's *Washington Square*, or Joseph Conrad's *Heart of Darkness*, or Virginia Woolf's *Mrs Dalloway*?

Toni Morrison's *The Bluest Eye*, on the other hand, involves the final revelation that the two primary narrators (a so-called omniscient narrator and one of the characters, Claudia) are apparently the same: such a revelation does not serve to clarify or rationalize the nature of the storytelling but, on the contrary, exacerbates the reader's sense of the narrator-as-enigma. *The Bluest Eye* indeed begins with mystery – with the enigmatic presentation (and equally enigmatic repetition or re-presentation) of the text of what appears to be a US school primer: 'Here is the house. It is green and white. It has a red door. It is very pretty. Here is the family' (7). In a forcefully disjunctive way this opening switches, without any explanation, to a passage of italicized text which starts: 'Quiet as it's kept, there were no marigolds in the fall of 1941. We thought, at the time, that it was because Pecola was having her father's baby that the marigolds did not grow' (9). There is a sense here of a narrator speaking knowledgeably from a position of hindsight ('We thought, at the time'), of someone who knows things which may or may not be revealed as the narrative unfolds. More provocatively, however, we are left with the mysteriousness of the first four words, 'Quiet as it's kept'. What is 'it', Who or what is keeping quiet? Why are we being alerted to what appears to be secret and why should it be kept quiet? Is the narrator imparting information to the reader or keeping quiet about it?

If a logic of secrecy, concealment and revelation is crucial to the workings of any novel, it is also evident in less obviously narrative texts such as lyric poetry. Consider the following poem (No. 180), written around 1859, by Emily Dickinson:

> Our lives are Swiss—
> So still—so Cool—
> Till some odd afternoon
> The Alps neglect their Curtains
> And we look farther on!
>
> *Italy* stands the other side!
> While like a guard between—
> The solemn Alps—
> The siren Alps—
> Forever intervene!

This poem is about what is concealed or hidden from us: it gestures towards something secret. It suggests that there are moments of revelation or epiphany ('some odd afternoon') when we are able to 'look farther on' – beyond the Alps. These moments, or this moment (since technically only one 'odd afternoon' is mentioned), might be compared to what Wordsworth calls 'spots of time' or Hardy 'moments of vision'. Dickinson's poem appears, at least on one level, to describe or relate such a moment and to attribute great significance to it. But if there is a revelation, if the secret and perhaps the meaning of our lives is being referred to here, what is it? The poem says only that 'we look farther on' and that '*Italy* stands the other side': it remains unclear what it is that is being revealed at this moment when 'The Alps neglect their Curtains'. Is it '*Italy*' simply? But what does '*Italy*' mean? The word 'Forever' in the final line of the poem underlines the strangeness of what is going on here and the continuing or unresolved *enigma* of what the poem has to tell us. The definiteness and absoluteness of 'forever' confirms, in effect, the sense that this poem at once reveals and can never reveal its secret.

Dickinson's poem could in fact be described as exemplary of literary texts in general. In particular, it dramatizes the fact that the notion of a secret is paradoxical. Jacques Derrida has formulated the paradox as follows: '*There is something secret*. But it does not conceal itself' (Derrida 1992b, 21). In an essay called 'Derrida's Topographies', J. Hillis Miller offers a helpful account of this paradox. On the one hand, Miller points out, 'We normally think of a secret as in principle discoverable' (Miller 1994, 16): Kermode's 'satisfactions of closure' and 'the receipt of a message' and Barthes's 'hermeneutic code' make sense only if we accept this principle. There is closure and there is a message to the extent that 'All is revealed'. There is a valid hermeneutic effort or labour of interpretation because there is something to be interpreted, seized, comprehended. On the other hand, however, there is the question of what Miller calls a 'true secret'. He notes: 'a true secret, if there is such a thing, cannot ever, by any means, be revealed' (17). And Miller then elaborates on the Derridean paradox: 'A true secret . . . is not hidden somewhere . . . A true secret is all on the surface. This superficiality cannot by any hermeneutic procedures, material or linguistic, be gone behind. A literary text (and any text may be taken as literary) says what it says' (17). Thus, in Dickinson's poem, there would be the enigmatic, perhaps ultimately cryptic status of '*Italy*': there is nothing 'within' or 'behind' this appositely italicized '*Italy*'. The text says (only) what it says: '*Italy* stands the other side!' It does not say that 'Italy' symbolizes 'romance' or that it represents 'revolution' or even that it can be taken as a synonym for 'the secret'. However superficial or profound or elliptical, it simply says what it says. In these terms, then, it is not only a question of literature as involving secrets that are concealed and that are gradually or finally brought to light. It is also – and perhaps more enigmatically – a matter of a secrecy that does not involve any kind of concealment at all.

A literary text 'says what it says': it says, for example, that 'we look farther on!' Or it says, at the very outset, what its title is. Perhaps the secrecy of literary works begins with titles themselves. Perhaps what makes a work 'literary' is in part that its title remains enigmatic. A literary text says that it is called 'The Virgin and the Gipsy' or 'The Bluest Eye' or, say, 'The Shining'. What do these titles refer to? Does Lawrence's text, for example, finally and clearly establish what is to be understood by 'the dark, tremulous potent secret of . . . virginity' (207), or what is meant by the idea of a gipsy, of a figure that is apparently outside 'the vast and gruesome clutch of our law' (236)? And what is the status and significance of the conjunctive ('and') in the title of this Lawrence text? What does 'and' mean? Conversely, what is signified by 'the bluest eye' and in the eyes of which reader or beholder? Or again, what do those two words, 'the shining', have to tell us? Each of these examples, in fact, resists what Kermode refers to as 'the satisfactions of closure' and 'the receipt of a message'. It is their readability *and* their resistance to being read that makes them 'literary', in Hillis Miller's terms. This is in part at least why the question 'What is literature?' is inseparable from the question 'What is a secret?'

It has been traditional to think of meaning as something behind or within the words of a text. Reading has conventionally been thought of on the basis of a surface-depth model, with the words of the text as the surface and the meaning lurking somewhere inside or underneath. The text has secrets and often explicitly conveys and exploits the idea that it has the power to disclose or preserve these secrets. With poststructuralist accounts of literature, however, there has been an important shift away from this surface-depth model. This is not to say that the surface-depth model is no longer relevant. Indeed, it is very difficult to think about meaning or about reading without relying to a considerable extent on the values and assumptions of this model. Moreover, as we have been trying to suggest, virtually every literary text can be seen to work with this model. This is, in short, the theory and practice of secrets as (in principle) discoverable. Poststructuralism, however, is generally suspicious about any reading of a literary text that would equate a secret with the 'complete' or 'ultimate' meaning. Poststructuralism pays particular attention to the paradoxical nature of secrets – to the fact that secrets can be undiscoverable and yet at the same time unconcealed. In this sense the secrets of a literary text may be right in front of our eyes and yet they remain secret, like 'the purloined letter' on the mantelpiece in Edgar Allan Poe's story of that title, or like the solemn, siren Alps, some odd afternoon.

To conclude, we could briefly consider secrets in two further ways. At the beginning of this chapter we put forward the hypothesis that what attracts many people to the study of literature is a fascination with the idea of secrets. We have sought to elaborate on this by considering some of the many respects in which literary texts are bound up with the enigmatic, mysterious, secret and (in a double sense) occult. And we have attempted to emphasize the important paradox whereby secrets can be discoverable but that a 'true secret', if there is such a thing, can never be discovered. Our focus has been on texts and on how they compel, manipulate and fascinate their readers. But there is also another perspective from which to think about literature and secrets. This would be from that of the reader rather than the text, and in particular as regards the notion of a reader who is interested not so much in the idea of secrets *in the text* (whodunnit? what is going to happen next? and so on) but rather in the possibilities of secrets *within herself* or *within himself*, secrets that may have to do with dreams, memories, fantasies, speculations, apprehensions and desires set off by the text, thoughts and feelings that may never have been experienced before – that is to say, in a surprising way, secret thoughts and feelings. It is in this context that literary texts can be acknowledged as having uncanny powers, including an ability to alter people's very sense of themselves, of their identity and 'place'.

Secondly, we might try to think about the possibility of a 'true secret' within ourselves, about the paradox of what a 'true secret' might be. This touches on what we refer to in the following chapter as 'the unpresentable'. The name which is sometimes given to this notion of a true secret is 'death'. The Ghost of Hamlet's father comes to Hamlet and says:

But that I am forbid
To tell the secrets of my prison-house,
I could a tale unfold whose lightest word
Would harrow up thy soul, freeze thy young blood,
Make thy two eyes like stars start from their spheres,
Thy knotted and combined locks to part,
And each particular hair to stand an end
Like quills upon the fretful porpentine.
But this eternal blazon must not be
To ears of flesh and blood. (I, v, 14–21)

The Ghost at once tells and does not tell. The Ghost keeps the secrets of its prison-house even as it evokes the effects of their disclosure. This is another way of talking about the enigma of literature: whether in the form of Shakespearean tragedy or a contemporary whodunnit, literature is about what cannot be told, and in particular about that impossible package holiday which Hamlet refers to as that 'undiscover'd country, from whose bourn / No traveller returns' (III, i, 78–9). This undiscovered country is neither inside us nor outside us. It is a secret that does not conceal itself: the fact that we are going to die but that, as Freud puts it, 'It is indeed impossible to imagine our own death; and whenever we attempt to do so we can perceive that we are in fact still present as spectators' (Freud 1985a, 77).

Further reading

Besides the readable and stimulating essay on 'Secrets and Narrative Sequence' (1983), Frank Kermode has written an important study entitled *The Genesis of Secrecy* (1979) which deals with various questions about, for example, 'why narratives are obscure', why we prefer an enigma to 'a muddle', and so on. Barthes's *S/Z* (1990b) contains brilliant insights into senses of secrecy and enigma in reading. Especially in its focus on silence and the unspoken, Pierre Macherey's *A Theory of Literary Production* (1978) is a powerful account of literary secrets in relation to politics and ideology. On literary fiction and the omniscient narrator, see Royle's 'The "Telepathy Effect": Notes toward a Reconsideration of Narrative Fiction' (in Royle 2003) and Jonathan Culler, 'Omniscience' in *The Literary in Theory* (2007). From a quite different, intensively psychoanalytic perspective, Esther Rashkin's *Family Secrets* (1992) is a thought-provoking study of secrets and crypts in mainly nineteenth-century literary works. Jacques Derrida has written numerous essays about secrets: see, in particular, the fascinating but difficult 'Fors' (Derrida 1986b) and 'Passions' (Derrida 1992b), as well as the highly illuminating discussions in *A Taste for the Secret* (Derrida and Ferraris, 2001). In his essay on 'Derrida's Topographies' (1994), on the other hand, J. Hillis Miller provides an excellent account of Derrida's work on secrets (especially 'Fors') and more generally a rich and accessible introduction to 'Derrida and literature'. For a more difficult but also valuable study, Esther Rashkin's *Unspeakable Secrets and the Psychoanalysis of Culture* (2008) looks at examples of film and literature in relation to Abraham and Torok's notions of cryptonymy.

31. The postmodern

Since this book does not attempt to introduce different critical schools or historical periods of literature, it might seem odd to include a chapter on the postmodern. In the following pages, however, we wish to suggest that this topic provides us with an invaluable set of terms for thinking about literary and other cultural texts, that to a significant degree it involves ways of thinking which are unavoidable in the twenty-first century.

The word 'postmodern' itself seems odd, paradoxically evoking what is after ('post') the contemporary ('modern'). How can something be *after* the contemporary? In this respect, in as much as they are confronting the importance of paradox in relation to the contemporary study of literature, other chapters in this book are also dealing with the postmodern. But this paradox of the time of the postmodern also points to the fact that, strictly speaking, the postmodern should not be thought of as a term of periodization: the postmodern challenges our thinking about time, challenges us to see the present in the past, the future in the present, the present in a kind of no-time.

No doubt all periodizing terms (the Renaissance, the early modern period, the Romantic period, and so on) resist definition, but there is perhaps something additionally resistant, peculiar and (for many) maddening about the 'postmodern'. Indeed, the postmodern appears to welcome and embrace a thinking of itself in terms of multiplicity. It resists the totalizing gesture of a metalanguage, the attempt to describe it as a set of coherent explanatory theories. Rather than trying to explain it in terms of a fixed philosophical position or as a kind of knowledge, we shall instead present a 'postmodern vocabulary' in order to suggest its mobile, fragmented and paradoxical nature.

A postmodern vocabulary

Undecidability

Undecidability involves the impossibility of deciding between two or more competing interpretations. As we point out in Chapter 20, classical logic is founded on the law of non-contradiction: something cannot be both A and not A at the same time. The postmodern gives particular emphasis to ways in which this law may be productively questioned or suspended. A classical example of this is the Cretan liar paradox. If someone says 'I am a liar', how can we tell if that person is lying or not? The statement would seem to make him both a liar and not a liar at the same time. Our ability to make a decision about the validity of such a statement is, at least temporarily, suspended. According to classical logic, the Cretan liar paradox is an isolated and particular instance of a paradoxical statement. For the postmodern, by contrast, the suspension of the law of non-contradiction is endemic. In the postmodern, all absolute values – such as the traditional values of God, Truth, Reason, the Law and so on – become sites of questioning, of rethinking, of new kinds of affirmation. The postmodern, that is to say, does not simply reject the possibility of making decisions. Rather, it gives new attention to the value of the undecidable. What the new critics of the middle of the twentieth century called ambiguity or paradox is now considered in terms of undecidability. The difference is that for the new critics literary texts tended to exploit the polysemic potential of language to create a unified whole in which ambiguity produced an enriching of the text's final unity. For postmodern critics, by contrast, undecidability radically undermines the very principle of unity: these critics celebrate multiplicity, heterogeneity, difference. Undecidability splits the text, disorders it. Undecidability dislodges the principle of a single final meaning in a literary text. It haunts. As Derrida puts it, there is no decision, nor any kind of moral or political responsibility, that is not haunted by the '*experience and experiment of the undecidable*' (Derrida 1988, 116).

A new enlightenment

Theorists of the postmodern are drawn into that exhilarating as well as terrifying 'play' of a text thrown up by its forms of undecidability. For those nervous of the postmodern, this is deemed to amount simply to nihilism and chaos. But for postmodernists it is precisely those monolithic, unthinking assumptions about a fixed grounding for political, ethical and textual decisions that lead to abhorrent results. It is the belief in a transcendent explanatory system

– such as God, national identity or historical materialism, to name just three
– which leads to terror, persecution and oppression. In each case, there is a
transcendental value (God, the nation-state, a certain reading of the writings
of Marx) which can justify any excess. Postmodernists suggest that reason
itself has been used to justify all sorts of oppression. Reason may be said to lie
behind the Stalinist terror, for example, in the form of a rational or 'scientific'
development of Marx's thinking. Alternatively, in the science of eugenics,
'rational' argument or so-called empirical science helped to justify the Jewish
holocaust on grounds of racial difference. This is why, writing in 1944,
Theodor Adorno and Max Horkheimer argue that 'Enlightenment is totalit-
arian' (Horkheimer and Adorno 2002, 4). 'Enlightenment' here can be understood very generally as a way of characterizing Western thought since the
seventeenth century. Very simply, the notion of the Enlightenment entails
the assertion of the power of reason over both superstition and nature, the
belief that a combination of abstract reason and empirical science will lead to
knowledge and eventually to political and social progress. By contrast, the
postmodern is sceptical about claims of progress in history, not least because
of the necessary marginalization (of the apparently non-progressive) which
it entails.

A common misunderstanding of the postmodern is that it involves simply
an assertion and celebration of the irrational. The postmodern can more
helpfully be understood, however, as a *suspension and deconstruction* of the
opposition between the rational and the irrational. Irrationalism in itself is
only another form of rationalism because it is dependent for its definition on
its opposite (only someone who is *rational* could conceive of someone or
something as *irrational* and the irrational can only be defined in opposition to
the rational). The postmodern could be seen as concerned rather with what
Jacques Derrida calls 'a new enlightenment' (Derrida 1988, 141) concerned
to explore the value and importance of ways of thinking that cannot be
reduced to an opposition between the rational and the irrational.

Fragmentation, dissemination

Postmodern resistance to totalizing forces such as rationalism or irrationalism
means that its characteristic form is fragmentary. Fragmentation, in fact, is
commonly associated with the Romantic and modern periods: poems such as
Percy Bysshe Shelley's 'Ozymandias' (1818) from the Romantic period and
T.S. Eliot's *The Waste Land* (1922) from the modern period are crucially concerned with the notion of the fragment. In this sense, fragmentation is not
unique to the postmodern. But the postmodern entails a new kind of critique

of the very ideas of fragment and totality. This has taken the form of, among other things, a fundamental questioning of the notion of originality and correspondingly a new kind of emphasis on citation and intertextuality, parody and pastiche. In this respect, originality, which has been of particular importance as an aesthetic value since the eighteenth century, is seen as a kind of ideological fetish, rather than the overriding criterion in aesthetic judgements. Moreover, we might remark a significant difference between notions of fragmentation in the postmodern and those in Romanticism and Modernism: fragmentation in the postmodern does not depend on the possibility of an original 'unity' which has been lost. The Romantics and Modernists, by contrast, tend to figure fragmentation in terms of the loss of an original wholeness. Another way of thinking about postmodern fragmentation is in terms of dissemination. Dissemination involves a sense of scattering (as in a scattering of seeds or 'semes'), a scattering of origins and ends, of identity, centre and presence. Postmodern fragmentation is without origins, it is dissemination without any assurance of a centre or destination.

Little and grand narratives

One of the best-known distinctions in the postmodern is that made by Jean-François Lyotard concerning what he calls 'grand' narratives and 'little' narratives. 'Grand narratives' such as Christianity, Marxism, the Enlightenment attempt to provide a framework for everything. Such narratives follow a 'teleological' movement towards a time of equality and justice: after the last judgement, the revolution, or the scientific conquest of nature, injustice, unreason and evil will end. Lyotard argues that the contemporary 'world-view', by contrast, is characterized by 'little narratives'. Contemporary Western discourse is characteristically unstable, fragmented, dispersed – not a *world-view* at all. 'Little narratives' present local explanations of individual events or phenomena but do not claim to explain everything. Little narratives are fragmentary, non-totalizing and non-teleological. Lyotard claims that, in the West, grand narratives have all but lost their efficacy, that their legitimacy and their powers of legitimation have been dispersed. Legitimation is now plural, local and contingent. No supreme authority – Marx, Hegel or God – can sit in judgement. In his provocatively titled book *The Gulf War Did Not Take Place* (1995), for example, Jean Baudrillard offers an analysis of the way that the first Gulf War was as much a function of televisual and other media representations as of anything else. Despite the controversial nature of his title, Baudrillard is not so much suggesting that there was no war as that in an unprecedented way its very actuality was and remains indissoluble from media representations.

The phenomenon described here has also been described by the phrase 'legitimation crisis', borrowed from the German thinker Jürgen Habermas. Habermas uses this phrase to denote a situation in which all 'master codes' or grand narratives, all conventions, institutions, final authorities have been put into a state of crisis. And in the last century or so, the announcements of the death of God, 'man' and the author have successively dramatized this dissolution of authority.

Simulation

The Western philosophical tradition of aesthetics has relied heavily on a distinction between the real and its copy. This goes back at least as far as Plato, who argued that painters, actors, dramatists and so on, all produce representations or 'imitations' of the real world. (In fact, Plato argues that even a bed is an imitation of the concept or idea of a bed, so that a picture of a bed is a second-degree copy of an essential but unobtainable bed, the essence of bedness.) This way of thinking has given rise to a hierarchical opposition between the real and the copy. And the hierarchy corresponds to that of nature and fabrication, or nature and artifice. The postmodern, however, challenges such hierarchies and shows how the set of values associated with these oppositions can be questioned. As the film *Falling Down* (1993) starring Michael Douglas makes clear, the photograph of the hamburger in the fast-food restaurant is infinitely superior to the rather sad and surprisingly expensive artifact that you have just bought. Even nature, in this postmodern reversal, is subject to improvement. To adopt Umberto Eco's words, 'technology can give us more reality than nature can' (Eco 1993, 203). Films such as *The Truman Show* (1998) and the *Matrix* trilogy (1999–2003) demonstrate a postmodern fascination with the technologies of virtual reality. In the first a man unwittingly lives his life in the fabricated studio world of a 24-hour-a-day soap opera, while in the second humankind has been enslaved by robots who feed off their energy, keeping them subservient by plugging them into a virtual world, the matrix.

Another way of thinking about this phenomenon is to use Jean Baudrillard's term 'simulation' (or 'the simulacrum'). Simulation is contrasted with representation. The latter works on the basis that there is a distinction between what the linguist Ferdinand de Saussure calls the signifier and the signified, between a word or 'sound-image', and the idea or the 'mental concept' that it represents. In classical terms, there is an absolute distinction between the word 'hamburger' and what that word represents. Similarly, common sense tells us that there is a clear and necessary distinction between a photograph of a hamburger and a hamburger. Simulation, by contrast, short-circuits such distinctions. Saturated by images – on computers, TV, advertising hoardings, magazines, newspapers and so on – the 'real' becomes unthinkable without the copy. In other words, simulation involves the disturbing idea that the copy is not a copy of something real; the real is inextricable from the significance and effects of the copy. That hamburger that looks so tempting is far more delicious than any you could ever taste. But, paradoxically, when you taste *your* hamburger, you are at the same time tasting what is created by advertising images of hamburgers. If Coke really is it, then it is because our experience of drinking Coca-Cola cannot be disengaged from the seductive lifestyle images of its advertising, from those insidious effects of the brand name, whereby the desirability of a given product is in a sense *branded* into our consciousness and unconscious. This leads to the world of what Jean Baudrillard calls the hyperreal, in which reality is fabricated by technology. As Baudrillard puts it: 'simulation is no longer that of a territory, a referential being or substance. It is the generation by models of a real without origin or reality; a hyperreal . . . Henceforth it is the map that precedes the territory' (Baudrillard 1988, 166).

Depthlessness

Another way of talking about simulation or the simulacrum is in terms of depthlessness. If one governing opposition for Western thought has been between the real and the copy, between nature and artifice, another has been between surface and depth. An obvious example of this would be the notion of 'expression', which involves the idea that the words which we write or speak *express* something 'inside' our heads (thoughts and feelings). The words are the surface, whereas our thoughts or consciousness represent depth. Similarly, the idea of the self, the very possibility of being human, has conventionally relied on such an opposition: the subject or self is constituted as a relation between surface and depth, inside and outside.

Fredric Jameson provides a useful account of four depth models that, he argues, have dominated the West in the twentieth century (Jameson 1993, 70):

1. Marxism: Marxism crucially depends on the notion of ideology. Put simply, this involves the idea that we do not see the reality of the world around us but only what we have been indoctrinated into seeing.
2. Psychoanalysis: Freud's theories are based on the distinction between the conscious and the unconscious, whereby the unconscious is held to be the truth behind or beneath the distorted representation which we call consciousness.

3. Existentialism: in its various forms, existentialism relies on a distinction between, on the one hand, authentic existence and, on the other hand, inauthenticity: authenticity is the truth of selfhood underlying the distortions effected by a state of inauthenticity.
4. Semiotics: as we have seen, Saussurean notions of language presuppose a distinction between the signifier on the one hand and the signified on the other. The word or sound-image indicates an underlying idea or mental concept.

In each case, the authentic or real is understood to be hidden or disguised, while the surface phenomenon, the façade, is an inauthentic distortion or arbitrary offshoot of the underlying truth. With the postmodern, all of these surface–depth models are shaken up. The postmodern suspends, dislocates and transforms the oppositional structures presupposed by major Western modes of thought – by classical Marxism, psychoanalysis, existentialism, semiotics.

Pastiche

Jameson also distinguishes between parody and pastiche. Both rely on imitation of earlier texts or objects. In parody, there is an impulse to ridicule by exaggerating the distance of the original text from 'normal' discourse. The postmodern, however, no longer accepts the notion of 'normal' language: pastiche is 'blank' parody in which there is no single model followed, no single impulse such as ridicule and no sense of a distance from any norm (see Jameson 1992, 166–7). Postmodern architecture, for example, borrows elements from various earlier periods of architecture and puts them in eclectic juxtaposition. In what the architectural critic Charles Jencks has termed 'radical eclecticism' (Jencks 1993, 283), there is no single stable reference. Similarly, a Madonna video parodies, for example, film noir, Marilyn Monroe, contemporary pornography, avant-garde erotic art and Catholic icons, in an apparently random dissonance of combination. Rather differently, the music of contemporary 'Bollywood' films supplies a potent mix of classical and folk music from the Indian subcontinent with the so-called 'Western' rhythms and sounds of soul, jazz, rock'n'roll, pop, disco, 1970s blaxploitation funk, trip hop, techno, ambient and house music. It is just such a sense of eclecticism that distinguishes contemporary culture for Lyotard:

> Eclecticism is the degree zero of contemporary general culture: one listens to reggae, watches a western, eats McDonald's food for lunch and local

cuisine for dinner, wears Paris perfume in Tokyo and retro clothes in Hong Kong; knowledge is a matter for TV games. (Lyotard 1992, 145)

This hybridization, a radical intertexuality mixing forms, genres, conventions, media, dissolves boundaries between high and low art, between the serious and the ludic. Genre becomes explicitly unstable, especially in such texts as Vladimir Nabokov's *Pale Fire* (1963), which mixes up a poem with a literary-critical analysis and political thriller, John Fowles's *The French Lieutenant's Woman* (1969), which uses history textbooks to tell a love story, D.M. Thomas's *The White Hotel* (1981), which exploits the genres of poetry and psychoanalytic case-study, or Dave Eggers's *A Heartbreaking Work of Staggering Genius* (2000), which infuriatingly resists our desire to categorize it as either autobiography or novel ('Based on a true story', the book proclaims on its cover). Two of the most creative and powerful television drama series of the 1980s and early 1990s are exemplary in this respect: David Lynch's *Twin Peaks* (1990) mixes up the detective story with forms such as horror, avant-garde or art-house movies, soap opera and so on, while Dennis Potter's *The Singing Detective* (1986) dissolves the borders between the detective story, Hollywood musicals, psychological dramas and the *Bildungsroman*. More recently, TV series such as *The Office, Green Wing, The Hills, The Sopranos* similarly take up and meddle with a plurality of styles, discourses, genres.

The unpresentable

Since the postmodern challenges the distinction between mimesis or copy and the real, it contests the modes of its own representation, of representation itself. Thus it paradoxically *defines* itself in terms of liminal phenomena which defy both categorization and, finally, expression – the unpresentable, or in some of its other formulations, the sublime (Lyotard), the abject (Kristeva), the unnamable (Beckett). Thus Samuel Beckett's writing, for example, may be said to be constituted by the paradoxical impossibility and necessity of discourse – 'I can't go on, I'll go on' (*The Unnamable*, 418).

If in 'going on' there are no clear rules of representation, mimesis, temporality, then the artist is working within the terms of the radically undecidable, or the yet to be decided, as Lyotard remarks:

> The postmodern would be that which, in the modern, puts forward the unpresentable in presentation itself: that which denies itself the solace of good forms, the consensus of a taste which would make it possible to share

collectively the nostalgia for the unattainable; that which searches for new presentations, not in order to enjoy them but in order to impart a stronger sense of the unpresentable . . . the artist and the writer, then, are working without rules in order to formulate the rules of what *will have been done*. Hence the fact that work and text have the characters of an *event* . . . *Post modern* would have to be understood according to the paradox of the future (*post*) anterior (*modo*). (Lyotard 1992, 149–50)

The unpresentable is an effect, not least, of a disturbance of temporality, of the linear progression of time. The postmodern is grammatically specified as inhabiting the future perfect, what will have been. There is no pure present on the basis of which re-presentation may take place.

Decentring

Everything that we have said in this chapter may be summarized in terms of the notion of decentring. The postmodern challenges the 'logo-centric' (the authority of the word, the possibility of final meanings or of being in the presence of pure 'sense'). It challenges the ethnocentric (the authority of one ethnic 'identity' or culture – such as Europe or 'the West' or Islam or Hinduism). It challenges the phallocentric (everything that privileges the symbolic power and significance of the phallus and therefore of masculinity). As Ihab Hassan remarks, the postmodern may be summarized by a list of words prefixed by 'de-' and 'di-':

deconstruction, decentring, dissemination, dispersal, displacement, difference, discontinuity, demystification, delegitimation, disappearance. (Hassan 1989, 309)

In place of the centre, but not in its place, there is alterity, otherness, a multiplicity and dispersal of centres, origins, presences.

Further reading

An excellent introduction to postmodernism is Christopher Butler's *Post-modernisn: A Very Short Introduction* (2002). Good collections of essays include Brooker's *Modernism/Postmodernism* (1992), Docherty's *Post-modernism* (1993), and Drolet's *The Postmodernism Reader* (2003); see also Stuart Sim, ed., *The Routledge Companion to Postmodernism* (2004). Bertens and Natoloi, eds, *Postmodernism: The Key Figures* (2001) provides useful entries on the key thinkers. Lyotard's *The Postmodern Condition* (1984) is, by now (paradoxically), a classic text to start with – 'Answering the Question: What is Postmodernism?' (1992) is particularly useful. His more recent *Postmodern Fables* (1997) offers a series of brief, elliptical and often enigmatic essays on postmodern topics. Jameson's 'The Politics of Theory' (1988) and Linda Hutcheon's books *A Poetics of Postmodernism* (1988) and *The Politics of Postmodernism* (1989) provide strong, politicized accounts of the post-modern. Steven Connor offers an excellent overview of the postmodern in his *Postmodernist Culture* (1997); on literature in particular, see Ian Gregson, *Postmodern Literature* (2004). For two accounts of the postmodern speci-fically in the context of literary narrative and narrative theory, see Andrew Gibson, *Towards a Postmodern Theory of Narrative* (1996) and Mark Currie, *Postmodern Narrative Theory* (1998). Readings and Schaber, eds, *Postmod-ernism Across the Ages* (1993) is a useful collection of essays which seek to challenge the common assumption that postmodernism is a period term referring to the current time.

32. Pleasure

Whether in a seminar or at the pub, often the first thing that gets asked about a book is: Did you enjoy it? This is not just a way of making conversation, but also suggests the fundamental importance of pleasure when it comes to reading. In fact, the question 'Did you enjoy it?', far from breaking the ice and starting a passionate discussion, is generally followed by a terse 'Yes' or 'No' and then forgotten. We may talk about things we enjoy in a work of literature – the gripping narrative, the appealing characters, the power of the language, the comedy and pathos – but we do not very often talk about the enjoyment itself, about what enjoyment or pleasure *is*. There are at least two reasons for this. In the first place, pleasure, enjoyment, emotional and indeed erotic excitement can be surprisingly difficult to talk about. Secondly, and no doubt related to this, such pleasures tend to border on the transgressive, censored or taboo. But as we hope to show in the course of this chapter, pleasure is crucial to, and even synonymous with, literature itself. This is perhaps why Sir Philip Sidney declares that the purpose of poetry is 'to teach and delight' (Sidney 2002, 86) and why, in his 1802 Preface to *Lyrical Ballads*, William Wordsworth uses the word 'pleasure' (and its cognates) more than 50 times, proposing that the 'end of poetry is to produce excitement in coexistence with an overabundance of pleasure' (Wordsworth 1984, 609). This is not to construe the literary as 'mere' play, as simply hedonistic or self-indulgent. Instead we will seek to describe a sense of pleasure and of literature that may be both disconcerting and subversive.

Take a text that might seem relatively innocuous, a story called 'Bliss' (1920) by the New Zealand writer Katherine Mansfield. 'Bliss' concerns a 30-year-old woman called Bertha Young and her feelings of extreme pleasure before and during a dinner-party at her home. She and her husband Harry entertain an erotically powerful blonde called Pearl Fulton, a ludicrous poet called Eddie Warren and a more or less equally risible couple, Mr and Mrs Norman Knight. Bertha is consistently described as feeling a 'fire of bliss' (311) inside her: 'Everything was good – was right. All that happened seemed to fill again her brimming cup of bliss' (311). She is 'as much in love as ever' (308) with her husband, but she has also fallen in love with the beautiful Pearl Fulton: 'she always did fall in love with beautiful women who had something strange about them' (307). Whether it is the lovely appearance of the dinner table or the blossoming pear tree which Bertha takes Pearl to look at from the drawing-room balcony, everything helps to give Bertha the feeling of being (like Keats in 'Ode to a Nightingale') 'too happy' (308). The story ends with an excruciating moment of revelation, however, as Bertha inadvertently discovers that her husband and Pearl Fulton are lovers: unaware that Bertha can see them, the couple exchange intimacies in the hall. Bertha's feelings of bliss are finally, brutally effaced.

This is how 'Bliss' begins:

> Although Bertha Young was thirty she still had moments like this when she wanted to run instead of walk, to take dancing steps on and off the pavement, to bowl a hoop, to throw something up in the air and catch it again, or to stand still and laugh at – nothing – at nothing, simply.
>
> What can you do if you are thirty and, turning the corner of your own street, you are overcome, suddenly, by a feeling of bliss – absolute bliss! – as though you'd suddenly swallowed a bright piece of that late afternoon sun and it burned in your bosom, sending out a little shower of sparks into every particle, into every finger and toe? (305)

Bertha can scarcely contain herself, she is overcome by such a feeling of bliss that she does not know what to do. The passage suggests a number of significant things about the nature of pleasure. First, there is an evocation of laughter which may complement some of the remarks we make about laughter in Chapter 12: Bertha wants 'to stand still and laugh at – nothing – at nothing, simply'. Laughter, the desire to laugh, is one manifestation of Bertha's feelings of extreme pleasure or 'bliss'. But more precisely laughter is identified with a sense of 'nothing, simply'. We may recall here Georges Bataille's remark: '[when I laugh,] I am in fact nothing other than the laughter which takes hold of me' (Bataille 1973, 364). There is, for Bertha, the desire to laugh but a desire for laughter that would be 'at nothing', a sense of laughter as pointless, as itself nothing.

Second, and related to this, there is the sense of bliss (like the force of uncontrollable laughter) as something by which a subject – Bertha Young – is 'overcome'. The subject is no longer in control, but rather is in danger of shattering, as if into a 'shower of sparks'. Third, the passage suggests a striking correlation between 'bliss' and the inexpressible. The language of the extract resorts to the metaphorical, figurative and paradoxical (it was '*as though* you'd suddenly swallowed a bright piece of that late afternoon sun') precisely because it would appear that there is no other way of describing this 'feeling of bliss'. This feeling of bliss is like having a foreign body inside you (as if you'd suddenly swallowed a piece of the sun): it's alien to yourself but burning inside you. Fourth, and leading on from this, there is the suggestion that pleasure can be painful at the same time: the burning bosom here might be compared with the 'aching Pleasure' evoked in Keats's 'Ode on Melancholy'.

Finally, and perhaps most crucially, the passage draws the reader into the experience that is being described. It intimates a subtle kind of performative (see Chapter 27), that is to say we can think about the passage as not only describing something but also *doing something*. Pleasure, up to and perhaps even beyond the extreme form of pleasure to which the narrator gives the name 'bliss', is not just a topic or theme *in* the text: it also *is* the text, it is the title of the text and it is a potential effect of reading. The text draws us into a sense of what Wordsworth refers to when he declares, of his experience of the first days of the French Revolution, in *The Prelude*: 'Bliss was it in that dawn to be alive' (Book XI, 108). Through its evocations of the loveliness of the world (a blue dish, a pear tree in blossom), Mansfield's story affirms and calls on us to affirm the inexpressible pleasures of being alive: it evokes a revolution in sensibility. It also gives us the pleasure of reading as romance, reading about romance, about the subtleties of erotic feelings between people. It gives us the pleasures of identification, irony, suspense and social satire. And 'Bliss' gives us all of these things in language: the experience of pleasure is an experience of words, a pleasure in words, even as it points towards a sense of pleasure that is inexpressible, beyond words.

The pleasure of reading 'Bliss' starts with the deceptive simplicity of its narrative perspective. We are confronted here with an apparently omniscient or telepathic narrator who is capable of inhabiting the mind, body and feelings of the protagonist. This is what narrative theorists call 'free indirect discourse', in which we are presented with a voice practising impersonation or ventriloquism, a voice that is undecidably both the narrator's and the character's. Bertha Young's thoughts and feelings are conveyed not only through a third-person narration ('she still had moments', 'she wanted to run') but also, in the second paragraph of the extract, in the second-person ('you are overcome'). This is unusual – though an important characteristic of Mansfield's work generally – and strangely insidious: the 'you', after all, may not finally stop short of *you*, the reader. The subtle, almost imperceptible way in which the text draws us into the experience of what is being described can be illustrated in the very opening words of the story: 'Although Bertha Young was thirty she still had moments like this.' The word 'this' seems to call on the reader to acknowledge or accept something already evident, already presented to her or him. Discreetly, deftly, it draws the reader into the immediate here and now of the experience of bliss.

Another aspect of the pleasure of Mansfield's story has to do with its creation of irony and suspense. The text works through suspense, through the pleasure of suspension and an ominous suspension of pleasure. For while the narrative perspective invites us to identify with Bertha and her feelings of bliss, the text also generates other, more specifically readerly kinds of pleasure. Bertha's feelings of 'bliss', for example, are at various moments represented in ironic terms. The reader is given a strong sense that – despite the repeated evocations of the 'fire of bliss', the incredible beauty of the table, the pear tree and so on – Bertha Young may have a rather limited experience of bliss, especially in sexual terms. Near the end of the story we are told that, as people are about to start leaving the party, 'For the first time in her life Bertha Young desired her husband' (314). Bliss in this case seems to have been postponed. The reader takes pleasure, then, in being able to identify with the protagonist but to experience at the same time a sense of ironic detachment. Above all, the reader's pleasure is generated by the pervasive sense that something is going to happen, that the narrator knows something (and soon perhaps the reader will know something too) which fundamentally complicates Bertha's feelings of 'bliss'. Bliss, then, seems to involve a state of suspension – for Bertha, for the reader and, differently, for the very structure of narration.

On this basis we can perhaps formulate one or two more general propositions about pleasure and literature. Literature is about the possibilities of pleasure. It is about the idea that readerly pleasure is erotic. Literature is erotic (even if it is not literally concerned with erotic or sexual topics or themes) because it is always concerned with seducing the reader. Literary texts can seduce us, or, put more strongly, they need to seduce us. In a sense there is no reason to read a literary text, it serves no purpose, has no function. And this is why, as Ross Chambers has argued, in his book *Story and Situation: Narrative Seduction and the Power of Fiction* (1984), the essential 'power' of a literary text is its power of seduction. In particular, literary seduction has to do with identification (the reader's identification with a character, narrator, author or situation), with a sense of intrigue, mystery or secrecy (what is this text about? Is it, in fact, about something different from what it appears to be about? What designs does it have on me?), and with the beauty of language (elegance of expression, lyricism, wit, poignant or provoking metaphors, and so on). Finally, a literary text can seduce us through a logic of what Freud calls 'disavowal'. Disavowal involves the situation in which someone knows that such and such is not true but nevertheless thinks, speaks or acts as if it is true. Disavowal involves thinking: 'I know, but still . . .' The process of disavowal whereby we can be seduced into the world of literature, into fictional worlds, has been neatly phrased by Roland Barthes in his book, *The Pleasure of the Text* (1973): the reader *disavows*, in other words he or she keeps thinking, '*I know these are only words, but all the same . . .*' (Barthes 1990a, 47). The logic of disavowal perhaps offers a more precise way of thinking about how we read works of literature than Coleridge's famous idea of a 'willing suspension of disbelief' (Coleridge 1975, 169): the notion of disavowal more dramatically highlights the contradictoriness of what is going on in the act of reading. The work of the text, its task of seduction, is to ensure this disavowal, to put the reader into this state of what is at once 'truth' and 'fiction'.

This principle of disavowal – of reading a work of fiction as though it were not only words – permits us to suggest a way of distinguishing between litera-ture and pornography. Both have a capacity for erotic and sexual stimulation but the difference between them could be said to consist in the fact that a liter-ary work does not allow the reader to forget the process by which he or she is being seduced, whereas pornography calls for the abolition of the 'as though' altogether. In other words, pornography entails what John Forrester (follow-ing Jean Baudrillard) describes as 'a fantasy of a real in which representation does not exist, i.e. a real without seduction' (Forrester 1990, 332). Katherine Mansfield's 'Bliss' is not likely to be classified as pornography; but it is certainly about erotic and sexual feelings – both in what it tells and in its telling. More particularly, the story explores some of the limits of pleasure: it dramat-izes the ways in which pleasure is concerned with strangeness (the nothing-ness of laughter), paradox (the inarticulable) and contradiction (disavowal). Fundamental to this is what Mansfield's text suggests about the curious tem-porality of pleasure. To recall the opening words once more: 'Although Bertha Young was thirty she still had moments like this when she wanted to run instead of walk, to take dancing steps on and off the pavement, to bowl a hoop, to throw something up in the air and catch it again, or to stand still and laugh at – nothing – at nothing, simply.' This sentence is set in the past tense, but the 'this' ('moments like this') suggests something immediate, here and now. In fact, the time of 'this' is uncertain and strange: it is as if the present of 'moments like this' is already gone. 'Moments like this' are presented in the past tense in such a way as to suggest that they are already 'moments like that' or 'moments like those'. The ambiguity of the this-ness of 'this' is compounded by multiplicity: Bertha wanted to run, to dance, to bowl a hoop, to throw and catch something, to stand still and laugh. Are these all different moments or are they different ways of figuring one single moment ('moments like this [one]')? The sense of time, in the context of extreme pleasure or 'bliss', seems to involve an undecidable, uncontainable multiplicity. Time cannot contain itself when it comes to bliss.

Katherine Mansfield's special focus on moments of intense feeling belongs to a specific historical context and in particular to the literary and cultural aftermath of late nineteenth-century aestheticism. This is to suggest that pleasure and bliss can be thought about in historical terms: they are experienced and represented differently at different times. A full-scale account of the aestheticism associated with such figures as Walter Pater, Oscar Wilde, Algernon Swinburne, Aubrey Beardsley and others need not detain us here. Its principal concerns were with the idea of art for art's sake, beauty as truth, and the appeal of the moment for the moment's sake (there is no past, no future, only the present moment). In the late nineteenth century the aesthetes made of pleasure a philosophy, a moral creed, a way of being. At the heart of aestheticism is a focus on the beauty and power of the moment. It is concerned with the experience and expression of the intense pleasure of the present. The most succinct and eloquent text for an understanding of aestheticism is Walter Pater's Conclusion to his book *The Renaissance* (1873). This Conclusion, only a few pages in length, offers us a way of understanding the work of many modernist writers, including Joseph Conrad, James Joyce, D.H. Lawrence, Virginia Woolf, Elizabeth Bowen, Ezra Pound, Wallace Stevens, T.S. Eliot and Mansfield herself. All of these writers are singularly concerned with the power of particular moments. On the one hand, they are concerned with exploring a sense that the only time of *any* feeling or experience (painful or pleasurable) is right now, this very moment now. On the other hand, however, these writers are concerned with showing that even the present moment is already a ghost of itself. In the Conclusion to *The Renaissance*, Pater puts this concisely when he describes the present moment as 'gone while we try to apprehend it'. The present moment is that 'of which it may ever be more truly said that it has ceased to be than that it is' (196). Pater's Conclusion urges us to make the most of the ecstatic and passionate possibilities of experience, given the 'awful brevity' of our lives: life is defined as 'this short day of frost and sun' (197) and (one of the things that made Pater's text quite scandalous at the time of its first publication) there is no sense of any afterlife or consolations beyond the grave. Here is the conclusion to Pater's Conclusion:

our one chance lies in expanding that interval [i.e. life], in getting as many pulsations as possible into the given time. Great passions may give us this quickened sense of life, ecstasy and sorrow of love, the various forms of enthusiastic activity, disinterested or otherwise, which come naturally to many of us. Only be sure it is passion – that it does yield you this fruit of a quickened, multiplied consciousness. Of such wisdom, the poetic passion, the desire of beauty, the love of art for its own sake, has most. For art comes to you proposing frankly to give nothing but the highest quality to your moments as they pass, and simply for those moments' sake. (198–9)

Pater's unprecedented emphasis on the present moment played a crucial role in the development of aestheticism in Britain, the United States and elsewhere. It haunts modernist writing in turn – whether in the form of epiphanies (in James Joyce's *A Portrait of the Artist as a Young Man* for example), or of what Virginia Woolf famously refers to as 'moments of being', or of what Mansfield, at the start of 'Bliss', refers to as 'moments like this'. All of these writers in their different ways are concerned with the uncontainable, delirious, ecstatic, inexpressible quality of individual moments, of time as (only) now. It is not simply a question of a '*carpe diem*' ('seize the day') motif in modern literature. Rather, it is a matter of how the present moment resists any attempt to appropriate or 'seize' it. It is a matter of how moments of extreme pleasure (including orgasm) are at the same time moments of loss: such moments involve, indeed, a kind of dissolution and more generally suggest a sense of experience in terms of what Pater calls 'that continual vanishing away, that strange, perpetual weaving and unweaving of ourselves' (196).

In other words, as Mansfield's story suggests, pleasure can be thought about in terms of a subversion of identity. It is for this reason, among others, that it is not possible to say that the kinds of pleasures with which this chapter is concerned are simply hedonistic. Nor can one say that the kind of thinking and experience valued by Pater constitutes mere self-indulgence or a contemptible neglect of political and social realities. As a way of illustrating this we will focus on what is perhaps the most important and most pleasurable work on the topic of pleasure and literature in recent years, Roland Barthes's *The Pleasure of the Text*. Barthes stresses that 'hedonism has been repressed by nearly every philosophy' (Barthes 1990a, 57) and he is at pleasurable pains to argue against such repression. The value and originality of his study consists not in the politically suspect project of advocating hedonism in a traditional sense but rather in the critical delineation of the paradoxes of pleasure, specifically in the experience of reading. Barthes offers a sort of critical anatomy of pleasure in reading. In particular, he distinguishes between two sorts of pleasure: pleasure of the 'comfortable' sort and pleasure of a more disturbing and subversive kind. Barthes writes:

> Text of pleasure: the text that contents, fills, grants euphoria; the text that comes from culture and does not break with it, is linked to a *comfortable* practice of reading. Text of bliss: the text that imposes a state of loss, the text that discomforts (perhaps to the point of a certain boredom), unsettles the reader's historical, cultural, psychological assumptions, the consistency of his tastes, values, memories, brings to a crisis his relation with language. (14)

Barthes's book suggests, then, that there are two ways in which we could think about pleasure. One is basically recuperative: it does not break with culture but rather reinforces traditional or comfortable notions of meaning, society, ideology, etc. The other sense of pleasure ('bliss') is more unsettling and strange. No doubt all literary and other cultural texts are susceptible to being read in both of these ways. Barthes's own emphasis, however, falls on 'bliss' ('jouissance' in French). 'Bliss' has to do with the inexpressible: 'pleasure can be expressed in words, bliss cannot' (21). Bliss has to do with a deconstruction of the political: it is thus engaged in 'de-politicizing what is apparently political, and in politicizing what apparently is not' (44). Or as Barthes puts it: 'The text is (should be) that uninhibited person who shows his behind to the *Political Father*' (53). Above all, bliss has to do with the subversion of identity itself. As with the uncontrollable force of laughter or the moment of orgasm, the extreme pleasure of bliss involves a collapse of self, a (momentary) dissolution of identity. The subject is thus 'never anything but a "living contradiction": a split subject, who simultaneously enjoys, through the text, the consistency of his selfhood and its collapse, its fall' (21).

By way of conclusion, we would like to suggest that – while Barthes refers to the reader as 'he' – the 'living contradiction' he describes may be thought about as, in the final analysis, undecidably gendered. Partly what makes Barthes's work unusual and challenging is that it explicitly centres on the importance of 'emotion', defining this as 'a disturbance, a bordering on collapse' (25). For Barthes, we could say, the pleasure of reading inevitably involves 'getting hysterical'. But the collapse of selfhood, the shattering force of bliss which he talks about, is a collapse in which it is no longer clear whether there is a subject, or what gender it might belong to. Mansfield's story can also be considered in these terms. Insofar as it is a text about 'women and hysteria', it suggests that 'getting hysterical' (306) is just as much a male as a female tendency. 'Bliss', that is to say, is as much about male hysteria as it is about female hysteria. This is evident, in particular, in Mansfield's characterization of

Eddie Warren, the poet who is '(as usual) in a state of acute distress', and whose first words, frenetically peppered with italics, provide a hysterical account of his journey to the Youngs':

> 'I have had such a *dreadful* experience with a taxi-man; he was *most* sinister. I couldn't get him to *stop*. The *more* I knocked and called the *faster* he went. And *in* the moonlight this *bizarre* figure with the *flattened* head *crouching* over the *lit-tle* wheel . . .' (309)

But it is also evident in Mansfield's characterization of Bertha's husband Harry, who is one moment 'rush[ing] into battle where no battle was' (310) and at others 'extravagantly [i.e. hysterically] cool and collected' (310, 315). More radically, however, 'Bliss' is a story about the condition of 'living contradiction' which Barthes evokes. It suggests that that extreme of pleasure called 'bliss' is our undoing, including the undoing of gender-identity.

The story concludes with Harry locking up and Bertha recalling Pearl Fulton's final words to her ('Your lovely pear tree!'):

> And then she was gone, with Eddie following, like the black cat following the grey cat.
> 'I'll shut up shop,' said Harry, extravagantly cool and collected.
> 'Your lovely pear tree—pear tree—pear tree!'
> Bertha simply ran over to the long windows.
> 'Oh, what is going to happen now?' she cried.
> But the pear tree was as lovely as ever and as full of flower and as still. (315)

'Bliss' ends with this 'still'. It leaves the question of bliss itself in suspense, inexpressible, unbearable. As Barthes remarks: 'Pleasure's force of *suspension* can never be overstated' (Barthes 1990a, 65). Pleasure remains resistant and enigmatic, like 'literature'. The pleasure of literature is perhaps less to do with the fact that it 'holds a mirror up to nature', offering a reflection of 'life', and more to do with an experience of 'living contradiction' – with what suspends or momentarily shatters our sense of ourselves. It is subversive, finally, in suggesting that nothing is obvious, that, as Stephen Melville puts it: 'nothing is obvious either in advance or after the fact' (Melville 1986, xxvi).

Further reading

For a contemporary classic account, see Michel Foucault's *The Use of Pleasure* (*The History of Sexuality*, vol. 2, 1985). On pleasure and reading in general, see Roland Barthes's *The Pleasure of the Text* (1990a). For reading and seduction, Ross Chambers's *Story and Situation: Narrative Seduction and the Power of Fiction* (1984) is a fascinating and quite accessible work. Jean Baudrillard's *Seduction* (1990) is an important study but difficult. On the power of the moment in modern literature a good place to start is Morris Beja's clear and very readable *Epiphany in the Modern Novel* (1971). For an advanced study of pleasure and self, see Carolyn J. Dean's *The Self and Its Pleasures* (1992). On literature and the gendering of hysteria, see Elaine Showalter's fine essay 'On Hysterical Narrative' (1993). For a useful collection of essays on pleasure in relation to cultural studies, see Stephen Regan, ed., *The Politics of Pleasure* (1992). On the politics of enjoyment, in particular regarding enjoyment as something ordered, imposed or 'superegotistical', see Slavoj Žižek, *For They Know Not What They Do: Enjoyment as a Political Factor* (1991).

33. War

Here's a poem that you probably won't like very much:

I

Half a league, half a league,
  Half a league onward,
All in the valley of Death
  Rode the six hundred.
5 'Forward, the Light Brigade!
Charge for the guns!' he said:
Into the valley of Death
  Rode the six hundred.

II

'Forward, the Light Brigade!'
10 Was there a man dismayed?
Not though the soldier knew
  Some one had blundered:
Theirs not to make reply,
Theirs not to reason why,
15 Theirs but to do and die:
Into the valley of Death
  Rode the six hundred.

III

Cannon to the right of them,
Cannon to the left of them,
20 Cannon in front of them
  Volleyed and thundered;

Stormed at with shot and shell,
Boldly they rode and well,
Into the jaws of Death,
25   Into the mouths of hell
Rode the six hundred.

IV
Flashed all their sabres bare,
Flashed as they turned in air
Sabring the gunner there,
30   Charging an army, while
All the world wondered:
Plunged in the battery-smoke
Right through the line they broke;
Cossack and Russian
35   Reeled from the sabre-stroke
Shattered and sundered.
Then they rode back, but not
Not the six hundred.

V
Cannon to the right of them,
40   Cannon to the left of them,
Cannon behind them
Volleyed and thundered;
Stormed at with shot and shell,
While horse and hero fell,
45   They that had fought so well
Came through the jaws of Death
Back from the mouth of hell,
All that was left of them,
Left of the six hundred.

VI
50   When can their glory fade?
O the wild charge they made!
All the world wondered.
Honour the charge they made!
Honour the Light Brigade,
55   Noble six hundred!

The poem recounts an incident from the Crimean War (1854–6): after a
'blunder' by an officer, 673 lightly-armed British cavalrymen charged the
Russian artillery, resulting in about 400 British casualties. 'The Charge of

the Light Brigade' was written on 2 December 1854 by Alfred Tennyson, the poet laureate – 'in a few minutes', he says, after reading a report of the incident in the *Times* newspaper. It is a famous poem that is invariably included in anthologies, so you'll probably know it or know of it. If you had gone to an English school in the early twentieth century you might well have been made to memorize and recite it. But what is it about the poem that you (probably) don't like and indeed that you may disapprove of? There are two things in particular. First, there are its militaristic repetitions and rhythms. This means that, despite its intricately varied form, the poem can seem somewhat crude or unsophisticated. And the formal, public nature of the poem might seem a little dated as well – just the kind of thing you might expect of a nineteenth-century poet laureate. Second, there is the sentiment that underlies the poem: it seems unreservedly to celebrate warfare, heroism, and perhaps above all an unthinking and unquestioning adherence to one's duty. Tennyson's poem seems to glorify the actions of those compatriots who fight and die in war, even – or especially – in the context of a futile, misguided, suicidal military manoeuvre. Someone has blundered, but the poem is not particularly interested in who that might be, or in holding anyone responsible for the error. Instead, Tennyson simply seeks to praise the soldierly virtues of those who carried out orders. For these reasons, the poem has come to seem (as one critic puts it) 'mildly ludicrous, slightly contemptible' (McGann 1985, 190–1).

You'll probably like Wilfred Owen's 'Futility' rather better:

> Move him into the sun –
> Gently its touch awoke him once,
> At home, whispering of fields half-sown.
> Always it woke him, even in France,
> 5 Until this morning and this snow.
> If anything might rouse him now
> The kind old sun will know.
>
> Think how it wakes the seeds –
> Woke once the clays of a cold star.
> 10 Are limbs, so dear achieved, are sides
> Full-nerved, still warm, too hard to stir?
> Was it for this the clay grew tall?
> – O what made fatuous sunbeams toil
> To break earth's sleep at all?

This First World War poem was written in May 1918 and published posthumously in 1920. It gradually becomes clear that the 'him' of the first line is in fact a dead soldier. Like Tennyson's poem, Owen's is very well known and like Tennyson's it focuses on a futile death. Like Tennyson's, Owen's is a poem of commemoration or mourning. In other respects, though, 'Futility' seems very different. It takes the form of an intimately personal, even private lyric, expressing the sadness of an individual (a soldier, rather than a civilian newspaper reader, we might surmise from the intimacy and directness of the poem). This contrasts with Tennyson's more detached, formal and public expression of pride, a kind of triumphant mourning. For Owen, as he famously said in a planned Preface to his poems, the poetry 'is in the pity' (Owen 1985, 192). In its own way, Owen's poem is just as much a piece of propaganda as Tennyson's jingoistic ballad. It is a matter of anti-war propaganda in this case – though it has been read by some critics as being, in its nostalgic evocation of 'home', a kind of pro-British propaganda (see for example Pittock 2001). 'Futility' works as public propaganda through its very privateness. It works as propaganda by appearing not to. Only at the very end of the poem does it become evident why it is called 'Futility'. The poem involves an almost abstract meditation on the futility of war, moving from the expression of mourning for an individual soldier to the question of the futility of human life. It shifts from curiously muted imperatives ('move him', 'Think how') to a series of plangently rhetorical questions. There is no narrative beyond this movement of the speaker's thoughts and we know next to nothing about the individual who died, an individual who in fact seems to stand (in a kind of synecdoche) for the many others, many British at least, who died in the First World War. The poem's form itself disavows any suggestion of militarism or of the celebration of battle: the subtly varied rhymes and half-rhymes ('sun', 'once', 'half-sown', 'France', 'snow', 'now', 'know') and the gently tripping rhythm ('Think how it wakes the seeds – / Woke once the clays of a cold star') themselves abrogate the strident uniformity of militarism. Even nationalism is subdued to a longing for English fields. The poem won't march in step, so to speak.

We think you'll like Owen's poem more than Tennyson's (though we might be wrong, of course, especially if you have the military in mind as a career option). In other words, we imagine you will be more inclined to assent to Owen's understated critique of war and militarism. It is easier to identify with the quiet, meditative, lyric poise of its individualized elegiac voice, its anti-militaristic rhythms. Such a preference would be in keeping with a more general change in literary and cultural taste over the last 150 years, especially in the wake of two world wars, the American trauma of Vietnam, and what many see as the disasters of the US and British invasions of Afghanistan and Iraq. The public, nationalistic celebration of military heroism of the nineteenth century has given way to a more contemporary appreciation of the significance of private sorrow and a resistance to the futility of war, any war, all war.

But things were not always so. Literature begins with war, with the rage of war. *Menis*: wrath, fury, rage. The first word of the first great poem in the Western literary tradition, Homer's *Iliad* (*c.* 700 BC), declares its topic: *menis*, the rage of Achilles. The Western tradition, in other words, starts up in rage and blood, the rage for war, the rage for rage – godlike, swift-footed, murderous Achilles' rage:

> Rage – Goddess, sing the rage of Peleus' son Achilles,
> murderous, doomed, that cost the Achaeans countless losses,
> hurling down to the House of Death so many sturdy souls,
> great fighters' souls, but made the bodies carrion,
> feasts for the dogs and birds,
> and the will of Zeus was moving towards its end.
> Begin, Muse, when the two first broke and clashed,
> Agamemnon lord of men and brilliant Achilles.
>   (Homer 1990: Book 1, lines 1–8)

What is striking about such a beginning, and about Homer's poem as a whole, is its keen enthusiasm for war, a celebration of war that is joined with loud regret for its murderous, bloody losses. The poet calls on the goddess, his muse, to 'sing the rage' of Achilles, attempting to summon up poetry that will itself be warrior-like, belligerent. Homer's narrative is driven by its tale of war, just as its readers are, and at the same time it is sickened by its own violence, just as its readers are. The language itself, in Robert Fagles's evocative translation, has a belligerence that is at once appalling, and appalled. Here, even at the very start of the Western literary tradition, there is a sense that war is all, that war is total and never ending. The *Iliad* is thoroughly immersed in warfare, with up to half of its 17,000 lines concerned with battles. Its set-piece battle-scenes and intricate, bloody evocations of hand-to-hand fighting make the *Iliad* seem like a multiplex conflation of *Bridge Over the River Kwai*, *Star Wars*, *Apocalypse Now*, *Saving Private Ryan*, and *Fight Club* – but in the hexameters of Homeric Greek verse rather than as a Dolby-enhanced cinematic experience. The opening to the *Iliad* takes place in the tenth year of the Achaean siege of Troy, and the sense that the war might never end is voiced early on by Agamemnon: 'We are still fighting it, / no end in sight' (Book 2, lines 142–3). Indeed, the end of Homer's poem is not the end of the war: victory and defeat are still looming. We leave, we are left, at the end of the *Iliad*, with the death of Hector, the Trojan leader. 'The *Iliad* is a poem that lives and moves and has its being in war', comments the classical scholar Bernard Knox, 'in that world of organized violence in which a man justifies his existence most clearly by killing others' (Homer 1990, 35). This war, Homer's war, is a war without end.

Amazingly, for much of the twentieth century the *Iliad* was read as anything but a war poem (see Tatum 2003, 49–50). In his classic study of the poem *Tradition and Design in the 'Iliad'* (1930), for example, Maurice Bowra analyses it as a 'profoundly moral story' that is 'tragic in character' (26). Why is it that a poem about a war has systematically been read differently, as if it was 'really' about something else, not about war at all? It may be that the answer has to do with the poem's obsessive focus on the very stuff of war, on rage, violence, blood and bodies in pieces, and with our desire to think of poetry in other terms, as celebrating other virtues, less polemical kinds of thinking. It may at least partly be explained, in other words, by the delight that the poem takes in gore, savagery, rage, violence. Here are some samples from Book 16, if you can stomach them:

> Brave Patroclus first –
> just as Areilycus swerved in sudden flight
> he gored him in the hip with a slashing spear
> and the bronze lancehead hammered through his flesh,
> the shaft splintering bone as he pitched face-first,
> pounding the ground –
> And the veteran Menelaus wounded Thoas,
> raking his chest where the shield-rim left it bare,
> and loosed his limbs –
> And Amphiclus went for Meges
> but Meges saw him coming and got in first by far,
> spearing him up the thigh where it joins the body,
> the point where a man's muscle bunches thickest:
> the tough sinews shredded around the weapon's point
> as the dark swirled down his eyes –
> . . .
> Idomeneus skewered Erymas straight through the mouth,
> the merciless brazen spearpoint raking through,
> up under the brain to split his glistening skull –
> teeth shattered out, both eyes brimmed to the lids
> with a gush of blood and both nostrils spurting,
> mouth gaping, blowing convulsive sprays of blood
> and death's dark cloud closed down around his corpse.
> (Homer 1990, Book 16, lines 362–74, 407–13)

In this respect, Homer's poem is the equivalent not of the sanitized violence of a Hollywood war movie, nor even of the discreetly edited images from 'war torn' countries that are beamed into your sitting room by CNN or the BBC, but of Goya's shocking images of the Spanish War of Independence in *Disasters of War* (1810–14): bodies in pieces, bodies hacked, sliced, torn apart, decapitated, dismembered, disembowelled. Homer's words, like Goya's pictures, are grotesque in their realism, appalling in their unflinching, even zealous, recording of human suffering, in their representation of *people* violently objectified as violated, hacked and pierced *bodies*.

So what is a war poem presenting us with? What are Homer, Tennyson and Owen commemorating? To what are they testifying or bearing witness? The question of commemoration and testimony, of poetry as bearing witness and the associated questions of trauma and trauma theory, have become important dimensions of literary studies in the past decade or so, both in relation to cultural representations of war and, more especially, in relation to Holocaust studies. 'How is the act of *writing* tied up with the act of *bearing witness?*' asks Shoshana Felman in *Testimony: Crises of Witnessing in Literature, Psychoanalysis, and History* (1992). 'Is the act of *reading* literary texts itself inherently related to the act of *facing horror?*' she ponders (2). Writing of Claude Lanzmann's film *Shoah* (1985), a film of first-hand testimonies by witnesses of – mostly victims of – the Holocaust, Felman defines our era as an '*age of testimony*', one in which witnessing itself 'has undergone a major trauma'. Lanzmann's film, Felman argues, presents 'a historical crisis of witnessing' out of which witnessing becomes 'in all senses of the word, a *critical* activity' (Felman 1992, 206). For Felman, this 'crisis' involves the sense that bearing witness to something of such unimaginable horror as the Holocaust puts the act of witnessing itself under extreme pressure. Susan Gubar expresses at least part of the difficulty in the subtitle to her recent book *Poetry After Auschwitz: Remembering What One Never Knew* (2003): the problem of testimony in the context of the Holocaust has to do with the difficulty of fully or properly 'knowing' what has been witnessed, even by those most directly involved as victims – or indeed as persecutors.

But the crisis of witnessing also involves the idea that, as Jacques Derrida puts it, testimony 'always goes hand in hand with at least the *possibility* of fiction, perjury, lie' (Derrida 2000, 27). As Derrida makes clear, this is *not* to say that all testimony is fiction, perjury, lie, not to dissolve the crucial distinction between truth and lie, truth and fiction, but to suggest nevertheless that they are inextricably linked. This is evident, not least, from the writings of the Holocaust, writings by victims and witnesses such as Primo Levi, who themselves struggle to make sense, to form narratives, out of their experiences, to piece their experiences together into coherent shapes. Levi's *If This Is A Man* (published in the USA as *Survival in Auschwitz*) (1958) is an extraordinary account of his time in Auschwitz – 'Auschwitz, *anus mundi*, ultimate drainage site of the German universe', as he calls it (Levi 1989, 65). Explaining the 'fragmentary character' of the book, Levi recounts that, at the time, the need to tell his story involved 'an immediate and violent impulse, to the point of competing with . . . other elementary needs'. The shaping of these fragments into a book only occurred later. The book could only retrospectively lend coherence to what took place in the arsehole of the world (Levi 1987, 15–16). Levi even proposes, in his later meditation on witnessing the Holocaust *The Drowned and the Saved* (1986), that the witnesses to the full horror of Auschwitz are precisely those who can never bear witness, since they are those who went under, who 'drowned', who were killed. As Paul Celan writes, in what is perhaps the most succinct but inexhaustibly provoking remark on this topic: 'No one / bears witness for / the witness' (Celan 1971, 241). The witness is always, in some sense, deprived. There is something eerie and ghostly about the solitude of bearing witness.

Derrida adds another perception to our thinking of testimony, however, a perception which is fundamental to the question of the *Shoah*, the destruction or burning, the Holocaust of World War Two in particular, but which will also take us back to the question of war literature, and to the poems of Tennyson, Owen and Homer. As Derrida argues, testimony involves a 'universalizable singularity' (Derrida 2000, 94). A testimony must in the first place be singular, unique:

> I am the only one to have seen this unique thing [the witness says], the only one to have heard or to have been put in the presence of this or that, at a determinate, indivisible instant; and you must believe me because you must believe me – this is the difference, essential to testimony, between belief and proof – you must believe me because I am irreplaceable. (40)

But at the same time, this singularity, this irreplaceability of testimony, of the witness, must also be 'exemplary', must also stand as an example. The witness implicitly announces that:

> I swear to tell the truth, where I have been the only one to see or hear and where I am the only one who can attest to it, this is true to the extent that anyone *in my place*, at that instant, would have seen or heard or touched the same thing and could repeat exemplarily, universally, the truth of my testimony. The exemplarity of the 'instant', that which makes it an 'instance', if you like, is that it is singular, singular *and* universal, singular

and universalizable. The singular must be universalizable; this is the testimonial condition. (41; translation modified)

Let us return to our three war poems and briefly consider how each is caught up in its own way with problems of testimony and exemplarity. The force of Homer's narration of violent hackings and gory deaths involves the specificity of those violations, the uniqueness of each slash, each stab. But the force also inheres in the exemplarity of these actions and these scenes, which means that one stab or slash has to take the place of thousands (just as in Hollywood movies, for different, for financial reasons, a handful of soldiers must take the place of thousands). The emotional, visceral effect on us as readers is surely to make us imagine what it would be like to receive or to deliver such violations of the body. And it is the terrible specificity, the graphic violence of the images that gives them their sense of authenticity, even as we understand that these acts take place in the realm of myth, that 'Homer' (whoever he was or they were) is not a witness, that 'Homer' is part of the myth. Part of what is remarkable about these scenes, perhaps, is our uncertainty about their undecidably mythic status (remembering that, as such critics as Paul Veyne have argued, in Ancient Greek culture myths were at the same time believed in and not believed in, seen as both true and not true (see Veyne 1988)). By contrast, through the intimacy of his language, his touching lyricism, Owen evokes a sense that this one soldier's death stands for the deaths of thousands of others and that the speaker's authentically personal witnessing of this death can stand as a wider argument about the futility of war. The 'Futility' of the title is not just of this death but of all war deaths. But in this case, it is on account of the 'authenticity effect' (as we might call it), the sense that the speaker has been a witness to this particular individual death, that he can speak with authority about war. Finally, Tennyson makes the opposite argument, an argument for war or at least for its heroism, when he witnesses, as a newspaper reader, the heroism of soldiers even in the face of blundering officers. And it is precisely because his witnessing is not unique and indeed not direct that his poem may seem to those living in the contemporary 'age of testimony' to be false, phoney, unconvincing, crass.

The different testamentary structures of the poems of Tennyson, Owen and Homer open up another question, the question of the 'aesthetic' pleasure that we might take from scenes of death, sacrifice, savagery. Why do we like to read and imagine such scenes? What is it about such scenes that is so compelling, even as they repel? It is in dealing with paradoxical questions such as these that psychoanalysis can be especially helpful. Freud's 'Psychopathic Characters on the Stage' (1904), for example, offers a rich exploration of drama and *agon* (or conflict), and of the reader's or speaker's suffering as a form of 'compensation' (Freud 1985h, 123). In fact, war haunts the work of Sigmund Freud. There are writings that specifically focus on its meanings and psychological effects, such as 'Thoughts for the Times on War and Death' (1915), 'On Transience' (1916), 'Mourning and Melancholia' (1917), and 'Why War?' (1933). But war is in fact everywhere in Freud's thinking. Freud is a great theorist of war and of *agon* more generally. Amongst his most remarkable, devastating essays in this context is 'Civilization and Its Discontents' (1930). Here he offers a compelling explanation for our delight in – and, to use Seamus Heaney's phrase from 'Punishment' (1975), our 'civilized outrage' at – images of war. Freud argues that aggression goes deep but that it conflicts with our sense of 'civilization', our sense of ourselves as civilized, cultured, rational and reasonable beings. In 'Civilization and Its Discontents', he argues that human beings are driven by what he calls the 'pleasure principle' but that the 'programme of becoming happy . . . cannot be fulfilled', and indeed that 'what we call our civilization is largely responsible for our misery' (Freud 1985e, 271, 274). Freud suggests that there is a fundamental conflict or contradiction between our primitive instincts – in particular our aggressiveness – and our desire or need for civilization (by which he means both what he calls 'Eros', the 'instinct' of love, fellowship, community, and the need for security). Rather than simply being 'gentle creatures who want to be loved', Freud tells us, human beings are, 'on the contrary, creatures among whose instinctual endowments is to be reckoned a powerful share of aggressiveness' (302). It is 'not easy for men to give up the satisfaction of this inclination to aggression', Freud argues, and they 'do not feel comfortable without it' (304–5). The reason for our unhappiness, Freud suggests, is that 'civilization' demands that we forgo our 'natural aggressive instinct, the hostility of each against all and of all against each' (313). 'The price we pay for our advance in civilization', he declares, 'is a loss of happiness through the heightening of the sense of guilt' (327). In so-called 'civilized' society, our instinctual aggression is turned inward, it becomes that kind of psychic violence of the 'conscience' experienced as feelings of 'guilt'. Freud's analysis of human aggression and its conflict with the social or 'civilized' might help us to understand something of the problem of the literature of war, and our ambivalence in reading it.

Freud helps us to think differently about literature and war – more polemically, perhaps ('polemic' comes from the Greek *polemos*, war). In particular, his work serves to challenge two perhaps rather naive, sentimental or unhistorical conceptions about war literature. In the first place it allows us to question the assumption that war is the opposite of peace and that peace is the natural or normal condition of society. 'War and Peace': Leo Tolstoy's title can easily be read as articulating a contrast, an opposition. But it can also, and perhaps more productively, be construed as a conjunction, a joining up. We might thus start to explore the idea that there is no literature that is not war literature. War in the *Iliad*, remember, never ends. And war in 'post-war' Europe and beyond has never stopped – in colonial, neocolonial and postcolonial arenas; as the 'cold war' (in which 'real' war was displaced to other, mostly developing, countries); in tribal conflicts, civil wars and inter-ethnic killings in Europe and across the globe; and as the so-called 'war against terror', our new war of religion. Second, Freud's work encourages us to question the assumption that the literature of war is, or should be, somehow 'naturally' or normally against war, anti-war, pacifist or non-combatant. In fact, something of the opposite is true: the history of Western literature is a history of warfare and belligerence, of *agon* and *polemos*. From Homer's *Iliad* to Virgil's *Aeneid* to Chaucer's *Troilus and Criseyde* to Milton's *Paradise Lost*, the epic tradition in particular, that most elevated of genres, has celebrated the heroes of warfare and celebrated the victory of the mighty. And traces of war are found in more recent epics even when they appear to be about other things than war. We could consider, for example, William Wordsworth's *The Prelude* (with its turning point of the French Revolution), Keats's *Hyperion* (a poem on the war of the gods), Byron's *Don Juan* (with its fascination with the Napoleonic Wars), Walt Whitman's *Leaves of Grass* (which according to Whitman himself 'revolves around' the American Civil War), Ezra Pound's *The Cantos* (which spans two world wars), or David Jones's *In Parenthesis* (recounting the poet's experience as a soldier in the First World War).

We might remember Doris Lessing's remark that it is 'sentimental to discuss the subject of war, or peace, without acknowledging that a great many people enjoy war – not only the idea of it, but the fighting itself' and that this is true 'even of people whose experiences in war were terrible, and which ruined their lives' (quoted in Tatum 2003, 116). That certainly seems to have been the case in the early twentieth century, at the beginning of its first 'great' war: Bertrand Russell expresses pacifist horror at finding in 1914 that 'the anticipation of carnage was delightful to something like ninety per cent of the population' (Russell 1968, 2:17). It is for this reason, perhaps, that literature is not simply *against* war, the poetry is not only in the 'pity'. And an understanding of this fact will perhaps better help us to understand the strange double-talk and double-dealings of literature, and to appreciate the deep, troubled and incessant conjunction of literature and war.

Further reading

For fascinating recent work on literature and the Holocaust see Geoffrey Hartman's *Scars of the Spirit* (2002), Daniel Schwartz's *Imagining the Holocaust* (1999), Susan Gubar's *Poetry After Auschwitz* (2003) and Robert Eaglestone, *The Holocaust and the Postmodern* (2004). More generally on trauma and writing in relation to psychoanalysis, literature and history, see Cathy Caruth's *Unclaimed Experience* (1996); for an interesting discussion of the significance of trauma in contemporary literature and culture, see Roger Luckurst, *The Trauma Question* (2008); and for a helpful study of the term and concept in Western cultural history more generally, see Ruth Leys, *Trauma: A Genealogy* (2000). For a fascinating if challenging meditation on AIDS writing, autobiography, writing about war, and on responses to trauma generally, see Ross Chambers, *Untimely Meditations* (2004). For a psycho-analytic approach to the question of aggression and war, see the title essay in Jacqueline Rose's *Why War?* (1993). James Tatum's excellent study of the culture of war in *The Mourner's Song* (2003) focuses in particular on Homer and the Vietnam war and touches on a number of points raised in this chapter; James Winn's *The Poetics of War* (2008) is a very readable book on what he calls 'the terrible beauty of war'. There are very many interesting and valuable studies of literature and the First World War in particular: see, for example, Paul Fussell's *The Great War and Modern Memory* (1975), Samuel Hynes's *A War Imagined: The First World War and English Culture* (1990), Allyson Booth's *Postcards from the Trenches* (1996), Vincent Sherry, ed., *The Cambridge Companion to the Literature of the First World War* (2005), and more generally Tim Kendall, ed., *The Oxford Companion to British and Irish War Poetry* (2007).

34. The end

Fin. The British comedians French and Saunders once did a parody of Ingmar Bergman films, in which they occupy an isolated clifftop house and moan at one another about alienation, death and damnation. The skit – shot, naturally, in black and white – concludes as the two women look out at the dismal grey seascape and see the letters 'FIN' appear amid the waves. One turns to the other and asks, 'What does it mean?' As with all witticisms perhaps, amusement here depends on a force of recognition: 'fin' is not a dorsal fin or an abbreviation for 'Finland' but is immediately recognizable as a word (rather pretentiously taken from the French language) meaning 'The End'. And we all know what 'The End' means. It's obvious. Or is it? What is an end?

In 'Little Gidding' (1942), T.S. Eliot observes that 'to make an end is to make a beginning. / The end is where we start from.' Certainly when it comes to reflecting critically on our reading of a literary text, thinking about the end is a good way of starting. We can ask ourselves various questions: How does the text end? What effects does this ending have? Where does the text leave *us* as readers? More specifically, what *kind* of ending does the text have? Is it abrupt, surprising, inevitable, apocalyptic, bathetic? And why? All of these are questions which assume that the end or ending is indeed final, conclusive, closed. But what happens when we think about texts as having open endings? In what ways might the text be seen as having an ending that is haunting, ambiguous, suspenseful, unfinished, equivocal, undecidable? Inevitably perhaps, the end of a literary text is both obvious and not so obvious – in some senses closed, but in others open. In any case, a particularly helpful way of reflecting on the overall force of a literary text is to analyse the nature and impact of its ending.

To provide a typology or systematic account of different kinds of endings, in poems, plays, short stories and novels, would be an endless task, since every ending is different from every other and each calls on the reader to respond to this singularity. It may be a characteristic of many short stories that they end with a twist, and it may be a characteristic of many sonnets that they end with a rhyming couplet, but every short story and every sonnet still has to be thought about on its own terms. In this way we might take the final line of Adrienne Rich's poem, 'A Valediction Forbidding Mourning' (1970), to be emblematic: 'To do something very common, in my own way.' Every poem, every literary work, must have an ending – however open, suspended or apparently non-conclusive – but each one has its own way of doing this 'very common' thing.

More than this, every literary work is open to rereading, and the way in which its ending is appreciated or understood will vary, however imperceptibly, not only from one reader to another but from one reading to another. The idea of rereading can help us to clarify two important points about endings. First, to consider the end, to reflect critically on how a text ends and what effects it produces, is already to reread and, consequently, to recognize that there is no single end to a literary work: the end is always multiple. It is always possible to consider the end as happening in a number of different ways and in the light of more than one reading. Second, to reflect critically on how a text ends, and what impact it produces, is inevitably to think back, to think again and in effect to reread everything that has led up to this end. Thus it may be argued that, rather than being unusual or perverse, rereading is perhaps unavoidable. In this sense we never get to the end of a text.

Literary texts call for rereading in various ways. Elizabeth Taylor's short story 'Mr Wharton' (1965) is about a girl called Pat Provis who has left her home near Nottingham to work in London, and about her mother Hilda who insists on coming down to help her move into a new flat in the suburbs. Pat rather reluctantly puts up with her mother's presence and begrudgingly accepts her maternal attentions and assistance. A significant topic of conversation, when Pat gets back from her day working as a secretary in an office, is how disgusting her boss, Mr Wharton, is. He is one of those sorts of men who (in Pat's words) go out for lunch, 'eat and drink themselves stupid, and then go home and tell their wives what a hard day they've had' (229). The story ends with Hilda Provis on the train back to Nottingham and her daughter returning home to the flat. Here is the twist:

> In a positive deluge, Pat and Mr Wharton drove up to Number Twenty. He, too, had an umbrella, and held it carefully over her as they went down the garden path and round the side of the house.

'Excusez-moi,' she said, stooping to get the key from under the dustbin.
'Could be a nice view on a nice day,' he said.
'Could be,' she agreed, putting the key in the door. (234)

The revelation that Pat and her boss are apparently having (or are about to begin having) an affair overturns the sense that we had been given that Pat finds Mr Wharton repulsive. The twist, then, calls for a rethinking or rereading of the text, even as it provides a final justification or clarification as to why the text should be entitled 'Mr Wharton'. It is also worth stressing, however, that while this is an apparently straightforward, even banal example of what Jeffrey Archer would call a story with 'a twist in the tale', and while it ends in a clear and specific way, still the ending is open and multiple. It is not, for example, entirely clear how these two characters feel about one another or what kind of relationship is involved. More generally, this ending forces us to rethink everything in the story up to that point: we cannot help but revise our reading of the text. Finally, it is important to recognize that the end of Taylor's text, like that of many literary works, is explicitly future-oriented. The words 'Could be' mark an openness to the future in relation to the recounted time of the narrative but they also mark an openness of ending and of interpretation.

Other texts call for other kinds of thinking about ends and rereading. Samuel Taylor Coleridge's 'The Rime of the Ancient Mariner' (1798; revised 1817) ends with a description of the effect of the tale of the Ancient Mariner on the Wedding-Guest who has been forced to listen to it:

> He went like one that hath been stunned,
> And is of sense forlorn:
> A sadder and a wiser man,
> He rose the morrow morn. (ll.622–5)

The final stanzas of Coleridge's poem constitute a sort of epilogue. We might reasonably ask ourselves what status such an epilogue has in relation to the idea of the end of a work: does the end come before the epilogue or is the epilogue itself the end? As in many of Shakespeare's plays (*As You Like It, All's Well That Ends Well* and *The Tempest*, for instance), the epilogue functions as a kind of supplement, and thus conforms to the paradoxical logic of both coming *after* the end and at the same time *being the end*. Such a supplement is paradoxical in that it both completes and adds to the story. More generally, such endings are self-referential: just as the epilogues to Shakespeare's plays are explicitly about the fact that (as the King puts it, at the end of *All's Well That Ends Well*) 'the play is done', so the end of 'The Rime of the Ancient

Mariner' specifically talks about the telling of the tale and the effect of this telling on its listener ('He went like one that hath been stunned / And is of sense forlorn'). The Mariner's tale, in other words, has already ended. Or has it? These are the words that come after his tale is told:

> 'Since then, at an uncertain hour,
> That agony returns:
> And till my ghastly tale is told,
> This heart within me burns.
>
> I pass, like night, from land to land;
> I have strange power of speech;
> That moment that his face I see,
> I know the man that must hear me:
> To him my tale I teach.' (ll.582–90)

In a transfixing and haunting way, the tale of the Ancient Mariner both ends and does not end. The 'ghastly tale is told' but what the tale tells is that it can never finally be told: it is at once the product and the articulation of an interminably recurring 'agony'. It is a tale about demonization, about being possessed by an 'agony' and by 'strange power of speech': it is a tale about its own telling and, in situating the reader in the position of the Wedding-Guest, it suggests that the end is only a beginning. Reading, or rereading, is interminable. From start to finish, reading is *it*: to recall the bizarre first word of Coleridge's poem, 'It is an Ancient Mariner . . .' (l.1).

In a very different fashion, Jean Rhys's novel *Wide Sargasso Sea* (1966) ends with the Creole female narrator (Bertha or, more correctly perhaps, Antoinette) preparing to set fire to the house in England belonging to the male narrator (the never specifically named Mr Rochester). Antoinette/Bertha waits for her guard, Grace Poole, to fall asleep:

> I waited a long time after I heard her snore, then I got up, took the keys and unlocked the door. I was outside holding my candle. Now at last I know why I was brought here and what I have to do. There must have been a draught for the flame flickered and I thought it was out. But I shielded it with my hand and it burned up again to light me along the dark passage. (124)

Rhys's novel depends on the reader's acknowledgement of an intertextual relationship with Charlotte Brontë's *Jane Eyre*, but it is only at the end that the two dramatically collide. One of the things that makes this final passage so extraordinary is the fact that it is *not* final. Rather, it leads us directly into another text, into the fire that engulfs Thornfield Hall and kills Bertha Mason, in *Jane Eyre*. More fundamentally still, it puts a light to all our assumptions about Brontë's novel, it calls on us to reread and rethink the whole of *Jane Eyre* and its place and significance in the (white, middle-class or aristocratic) English literary canon. With the end of *Wide Sargasso Sea, Jane Eyre* can never be the same again.

The end of *Wide Sargasso Sea* is both an end and not an end. It is both closed and open. It is closed or conclusive in the sense that it leads us to the dramatic and terrible moment of setting fire to the house, and of the narrator in effect setting fire to herself. And it is open in the sense that it leads us into a radically different encounter with another text. *Wide Sargasso Sea* dislocates everything in *Jane Eyre* that marginalizes or silences the otherness of a non-white (in this case West Indian Creole) subject and everything that marginal-izes or silences the otherness of madness. The ending of Rhys's novel is also open in the sense that it calls for a rereading or for rereadings that are, in prin-ciple, limitless. What is involved here is a notion of intertextuality not only in its weak sense (*Wide Sargasso Sea* 'quotes' or alludes to *Jane Eyre*) but also in the strong sense of a text's strictly unbounded capacity for referring to or link-ing up with other texts. Thus the text of *Wide Sargasso Sea* is linked up not only with the text of *Jane Eyre*, for example, but with any and every other text that might be classified as representative of 'the traditional English novel', with any and every other text that portrays what Gilbert and Gubar call 'the madwoman in the attic', with any and every text that ends with fire or entails a holocaust, and so on. The end of Rhys's text is open, above all perhaps, in the sense that it is future-oriented. The novel ends with a suspension of time: 'Now at last I know why I was brought here and what I have to do.' It leads us towards a terrible event, it leads us (in short) towards death, but it leaves us on the threshold – or rather, to recall the very last words of the text, it leaves us with suspended movement, in a 'dark passage'.

Jane Eyre itself 'ends' with intertextuality. Specifically, it cites the end of what is probably the most intertextually pervasive book in Western culture, the Bible: ' "Amen; even so come, Lord Jesus!" ' (Revelation 22:20). The end of *Jane Eyre*, like the end of *Wide Sargasso Sea*, would then seem to confirm a sense that texts are inevitably linked up with other texts and that there is no simple end (or beginning) to any text. It may be, in fact, that to emphasize texts as unfinished and unfinishable is characteristically modern or, perhaps, postmodern. The writings of Franz Kafka and Samuel Beckett are often thought of as being especially representative of twentieth-century European literature. In this respect it should not seem surprising that Kafka's novels are unfinished and that they are about experiencing the interminable, or that Beckett's great trilogy (*Molloy, Malone Dies, The Unnamable*) ends with the paradoxical words, 'I can't go on, I'll go on' (418). Poststructuralism in particular challenges us to think critically about the ways in which the idea of the end is in various ways paradoxical. It calls on us to acknowledge – rather than to deny or ignore, or explain so as to defuse, as more traditional literary criticism has done – the intractable complexities of aporia, suspense and the undecidable.

We can briefly illustrate this in terms of the endings of two very different twentieth-century novels, Elizabeth Bowen's *The Death of the Heart* (1938) and J.D. Salinger's *The Catcher in the Rye* (1951). Bowen's magnificent novel ends with a housemaid called Matchett taking a taxi to an obscure hotel somewhere in Kensington, intending to collect and take home the heartbroken heroine of the novel, the 16-year-old orphan called Portia:

> Matchett straightened her hat with both hands, gripped her bag more firmly, mounted the steps. Below the steps the grey road was all stucco and echoes – an occasional taxi, an occasional bus. Reflections of evening made unlit windows ghostly; lit lights showed drawing-rooms pallid and bare . . .
> Through the glass door, Matchett saw lights, chairs, pillars – but there was no buttons, no one. She thought: 'Well, what a place!' Ignoring the bell, because this place was public, she pushed on the brass knob with an air of authority. (318)

Bowen's novel ends with this endless moment of suspense – before Matchett enters the hotel. In this way Bowen's novel dramatizes the idea that the end of a text always figures a threshold, a place that is liminal and uncertain. Moreover it is a threshold which we can never go beyond: Matchett never goes into the hotel. Her intention (of collecting Portia) is never fulfilled.

Uncertainty or undecidability also marks the end of *The Catcher in the Rye*. Its final chapter is a kind of epilogue, which begins with Holden Caulfield declaring 'That's all I'm going to tell about' and goes on to conclude:

> . . . D.B. [Holden's brother] asked me what I thought about all this stuff I just finished telling you about. I didn't know what the hell to say. If you want to know the truth, I don't *know* what I think about it. I'm sorry I told so many people about it. About all I know is, I sort of *miss* everybody I told about. Even old Stradlater and Ackley, for instance. I think I even miss that goddam Maurice. It's funny. Don't ever tell anybody anything. If you do, you start missing everybody. (220)

The ending of Salinger's novel emphasizes that the narrator is in some kind of psychiatric institution but leaves in suspense the question of whether or not he will stay there or what will happen if he leaves. The final passage is equivocal and paradoxical: it suggests that the story or 'stuff' is 'finished' but that there is more 'to tell about'. We are presented not only with the narrator's own powerful ambivalence ('I don't *know* what I think') but also with a sense of uncertainty as to whether or not we as readers have really been told anything or where we are being left. What kind of end is this? Is it an end?

Poststructuralism entails a kind of thinking that tries to proceed by putting the very idea of the end into question. 'End' here involves not only the sense of 'conclusion' (the end of a text, for instance) but also the sense of 'goal' and 'purpose' (the goal or purpose of reading a text, for instance). As regards the sense of 'the end' as 'the conclusion of the text', we can see how this is problematic and even impossible: as we have been trying to make clear, intertextuality and rereading (or rereadability) mean that, in important respects, there is no end to any text. As regards the sense of 'the end' as 'the goal' or 'purpose', poststructuralist thinking highlights what is paradoxical. At issue here is the very nature of human desire and the paradox of the idea that, as we argue in greater detail in Chapter 21, desire is endless. Jacques Derrida, for example, emphasizes that we cannot do without the notion of end as goal or purpose (or, in its Greek form, *telos*). Nor can we do without the idea of a fulfilment or plenitude of desire. As he puts it: 'Plenitude is the end (the goal), but were it attained, it would be the end (death)' (Derrida 1988, 129).

The poetry of John Ashbery is suggestive in this context. In a poem entitled 'Soonest Mended' (1970), he writes:

> To step free at last, minuscule on the gigantic plateau –
> This was our ambition: to be small and clear and free.

Part of what makes Ashbery's poetry 'postmodern' is that it repeatedly articulates the desire to 'step free at last' but at the same time repeatedly ironizes, dislocates, writes off this gesture or 'ambition'. Ashbery has described his poems as being like dreams, and as texts for a reader to pick up, to start reading and put down again at whatever point she or he chooses: like dreams, Ashbery's poems tend to give no coherent or comforting sense of how or why they end, and yet they also convey a strong sense of the desire and need to think in terms of ends.

In the end, of course, the end is death and, more generally perhaps, the end of the world. It is not surprising, in this respect, that *Jane Eyre* should end with a quotation from the end of the book which tells of the end of the world

('The Book of Revelation' or, in Greek, 'The Apocalypse'). As Frank Kermode demonstrates, in his brief classic *The Sense of an Ending* (1967), 'the paradigms of apocalypse continue to lie under our ways of making sense of the world' (Kermode 1967, 28). Thus, for example, the great systems of Western philosophy – such as Christianity and Marxism – make sense of the world by imagining a future in which the world is fundamentally different, in which *our* world has ended forever. Christianity and Marxism, then, engage with desires that can be called apocalyptic. Such desires are crucial, also, for an appreciation of literature. Literature offers at once an imaginative experiencing and a critical questioning of the end, and it does so in ways that can be both at once exhilarating and unnerving. Literary texts, and particularly the ends of literary texts, open on to the future. And as Derrida has observed: 'The future can only be anticipated in the form of an absolute danger' (Derrida 1976, 5). The end is coming, this is it, it's now, right now, any moment now.

Further reading

Frank Kermode's *The Sense of an Ending* (1967) is a remarkable and thought-provoking account of literature and what he sees as the human need for ends. Norman Cohn's *The Pursuit of the Millennium* (1970) remains a standard and accessible work of reference for the apocalyptic nature of religious and political systems (especially Christianity and Nazism). Jacques Derrida's entire œuvre can be described as a sustained meditation on 'the end': see, in particular, 'The Ends of Man', in *Margins of Philosophy* (Derrida 1982), 'No Apocalypse, Not Now (full speed ahead, seven missiles, seven missives)' (1984), and 'Of an Apocalyptic Tone' (Derrida 1992c). On the way that poems end, see Barbara Herrnstein Smith, *Poetic Closure* (1968). For a highly engaging account of gender and culture at the *fin de siècle*, see Elaine Showalter's *Sexual Anarchy* (1991). Finally, see D.A. Miller, *Narrative and its Discontents* (1981), a fascinating book on the endings of traditional nineteenth-century novels. And then, to end yet again, death: see Peter Brooks's remarkable cogitations on death, narrative and the end-of-the-story, in the essay 'Freud's Masterplot' (in Brooks 1984), and Garrett Stewart's brilliant study of ending it all in fiction, *Death Sentences* (1984).

Glossary

Affective fallacy: term used by W.K. Wimsatt and Monroe Beardsley to designate what they see as the error of making subjective responses (cognitive or emotional) the criteria for interpretive, critical or aesthetic judgements.

Allegory: (Gk. 'other speaking') a narrative which – through allusion, metaphor, symbolism, etc. – can be read not simply on its own terms but as telling another, quite different story at the same time.

Alliteration: repeated consonant sounds, particularly at the beginning of words, e.g. 'kiddies' clobber', 'mountains of moonstone'. (See also *assonance*.)

Allusion: a reference, often only implicit or indirect, to another work of literature or art, person, event, etc.

Ambiguity: where a word, phrase or text may be interpreted in more than one way, but often taken to suggest an uncertainty between two (rather than three or more) meanings or readings. (See also *equivocality, polysemia, undecidability*.)

Animism: the rhetorical figure whereby something inanimate or lifeless is given attributes of life or spirit, e.g. Emily Brontë, *Wuthering Heights*: 'I believe at Wuthering Heights the kitchen is forced to retreat altogether into another quarter . . . the chairs, high-backed, primitive structures, painted green, one or two heavy black ones lurking in the shade . . .'; or the opening of Shelley's 'Ode to the West Wind': 'O wild West Wind, thou breath of Autumn's being . . .'

Anthropocentrism: refers to everything in a culture that asserts or assumes that the human (Gk. *anthropos*, 'man') is at the centre – whether of the universe, the world, or the meaning of a text.

Anthropomorphism: the rhetorical figure whereby the non-human is described in human terms (e.g. the legs of a table, the face of truth).

Aporia: a rhetorical figure for doubt. Especially associated with deconstructive thinking, an aporia may arise when the reader encounters two or more contradictory codes, 'messages' or 'meanings' in a text. It involves an impasse or site of undecidability. (See also *undecidability*.)

Assonance: correspondence or 'rhyming' of vowel sounds, e.g. eat, sleep; ooze, droop.

Bathos: artistic falling-away; a sense of disappointment or anticlimax, expressed by the writer or felt by the reader, e.g. the bathos in Matthew Arnold's 'The Buried Life', in the use of the word 'melancholy' at the culmination of a sentence which might have been expected to conclude on a note of triumph or joy: 'Yet still . . . / As from an infinitely distant land, / Come airs, and floating echoes, and convey / A melancholy into all our day'.

Catachresis: (Gk. 'misuse') rhetorical term for misuse or misapplication of language.

Catharsis: (Gk. 'purgation', 'purification') according to Aristotle, something that can happen to a spectator or reader at the end of a tragedy, due to a release of emotional tension arising from the experience of a paradoxical mixture of pity and terror.

Chiasmus: (from the Gk. letter χ) a rhetorical figure involving repetition and reversal, e.g. 'If you fail to plan, you plan to fail'. More broadly the term is used to refer to forms of intercrossing or reversal whereby each of the two sides of a conceptual opposition (e.g. man/woman, text/world, etc.) is shown to be reversible and paradoxically to be present and functionally active in its opposite.

Close reading: 'method' of reading emphasized by new critics which pays careful attention to 'the words on the page' rather than the historical and ideological context, the biography or intentions of the author and so on. Close reading, despite its name, brackets questions of readers and reading as arbitrary and irrelevant to the text as an artifact (see *affective fallacy*). It assumes that the function of reading and criticism is simply to read carefully what is already 'there' in the text.

Closure: an ending, the process of ending.

Connotation: an association, idea or image evoked by a word or phrase. Roughly equivalent to 'suggestion', connotation is distinct from denotation (what words denote or signify).

Couplet: two successive rhyming lines in a poem, e.g. Alexander Pope's 'Epigram Engraved on the Collar of a Dog I Gave to His Royal Highness': 'I am his Highness' Dog at Kew: / Pray tell me, sir, whose dog are you?'

Crypt: (Gk. *kryptein*, to hide) a term developed by the psychoanalysts Nicolas Abraham and Maria Torok to describe effects of transgenerational haunting. A crypt is a sort of 'false unconscious', the means by which a child is unknowingly preoccupied by a secret or secrets transmitted by a parent.

Cultural materialism: cultural materialism may be considered as the British version of new historicism. Both schools of criticism are characterized by newly theorized and politicized readings of history and of literary texts. While new historicism is particularly concerned with the textuality of history, however, cultural materialism, influenced by Raymond Williams's version of Marxist criticism, focuses on the material conditions of the production and reception of literary texts. Cultural materialists are thus concerned to expose the ideological and political dimensions of such texts.

Deconstruction: a term particularly associated with the work of Jacques Derrida. Roughly speaking, deconstruction is desedimentation: to deconstruct is to shake up and transform.

Defamiliarization: the Russian formalist critic Viktor Shklovsky uses the term *ostranenie*, usually translated as 'making strange' or 'defamiliarization', to denote what he sees as the primary function of literary texts – to make the familiar unfamiliar, to renew the old, or make the habitual appear fresh or strange.

Deixis: a term from linguistics, referring to the use of words concerning the place and time of utterance, e.g. 'this', 'here'.

Denouement: (Fr: 'unknotting') either the events following the climax of a plot, or the resolution of this plot's complications at the end of a short story, novel or play.

Discourse: can mean simply 'speech or language generally', or 'language as we use it'. But the term is often used in more theoretical contexts to signify the use of language associated with a particular institution, cultural identity, profession, practice or discipline. In this way each discourse is one of a number of discourses (the discourse of the colonizer, for instance, as distinct from that of the colonized). Whether general or particular, discourse is always inscribed within relations of power, within the structures and strictures of institutions.

Double bind: a double bind involves the kind of double or contradictory statement or order which deconstructive criticism tends to focus on, e.g. the sentence 'This sentence is not true' is both true and not true at the same time (if it's true then it's not true and if it's not true then it's true). Rather differently, the sentence 'Do not read this sentence' involves an order which can only be obeyed if it is disobeyed (we have to read the sentence in order to know that we should not read it).

Ecocriticism: the study of literature from the perspective of the relationship between humans and their environment.

Ekphrasis: (Gk. 'description') narrowly defined, ekphrasis involves the attempt to describe a visual work of art in words; more generally, however, ekphrasis denotes any attempt to encapsulate a visual image or perception or effect in language.

Elegy: (Gk. 'lament') a poem of mourning for an individual or a lament for a tragic event; the adjective 'elegiac' may be used to describe a sense of mourning or loss encountered in any text – poem or prose.

End-stopping: where lines of poetry end with punctuation, usually with strong punctuation such as full stops, semi-colons or colons, e.g. in the penultimate section of Wallace Stevens's 'An Ordinary Evening in New Haven': 'The wind has blown the silence of summer away. / It buzzes beyond the horizon or in the ground: / In mud under ponds, where the sky used to be reflected'. End-stopping is the opposite of *enjambement*.

Enjambement: the phenomenon whereby one line of poetry carries over into the next line without any punctuation whatsoever. Especially characteristic of poetry such as Milton's, Wordsworth's and Shelley's.

Epic: long narrative dealing with heroic deeds usually employing elevated language and traditionally involving a heroic or 'superhuman' protagonist, e.g. *The Odyssey, Paradise Lost.*

Epistemophilia: (Gk. 'a love of knowledge') epistemophilia is the desire for knowledge which literary texts produce in readers – the desire for the 'truth' or 'meaning' of the text, for example. Peter Brooks argues that epistemophilia is a dimension of the sex drive, and that it involves a 'dynamic of curiosity' which may be thought to be 'the foundation of all intellectual activity' (Brooks 1993, xiii).

Equivocality: like 'ambiguity', this suggests that a word, phrase, etc. has more than one meaning but, while 'ambiguous' suggests that it may be possible to decide on one primary meaning, 'equivocal' suggests that the meaning cannot be resolved. (See also *undecidability, polysemia*.)

Essentialism: refers to ways of conceiving people, cultures, etc. as having certain innate, natural or universal characteristics. Essentialism is strongly contested in most contemporary literary theory. The following three statements are all examples of essentialist thinking: (1) 'I have a personality and individuality which is completely unaffected by anything out there in the "real" world, such as language, economics, education, nationality, etc.'; (2) 'Women are more intelligent, caring and sensitive than men'; and (3) 'At bottom, you are either white or black, and that's all there is to it'.

Fabula: (also referred to as 'story' or '*histoire*') the events of a narrative.

Feminist criticism: feminist criticism seeks on the one hand to investigate and analyse the differing representations of women and men in literary texts and, on the other hand, to rethink literary history by exploring an often marginalized tradition of women's writing. Feminist criticism is concerned to question and challenge conventional notions of masculinity and femininity; to explore ways in which such conventions are inscribed in a largely patriarchal canon; and to consider the extent to which writing, language and even literary form itself are themselves bound up with issues of gender difference.

Figure (of speech), figurative language: this is usually defined in negative terms – that is to say, as non-literal language. Figurative language involves the entire field of what is known as rhetoric and includes, for example, metaphor, simile, hyperbole, anthropomorphism, etc.

Formalism: refers generally to kinds of criticism that emphasize the importance of the formal dimensions of literary texts, such as prose style, rhyme, narrative structure, verse-form and so on. In this respect formalism is seen to stress the importance of form as (supposedly) distinct from content, meaning, social and historical context, etc. The term can be encountered in two quite different contexts, namely Russian formalism and the formalist concerns of American new criticism (or 'close reading'). In fact, the Russian formalists were not simply formalist: their close attention to the specificity of literary form was consistently subordinate to more general political, even revolutionary concerns.

Genre: a kind; a literary type or style. Poetry, drama, novel may be subdivided into lyric (including elegy, ode, song, sonnet, etc.), epic, tragedy, comedy, short story, biography, etc.

Hermeneutic: a term formerly used to designate attempts to establish a set of rules governing the interpretation of the Bible in the nineteenth century; in the context of contemporary criticism, the term refers to theories of interpretation more generally.

Heteroglossia: (Gk. 'other/different tongues') term used by Mikhail Bakhtin to describe the variety of voices or languages within a novel, but can be used of any text to give the sense that language use does not come from one origin but is multiple and diverse, a mixing of heterogeneous discourses, sociolects, etc. (See also *polyphony*.)

Humanism: any system of thought that accords human beings central importance can be called humanism. Humanism involves the belief that humans are unique among animals (that they are not, in a sense, animals at all), as well as a resistance to superstitious or religious thinking.

Hyperbole: a figure of speech which involves exaggeration, excess or extravagance, e.g. 'I'm starving' instead of simply 'I am hungry', 'incredible' instead of 'very good'.

Ideology: while the term 'ideology' has a long history, its most common usage in contemporary literary criticism and theory originates in Marx's distinction between base and superstructure and refers to the way in which literary texts may be said to engage with – to reinforce or resist – the governing social, cultural and especially political ideas, images and representations of a society. Ideology, in the work of writers such as Louis Althusser and Pierre Macherey, is seen as fundamental to the very production of subjectivity itself, and for these writers, all cultural signification (including that of literary texts) is 'ideological'. According to this thinking, ideology reflects the fact that no writer is merely 'free' to express him- or herself, but is necessarily constrained by the conditions of the production of his or her text, by his or her social, cultural, economic and political circumstances. Ideology is thus held to be ineradicably inscribed in the literary text and the task of the critic is to analyse the work's often disguised or hidden ideological subtext.

Implied reader: Wolfgang Iser uses this term to denote a hypothetical reader towards whom the text is directed. The implied reader is to be distinguished from the so-called 'real reader'.

Indeterminacy: see *undecidability*.

In medias res: (L. 'in the middle of things') starting a story in the middle of the action.

Intentional fallacy: W.K. Wimsatt and Monroe Beardsley's term for what they see as the mistake of attempting to interpret a literary text by appealing to the supposed intentions of its author.

Interpretation: usually understood to involve an attempt to define the meaning or meanings of a specific text, with the assumption that a text has a limited meaning or meanings.

Intertextuality: a term coined by Julia Kristeva to refer to the fact that texts are constituted by a 'tissue of citations', that every word of every text refers to other texts and so on, limitlessly. Often used in an imprecise or weak sense to talk about echoes or allusions.

Irony: a rhetorical figure referring to the sense that there is a discrepancy between words and their meanings, between actions and their results, or between appearance and reality: most simply, saying one thing and meaning another.

Jouissance: (Fr. 'bliss', 'pleasure', including sexual bliss or orgasm) a term introduced into psychoanalytic theory by Jacques Lacan, to refer to extreme pleasure, but also to that excess whereby pleasure slides into its opposite. Roland Barthes uses the term to suggest an experience of reading as textual bliss. Similarly, Jacques Derrida suggests that the effect of deconstruction is to liberate forbidden jouissance.

Logocentrism: term introduced by Jacques Derrida in order to refer to everything in Western culture that puts *logos* (the Gk. term for 'word', more broadly translatable as 'meaning' or 'sense') at the centre. As Derrida argues, there is no simple escape from logocentric thinking.

Lyric: usually a fairly short poem supposedly expressing the thoughts and emotions of a speaker. Lyrics tend to be non-narrative in form.

Metafiction: a short story or novel which exploits the idea that it is (only) fiction, a fiction about fiction. Arguably, however, there are metafictional dimensions in any work of fiction. (See also *self-reflexivity*.)

Metaphor: a basic trope or figure of speech in which one thing is described in terms of its resemblance to another thing, e.g. the verb 'to fly' in 'she flew into his arms'. (See also *simile*.)

Metonymy: a basic trope or figure of speech in which the name of an attribute of an object is given for the object itself (e.g. in 'the pen is mightier than the sword', pen is a metonym for writing; sword is a metonym, for fighting or war).

Metre: the pattern of stressed and unstressed syllables in verse – one of the primary characteristics which may be said to distinguish verse from prose.

Mimesis: (Gk. 'imitation') the idea that literature attempts to represent 'life' or 'the world' more or less accurately, as it 'actually' is, etc. (See also *realism*.)

Monologue: a text (or part of a text) consisting of the speech of a single person (usually a fictional narrator, character or persona) speaking in actual or virtual solitude. In drama, referred to as a 'soliloquy'.

Narrative: may be defined in terms of the recounting of a series of events and the establishing of some (causal/temporal) relation between them.

Narratology: the field of critical and theoretical inquiry concerned with analysis of the underlying narrative structure or form of literary and other texts. Originating in the structuralist desire to produce a quasi-mathematical modelling of the deep structure of all narrative texts, recent developments in the field have encompassed poststructuralism, psychoanalytic criticism, feminism and other tendencies and have tended to move away from such scientism to examine the cultural and political significance of the workings of specific narrative texts in their historical context.

Narrator: the person or persona (as distinguished from the author) who is telling a story. Narrators can be variously categorized: a so-called omniscient narrator appears to know everything, an intrusive narrator gives his or her own comments and opinions on the story, an unreliable narrator cannot be trusted for some reason (e.g. he or she is prejudiced, exaggerating, lying), a first-person narrator presents himself or herself in the story as 'I', a third-person narrator speaks of his or her characters as 'she', 'he', etc.

New historicism: like its British version, cultural materialism, new historicism in the USA is concerned with a newly politicized and theorized historical criticism. While cultural materialism traces its roots back to Raymond Williams, new historicism is particularly influenced by Foucault's investigations of the workings of the institutions and discursive practices of medicine, psychology, the law, the university and so on, by which subjects are constructed, by which ideas are formed, and within which contexts literary texts are produced. New historicists are concerned with what Louis Montrose, in a now famous chiasmus, calls the 'historicity of texts and the textuality of history' (in Veeser 1989): history is itself 'textual' and open to interpretation, while literary texts are subject to the circulation of political and other currents of power.

Oxymoron: (Gk. 'wise foolishness') a trope which combines contradictory words or ideas, e.g. 'bittersweet', 'darkness visible'.

Paradox: an apparently contradictory or strange statement of how things are: that which is apparently illogical or absurd but may be understood to be meaningful or 'true'.

Parody: an imitation of another work of literature (usually with exaggeration) in order to make it seem ridiculous and/or amusing.

Paronomasia: word play. (See also *pun*.)

Pastiche: a work made up of imitation of other work(s); unlike parody, pastiche is not necessarily designed to ridicule.

Performative: pertaining generally to performance and, in the context of drama, to the active, dynamic effects of theatre. More specifically in the context of speech-act theory and the analysis of literary texts, however, 'performative' is an adjective referring to the capacity that statements have for *doing* as well as *saying* things. A promise or an act of naming, for example, is a performative.

Peritext: term used by the narratologist Gerard Genette (1987) to denote elements on the 'threshold' of a text such as the title, author's name, preface, chapter titles, indicators of generic identity ('A Novel', 'A Memoir', 'A Romance' and so on), epigraph, footnotes, or indeed glossary.

Phallocentrism: refers to everything in a culture that asserts or assumes that the phallus (the symbolic significance of a penis and more generally the patriarchy linked to this) is at the centre.

Phallogocentrism: a term conflating logocentrism and phallocentrism, used to refer to everything in language or meaning (*logos*) which is phallocentric. See also *logocentrism* and *phallocentrism*.

Point of view: refers to the way in which the narrator 'sees' or interprets her or his material: also referred to as 'narrative perspective'.

Polyphony: literally, 'having many voices': the idea that, rather than originating in a 'single voice' (cf. 'univocal'), a literary text has multiple origins or voices. Cf. *heteroglossia, intertextuality.*

Polysemia or polysemy: (Gk. 'many meanings') the quality of having several or many meanings.

Poststructuralism: Term used to describe those kinds of thinking and writing that disturb or exceed the 'merely' rational or scientific, self-assuredly 'systematic' work of structuralists. It is primarily associated with the work of Derrida, Lacan, Foucault, Deleuze and Guattari, Cixous and (post-1967) Barthes. Poststructuralism entails a rigorous and, in principle, interminable questioning of every centrism (logocentrism, ethnocentrism, anthropocentrism, etc.), of all origins and ends, meaning and intention, paradigm or system.

Protagonist: the leading character in a story (hero or heroine).

Pun: a play on words alike or nearly alike in sound but different in meaning (e.g. the word 'grave' in 'Ask for me tomorrow and you shall find me a grave man', *Romeo and Juliet*, III, i).

Queer theory: taking as its starting point an assumption about the constructedness of human sexualities, queer theory argues that sexuality is neither 'innate' nor 'natural' but subject to social, cultural, religious, educational, intellectual and other influences. Following Michel Foucault, theorists such as Eve Kosofsky Sedgwick, Judith Butler, Jonathan Dollimore and Joseph Bristow examine ways in which masculinity and femininity, and homo- and heterosexuality, are represented in literary and other texts and question traditional notions of the stability of such categories. In the work of such critics, 'queer theory' is in fact central to any thinking about literary representation, homosexual, heterosexual or other.

Realism: a descriptive term particularly associated with the nineteenth-century novel to refer to the idea that texts appear to represent 'the world' 'as it really is'.

Rhyme: like assonance and alliteration, rhymes are everywhere, in prose as well as in strictly 'poetic' texts. There are several varieties of rhyme, of which the most common are (i) full rhyme, e.g. 'cat'/'sat'; (ii) half-rhyme or off-rhyme, e.g. 'beat'/'keep', 'crime'/'scream'; (iii) internal rhyme, where a rhyme occurs within a line of verse, e.g. the '-ell' rhymes in Keats's ode 'To Autumn': 'To swell the gourd, and plump the hazel shells / With a sweet kernel; to set budding . . . /'; (iv) eye-rhyme, which should be seen but not heard, e.g. 'love'/'prove'; (v) masculine or strong rhymes, that is, words of one syllable, e.g. 'cat'/'sat', etc.; (vi) feminine or weak rhymes, which extend over more than one syllable, e.g. 'follow'/'hollow', 'qualify'/'mollify', etc.

Satire: the humorous presentation of human folly or vice in such a way as to make it look ridiculous, e.g. Jonathan Swift's *A Modest Proposal*.

Self-reflexivity: the phenomenon whereby a piece of writing refers to or reflects on itself. Often used interchangeably with 'self-referentiality'. (See also *metafiction*.)

Sibilance: an emphatic presence of 's' or 'z' sounds.

Simile: a trope in which one thing is likened to another, specifically through the use of 'like' or 'as' (a species of metaphor): in 'The barge she sat in, like a burnish'd throne / Burn'd on the water' (*Antony and Cleopatra*, II, ii) there is a metaphor in 'The barge . . . burn'd' (it is not literally on fire), and a simile in 'the barge . . . like a burnish'd throne'.

Simulacrum: (L. 'to make like') in the postmodernism of Jean Baudrillard the simulacrum is defined in terms of the substitution of the sign of the real for the real itself, in terms of a copy without origin.

Sjuzhet: (Russian 'plot') term used by the Russian formalist critics and borrowed by certain narratologists to denote the way in which a story is told, its 'discourse' or telling, as opposed to the events of the narrative, the *fabula* or story.

Sonnet: a lyric poem of (usually) fourteen lines, most commonly divided into units of eight lines (octave) plus six (sestet), or of three quatrains (four lines each) and a couplet.

Stanza: a grouping of lines of verse, usually forming a self-contained pattern of rhymed lines – thus stanzas of a poem are normally of equal length.

Symbol: a figure in which one object represents another object (often an abstract quality): conventional symbols include, for example, scales for justice, a dove for peace, a goat for lust, a lion for strength, a rose for beauty or love, etc. A symbol is a kind of metaphor in which the subject of the metaphor is not made explicit, and may be mysterious or undecidable.

Teleology: literally, 'to do with the study of the end, goal or purpose'. In contemporary literary studies, 'teleology' has to do with the idea that we think about texts (or about our activities as readers) as having a particular kind or particular kinds of *telos* (goal, purpose or end). One way of defining deconstruction or poststructuralism would be as a sustained questioning of the meaning, value and effects of teleological assumptions and ideas.

Trauma theory: ('trauma' from Gk. 'a wound') trauma theory is concerned with ways in which traumatic events are represented in language. It is particularly concerned with the difficulty or impossibility of such representations, particularly in the context of a sense of the unspeakable or untellable and of Freud's notion of *Nachträglichkeit* or deferred action, whereby the trauma may properly be said to be experienced only after it is retrospectively (re)interpreted.

Trope: (Gk. 'turn'): any rhetorical figure or device.

Undecidability: the phenomenon or experience of being unable to come to a decision when faced with two or more possible readings or interpretations. In a weak and imprecise sense, used interchangeably with 'indeterminacy'. 'Indeterminacy' is a negative term, however, implying that a decision (about being unable to determine a reading or interpretation) has already been reached. 'Undecidability', on the other hand, stresses the active, continuing challenge of being unable to decide.

Univocal: the quality of supposedly having only one meaning. 'The cat sat on the mat' might (and at some level must) be considered as a statement with univocal meaning: everyone knows what it is referring to. But at another level univocality is always open to question, in particular insofar as the context of a statement is never stable but is always susceptible to alteration or recontextualization. For example: Does 'cat' mean 'lion' here? One person's sense of 'mat' may not be someone else's (it may be their prize Persian rug). And so on.

Select bibliography of other introductory texts, reference works and anthologies

Introductions

Barry, Peter. 2002. *Beginning Theory: An Introduction to Literary and Cultural Studies*. 2nd edn. Manchester: Manchester University Press.

Bertens, Hans. 2001. *Literary Theory: The Basics*. London: Routledge.

Castle, Gregory. 2007. *The Blackwell Guide to Literary Theory*. Oxford: Blackwell.

Culler, Jonathan. 1997. *Literary Theory: A Very Short Introduction*. Oxford: Oxford University Press.

Eagleton, Terry. 1996. *Literary Theory: An Introduction*. 2nd edn. Oxford: Basil Blackwell.

Furniss, Tom and Michael Bath. 1996. *Reading Poetry: An Introduction*. London: Harvester Wheatsheaf.

Selden, Raman, Peter Widdowson and Peter Brooker. 1997. *A Reader's Guide to Contemporary Literary Theory*. 4th edn. Hemel Hempstead: Prentice Hall.

Wolfreys, Julian. 2004. *Critical Keywords in Literary and Cultural Theory*. Basingstoke: Palgrave Macmillan.

Reference works

Brogan, T.V.F. 1994. *The New Princeton Handbook of Poetic Terms*. Princeton: Princeton University Press.

Coyle, Martin, Peter Garside, Malcolm Kelsall and John Peck, eds. 1990. *Encyclopaedia of Literature and Criticism*. London and New York: Routledge.

Cuddon, J.A., ed. 1992. *The Penguin Dictionary of Literary Terms and Literary Theory*. Harmondsworth: Penguin.

Evans, Dylan. 1996. *An Introductory Dictionary of Lacanian Psychoanalysis*. London: Routledge.

Gray, Martin. 1992. *A Dictionary of Literary Terms*. 2nd edn. Harlow, Essex and Beirut: Longman York Press.

Groden, Michael and Martin Kreiswirth, eds. 1994. *The Johns Hopkins Guide to Literary Theory and Criticism*. Baltimore: Johns Hopkins University Press.

Laplanche, J. and J.-B. Pontalis. 1973. *The Language of Psycho-Analysis*, trans. Donald Nicholson-Smith. London: Hogarth Press and the Institute of Psycho-Analysis.

Macey, David. 2000. *The Penguin Dictionary of Critical Theory*. London: Penguin.

Makaryk, Irena R., ed. 1993. *Encyclopaedia of Contemporary Literary Theory: Approaches, Scholars, Terms*. Toronto: University of Toronto Press.

Sim, Stuart. 1995. *The A–Z Guide to Modern Literary and Cultural Theorists*. Hemel Hempstead: Prentice Hall/Harvester Wheatsheaf.

Wolfreys, Julian, ed. 2002. *The Edinburgh Encyclopaedia of Modern Criticism and Theory*. Edinburgh: Edinburgh University Press.

Wright, Elizabeth, ed. 1992. *Feminism and Psychoanalysis: A Critical Dictionary*. Oxford and Cambridge, MA: Basil Blackwell.

Anthologies

Leitch, Vincent B., ed., 2001. *The Norton Anthology of Theory and Criticism*. New York: Norton.

Lentricchia, Frank and Thomas McLaughlin, eds. 1995. *Critical Terms for Literary Study*. 2nd edn. London and Chicago: Chicago University Press.

Lodge, David, and Nigel Wood., eds., 2008. *Modern Criticism and Theory*. 3rd edn. London: Longman.

McQuillan, Martin. 2000. *Deconstruction: A Reader*. Edinburgh: Edinburgh University Press.

Rice, Philip, and Patricia Waugh. 2001. *Modern Literary Theory: A Reader*. 4th edn. London: Arnold.

Ryan, Michael and Julie Rivkin, eds. 2004. *Literary Theory: An Anthology*. 2nd edn. Oxford: Blackwell.

Walder, Dennis, ed. 2004. *Literature in the Modern World: Critical Essays and Documents*. 2nd edn. Oxford: Oxford University Press.

Waugh, Patricia, ed., 2006. *Literary Theory and Criticism: An Oxford Guide*. Oxford: Oxford University Press.

Literary works discussed

Achebe, Chinua. *Things Fall Apart*. London: Heinemann, 1986.

Achebe, Chinua. *Anthills of the Savannah*. London: Heinemann, 1987.

Anon. 'Sir Patrick Spens', in *The Penguin Book of Ballads*, ed. Geoffrey Grigson. Harmondsworth: Penguin, 1975.

Arnold, Matthew. Preface to *Poems* (1835), 'To Marguerite – Continued', 'Dover Beach', in *The Poems of Matthew Arnold*, ed. Kenneth Allott. London: Longman, 1965.

Ashbery, John. 'Soonest Mended', in *The Double Dream of Spring*. New York: Ecco Press, 1975.

Atwood, Margaret. 'Giving Birth', in *Dancing Girls and Other Stories*. London: Virago, 1985.

Auden, W.H. 'In Memory of W.B. Yeats (d. Jan. 1939)', in *Collected Poems*, ed. Edward Mendelson. London: Faber and Faber, 1991.

Austen, Jane. *Pride and Prejudice*, ed. Frank W. Bradbrook. London: Oxford University Press, 1970.

Ayres, Michael. 'Bittersweet', in *Poems 1987–1992*. Nether Stowey, Somerset: Odyssey Poets, 1994.

Beckett, Samuel. *Molloy, Malone Dies, The Unnamable*. London: Calder and Boyars, 1959.

Beckett, Samuel. *Murphy*. London: Picador, 1973.

Beckett, Samuel. *Waiting for Godot*. London: Faber and Faber, 1986.

Blake, William. 'The Marriage of Heaven and Hell', in *Blake: The Complete Poems*, 2nd edn, ed. W.H. Stevenson. London: Longman, 1989.

Bowen, Elizabeth. *Friends and Relations*. Harmondsworth: Penguin, 1943.

Bowen, Elizabeth. *The Heat of the Day*. Harmondsworth: Penguin, 1976.

Bowen, Elizabeth. *The Death of the Heart*. Harmondsworth: Penguin, 1987.

Bowen, Elizabeth. *A World of Love*. Harmondsworth: Penguin, 1988.

Brontë, Charlotte. *Jane Eyre*. Harmondsworth: Penguin, 1966.

Brontë, Emily. *Wuthering Heights*. Harmondsworth: Penguin, 1965.

Browning, Robert. 'Two in the Campagna', in *Robert Browning: Selected Poetry*, ed. Daniel Karlin. Harmondsworth: Penguin, 1989.

Byron. *Poetical Works*. Oxford: Oxford University Press, 1970.

Carver, Raymond. 'Fat' and 'Cathedral' in *Where I'm Calling From: The Selected Stories*. London: Harvill, 1993.

Celan, Paul. *Speech-Grille and Selected Poems, trans. Joachim Neugroschel*. New York: Dutton, 1971.

Chandler, Raymond. *The Little Sister*. New York: Vintage Books, 1988.

Chaucer, Geoffrey. *The Canterbury Tales: Nine Tales and the General Prologue*, eds V.A. Kolve and Glending Olson. New York: Norton, 1989.

Coleridge, S.T. *Collected Letters of Samuel Taylor Coleridge*, 6 vols, ed. Earl Leslie Griggs. Oxford: Oxford University Press, 1956–71.

Coleridge, S.T. 'The Rime of the Ancient Mariner', 'Kubla Khan', in *The Oxford Authors Samuel Taylor Coleridge*, ed. H.J. Jackson. Oxford: Oxford University Press, 1985.

Conrad, Joseph. *Heart of Darkness*. Harmondsworth: Penguin Popular Classics, 1994.

Dante Alighieri. *The Divine Comedy. Inferno I: Italian Text and Translation*, trans. Charles S. Singleton. New Jersey: Princeton University Press, 1970.

DeLillo, Don. *The Body Artist*. London: Picador, 2001.

Dickens, Charles. *Great Expectations*. Harmondsworth: Penguin, 1965.

Dickinson, Emily. 'Our Lives are Swiss', 'I taste a liquor never brewed', 'A Bird came Down the Walk', in *The Complete Poems of Emily Dickinson*, ed. Thomas H. Johnson. London: Faber and Faber, 1970.

Eliot, George. *Middlemarch*. Harmondsworth: Penguin, 1965.

Eliot, George. *The Lifted Veil*. London: Virago, 1985.

Eliot, George. *Daniel Deronda*. Harmondsworth: Penguin, 1987.

Eliot, T.S. *The Waste Land*, 'Little Gidding', in *Complete Poems and Plays*. London: Faber and Faber, 1975.

Ellison, Ralph. *Invisible Man*. New York: Random House, 1952.

Eugenides, Jeffrey. *Middlesex*. London: Bloomsbury, 2003.

Ford, Ford Madox. *The Good Soldier* in *The Bodley Head Ford Madox Ford*, vol. 1. London: Bodley Head, 1962.

Gilman, Charlotte Perkins. *The Yellow Wallpaper*. London: Virago, 1981.

Hardy, Thomas. 'Neutral Tones', 'The Voice', 'The Darkling Thrush', in *The Oxford Authors Thomas Hardy*, ed. Samuel Hynes. Oxford: Oxford University Press, 1984.

Hazlitt, William. *The Complete Works of William Hazlitt*, 21 vols, ed. P.P. Howe. London: Dent, 1930–34.

Heaney, Seamus. *North*. London: Faber and Faber, 1975.

Homer. *The Iliad*, trans. Robert Fagles, introduction and notes by Bernard Knox. New York: Penguin, 1990.

Ibsen, Henrik. *Four Major Plays*. Oxford: Oxford University Press, 1981.

James, Henry. *The Turn of the Screw*, in *The Bodley Head Henry James*, vol. XI, ed. Leon Edel. London: Bodley Head, 1974.

James, Henry. 'The Jolly Corner', in *Major American Short Stories*, ed. A. Walton Litz. Oxford: Oxford University Press, 1994.

Jonson, Ben. *A Critical Edition of the Major Works*, ed. Ian Donaldson. Oxford: Oxford University Press, 1988.

Joyce, James. 'The Dead', in *Dubliners*. London: Everyman, 1991.

Kafka, Franz. *The Collected Aphorisms*, trans. Malcolm Pasley. Syrens: London, 1994.

Kafka, Franz. 'In the Penal Colony', and 'The Burrow' in *The Complete Short Stories of Franz Kafka*, ed. Nabu N. Glatzer. London: Minerva, 1992.

Keats, John. *The Letters of John Keats, 1814–1821*, 2 vols, ed. Hyder Edward Rollins. Cambridge, MA: Harvard University Press, 1958.

Keats, John. 'Ode to a Nightingale', 'Ode on Melancholy', 'This Living Hand', in *The Poems of John Keats*, ed. Jack Stillinger. London: Heinemann, 1978.

Larkin, Philip. 'This Be The Verse', in *Collected Poems*, ed. Anthony Thwaite. London: Faber and Faber, 1988.

Lawrence, D.H. 'The Mosquito', in *The Complete Poems of D. H. Lawrence*, ed. Vivian de Sola Pinto and F. Warren Roberts. New York: Viking Press, 1975.

Lawrence, D.H. 'The Rocking-Horse Winner', in *The Collected Short Stories of D.H. Lawrence*. London: Heinemann, 1974.

Lawrence, D.H. *St. Mawr. The Virgin and the Gipsy*. Harmondsworth: Penguin, 1950.

McCarthy, Cormac. 2007. *The Road*. Basingstoke: Picador.

Mansfield, Katherine. 'Bliss', in *The Stories of Katherine Mansfield*, ed. Antony Alpers. Oxford: Oxford University Press, 1984.

Marvell, Andrew. 'To His Coy Mistress', in *The Oxford Authors Andrew Marvell*, ed. Frank Kermode and Keith Walker. Oxford: Oxford University Press, 1990.

Melville, Herman. *Moby-Dick; or, The Whale*, ed. Harold Beaver. Harmondsworth: Penguin, 1972.

Miller, Arthur. *The Crucible*. Harmondsworth: Penguin, 1988.

Milton, John. *Complete Shorter Poems*, ed. John Carey. London: Longman, 1971.

Milton, John. *Paradise Lost*, ed. Scott Elledge, 2nd edn. New York: Norton, 1993.

Monty Python's Flying Circus. *Just the Words*, 2 vols. London: Methuen, 1989.

Morrison, Toni. *The Bluest Eye*. London: Triad/Panther, 1981.

Morrison, Toni. *Beloved*. London: Picador, 1988.

Murray, Les. 'Cuttlefish', in *Translations from the Natural World*. Manchester: Carcanet Press, 1992.

O'Connor, Flannery. 'Revelation', in *The Secret Self: Short Stories by Women*, ed. Hermione Lee. London: Everyman, 1991.

Owen, Wilfred. 'Futility', in *The Poems of Wilfred Owen*, ed. John Stallworthy. London: Hogarth, 1985.

Plath, Sylvia. 'Daddy', in *Collected Poems*, ed. Ted Hughes. London: Faber and Faber, 1981.

Poe, Edgar Allan. 'The Premature Burial', 'The Purloined Letter', in *Tales of Mystery and Imagination*. London: Dent, 1984.

Ponge, Francis. 'The New Spider', in *Things: Selected Writings*, trans. Cid Corman. New York: White Pine Press, 1986.

Pope, Alexander. 'An Essay on Criticism', in *The Poems of Alexander Pope*, ed. John Butt. London: Methuen, 1963.

Proust, Marcel. *A la recherche du temps perdu*. Paris: Gallimard, 1954.

Rhys, Jean. 'Let Them Call It Jazz', in *The Secret Self: Short Stories by Women*, ed. Hermione Lee. London: Everyman, 1991.

Rhys, Jean. *Wide Sargasso Sea*, ed. Angela Smith. Harmondsworth: Penguin, 1997.

Rich, Adrienne. 'A Valediction Forbidding Mourning', in *The Fact of a Doorframe: Poems Selected and New, 1950–84*. New York: Norton, 1984.

Rushdie, Salman. *Midnight's Children*. London: Picador, 1982.

Rushdie, Salman. *The Satanic Verses*. New York: Viking, 1988.

Salinger, J.D. *The Catcher in the Rye*. Harmondsworth: Penguin, 1987.

Shakespeare, William. *All's Well That Ends Well, Romeo and Juliet, Twelfth Night, Hamlet, Othello, King Lear, Macbeth, The Tempest*, 'Sonnet 20', 'Sonnet 55', in *The Riverside Shakespeare*. Boston: Houghton Mifflin, 1974.

Shelley, Mary Wollstonecraft. *Frankenstein; Or, The Modern Prometheus*, eds D.L. Macdonald and Kathleen Scherf. Peterborough, Ontario: Broadview, 1994.

Shelley, Percy Bysshe. 'Ozymandias', 'To a Sky-Lark', 'A Defence of Poetry', in *Shelley's Poetry and Prose*, eds Donald H. Reiman and Sharon B. Powers. New York: Norton, 1977.

Sheridan, Richard Brinsley. *The Rivals*, ed. Elizabeth Duthie. London: Ernest Benn, 1979.

Sheridan, Richard Brinsley. *The School for Scandal*, ed. F.W. Bateson. New York: Norton, 1979.

Sidney, Sir Philip. *An Apology for Poetry*, ed. Geoffrey Shepherd. London: Nelson, 1965.

Sophocles. *The Three Theban Plays: Antigone, Oedipus the King, Oedipus at Colonus*, trans. Robert Fagles. Harmondsworth: Penguin, 1984.

Sterne, Laurence. *The Life and Opinions of Tristram Shandy, Gentleman*, ed. Ian Campbell Ross. Oxford: Clarendon Press, 1983.

Stevens, Wallace. 'Large Red Man Reading', 'The Man with the Blue Guitar' and 'Tea at the Palaz of Hoon', in *The Collected Poems of Wallace Stevens*. New York: Alfred Knopf, 1954.

Stevens, Wallace. 'Adagia', in *Opus Posthumous*. New York: Alfred A. Knopf, 1957.

Stevens, Wallace. *Letters of Wallace Stevens*, ed. Holly Stevens. New York: Alfred Knopf, 1966.

Swift, Jonathan. 'A Modest Proposal', in *The Writings of Jonathan Swift*, eds Robert A. Greenberg and William Bowman Piper. New York: Norton, 1973.

Taylor, Elizabeth. 'Mr Wharton', in *The Secret Self: Short Stories by Women*, ed. Hermione Lee. London: Everyman, 1991.

Tennyson, Alfred Lord. 'The Charge of the Light Brigade', in *The Poems of Tennyson*, ed. Christopher Ricks. London: Longman, 1987.

Traherne, Thomas. 'Centuries of Meditations', in *Selected Poems and Prose*, ed. Alan Bradford. Harmondsworth: Penguin, 1991.

Twain, Mark. *The Adventures of Huckleberry Finn*, eds Walter Blair and Victor Fischer. Berkeley: University of California Press, 1988.

Wertenbaker, Timberlake. *Our Country's Good*. London: Methuen, 1988.

Whitman, Walt. 'Song of Myself', in *Leaves of Grass*. New York: Signet, 2000.

Winterson, Jeanette. *Sexing the Cherry*. London: Bloomsbury, 1989.

Winterson, Jeanette. *Written on the Body*. London: Jonathan Cape, 1992.

Woolf, Virginia. 'The Mark on the Wall', in *A Haunted House and Other Short Stories*. London: Grafton, 1982.

Woolf, Virginia. *Orlando: A Biography*. Oxford: Oxford University Press, 1992.

Wordsworth, William. *The Prelude 1799, 1805, 1850*, eds Jonathan Wordsworth, M.H. Abrams and Stephen Gill. London: Norton, 1979.

Wordsworth, William. 'Alice Fell', 'A Slumber did my Spirit Seal', 'Ode: Intimations of Immortality', in *The Oxford Authors William Wordsworth*, ed. Stephen Gill. Oxford: Oxford University Press, 1984.

Wordsworth, William. 'Nutting', in *Lyrical Ballads and Other Poems, 1797–1800*, ed. James Butler and Karen Green. Ithaca: Cornell University Press, 1992.

Wyatt, Sir Thomas. 'Whoso List to Hunt', in *Collected Poems*, ed. Joost Daalder. London: Oxford University Press, 1975.

Yeats, W.B. 'The Wheel', in *The Collected Poems of W.B. Yeats*. London: Macmillan, 1977.

Bibliography of critical and theoretical works

Abbott, H. Porter. 2002. *The Cambridge Introduction to Narrative*. Cambridge: Cambridge University Press.

Abraham, Nicolas. 1994. 'Notes on the Phantom: A Complement to Freud's Metapsychology' (1975) and 'The Phantom of Hamlet *or* The Sixth Act, *preceded by* The Intermission of "Truth"'' (1975), in *The Shell and the Kernel: Renewals of Psychoanalysis*, Nicolas Abraham and Maria Torok, trans. Nicholas Rand. Chicago: Chicago University Press.

Abrams, M.H. 1953. *The Mirror and the Lamp: Romantic Theory and the Critical Tradition*. Oxford: Oxford University Press.

Afzal-Khan, Fawzia and Kalpana Seshadri-Crooks, ed. 2000. *The Pre-Occupation of Postcolonial Studies*. Durham: Duke University Press.

Ahmed, Sara. 2006. *Queer Phenomenology: Orientations, Objects, Others*. Durham: Duke University Press.

Allen, Graham. 2000. *Intertextuality*. London: Routledge.

Alter, Robert. 1981. *The Art of Biblical Narrative*. London: George Allen and Unwin.

Alter, Robert. 1985. *The Art of Biblical Poetry*. New York: Basic Books.

Althusser, Louis. 1969. 'Ideology and Ideological State Apparatuses' and 'A Letter on Art', in *Lenin and Philosophy and Other Essays*, trans. Ben Brewster, 2nd edn. London: New Left Books, 1977.

Appelbaum, David. 1990. *Voice*. Albany: State University of New York.

Apter, Terry E. 1982. 'The Uncanny', in *Fantasy Literature: An Approach to Reality*. London: Macmillan.

Aristotle. 1941. *The Basic Works of Aristotle*, ed. Richard McKeon. New York: Random House.

Aristotle. 1965. *On the Art of Poetry*, in *Classical Literary Criticism*, Trans. T.S. Dorsch. Harmondsworth: Penguin.

Aristotle. 2001. *On the Parts of Animals*, trans. James G. Lennox. Oxford: Oxford University Press.

Armbruster, Karla, and Kathleen R. Wallace, eds. 2001. *Beyond Nature Writing: Expanding the Boundaries of Ecocriticism*. Charlottesville, VA: University of Virginia Press.

Armstrong, Philip. 2008. *What Animals Mean in the Fiction of Modernity*. London: Routledge.

Armstrong, Tim. 1998. *Modernism, Technology and the Body: A Cultural Study*. Cambridge: Cambridge University Press.

Arnold, Matthew. 1964. 'The Function of Criticism at the Present Time', in *Essays in Criticism*. New York: Everyman's Library.

Ashcroft, Bill, Gareth Griffiths and Helen Tiffin, eds. 1989. *The Empire Writes Back*. London: Routledge.

Ashcroft, Bill, Gareth Griffiths and Helen Tiffin, eds. 1995. *The Post-Colonial Studies Reader*. 2nd edn. London: Routledge.

Attridge, Derek. 1992. *Poetic Rhythm*. Cambridge: Cambridge University Press.

Audi, Robert, ed. 1999. *The Cambridge Dictionary of Philosophy*, 2nd edn. Cambridge: Cambridge University Press.

Austin, J.L. 1962. *How to do Things with Words*. Oxford: Clarendon Press.

Austin, J.L. 1970. 'Performative Utterances', in *Philosophical Papers*, 2nd edn, eds J.O. Urmson and G.J. Warnock. Oxford: Oxford University Press.

Badmington, Neil, ed. 2000. *Posthumanism*. London: Palgrave.

Badmington, Neil, ed. 2007. *Derridanimals*. Special issue of the *Oxford Literary Review*, vol. 29.

Baker, Steve. 2000. *The Postmodern Animal*. London: Reaktion.

Bakhtin, M.M. 1981. *The Dialogic Imagination: Four Essays*, trans. M. Holquist and C. Emerson. Austin: University of Texas Press.

Bakhtin, M.M. 1992. From 'Discourse in the Novel', in *Modern Literary Theory: A Reader*, eds Philip Rice and Patricia Waugh. London: Edward Arnold.

Baldick, Chris. 1987. *In Frankenstein's Shadow: Myth, Monstrosity, and Nineteenth-Century Writing*. Oxford: Oxford University Press.

Balibar, Étienne and Pierre Macherey. 1981. 'On Literature as an Ideological Form', in *Untying the Text: A Post-Structuralist Reader*, ed. Robert Young. London: Routledge and Kegan Paul.

Barker, Francis and Peter Hulme. 1985. 'Nymphs and Reapers Heavily Vanish: The Discursive Con-Texts of *The Tempest*', in *Alternative Shakespeares*, ed. John Drakakis. London: Routledge.

Barker, Howard. 1989. *Arguments for a Theatre*. London: John Calder.

Barthes, Roland. 1972. *Mythologies*, trans. Annette Lavers. London: Jonathan Cape.

Barthes, Roland. 1977a. 'The Death of the Author', in *Image Music Text*, trans. Stephen Heath. London: Fontana.

Barthes, Roland. 1977b. 'From Work to Text', in *Image Music Text*, trans. Stephen Heath. London: Fontana.

Barthes, Roland. 1977c. *Roland Barthes by Roland Barthes*, trans. Richard Howard. New York: Hill and Wang.

Barthes, Roland. 1981. 'Theory of the Text', in *Untying the Text: A Post-Structuralist Reader*, ed. Robert Young. London: Routledge and Kegan Paul.

Barthes, Roland. 1990a. *The Pleasure of the Text*, trans. Richard Miller. Oxford: Basil Blackwell.

Barthes, Roland. 1990b. *S/Z*, trans. Richard Miller. Oxford: Basil Blackwell.

Barthes, Roland. 1990c. *A Lover's Discourse: Fragments*, trans. Richard Howard. Harmondsworth: Penguin.

Bataille, Georges. 1973. *Oeuvres Complètes*, vol. V. Paris: Gallimard.

Bataille, Georges. 1985. *Literature and Evil*, trans. Alistair Hamilton. London: Marion Boyars.

Bate, Jonathan. 1991. *Romantic Ecology: Wordsworth and the Environmental Tradition*. London: Routledge.

—. 2000. *The Song of the Earth*. London: Picador.

Baudrillard, Jean. 1988. 'Simulacra and Simulations', in *Selected Writings*, ed. Mark Poster. Cambridge: Polity.

Baudrillard, Jean. 1990. *Seduction*, trans. Brian Singer. London: Macmillan.

Baudrillard, Jean. 1995. *The Gulf War Did Not Take Place*, trans. Paul Patton. Sydney: Power Publications.

Beckett, Samuel. 1983. *Disjecta: Miscellaneous Writings and a Dramatic Fragment*. London: John Calder.

Beja, Morris. 1971. *Epiphany in the Modern Novel*. London: Peter Owen.

Belfiore, Elizabeth S. 1992. *Tragic Pleasures: Aristotle on Plot and Emotion*. Princeton, NJ: Princeton University Press.

Belsey, Catherine. 1994. *Desire: Love Stories in Western Culture*. Oxford: Blackwell.

Bertens, Hans, and Joseph Natoli, eds. 2001. *Postmodernism: The Key Figures*. Oxford: Blackwell.

Bennett, Andrew, ed. 1995. *Readers and Reading*. London: Longman.

Bennett, Andrew. *The Author*. London: Routledge. 2005.

Bennett, Tony. 1979. *Formalism and Marxism*. London: Methuen.

Berger, Anne-Emmanuelle. 2005. 'Sexing Differances', in *Derrida's Gift* (special issue), *differences*, 16: 3.

Berger, Anne and Marta Segarra, eds. 2009. *Demenageries*. Amsterdam: Rodopi.

Bergson, Henri. 1921. *Laughter: An Essay on the Meaning of the Comic*, trans. Cloudesley Brereton and Fred Rothwell. London: Macmillan.

Berry, Francis. 1962. *Poetry and the Physical Voice*. London: Routledge and Kegan Paul.

Bersani, Leo. 1978. *A Future for Astyanax: Character and Desire in Literature*. Boston: Little Brown.

Bersani, Leo. 1990. *The Culture of Redemption*. Cambridge, MA: Harvard University Press.

Bersani, Leo. 1995. *Homos*. Cambridge, MA: Harvard University Press.

Bhabha, Homi, ed. 1990. *Nation and Narration*. London: Routledge.

Bersani, Leo and Adam Phillips. 2008. *Intimacies*. Chicago: Chicago University Press.

Bhabha, Homi K. 1996. 'Of Mimicry and Man: The Ambivalence of Colonial Discourse', in eds Philip Rice and Patricia Waugh, *Modern Literary Theory: A Reader*, 3rd edn. London: Edward Arnold.

Biriotti, Maurice and Nicola Miller, eds. 1993. *What is an Author?* Manchester: Manchester University Press.

Blanchot, Maurice. 1981. 'The Narrative Voice (the "he", the neuter)', in *The Gaze of Orpheus and Other Literary Essays*, trans. Lydia Davis. New York: Station Hill.

Blanchot, Maurice. 1995. *The Work of Fire*, trans. Charlotte Mandell. Stanford: Stanford University Press.

Blanchot, Maurice. 1999. *The Station Hill Blanchot Reader: Fiction and Literary Essays*, trans. Lydia Davis, Paul Auster and Robert Lamberton, ed. George Quasha. Barrytown, New York: Station Hill Press.

Blair, Hugh. 1842. *Lectures on Rhetoric and Belles Lettres*, ed. William Milner.

Bloom, Harold. 1973. *The Anxiety of Influence: A Theory of Poetry*. Oxford: Oxford University Press.

Bloom, Harold. 1990. 'The Analysis of Character', in *Holden Caulfield*, ed. Harold Bloom. New York: Chelsea House.

Bloom, Harold. 1994. *The Western Canon: The Book and School of the Ages*. London: Macmillan.

Bloom, Harold. 2000. *How to Read and Why*. London: Fourth Estate.

Boden, Margaret A. 2004. *The Creative Mind: Myths and Mechanisms*, 2nd edn. London and New York: Routledge.

Boone, Joseph Allen. 1987. *Tradition and Counter Tradition: Love and the Form of Fiction*. Chicago: University of Chicago Press.

Boone, Joseph Allen. 1988. *Libidinal Currents. Sexuality and the Shaping of Modernism*. Chicago: Chicago University Press.

Booth, Allyson. 1996. *Postcards from the Trenches: Negotiating the Space Between Modernism and the First World War*. New York: Oxford University Press.

Borch-Jacobsen, Mikkel. 1987. 'The Laughter of Being', in *Modern Language Notes*, 102, no. 4: 737–60.

Borch-Jacobsen, Mikkel. 1988. *The Freudian Subject*, trans. Catherine Porter. Stanford: Stanford University Press.

Botting, Fred, ed. 1995. *Frankenstein: New Casebook*. Basingstoke: Macmillan.

Botting, Fred. 1997. *Gothic*. London: Routledge.

Bourdieu, Pierre. 1984. *Distinction: A Social Critique of the Judgment of Taste*, trans. Richard Nice. Cambridge, MA: Harvard University Press.

Bowen, Elizabeth. 1986. *The Mulberry Tree*. London: Virago.

Bowen, Elizabeth. 1970. 'A Novelist and His Characters', in *Essays by Divers Hands: Being the Transactions of the Royal Society of Literature*, vol. 26, ed. Mary Stocks. Oxford: Oxford University Press.

Bowie, Malcolm. 1991. *Lacan*. London: Fontana.

Bowra, Maurice. 1930. *Tradition and Design in 'The Iliad'*. London: Oxford University Press.

Bradley, A.C. 1904. *Shakespearean Tragedy: Lectures on Hamlet, Othello, King Lear, Macbeth*. London: Macmillan.

Brannigan, John. 1998. *New Historicism and Cultural Materialism*. London: Macmillan.

Brecht, Bertolt. 1978. 'A Short Organum for the Theatre', in *Brecht on Theatre: The Development of an Aesthetic*, ed. and trans. John Willett. London: Eyre Methuen.

Brewster, Scott, John L. Joughin, David Owen and Richard Walker, eds. 2000. *Inhuman Reflections: Thinking the Limits of the Human*. Manchester: Manchester University Press.

Bristow, Joseph. 1992a. 'Introduction' to Oscar Wilde, *The Importance of Being Earnest and Related Writings*. London: Routledge.

Bristow, Joseph, ed. 1992b. *Sexual Sameness: Textual Differences in Lesbian and Gay Writing*. London: Routledge.

Bristow, Joseph. 1995. *Effeminate England: Homoerotic Writing after 1885*. Buckingham: Open University Press.

Bristow, Joseph. 1997. *Sexuality*. London: Routledge.

Bronfen, Elisabeth. 1992. *Over Her Dead Body: Death, Femininity and the Aesthetic*. Manchester: Manchester University Press.

Brooke-Rose, Christine. 1958. *A Grammar of Metaphor*. London: Secker and Warburg.

Brooker, Peter, ed. 1992. *Modernism/Postmodernism*. London: Longman.

Brooks, Peter. 1984. *Reading for the Plot: Design and Intention in Narrative*. Oxford: Oxford University Press.

Brooks, Peter. 1993. *Body Work: Objects of Desire in Modern Narrative*. Cambridge, MA: Harvard University Press.

Broswimmer, Franz J. 2002. *Ecocide: A Short History of the Mass Extinction of Species*. London: Pluto.

Brown, Paul. 1994. ' "This thing of darkness I acknowledge mine": *The Tempest* and the Discourse of Colonialism', in *Political Shakespeare: Essays in Cultural Materialism*, eds Jonathan Dollimore and Alan Sinfield, 2nd edn. Manchester: Manchester University Press.

Buchanan, Ian and John Marks. 2000. *Deleuze and Literature*. Edinburgh: Edinburgh University Press.

Burke, Seán. 1998. *The Death and Return of the Author: Criticism and Subjectivity in Barthes, Foucault and Derrida*, 2nd edn. Edinburgh: Edinburgh University Press.

Burke, Seán, ed. 1995. *Authorship: From Plato to the Postmodern: A Reader*. Edinburgh: Edinburgh University Press.

Burnett, Mark Thornton. 2002. *Constructing 'Monsters' in Shakespearean Drama and Early Modern Culture*. Basingstoke: Palgrave.

Buse, Peter and Andrew Stott, eds. 1999. *Ghosts: Deconstruction, Psychoanalysis, History*. Basingstoke: Macmillan.

Butler, Judith. 1990. *Gender Trouble: Feminism and the Subversion of Identity*. London: Routledge.

Butler, Judith. 1991. 'Imitation and Gender Insubordination', in *Inside/Out: Lesbian Theories, Gay Theories*, ed. Diana Fuss. New York: Routledge.

Butler, Judith. 1993. *Bodies that Matter: On the Discursive Limits of 'Sex'*. New York: Routledge.

Butler, Judith. 1997. *Excitable Speech: A Politics of the Performative*. New York: Routledge.

Calarco, Matthew. 2008. *Zoographies: The Question of the Animal from Heidegger to Derrida*. New York: Columbia University Press.

Campbell, Sueellen. 1996. 'The Land and Language of Desire: Where Deep Ecology and Post-Structuralism Meet'. In Glotfelty and Fromm, eds. *The Ecocriticism Reader*.: P 124–36.

Caputo, John D. and Gianni Vattimo. 2007. *After the Death of God*. New York: Columbia University Press.

Carper, Thomas and Derek Attridge. 2003. *Meter and Meaning: An Introduction to Rhythm in Poetry*. New York: Routledge.

Caruth, Cathy. 1996. *Unclaimed Experience: Trauma, Narrative, and History*. Baltimore: Johns Hopkins University Press.

Carver, Raymond. 1986. 'On Writing', in *Fires: Essays, Poems, Stories*. London: Picador.

Castle, Terry. 1992. 'Sylvia Townsend Warner and the Counterplot of Lesbian Fiction', in *Sexual Sameness: Textual Differences in Lesbian and Gay Writing*, ed. Joseph Bristow. London: Routledge.

Castle, Terry. 1995. *The Female Thermometer: Eighteenth-Century Culture and the Invention of the Uncanny*. Oxford: Oxford University Press.

Caughie, John, ed. 1981. *Theories of Authorship: A Reader*. London: Routledge and Kegan Paul.

Cavaliero, Glen. 2005. *The Alchemy of Laughter*. Houndmills: Palgrave.

Celan, Paul. 1986. *Collected Prose*, trans. Rosemarie Waldrop. Manchester: Carcanet Press.

Chambers, Ross. 1984. *Story and Situation: Narrative Seduction and the Power of Fiction*. Manchester: Manchester University Press.

Chambers, Ross. 1991. *Room for Maneuver: Reading (the) Oppositional (in) Narrative*. Chicago: University of Chicago Press.

Chandler, David. 2007. *Semiotics: The Basics*. 2nd edn. London: Routledge.

Chandler, James. 1998. *England in 1819: The Politics of Literary Culture and the Case of Romantic Historicism*. Chicago: University of Chicago Press.

Chase, Cynthia. 1986. *Decomposing Figures: Rhetorical Readings in the Romantic Tradition*. Baltimore: The Johns Hopkins University Press.

Chasseguet-Smirget, Janine. 1985. *Creativity and Perversion*. Foreword by Otto Kernberg. London: Free Association Books.

Chatman, Seymour. 1990. *Coming to Terms: The Rhetoric of Narrative in Fiction and Film*. Ithaca: Cornell University Press.

Chomsky, Noam. 1957. *Syntactic Structures*. S-Gravenhage: Mouton.

Chow, Rey. 2003. *Writing Diaspora: Tactics of Intervention in Contemporary Cultural Studies*. Bloomington: Indiana University Press.

Cixous, Hélène. 1974. 'The Character of "Character"', *New Literary History*, 5: 383–402.

Cixous, Hélène. 1976. 'Fiction and Its Phantoms: A Reading of Freud's *Das Unheimliche*', *New Literary History*, 7: 525–48.

Cixous, Hélène. 1990. 'The Laugh of the Medusa', trans. Keith Cohen and Paula Cohen, in *New French Feminisms: An Anthology*, eds Elaine Marks and Isabelle de Courtivron. Amherst: University of Massachusetts Press.

Cixous, Hélène. 1993. *Three Steps on the Ladder of Writing*, trans. Sarah Cornell and Susan Sellers. New York: Columbia University Press.

Cixous, Hélène. 1998. *Stigmata: Escaping Texts*, trans. Eric Prenowitz. London and New York: Routledge.

Cixous, Hélène. 2008. *White Ink: Interviews on Sex, Text and Politics*, ed. Susan Sellers. Stocksfield: Acumen.

Claridge, Laura P. and Elizabeth Langland, eds. 1991. *Out of Bounds: Male Writers and Gender(ed) Criticism*. Amherst: University of Massachusetts Press.

Clark, Timothy. 1997. *The Theory of Inspiration: Composition as a Crisis of Subjectivity in Romantic and Post-Romantic Writing*. Manchester: Manchester University Press.

Clark, Timothy and Nicholas Royle, eds. 2002. 'Monstrism', *The Oxford Literary Review* 23.

Clark, Tim. Forthcoming. *The Cambridge Introduction to Literature and the Environment*. Cambridge: Cambridge University Press.

Cohen, Tom. 1994. *Anti-Mimesis from Plato to Hitchcock*. Cambridge: Cambridge University Press.

Cohn, Dorrit. 1978. *Transparent Minds: Narrative Modes for Presenting Consciousness in Fiction*. Princeton, NJ: Princeton University Press, 1978.

Cohn, Norman. 1970. *The Pursuit of the Millennium: Revolutionary Millenarians and Mystical Anarchists of the Middle Ages*. Oxford: Oxford University Press.

Colebrook, Claire. 2002. *Gilles Deleuze*. London and New York: Routledge.

Colebrook, Claire. 2004. *Gender*. Houndmills: Palgrave.

Coleridge, Samuel Taylor. 1975. *Biographia Literaria, or Biographical Sketches of my Literary Life and Opinions*, ed. George Watson. London: Dent.

Connor, Steven. 1992. *Theory and Cultural Value*. Oxford: Blackwell.

Connor, Steven. 1997. *Postmodernist Culture: An Introduction to Theories of the Contemporary*, 2nd edn. Oxford: Blackwell.

Connor, Steven. 2000. *Dumbstruck – A Cultural History of Ventriloquism*. Oxford: Oxford University Press.

Cordner, Michael, Peter Holland and John Kerrigan, eds. 1994. *English Comedy*. Cambridge: Cambridge University Press.

Coupe, Laurence, ed., 2000. *The Green Studies Reader: From Romanticism to Ecocriticism*. London: Routledge.

Crane, R.S. 1967. 'History Versus Criticism in the Study of Literature', in *The Idea of the Humanities and Other Essays Critical and Historical*, vol. 2. Chicago: University of Chicago Press.

Critchley, Simon. 2002. *On Humour*. London and New York: Routledge.

Culler, Jonathan. 1981. 'Story and Discourse in the Analysis of Narrative', in *The Pursuit of Signs: Semiotics, Literature, Deconstruction*. London: Routledge and Kegan Paul.

Culler, Jonathan. 1983. *On Deconstruction: Theory and Criticism After Structuralism*. London: Routledge and Kegan Paul.

Culler, Jonathan, ed. 1988a. *On Puns: The Foundation of Letters*. Oxford: Basil Blackwell.

Culler, Jonathan. 1988b. 'Political Criticism: Confronting Religion', in *Framing the Sign: Criticism and Its Institutions*. Oxford: Basil Blackwell.

Culler, Jonathan. 1997. *Literary Theory: A Very Short Introduction*. Oxford: Oxford University Press.

Culler, Jonathan. 2007. *The Literary in Theory*. Stanford: Stanford University Press.

Cupitt, Don. 1997. *After God: The Future of Religion*. London: Weidenfeld and Nicolson.

Currie, Mark, ed. 1995. *Metafiction*. London: Longman.

Currie, Mark. 1998. *Postmodern Narrative Theory*. Basingstoke: Macmillan.

Curti, Lidia. 1998. *Female Stories, Female Bodies: Narrative, Identity and Representation*. London: Macmillan.

Darwin, Charles. 1866. *On the Origin of the Species By Means of Natural Selection, Or, The Preservation of Favoured Races in the Struggle for Life*, 4th edn, London: Murray.

Davies, Colin. 2004. *After Poststructuralism: Reading, Stories and Theory*. London: Routledge.

Davies, Tony. 1997. *Humanism*. London: Routledge.

Day, Gary. 1996. *Re-Reading F.R. Leavis: Culture and Literary Criticism*. Basingstoke: Macmillan.

Dean, Carolyn J. 1992. *The Self and Its Pleasures: Bataille, Lacan, and the History of the Decentered Subject*. Ithaca: Cornell University Press.

Decker, James M. 2004. *Ideology*. Basingstoke: Palgrave Macmillan.

Deitering, Cynthia. 1996. 'The Postnatal Novel: Toxic Consciousness in Fiction of the 1980s'. In Glotfelty and Fromm, eds. *The Ecocriticism Reader*: 196–203.

Deleuze, Gilles. 1986. *Cinema 1: The Movement-Image*, trans. Hugh Tomlinson and Barbara Habberjam. London: Athlone Press.

Deleuze, Gilles. 1989. *Cinema 2: The Time-Image*, trans. Hugh Tomlinson and Robert Galeta. London: Athlone Press.

Deleuze, Gilles. 1998. 'Literature and Life', 'He Stuttered' and 'The Exhausted', in *Essays Critical and Clinical*, trans. Daniel W. Smith and Michael A. Greco. London: Verso.

Deleuze, Gilles. 2000. 'The Brain Is the Screen: An Interview with Gilles Deleuze' [1986], trans. Marie Therese Guirgis, in *The Brain Is the Screen: Deleuze and the Philosophy of Cinema*, ed. Gregory Flaxman. Minneapolis: University of Minnesota Press.

Deleuze, Gilles and Félix Guattari. 1983. *Anti-Oedipus: Capitalism and Schizophrenia*, trans. Robert Hurley *et al*. Minneapolis: University of Minnesota Press.

Deleuze, Gilles and Félix Guattari. 1986. *Kafka: Toward a Minor Literature*, trans. Dana Polan. Minneapolis: University of Minnesota Press.

de Man, Paul. 1979. *Allegories of Reading: Figural Language in Rousseau, Nietzsche, Rilke, and Proust*. New Haven: Yale University Press.

de Man, Paul. 1983. *Blindness and Insight: Essays in the Rhetoric of Contemporary Criticism*, 2nd edn. London: Methuen.

de Man, Paul. 1984. *The Rhetoric of Romanticism*. New York: Columbia University Press.

De Man, Paul. 1986. *The Resistance to Theory*. Minneapolis: University of Minnesota Press.

Derrick, Scott S. 1997. *Monumental Anxieties: Homoerotic Desire and Feminine Influence in Nineteenth-Century U.S. Literature*. New Brunswick: Rutgers University Press.

Derrida, Jacques. 1976. *Of Grammatology*, trans. Gayatri Chakravorty Spivak. Baltimore: Johns Hopkins University Press.

Derrida, Jacques. 1978. 'Force and Signification', in *Writing and Difference*, trans. Alan Bass. London: Routledge and Kegan Paul.

Derrida, Jacques. 1979. 'Living On', trans. James Hulbert, in *Deconstruction and Criticism*, eds Harold Bloom *et al*. New York: Seabury Press.

Derrida, Jacques. 1981. *Positions*, trans. Alan Bass. Chicago: University of Chicago Press.

Derrida, Jacques. 1982. 'White Mythology', in *Margins of Philosophy*, trans. Alan Bass. Chicago: University of Chicago Press.

Derrida, Jacques. 1983. 'The Principle of Reason: The University in the Eyes of Its Pupils', trans. Catherine Porter and Edward P. Morris, in *Diacritics*, vol. 13, no. 3: 3–20.

Derrida, Jacques. 1984. 'No Apocalypse, Not Now (full speed ahead, seven missiles, seven missives)', trans. Catherine Porter and Philip Lewis, *Diacritics*, vol. 14, no. 3: 20–31.

Derrida, Jacques. 1985a. 'Des Tours de Babel', trans. Joseph F. Graham, in *Difference in Translation*, ed. Graham. Ithaca: Cornell University Press.

Derrida, Jacques. 1985b. *The Ear of the Other: Otobiography, Transference, Translation. Texts and Discussions with Jacques Derrida*, trans. Peggy Kamuf. New York: Schocken Books.

Derrida, Jacques. 1986a. *Mémoires: for Paul de Man*, trans. Cecile Lindsay, Jonathan Culler and Eduardo Cadava. New York: Columbia University Press.

Derrida, Jacques. 1986b. 'Fors: The Anglish Words of Nicolas Abraham and Maria Torok', trans. Barbara Johnson, in Nicolas Abraham and Maria Torok, *The Wolf Man's Magic Word: A Cryptonymy*, trans. Nicholas Rand. Minneapolis: University of Minnesota Press.

Derrida, Jacques. 1988. 'Afterword: Toward an Ethic of Discussion', trans. Samuel Weber, in *Limited Inc.* Evanston: Northwestern University Press.

Derrida, Jacques. 1989. 'The Ghost Dance: An Interview with Jacques Derrida', trans. Jean-Luc Svobada, in *Public*, no. 2: 60–73.

Derrida, Jacques. 1992a. *Acts of Literature*, ed. Derek Attridge. London: Routledge.

Derrida, Jacques. 1992b. 'Passions: "An Oblique Offering"', trans. David Wood, in *Derrida: A Critical Reader*, ed. David Wood. Oxford: Basil Blackwell.

Derrida, Jacques. 1992c. 'Of an Apocalyptic Tone Newly Adopted in Philosophy', trans. John P. Leavey, Jr, in *Derrida and Negative Theology*, eds Harold Coward and Toby Foshay. Albany, NY: State University of New York Press.

Derrida, Jacques. 1994. *Spectres of Marx: The State of the Debt, the Work of Mourning, and the New International*, trans. Peggy Kamuf. New York: Routledge.

Derrida, Jacques. 1995a. *Archive Fever: A Freudian Impression*, trans. Eric Prenowitz. Chicago: Chicago University Press.

Derrida, Jacques. 1995b. 'Che cos'è la poesia?', trans. Peggy Kamuf, in *Points . . . Interviews, 1974–1994*, ed. Elisabeth Weber. Stanford: Standord University Press.

Derrida, Jacques. 1998. *Monolingualism of the Other; or, The Prosthesis of Origin*, trans. Patrick Mensah. Stanford: Stanford University Press.

Derrida, Jacques. 2000. *Demeure: Fiction and Testimony*, trans. Elizabeth Rottenberg. Stanford: Stanford University Press.

Derrida, Jacques. 2002a. 'The University Without Condition', in *Without Alibi*, ed., trans., and with an Introduction by Peggy Kamuf. Stanford: Stanford University Press.

Derrida, Jacques. 2002b. *Acts of Religion*, ed. Gil Anidjar. London and New York: Routledge.

Derrida, Jacques. 2003. 'Autoimmunity: Real and Symbolic Suicides. A Dialogue with Jacques Derrida', trans. Pascale-Anne Brault and Michael Naas, in Giovanna Borradori, *Philosophy in a Time of Terror: Dialogues with Jürgen Habermas and Jacques Derrida*. Chicago and London: Chicago University Press.

Derrida, Jacques. 2008. *The Animal That Therefore I Am*. Ed. Marie-Louise Mallet, trans. David Wills. New York: Fordham University Press.

Derrida, Jacques and Maurizio Ferraris. 2001. *A Taste for the Secret*, trans. Giacomo Donis. Cambridge: Polity Press.

Derrida, Jacques and Gianni Vattimo, eds. 1998. *Religion*. Cambridge: Polity.

Descartes, René. 1977. *Discourse on Method and the Meditations*, trans. F.E. Sutcliffe. Harmondsworth: Penguin.

de Vries, Hent. 1999. *Philosophy and the Turn to Religion*. Baltimore: Johns Hopkins University Press.

Doane, Mary Ann. 2002. *The Emergence of Cinematic Time: Modernity, Contingency, The Archive*. Cambridge, MA: Harvard University Press.

Dobson, Michael. 1992. *The Making of the National Poet: Shakespeare, Adaptation and Authorship, 1660–1769*. Oxford: Oxford University Press.

Docherty, Thomas. 1983. *Reading (Absent) Character: Towards a Theory of Characterization in Fiction*. Oxford: Oxford University Press.

Docherty, Thomas, ed. 1993. *Postmodernism: A Reader*, 2nd edn. Hemel Hempstead: Harvester Wheatsheaf.

Dolar, Mladen. 1991. ' "I Shall Be with You on Your Wedding-night": Lacan and the Uncanny', *October*, vol. 58.

Dolar, Mladen. 1996. 'The Object Voice', in *Gaze and Voice as Love Objects*, eds Renata Salecl and Slavoj Zizek. Durham: Duke University Press.

Dollimore, Jonathan. 1991. *Sexual Dissidence: Augustine to Wilde, Freud to Foucault*. Oxford: Clarendon Press.

Dollimore, Jonathan. 1998. *Death, Desire and Loss in Western Culture*. London: Penguin.

Dollimore, Jonathan. 2001. *Sex, Literature and Censorship*. Cambridge: Polity.

Dollimore, Jonathan. 2004. *Radical Tragedy: Religion, Ideology and Power in the Drama of Shakespeare and his Contemporaries*. 3rd edn. Houndmills: Palgrave.

Dollimore, Jonathan and Alan Sinfield, eds. 1994. *Political Shakespeare: New Essays in Cultural Materialism*, 2nd edn. Manchester: Manchester University Press.

Donaldson, Ian, ed. 1988. *Ben Jonson: A Critical Edition of the Major Works*. Oxford: Oxford University Press.

Drakakis, John, ed. 1992. *Shakespearean Tragedy*. London: Longman.

Drakakis, John and Naomi Liebler, eds. 1998. *Tragedy*. London: Longman.

Drolet, Michael. 2003. *The Postmodernism Reader*. London: Routledge.

During, Simon. 1992. *Foucault and Literature: Towards a Genealogy of Writing*. London: Routledge.

Eaglestone, Robert. 2004. *The Holocaust and the Postmodern*. Oxford: Oxford University Press.

Eagleton, Terry. 1976. *Marxism and Literary Criticism*. London: Routledge.

Eagleton, Terry. 1990. *The Ideology of the Aesthetic*. Oxford: Blackwell.

Eagleton, Terry. 1991. *Ideology: An Introduction*. London: Verso.

Eagleton, Terry, ed. 1994. *Ideology*. London: Longman.

Eagleton, Terry. 1996. *Literary Theory: An Introduction*, 2nd edn. Oxford: Basil Blackwell.

Eagleton, Terry. 2003. *Sweet Violence: The Idea of the Tragic*. Oxford: Blackwell.

Eco, Umberto. 1979. 'The Poetics of the Open Work', in *The Role of the Reader: Explorations in the Semiotics of Texts*. Bloomington: Indiana University Press.

Eco, Umberto. 1992. 'Postmodernism, Irony, the Enjoyable', in *Modernism/Postmodernism*, ed. Peter Brooker. London: Longman.

Eco, Umberto. 1993. 'The City of Robots', in *Postmodernism: A Reader*, ed. Thomas Docherty. Hemel Hempstead: Harvester Wheatsheaf.

Edelman, Lee. 2004. *No Future: Queer Theory and the Death Drive*. Durham: Duke University Press.

Edmundson, Mark. 1990. *Towards Reading Freud: Self-Creation in Milton, Wordsworth, Emerson and Sigmund Freud*. Princeton: Princeton University Press.

Edwards, Justin. 2008. *Postcolonial Literature*. Houndmills: Palgrave.

Egan, Gabriel. 2006. *Green Shakespeare: From Ecopolitics to Ecocriticism*. London: Routledge.

Elam, Diane. 1992. *Romancing the Postmodern*. London: Routledge.

Eliot, T.S. 1975. *Selected Prose of T.S. Eliot*, ed. Frank Kermode. London: Faber and Faber.

Ellmann, Maud, ed. 1994. *Psychoanalytic Literary Criticism*. London: Longman.

Empson, William. 1953. *Seven Types of Ambiguity*, 3rd edn. London: Chatto and Windus.

Empson, William. 1965. *Milton's God*. London: Chatto and Windus.

Esterhammer, Angela. 2000. *The Romantic Performative: Language and Action in British and German Romanticism*. Stanford: Stanford University Press.

Fanon, Frantz. 1967. *The Wretched of the Earth*, trans. Constance Farrington. Harmondsworth: Penguin.

Felman, Shoshana. 1983. *The Literary Speech Act: Don Juan with J.L. Austin, or Seduction in Two Languages*, trans. Catherine Porter. Ithaca: Cornell University Press.

Felman, Shoshana. 1987. *Jacques Lacan and the Adventure of Insight: Psychoanalysis in Contemporary Culture*. Cambridge, MA: Harvard University Press.

Felman, Shoshana. 1993. *What Does a Woman Want? Reading and Sexual Difference*. Baltimore: The Johns Hopkins University Press.

Felman, Shoshana. 2003. *The Scandal of the Speaking Body: Don Juan with J.L. Austin or, Seduction in Two Languages*, trans. Catherine Porter. Stanford: Stanford University Press.

Felman, Shoshana and Dori Laub. 1992. *Testimony: Crises of Witnessing in Literature, Psychoanalysis and History*. New York: Routledge.

Felski, Rita. 2003. *Literature After Feminism*. Chicago: Chicago University Press.

Felski, Rita, ed. 2008. *Rethinking Tragedy*. Baltimore: Johns Hopkins.

Fetterley, Judith. 1978. *The Resisting Reader: A Feminist Approach to American Fiction*. Bloomington: Indiana University Press.

Fineman, Joel. 1991. *The Subjectivity Effect in Western Literary Tradition: Essays Toward the Release of Shakespeare's Will*. Cambridge, MA: MIT Press.

Fink, Bruce. 1996. 'Reading Hamlet with Lacan', in Willy Apollon and Richard Feldstein, eds, *Lacan, Politics, Aesthetics*. Albany, NY: State University of New York Press.

Finkelstein, David and Alistair McCleery, eds. 2006. *The Book History Reader*. 2nd edn. London: Longman.

Fish, Stanley. 1980. *Is There A Text in This Class? The Authority of Interpretive Communities*. Cambridge, MA: Harvard University Press.

Floyd-Wilson, Mary, and Garrett A. Sullivan, Jr,. 2007. *Environment and Embodiment in Early Modern England*. Basingstoke: Palgrave.

Forrester, John. 1990. *The Seductions of Psychoanalysis: Freud, Lacan and Derrida*. Cambridge: Cambridge University Press.

Forster, E.M. 1976. *Aspects of the Novel*. Harmondsworth: Penguin.

Foster, Jeanette H. 1958. *Sex Variant Women in Literature: A Historical and Quantitative Survey*. London: Frederick Muller.

Foucault, Michel. 1970. *The Order of Things: An Archeology of the Human Sciences*. New York: Random House.

Foucault, Michel. 1979. 'What Is an Author?' in *Textual Strategies: Perspectives in Post-Structuralist Criticism*, ed. Josué V. Harari. London: Methuen.

Foucault, Michel. 1980a. 'The History of Sexuality: Interview', trans. Geoff Bennington, in *Oxford Literary Review*, vol. 4, no. 2: 3–14.

Foucault, Michel. 1980b. Introduction to *Herculine Barbin: Being the Recently Discovered Memoirs of a Nineteenth-Century French Hermaphrodite*, trans. Richard McDougall. New York: Pantheon Books.

Foucault, Michel. 1981. *The History of Sexuality: An Introduction*, trans. Robert Hurley. Harmondsworth: Penguin.

Foucault, Michel. 1983. 'The Subject and Power', in *Michel Foucault: Beyond Structuralism and Hermeneutics*, eds Hubert L. Dreyfus and Paul Rabinow. Chicago: University of Chicago Press.

Foucault, Michel. 1985. *The Use of Pleasure* (*The History of Sexuality*, vol. 2). Harmondsworth: Penguin.

Fowler, Roger. 1986. *Linguistic Criticism*. Oxford: Oxford University Press.

Freeden, Michael. 2003. *Ideology: A Very Short Introduction*. Oxford: Oxford University Press.

Freud, Sigmund. 1957a. 'The Antithetical Meaning of Primal Words' (1910), in *The Standard Edition of the Complete Psychological Works of Sigmund Freud*, vol. XI, trans. James Strachey. London: Hogarth.

Freud, Sigmund. 1957b. 'Findings, Ideas, Problems', in *The Standard Edition of the Complete Psychological Works of Sigmund Freud*, vol. XXIII, trans. James Strachey. London: Hogarth.

Freud, Sigmund. 1976. *Jokes and their Relation to the Unconscious* (1905), in *Pelican Freud Library*, vol. 6, trans. James Strachey. Harmondsworth: Penguin.

Freud, Sigmund. 1977. *On Sexuality: Three Essays on the Theory of Sexuality* (1905), in *Pelican Freud Library*, vol. 7, trans. James Strachey. Harmondsworth: Penguin.

Freud, Sigmund. 1984. 'Beyond the Pleasure Principle', in *Pelican Freud Library*, vol. 11, trans. James Strachey. Harmondsworth: Penguin.

Freud, Sigmund. 1985a. 'Thoughts for the Times on War and Death' (1915), in *Pelican Freud Library*, vol. 12, trans. James Strachey. Harmondsworth: Penguin.

Freud, Sigmund. 1985b. 'The "Uncanny"' (1919), in *Pelican Freud Library*, vol. 14, trans. James Strachey. Harmondsworth: Penguin.

Freud, Sigmund. 1985c. 'A Seventeenth-Century Demonological Neurosis' (1923), in *Pelican Freud Library*, vol. 14, trans. James Strachey. Harmondsworth: Penguin.

Freud, Sigmund. 1985d. 'Humour' (1927), in *Pelican Freud Library*, vol. 14, trans. James Strachey. Harmondsworth: Penguin.

Freud, Sigmund. 1985e. 'Civilization and Its Discontents' (1930), in *Pelican Freud Library*, vol. 12, trans. James Strachey. Harmondsworth: Penguin.

Freud, Sigmund. 1985f. 'Creative Writers and Day-Dreaming', in *Pelican Freud Library*, vol. 14, trans. James Strachey. Harmondsworth: Penguin.

Freud, Sigmund. 1985g. 'Leonardo da Vinci and a Memory of his Childhood', in *Pelican Freud Library*, vol. 14, trans. James Strachey. Harmondsworth: Penguin.

Freud, Sigmund. 1985h. 'Psychopathic Characters on the Stage', in *Pelican Freud Library*, vol. 14, trans. James Strachey. Harmondsworth: Penguin.

Freud, Sigmund. 1986. 'Psychoanalysis' (1923) and 'The Resistances to Psychoanalysis' (1925), in *Pelican Freud Library*, vol. 15, trans. James Strachey. Harmondsworth: Penguin.

Freud, Sigmund. 2003. *The Uncanny*, trans. David McLintock, with an Introduction by Hugh Haughton. London: Penguin.

Freund, Elizabeth. 1987. *The Return of the Reader: Reader-Response Criticism*. London: Methuen.

Fudge, Erica. 2002. *Perceiving Animals: Humans and Beasts in Early Modern English Culture*. Champaign: University of Illinois Press.

Fuss, Diana. 1995. *Identification Papers*. New York: Routledge.

Fuss, Diana, ed. 1996. *Human, All Too Human*. New York: Routledge.

Fussell, Paul. 1975. *The Great War and Modern Memory*. Oxford: Oxford University Press.

Gallagher, Catherine and Stephen Greenblatt. 2000. *Practising New Historicism*. Chicago: University of Chicago Press.

Garrard, Greg. 2004. *Ecocriticism*. London: Routledge.

Gates, Henry Louis, Jr, ed. 1984. *Black Literature and Literary Theory*. London: Methuen.

Gates, Henry Louis, Jr, ed. 1986. *'Race', Writing, and Difference*. Chicago: University of Chicago Press.

Gates, Henry Louis, Jr, 1988. *The Signifying Monkey: A Theory of Afro-American Literary Criticism*. Oxford: Oxford University Press.

Gates, Henry Louis, Jr, 1992. *Loose Canons: Notes on the Culture Wars*. New York: Oxford University Press.

Gee, Henry. 1996. 'How Humans Behaved Before they Behaved like Humans'. *London Review of Books* 18: 21 (31 October): 36–8.

Genette, Gérard. 1986. *Narrative Discourse: An Essay in Method*, trans. Jane E. Lewin. Oxford: Basil Blackwell.

Genette, Gérard. 1987. *Seuils*. Paris: Seuil.

Gerstner, David A. and Janet Staiger, eds. 2003. *Authorship and Film*. New York: Routledge.

Giffney, Noreen and Myra J. Hird, eds. 2008. *Queering the Non/Human*. Aldershot: Ashgate.

Gibson, Andrew. 1996. *Towards a Postmodern Theory of Narrative*. Edinburgh: Edinburgh University Press.

Gilbert, Sandra M. and Susan Gubar. 1979. *The Madwoman in the Attic: The Woman Writer and the Nineteenth-Century Literary Imagination*. New Haven: Yale University Press.

Girard, René. 1965. *Deceit, Desire, and the Novel: Self and Other in Literary Structure*, trans. Yvonne Freccero. Baltimore: Johns Hopkins University Press.

Girard, René. 1986. 'Hamlet's Dull Revenge', in *Literary Theory/Renaissance Texts*, eds. Patricia Parker and David Quint. Baltimore: Johns Hopkins University Press.

Glotfelty, Cheryll and Harold Fromm, eds. 1996. *The Ecocriticism Reader: Landmarks in Literary Ecology*. Athens: The University of Georgia Press.

Glover, David and Cora Kaplan. 2000. *Genders*. London: Routledge.

Glut, D.F. 1984. *The Frankenstein Catalogue*. Jefferson NC: McFarland.

Goldberg, David Theo. 2002. *The Racial State*. Oxford: Blackwell.

Graham, Elaine L. 2002. *Representations of the Post/Human: Monsters, Aliens and Others in Popular Culture*. Manchester: Manchester University Press.

Gray, Frances. 1994. *Women and Laughter*. London: Macmillan.

Gray, John. 2002. *Straw Dogs: Thoughts on Humans and Other Animals*. London: Granta Books.

Green, André. 1979. *The Tragic Effect: The Oedipus Complex in Tragedy*, trans. Alan Sheridan. Cambridge: Cambridge University Press.

Greenblatt, Stephen. 1988. *Shakespearean Negotiations: The Circulation of Social Energy in Renaissance England*. Oxford: Clarendon Press.

Greenblatt, Stephen. 1990a. 'Toward a Poetics of Culture', in *Learning to Curse: Essays in Early Modern Culture*. London: Routledge.

Greenblatt, Stephen. 1990b. 'Culture', in *Critical Terms for Literary Study*, eds Frank Lentricchia and Thomas McLaughlin. Chicago: University of Chicago Press.

Greenblatt, Stephen. 1991. *Marvelous Possessions: The Wonder of the New World*. Oxford: Clarendon Press.

Gregson, Ian. 2004. *Postmodern Literature*. London: Arnold.

Griffiths, Eric. 1989. *The Printed Voice of Victorian Poetry*. Oxford: Clarendon Press.

Gubar, Susan. 2003. *Poetry After Auschwitz: Remembering What One Never Knew*. Bloomington: Indiana University Press.

Guillory, John. 1993. *Cultural Capital: The Problem of Literary Canon Formation*. Chicago: Chicago University Press.

Gutting, Gary. 2005. *Foucault: A Very Short Introduction*. Oxford: Oxford University Press.

Hall, Donald E. 2003. *Queer Theories*. Basingstoke: Palgrave Macmillan.

Halperin, David. 1990. *One Hundred Years of Homosexuality and Other Essays on Greek Love*. New York: Routledge.

Halperin, David. 2002. *How to Do the History of Homosexuality*. Chicago: University of Chicago Press.

Hamilton, Paul. 1996. *Historicism*. London: Routledge.

Harari, Josué V. 1979. 'Critical Factions/Critical Fictions', in *Textual Strategies: Perspectives in Post-Structuralist Criticism*, ed. Josué V. Harari. London: Methuen.

Haraway, Donna. 1985. 'A Cyborg Manifesto: Science, Technology, and Socialist-Feminism in the Late Twentieth Century', reprinted in Badmington, ed., *Posthumanism*.

Harrison, Nicholas. 2003. *Postcolonial Criticism: History, Theory and the Work of Fiction*. Cambridge: Polity Press.

Hartman, Geoffrey H. 1981. 'Words and Wounds', in *Saving the Text: Literature/Derrida/Philosophy*. Baltimore: Johns Hopkins University Press.

Hartman, Geoffrey. 2002. *Scars of the Spirit: The Struggle Against Inauthenticity*. New York: Palgrave Macmillan.

Hassan, Ihab. 1989. 'Beyond Postmodernism? Theory, Sense, and Pragmatism', in *Making Sense: The Role of the Reader in Contemporary American Fiction*, ed. Gerard Hoffmann. München: Wilhelm Fink.

Hawkes, David. 1996. *Ideology*. London: Routledge.

Hawkes, Terence. 1972. *Metaphor*. London: Methuen.

Hawley, John C., ed. 2001. *Postcolonial Queer*: Theoretical Intersections.

Hazlitt, William. 1910. 'On Shakespeare and Milton', in *Lectures on the English Poets and The Spirit of the Age*. London: Dent.

Heffernan, James A.W. 1993. *Museum of Words: The Poetics of Ekphrasis from Homer to Ashbery*. Chicago: University of Chicago Press.

Heidegger, Martin. 1962. *Being and Time*, trans. John Macquarrie and Edward Robinson. New York: Harper.

Heidegger, Martin. 1967. *What Is A Thing?* trans. W.B. Barton, Jr and Vera Deutsch. Chicago: Henry Regnery.

Heidegger, Martin. 1977. 'The Word of Nietzsche: "God Is Dead"', 'The Question Concerning Technology', in *The Question Concerning Technology and Other Essays*, trans. William Lovitt. New York: Harper Torchbooks.

Heidegger, Martin. 2001. 'The Thing', in *Poetry, Language, Thought*, trans. Albert Hofstadter. New York: Harper Perennial Modern Classics.

Hemingway, Ernest. 2000. 'Ernest Hemingway: An Interview', in *The Norton Anthology of Short Fiction*. New York: Norton.

Henderson, Mae Gwendolyn. 1993. 'Speaking in Tongues: Dialogics, Dialectics and the Black Woman Writer's Literary, Tradition', in *Colonial Discourse and Post-Colonial Theory: A Reader*, eds Patrick Williams and Laura Chrisman. Hemel Hempstead: Harvester Wheatsheaf.

Herman, David, ed. 2007. *The Cambridge Companion to Narrative*. Cambridge: Cambridge University Press.

Herman, David, Manfred John, and Marie-Laure Ryan, eds. 2005. *The Routledge Encyclopaedia of Narrative Theory*. London: Routledge.

Hertz, Neil. 1979. 'Freud and the Sandman', in *Textual Strategies: Perspectives in Post-Structuralist Criticism*, ed. Josué V. Harari. London: Methuen.

Hirst, Paul and Penny Woolley. 1982. *Social Relations and Human Attributes*. London: Tavistock.

Hobbes, Thomas. 1840. *The English Works of Thomas Hobbes*, ed. Sir William Molesworth, vol. IV. London: John Bohn.

Holland, Norman N. 1980. 'Unity Identity Text Self', in *Reader-Response Criticism: From Formalism to Post-Structuralism*, ed. Jane P. Tompkins, Baltimore: Johns Hopkins University Press.

Hollander, John. 1985. *Vision and Resonance: Two Senses of Poetic Form*, 2nd edn. New Haven: Yale University Press.

Homans, Margaret. 1994. 'Feminist Fictions and Feminist Theories of Narrative', in *Narrative* 2: 3–16.

Hough, Graham. 1967. *The Romantic Poets*, 3rd edn. London: Hutchinson.

Horkheimer, Max and Theodor W. Adorno. 2002. *Dialectic of Enlightenment: Philosophical Fragments*, trans. Gunzelin Schmid Noerr and Edmund Jephcott. Stanford: Stanford University Press.

Hughes, Ted. 1967. *Poetry in the Making*. London: Faber.

Hurley, Kelly. 1996. *The Gothic Body: Sexuality, Materialism, and Degeneration at the Fin de Siècle*. Cambridge: Cambridge University Press.

Hutcheon, Linda. 1988. *A Poetics of Postmodernism: History, Theory, Fiction*. London: Routledge.

Hutcheon, Linda. 1989. *The Politics of Postmodernism*. London: Routledge.

Hynes, Samuel. 1990. *A War Imagined: The First World War and English Culture*. London: Bodley Head.

Irigaray, Luce. 1977. 'Women's Exile', in *Ideology and Consciousness*, no. 1: 62–76.

Irigaray, Luce. 1985. 'This Sex Which Is Not One', in *This Sex Which Is Not One*, trans. Catherine Porter and Carolyn Burke. Ithaca: Cornell University Press.

Irvine, William. 2005. *On Desire: Why We Want What We Want*. Oxford: Oxford University Press.

Iser, Wolfgang. 1995. 'Interaction Between Text and Reader', in *Readers and Reading*, ed. Andrew Bennett. London: Longman.

Irwin, William. 1999. *Intentionalist Interpretation: A Philosophical Explanation and Defense*. Westport, CN: Greenwood Press.

Irwin, William, ed. 2002. *The Death and Resurrection of the Author?* Westport, CN: Greenwood Press.

Jacobus, Mary. 1986. *Reading Woman: Essays in Feminist Criticism*. London: Methuen.

Jakobson, Roman. 1960. 'Closing Statement: Linguistics and Poetics', in *Style in Language*, ed. Thomas A. Sebeok. Cambridge, MA: MIT.

James, Henry. 1986. *The Art of Criticism: Henry James on the Theory and Practice of Fiction*, eds William Veeder and Susan M. Griffin. Chicago: University of Chicago Press.

Jameson, Fredric. 1988. 'The Politics of Theory: Ideological Positions in the Postmodernism Debate', in David Lodge, ed., *Modern Literary Theory*. London: Longman.

Jameson, Fredric. 1992. 'Postmodernism and Consumer Society', in *Modernism/ Postmodernism*, ed. Peter Brooker. London: Longman.

Jameson, Fredric. 1993. 'Postmodernism, or the Cultural Logic of Late Capitalism', in *Postmodernism: A Reader*, ed. Thomas Docherty. Hemel Hempstead: Harvester Wheatsheaf.

Jay, Martin. 1993. *The Denigration of Vision in Twentieth-Century French Thought*. Berkeley: University of California Press.

Jencks, Charles. 1993. 'The Emergent Rules', in *Postmodernism: A Reader*, ed. Thomas Docherty. Hemel Hempstead: Harvester Wheatsheaf.

Johnson, Samuel. 1969. *Dr Johnson on Shakespeare*, ed. W.K. Wimsatt. Harmondsworth: Penguin.

Jolly, Roslyn. 1993. *Henry James: History, Narrative, Fiction*. Oxford: Clarendon.

Jones, Ernest. 1953–7. *Sigmund Freud: Life and Work*. London: Hogarth.

Judovitz, Dalia. 1988. *Subjectivity and Representation in Descartes: The Origins of Modernity*. Cambridge: Cambridge University Press.

Kant, Immanuel. 1988. *The Critique of Judgement*, trans. James Creed Meredith. Oxford: Clarendon Press.

Kendall, Tim. ed. 2007. *The Oxford Companion to British and Irish War Poetry*. Oxford: Oxford University Press.

Kermode, Frank. 1967. *The Sense of an Ending: Studies in the Theory of Fiction*. Oxford: Oxford University Press.

Kermode, Frank. 1975. *The Classic*. London: Faber and Faber.

Kermode, Frank. 1979. *The Genesis of Secrecy: On the Interpretation of Narrative*. Cambridge, MA: Harvard University Press.

Kermode, Frank. 1983. 'Secrets and Narrative Sequence', in *Essays on Fiction 1971–82*. London: Routledge and Kegan Paul.

Kerridge, Richard and Neil Sammells, eds. 1998. *Writing the Environment: Ecocriticism and Literature*. London: Zed Books.

Kittler, Friedrich. 1997. 'Romanticism – Psychoanalysis – Film: A History of the Double', in *Literature, Media, Information Systems*, ed. John Johnston. Amsterdam: G + B Arts International.

Knight, Stephen. 1980. *Form and Ideology in Detective Fiction*. London: Macmillan.

Knopp, Sherron E. 1992. ' "If I saw you would you kiss me?": Sapphism and the Subversiveness of Virginia Woolf's *Orlando*', in *Sexual Sameness: Textual Differences in Lesbian and Gay Writing*, ed. Joseph Bristow. London: Routledge.

Knowles, Murray and Rosamund Moon. 2006. *Introducing Metaphor*. London: Routledge.

Koestler, Arthur. 1964. *The Act of Creation*. London: Hutchinson.

Kolodny, Annette. 1996. 'Unearthing Herstory: An Introduction'. In Cheryll Glotfelty and Harold Fromm, eds. *The Ecocriticism Reader: Landmarks in Literary Ecology*. Athens: University of Georgia Press.

Kramnick, Jonathan Brody. 1998. *Making the English Canon: Print-capitalism and the Cultural Past, 1700–1770*. Cambridge: Cambridge University Press.

Krieger, Murray. 1992. *Ekphrasis: The Illusion of the Natural Sign*. Baltimore: Johns Hopkins University Press.

Kristeva, Julia. 1986. 'Word, Dialogue and Novel', in *The Kristeva Reader*, ed. Toril Moi. Oxford: Basil Blackwell.

Kristeva, Julia. 1991. *Strangers to Ourselves*, trans. Leon C. Roudiez. Hemel Hempstead: Harvester Wheatsheaf.

Lacan, Jacques. 1977a. *Écrits: A Selection*, trans. Alan Sheridan. London: Tavistock.

Lacan, Jacques. 1977b. 'Desire and the Interpretation of Desire in *Hamlet*', trans. James Hulbert, *Yale French Studies*, no. 55/56. *Literature and Psychoanalysis. The Question of Reading: Otherwise*, ed. Shoshana Felman.

Lakoff, George and Mark Johnson. 1980. *Metaphors We Live By*. Chicago: University of Chicago Press.

Lane, Christopher. 1995. *The Ruling Passion: British Colonial Allegory and the Paradox of Homosexual Desire*. Durham: Duke University Press.

Leavis, F.R. 1948. *The Great Tradition*. London: Chatto and Windus.

Leavis, F.R. 1972. *Revaluation: Tradition and Development in English Poetry*. Harmondsworth: Penguin.

Leavis, F.R. and Denys Thompson. 1964. *Culture and Environment: The Training of Critical Awareness*. London: Chatto and Windus.

Lecercle, Jean-Jacques. 1990. *The Violence of Language*. London: Routledge.

Lentricchia, Frank and Andrew DuBois. 2003. *Close Reading: The Reader*. Durham, NC: Duke University Press.

Levi, Primo. 1987. *If This Is A Man* and *The Truce*, trans. Stuart Woolf. London: Abacus.

Levi, Primo. 1989. *The Drowned and the Saved*, trans. Raymond Rosenthal. New York: Vintage.

Leys, Ruth. 2000. *Trauma: A Genealogy*. Chicago: University of Chicago Press.

Lippit, Akira Mazuta. 2000. *Electric Animal: Toward a Rhetoric of Wildlife*. Minneapolis: University of Minnesota Press.

Littau, Karin. 2006. *Theories of Reading: Books, Bodies and Bibliomania*. Cambridge: Polity.

Liu, Alan. 1989. *Wordsworth: The Sense of History*. Stanford: Standord University Press.

Loomba, Ania. 1998. *Colonialism/Postcolonialism*. London: Routledge.

Luckhurst, Roger. 2008. *The Trauma Question*. London: Routledge.

Lyotard, Jean-François. 1984. *The Postmodern Condition: A Report on Knowledge*, trans. Geoff Bennington and Brian Massumi. Manchester: Manchester University Press.

Lyotard, Jean-François. 1992. 'Answering the Question: What is Postmodernism?' in *Modernism/Postmodernism*, ed. Peter Brooker. London: Longman.

Lyotard, Jean-François. 1997. *Postmodern Fables*, trans. Georges van den Abbeele. Minneapolis: University of Minnesota Press.

MacCabe, Colin. 2003. 'On Impurity: the Dialectics of Cinema and Literature', in *Literature and Visual Technologies: Writing After Cinema*, ed. Julian Murphet and Lydia Rainford. Basingstoke: Palgrave Macmillan.

Macherey, Pierre. 1978. *A Theory of Literary Production*, trans. Geoffrey Wall. London: Routledge and Kegan Paul.

Machor, James L., ed. 1993. *Readers in History: Nineteenth-Century American Literature and the Contexts of Response*. Baltimore: Johns Hopkins University Press.

Mahony, Patrick J. 1987. *Freud as a Writer*, expanded edition. New Haven: Yale University Press.

Mahood, M.M. 1957. *Shakespeare's Wordplay*. London: Methuen.

Manguel, Alberto. 1997. *A History of Reading*. London: HarperCollins.

Mansfield, Katherine. 1930. *Novels and Novelists*, ed. Middleton Murry. London: Constable.

Marcus, Laura. 2007. *The Tenth Muse: Writing About Cinema in the Modernist Period*. Oxford: Oxford University Press.

Margolis, Uri. 2007. 'Character'. In Herman, ed., *The Cambridge Companion to Narrative*.

Marriott, David. 2000. *On Black Men*. Edinburgh: University of Edinburgh Press.

Martin, Wallace. 1986. *Recent Theories of Narrative*. Ithaca: Cornell University Press.

Marx, Karl. 1973. *Grundrisse: Foundations of the Critique of Political Economy*, trans. Martin Nicolaus. London: Allen Lane.

Marx, Karl. 1976. *The German Ideology*, in Karl Marx and Frederick Engels, *Collected Works*, vol. 5. London: Lawrence and Wishart.

McGann, Jerome J. 1985. *The Beauty of Inflections: Literary Investigations in Historical Method and Theory*. Oxford: Clarendon.

McQuillan, Martin, ed. 2000. *The Narrative Reader*. London: Routledge.

Melville, Stephen. 1986. *Philosophy Beside Itself: On Deconstruction and Modernism*. Minneapolis: University of Minnesota Press.

Melville, Stephen and Bill Readings, eds. 1995. *Vision and Textuality*. Basingstoke: Macmillan.

Meltzer, Françoise. 1994. *Hot Property: The Stakes and Claims of Literary Originality*. Chicago: University of Chicago Press.

Miller, D.A. 1981. *Narrative and its Discontents: Problems of Closure in the Traditional Novel*. New Jersey: Princeton University Press.

Miller, D.A. 1989. ' "Cage aux folles": Sensation and Gender in Wilkie Collins's *The Woman in White*', in *Speaking of Gender*, ed. E. Showalter. London: Routledge.

Miller, J. Hillis. 1963. *The Disappearance of God: Five Nineteenth-Century Writers*. Cambridge, MA: Belknap Press.

Miller, J. Hillis. 1980. 'The Figure in the Carpet', in *Poetics Today* 1, 3: 107–18.

Miller, J. Hillis. 1982. '*Wuthering Heights*: Repetition and the "Uncanny" ', in *Fiction and Repetition: Seven English Novels*. Oxford: Basil Blackwell.

Miller, J. Hillis. 1987. *The Ethics of Reading: Kant, de Man, Eliot, Trollope, James, and Benjamin*. New York: Columbia University Press.

Miller, J. Hillis. 1990. 'Narrative', in *Critical Term for Literary Study*, eds Frank Lentricchia and Thomas McLaughlin. Chicago: University of Chicago Press.

Miller, J. Hillis. 1991. 'Thomas Hardy, Jacques Derrida, and the "Dislocation of Souls"', in *Tropes, Parables, Performatives: Essays in Twentieth-Century Literature*. Hemel Hempstead: Harvester Wheatsheaf.

Miller, J. Hillis. 1992. *Ariadne's Thread: Story Lines*. New Haven: Yale University Press.

Miller, J. Hillis. 1994. 'Derrida's Topographies', in *South Atlantic Review*, 59, 1: 1–25.

Miller, J. Hillis. 2000. 'Deconstruction and a Poem', in *Deconstructions: A User's Guide*, ed. Nicholas Royle. Basingstoke: Palgrave.

Miller, J. Hillis. 2001. *Speech Acts in Literature*. Stanford: Stanford University Press.

Miller, J. Hillis. 2002. *On Literature*. London: Routledge.

Millett, Kate. 1969. *Sexual Politics*. London: Rupert Hart-Davis.

Mills, Sara, ed. 1994. *Gendering the Reader*. Hemel Hempstead: Harvester Wheatsheaf.

Mills, Sara. 2003. *Michel Foucault*. London: Routledge.

Mitchell, W.J.T. 1986. *Iconology: Image, Text, Ideology*. Chicago: University of Chicago Press.

Mitchell, W.J.T. 1994. *Picture Theory: Essays on Verbal and Visual Representation*. Chicago: University of Chicago Press.

Moi, Toril. 1985. *Sexual/Textual Politics: Feminist Literary Theory*. London: Routledge.

Monbiot, George. 2004. 'Born Yesterday' (review for the *Guardian* newspaper of *The Day After Tomorrow*). www.monbiot.com/archives/2004/05/14/born-yesterday/

Monbiot, George. 2007. 'The Road Well Travelled' (review for the *Guardian* newspaper of Cormac McCarthy's *The Road*). www.monbiot.com/archives/2007/10/30/the-road-well-travelled/

Montag, Warren. 2003. *Louis Althusser*. Basingstoke: Palgrave Macmillan.

Morrison, Toni. 1993. *Playing in the Dark: Whiteness and the Literary Imagination*. London: Picador.

Morton, Timothy. 2007. *Ecology Without Nature: Rethinking Environmental Aesthetics*. Cambridge, MA: Harvard University Press.

Mulhern, Francis, ed. 1992. *Contemporary Marxist Literary Criticism*. London: Longman.

Mulvey, Laura. 2006. *Death 24x a Second: Stillness and the Moving Image*. London: Reaktion Books.

Münsterberg, Hugo. 1916. *The Photoplay: A Psychological Study*. New York: Appleton.

Munt, Sally, ed. 1992. *New Lesbian Criticism: Literary and Cultural Readings*. Hemel Hempstead: Harvester Wheatsheaf.

Murphet, Julian and Lydia Rainford. 2003. 'Introduction', *Literature and Visual Technologies: Writing After Cinema*, eds. Murphet and Rainford. Basingstoke: Palgrave Macmillan.

Nagel, Thomas. 1974. 'What is it Like to be a Bat?' *Philosophical Review* 83:4. 435–50.

Nancy, Jean-Luc. 1987. 'Wild Laughter in the Throat of Death', in *Modern Language Notes*, vol. 102, no. 4: 719–36.

Nancy, Jean-Luc. 1993. 'Laughter, Presence', in *The Birth to Presence*, trans. Brian Holmes *et al.* Stanford: Stanford University Press.

Nero, Brian. 2003. *Race.* Basingstoke: Palgrave Macmillan.

Newton, K.M. 2008. *Modern Literature and the Tragic.* Edinburgh: Edinburgh University Press.

Nicholls, Peter. 1996. 'The Belated Postmodern: History, Phantoms and Toni Morrison', in Sue Vice, ed., *Psychoanalytic Criticism: A Reader.* Oxford: Polity.

Nietzsche, Friedrich. 1968. *The Will to Power*, trans. Walter Kaufmann and R.J. Hollingdale. New York: Vintage.

Nietzsche, Friedrich. 1980. 'On Truth and Lie in an Extra-Moral Sense', in *The Portable Nietzsche*, ed. Walter Kaufmann. New York: Random.

Nietzsche, Friedrich. 1989. *Beyond Good and Evil: Prelude to a Philosophy of the Future*, trans. Walter Kaufmann. New York: Vintage.

Nietzsche, Friedrich. 2003. *Twilight of the Idols* and *The Anti-Christ*, trans. R.J. Hollingdale. London: Penguin.

Nuttall, A.D. 1992. *Openings: Narrative Beginnings from the Epic to the Novel.* Oxford: Clarendon Press.

Nuttall, A.D. 1996. *Why Does Tragedy Give Pleasure?* Oxford: Oxford University Press.

Orr, Mary. 2003. *Intertextuality: Debates and Contexts.* Oxford: Polity.

Partridge, Eric. 2001. *Shakespeare's Bawdy.* London and New York: Routledge.

Pask, Kevin. 1996. *The Emergence of the English Author: Scripting the Life in Early Modern England.* Cambridge: Cambridge University Press.

Pater, Walter. *The Renaissance.* New York: Modern Library, 1919.

Patterson, Annabel. 1990. 'Intention', in *Critical Terms for Literary Study*, eds Frank Lentricchia and Thomas McLaughlin. Chicago: Chicago University Press.

Payne, Michael, ed. 2005. *The Greenblatt Reader.* Oxford: Blackwell.

Pfister, Manfred, ed. 2002. *A History of English Laughter: Laughter from Beowulf to Beckett and Beyond*, ed Amsterdam: Rodopi.

Phelan, James, ed. 1989. *Reading Narrative: Form, Ethics, Ideology.* Columbus: Ohio State University Press.

Phelan, James, and Peter Rabinowitz, eds. 2005. *A Companion to Narrative Theory.* Oxford: Blackwell.

Pinker, Steven. 1995. *The Language Instinct: The New Science of Language and Mind.* London: Penguin.

Pittock, Malcolm. 2001. 'The War Poetry of Wilfred Owen: A Dissenting Reappraisal', in *The Literature of the Great War Reconsidered: Beyond Modern Memory* ed. Patrick J. Quinn and Steven Trout. Basingstoke: Palgrave.

Plato. 1961. *The Collected Dialogues of Plato, Including the Letters*, eds Edith Hamilton and Huntington Cairns. New Jersey: Princeton University Press.

Politzer, Heinz. 2006. *Freud and Tragedy*, trans. Michael Mitchell. Riverside, CA: Ariadne Press.

Price, Martin. 1983. *Forms of Life: Character and Moral Imagination in the Novel*. New Haven: Yale University Press.

Prince, Gerald. 2004. *A Dictionary of Narratology*. 2nd edn. Nebraska: University of Nebraska Press.

Procter, James, ed. 2000. *Writing Black Britain 1948–1998: An Interdisciplinary Anthology*. Manchester: Manchester University Press.

Procter, James. 2003. *Dwelling Places: Postwar Black British Writing*. Manchester: Manchester University Press.

Punter, David. 1996. *The Literature of Terror*, 2nd edn, 2 vols. London: Longman.

Punter, David. 2008. *Metaphor*. London: Routledge.

Punter, David and Glennis Byron. 2003. *The Gothic*. Oxford: Blackwell.

Quinn, Arthur. 1993. *Figures of Speech: 60 Ways to Turn a Phrase*. Davis, CA: Hermagoras Press.

Rabaté, Jean-Michel. 1996. *The Ghosts of Modernity*. Gainesville: Florida University Press.

Rabaté, Jean-Michel. 2001. *Jacques Lacan*. Basingstoke: Palgrave Macmillan.

Rashkin, Esther. 1992. *Family Secrets and the Psychoanalysis of Narrative*. Princeton, NJ: Princeton University Press.

Rashkin, Esther. 2008. *Unspeakable Secrets and the Psychoanalysis of Culture*. Albany: State University of New York Press.

Raven, James, Helen Small and Naomi Tadmor, eds. 1995. *The Practice and Representation of Reading in England*. Cambridge: Cambridge University Press.

Readings, Bill and Bennet Schaber, eds. 1993. *Postmodernism Across the Ages*. Syracuse, NY: Syracuse University Press.

Regan, Stephen, ed. 1992. *The Politics of Pleasure: Aesthetics and Cultural Theory*. Buckingham: Open University Press.

Regan, Tom. *The Case for Animal Rights*. Berkeley: University of California Press, 1983.

Rich, Adrienne. 1986. 'Compulsory Heterosexuality and Lesbian Existence', in *Blood, Bread, and Poetry: Selected Prose, 1979–1985*. London: Virago.

Ricks, Christopher. 1984. 'William Wordsworth 1: "A pure organic pleasure from the lines"', in *The Force of Poetry*. Oxford: Clarendon Press.

Ricks, Christopher. 2002. *Allusion to the Poets*. Oxford: Oxford University Press.

Ricoeur, Paul. 1978. *The Rule of Metaphor: Multi-Disciplinary Studies of the Creation of Meaning in Language*, trans. Robert Czerny. London: Routledge and Kegan Paul.

Ridley, Matt. 1994. *The Red Queen: Sex and the Evolution of Human Nature*. London: Penguin.

Riley, Denise. 1988. *'Am I That Name?': Feminism and the Category of 'Women' in History*. Basingstoke: Macmillan.

Rimmon-Kenan, Shlomith. 2002. *Narrative Fiction*, 2nd edn. London and New York: Routledge.

Robson, Mark. 2008. *Stephen Greenblatt*. London: Routledge.

Rogin, Michael. 1994. 'Sucking Up'. *London Review of Books*, 16, 9 (12 May): 26.

Ronell, Avital. 1989. *The Telephone Book: Technology, Schizophrenia, Electric Speech*. Lincoln: Nebraska University Press.

Rorty, Amélie Oksenberg, ed. 2001. *The Many Faces of Evil: Historical Perspectives*. London and New York: Routledge.

Rose, Jacqueline. 1993. *Why War?* Oxford: Blackwell.

Rose, Jacqueline. 1996. *States of Fantasy*. Oxford: Clarendon Press.

Rose, Mark. 1993. *Authors and Owners: The Invention of Copyright*. Cambridge, MA: Harvard University Press.

Rosen, Philip. 2001. *Change Mummified: Cinema, Historicity, Theory*. Minneapolis: University of Minnesota.

Ross, Thomas W. 1972. *Chaucer's Bawdy*. New York: Dutton.

Ross, Trevor. 1998. *The Making of the English Literary Canon: From the Middle Ages to the Late Eighteenth Century*. Montreal: McGill-Queens University Press.

Royle, Nicholas. 1991. *Telepathy and Literature: Essays on the Reading Mind*. Oxford: Basil Blackwell.

Royle, Nicholas. 2003. *The Uncanny*. Manchester and New York: Manchester University Press/Routledge.

Rushdie, Salman. 1990. *Is Nothing Sacred?* Cambridge: Granta.

Russell, Bertrand. 1968. *The Autobiography of Bertrand Russell*, 3 vols. London: George Allen and Unwin.

Russett, Margaret. 2006. *Fictions and Fakes: Romantic Authenticity, 1760–1845*. Cambridge: Cambridge University Press.

Ryan, Kiernan, ed. 1996. *New Historicism and Cultural Materialism: A Reader*. London: Arnold.

Sacks, Oliver. 1991. *Seeing Voices: A Journey into the World of the Deaf*. London: Picador.

Said, Edward W. 1975. *Beginnings: Intention and Method*. New York: Basic Books.

Said, Edward W. 1978. *Orientalism*. London: Routledge and Kegan Paul.

Said, Edward W. 1983. *The World, the Text, and the Critic*. London: Faber and Faber.

Said, Edward W. 1993. *Culture and Imperialism*. London: Chatto and Windus.

St Clair, William. 2007. *The Reading Nation in the Romantic Period*. Cambridge: Cambridge University Press.

Saunders, Barry. 1995. *Sudden Glory: Laughter as Subversive History*. Boston: Beacon.

Saussure, Ferdinand de. 1974. *Course in General Linguistics*, ed. Charles Bally and Albert Sechehayne, trans. Wade Baskin, with an introduction by Jonathan Culler. London: Fontana.

Scaggs, John. 2005. *Crime Fiction*. London: Routledge.

Scheese, Don. 1996. '*Desert Solitaire*: Counter-Friction to the Machine in the Garden'. in Glotfelty and Fromm, eds. *The Ecocriticism Reader*: 303–22.

Schwartz, Daniel R. 1999. *Imagining the Holocaust*. Basingstoke: Macmillan.

Schwartz, Hillel. 1996. *The Culture of the Copy: Striking Likenesses, Unreasonable Facsimiles*. New York: Zone Books.

Sedgwick, Eve Kosofsky. 1985. *Between Men: English Literature and Male Homosocial Desire*. New York: Columbia University Press.

Sedgwick, Eve Kosofsky. 1991. *Epistemology of the Closet*. Hemel Hempstead: Harvester Wheatsheaf.

Sedgwick, Eve Kosofsky. 1994. *Tendencies*. London: Routledge.

Sedgwick, Eve Kosofsky. 2003. *Touching Feeling: Affect, Pedagogy, Performativity*. Durham: Duke University Press.

Sherry, Vincent, ed. 2005. *The Cambridge Companion to the Literature of the First World War*. Cambridge: Cambridge University Press.

Shklovsky, Viktor. 1965. 'Art as Technique', in *Russian Formalist Criticism: Four Essays*, eds Lee T. Lemon and Marion J. Reis. Lincoln: University of Nebraska Press.

Showalter, Elaine. 1977. *A Literature of Their Own: British Women Novelists from Brontë to Lessing*. Princeton: Princeton University Press.

Showalter, Elaine, ed. 1989. *Speaking of Gender*. London: Routledge.

Showalter, Elaine. 1991. *Sexual Anarchy: Gender and Culture at the Fin de Siècle*. London: Virago.

Showalter, Elaine. 1993. 'On Hysterical Narrative', in *Narrative*, 1, 1: 24–35.

Sim, Stuart, ed. 2004. *The Routledge Companion to Postmodernism*. London: Routledge.

Simmons, Lawrence and Philip Armstrong, eds. 2007. *Knowing Animals*. Leiden and Boston: Brill.

Sinfield, Alan. 1994. *Cultural Politics – Queer Reading*. London: Routledge.

Sinfield, Alan. 1994. *The Wilde Century: Effeminacy, Oscar Wilde and the Queer Moment*. London: Cassell.

Singer, Peter. 1990. *Animal Liberation*. 2nd edition. London: Cape.

Singh, Amardeep. 2006. *Literary Secularism: Religion and Modernity in Twentieth-Century Fiction*. Newcastle: Cambridge Scholars Publishing.

Smith, Adam. 1986. *The Wealth of Nations*, Books I–III, ed. Andrew Skinner. Harmondsworth: Penguin.

Smith, Angela, ed. and introd. 1997. *Wide Sargasso Sea*. Harmondsworth: Penguin.

Smith, Barbara Herrnstein. 1968. *Poetic Closure: A Study of How Poems End*. Chicago: University of Chicago Press.

Smith, Barbara Herrnstein. 1981. 'Narrative Versions, Narrative Theories', in *On Narrative*, ed. W.J.T. Mitchell. Chicago: University of Chicago Press.

Smith, Barbara Herrnstein. 1988. *Contingencies of Value: Alternative Perspectives for Critical Theory*. Cambridge, MA: Harvard University Press.

Smith, Bruce R. 1994. *Homosexual Desire in Shakespeare's England: A Cultural Poetics*. Chicago: University of Chicago Press.

Smith, Grahame. 2003. *Dickens and the Dream of Cinema*. Manchester: Manchester University Press.

Smith, Marquard and Joanne Morra, eds. 2006. *The Prosthetic Impulse: From a Posthuman Present to a Biocultural Future*. Cambridge, MA: MIT Press.

Spargo, Tamsin, ed. 2000. *Reading the Past: Literature and History*. Basingstoke: Palgrave.

Spivak, Gayatri Chakravorty. 1987. *In Other Worlds: Essays in Cultural Politics*. London: Routledge.

Spivak, Gayatri Chakravorty. 1999. *A Critique of Postcolonial Reason: Towards a History of the Vanishing Present*. Cambridge, MA: Harvard University Press.

Steiner, George. 1961. *The Death of Tragedy*. London: Faber.

Steeves, H. Peter, ed. 1999. *Animal Others: On Ethics, Ontology, and Animal Life*. Albany, NY: State University of New York Press.

Stevens, Wallace. 1951. *The Necessary Angel: Essays on Reality and the Imagination*. New York: Alfred A. Knopf.

Stewart, Garrett. 1984. *Death Sentences: Styles of Dying in British Fiction*. Cambridge, MA: Harvard University Press.

Stewart, Garrett. 1990. *Reading Voices: Literature and the Phonotext*. Berkeley: University of California Press.

Still, Judith and Michael Worton, eds. 1990. *Intertextuality: Theories and Practices*. Manchester: Manchester University Press.

Suleiman, Susan R. and Inge Crosman, eds. 1980. *The Reader in the Text: Essays on Audience and Interpretation*. Princeton: Princeton University Press.

Sullivan, Nikki. 2001. *A Critical Introduction to Queer Theory*. Edinburgh: Edinburgh University Press.

Sword, Helen. 2001. *Ghostwriting Modernism*. Ithaca: Cornell University Press.

Sypher, Wylie, ed. 1956. *Comedy*. New York: Doubleday.

Syrotinski, Michael. 2007. *Deconstruction and the Postcolonial: At the Limits of Theory*. Liverpool: Liverpool University Press.

Tatum, James. 2003. *The Mourner's Song: War and Remembrance from the Iliad to Vietnam*. Chicago: University of Chicago Press.

Taylor, Charles. 1989. *Sources of the Self: The Making of Modern Identity*. Cambridge: Cambridge University Press.

Taylor, Gary. 1990. *Reinventing Shakespeare: A Cultural History from the Restoration to the Present*. London: Hogarth.

Thieme, John. 2001. *Postcolonial Con-texts: Writing Back to the Canon*. London: Continuum.

Thomas, Keith. 1971. *Religion and the Decline of Magic: Studies in Popular Beliefs in Sixteenth and Seventeenth Century England*. London: Weidenfeld and Nicolson.

Thomas, Sophie. 2008. *Romanticism and Visuality: Fragments, History, Spectacle*. London: Routledge.

Thomson, Alex. 2007. 'Derrida's *Rogues*: Islam and the Futures of Deconstruction', in *Derrida: Negotiating the Legacy*, ed. Madeleine Fagan, Ludovic Glorieux, Indira Hasimbegovic and Marie Suetsugu. Edinburgh: Edinburgh University Press.

Todd, Jane Marie. 1986. 'The Veiled Woman in Freud's *Das Unheimliche*', in *Signs* 2/3: 519–28.

Todd, Janet. 1988. *Feminist Literary History: A Defence*. Cambridge: Polity Press.

Todorov, Tzvetan. 1981. *Introduction to Poetics*, trans. Richard Howard, Minneapolis: University of Minnesota Press.

Todorov, Tzvetan. 1993. *On Human Diversity*. Cambridge, MA.: Harvard University Press.

Touval, Yonatan. 1997. 'Colonial Queer Something', in *Queer Forster*, eds Robert K. Martin and George Piggford. Chicago: University of Chicago Press.

Trotter, David. 2007. *Cinema and Modernism*. Oxford: Blackwell.

Veeser, H. Aram, ed. 1989. *The New Historicism*. New York: Routledge.

Veeser, H. Aram, ed. 1994. *The New Historicism Reader*. New York: Routledge.

Veyne, Paul. 1988. *Did the Greeks Believe in their Myths? An Essay on the Constitutive Imagination*, trans. Paula Wissing. Chicago: University of Chicago Press.

Vickers, Brian, ed. 1981. *Shakespeare: The Critical Heritage, Volume 6, 1774–1801*. London: Routledge and Kegan Paul.

Walder, Dennis. 1998. *Post-Colonial Literatures in English: History, Language, Theory*. Oxford: Blackwell.

Waller, Marguerite. 1987. 'Academic Tootsie: The Denial of Difference and the Difference It Makes', in *Diacritics*, vol. 17, no. 1: 2–20.

Ward, Graham. 1996. *Theology and Contemporary Critical Theory*. London: Macmillan.

Warhol, Robyn R. and Diane Price Herndl, eds. 1997. *Feminisms: An Anthology of Literary Theory and Criticism*, revised edn. London: Macmillan.

Watson, Robert N. 2006. *Back to Nature: The Green and the Real in the Late Renaissance*. Philadelphia: University of Pennsylvania Press.

Weber, Samuel. 1973. 'The Sideshow, or: Remarks on a Canny Moment', in *Modern Language Notes*, 88: 1102–33.

Weber, Samuel. 1987. 'Laughing in the Meanwhile', in *Modern Language Notes*, vol. 102, no. 4: 691–706.

Weber, Samuel. 1992. *The Return to Freud: Jacques Lacan and the Dislocations of Psychoanalysis*. Cambridge: Cambridge University Press.

Weber, Samuel. 2000. 'Uncanny Thinking', in *The Legend of Freud*, expanded edition. Stanford: Stanford University Press.

Weeks, Jeffrey. 1998. 'Introduction to Guy Hocquengham's *Homosexual Desire*', in *Literary Theory: An Anthology*, eds Julie Rivkin and Michael Ryan. Oxford: Blackwell.

Wellek, René. 1963. 'Literary Theory, Criticism, and History', in *Concepts of Criticism*. New Haven: Yale University Press.

Wesling, Donald and Tadeusz Slawek. 1995. *Literary Voice: The Calling of Jonah*. Albany, NY: State University of New York Press.

Wexman, Virginia Wright, ed. 2003. *Film and Authorship*. New Brunswick: Rutgers University Press.

White, Hayden. 1978. *Tropics of Discourse: Essays in Cultural Criticism*. Baltimore: Johns Hopkins University Press.

White, Susan. 1991. 'Allegory and Referentiality: *Vertigo* and Feminist Criticism', *Modern Language Notes*, vol. 106.

Whiteside, Anna and Michael Issacharoff, eds. 1987. *On Referring in Literature*. Bloomington: Indiana University Press.

Williams, Linda Ruth. 1995. *Critical Desire: Psychoanalysis and the Literary Subject*. London: Edward Arnold.

Williams, Patrick and Laura Chrisman, eds. 1993. *Colonial Discourse and Post-Colonial Theory: A Reader*. Hemel Hempstead: Harvester Wheatsheaf.

Williams, Raymond. 1969. *Modern Tragedy*. London: Chatto and Windus.

Williams, Raymond. 1973. *The Country and the City*. New York: Oxford University Press.

Williams, Raymond. 1983. *Keywords: A Vocabulary of Culture and Society*. Revised edn. London: Fontana.

Williams, Raymond. 1992. *The Long Revolution*. London: Hogarth.

Wilson, Richard and Richard Dutton, eds. 1992. *New Historicism and Renaissance Drama*. London: Longman.

Wilson, Scott. 1995. *Cultural Materialism: Theory and Practice*. Oxford: Blackwell.

Wimsatt Jr, W.K. and Monroe C. Beardsley. 1995. 'The Intentional Fallacy', in *Authorship From Plato to the Postmodern: A Reader*, ed. Seán Burke. Edinburgh: Edinburgh University Press.

Winters, Yvor. 1957. 'The Audible Reading of Poetry', in *The Function of Criticism: Problems and Exercises*, 2nd edn. Denver: Alan Swallow.

Wisker, Gina. 2007. *Key Concepts in Postcolonial Literature*. Basingstoke: Palgrave.

Wittgenstein, Ludwig. 1984. *Philosophical Investigations*. Oxford: Blackwell.

Wolfe, Cary, ed. 2003. *Zoontologies: The Question of the Animal*. Minneapolis: University of Minnesota Press.

Wolfe, Cary. 2003. *Animal Rites: American Culture, the Discourse of Species, and Posthumanism*. Chicago: Chicago University Press.

Wolfreys, Julian. 2002. *Victorian Hauntings: Spectrality, Gothic, the Uncanny and Literature*. Basingstoke: Palgrave.

Wood, Marcus. 2002. *Slavery, Empathy and Pornography*. Oxford: Oxford University Press.

Wood, Sarah, ed. 1995. *Home and Family*. Special issue of *Angelaki*, 2: 1.

Woolf, Virginia. 1942. *The Death of the Moth and Other Essays*. London: Hogarth Press.

Woolf, Virginia. 1988. 'Henry James's Ghost Stories', in *The Essays of Virginia Woolf*, vol. 3, 1919–1924, ed. Andrew McNeillie. New York: Harcourt Brace Jovanovich.

Wright, Elizabeth. 1998. *Psychoanalytic Criticism: A Reappraisal*, 2nd edn. Cambridge: Polity.

Young, Robert. 1981. 'Introduction', in *Untying the Text: A Post-Structuralist Reader*, ed. Robert Young. London: Routledge and Kegan Paul.

Young, Robert. 1990. *White Mythologies: Writing History and the West*. London: Routledge.

Young, Robert. 1991a. 'Poems That Read Themselves', *Tropismes* 5: 233–61.

Young, Robert, ed. 1991b. *Neocolonialism*. Special issue of *Oxford Literary Review*, 13.

Young, Robert. 1995. *Colonial Desire: Hybridity in Theory, Culture and Race*. London: Routledge.

Young, Robert. 1996. *Torn Halves: Political Conflict in Literary and Cultural Theory*. Manchester: Manchester University Press.

Young, Robert. 1999. 'Freud's Secret: *The Interpretation of Dreams* was a gothic novel', in *Sigmund Freud's The Interpretation of Dreams: New interdisciplinary essays*, ed. Laura Marcus. Manchester: Manchester University Press.

Young, Robert. 2000. *Postcolonialism: A History*. Oxford: Blackwell.

Zipes, Jack. 1988. *Fairy Tales and the Art of Subversion: The Classical Genre for Children and the Process of Civilization*. London: Methuen.

Žižek, Slavoj. 1991a. *Looking Awry: An Introduction to Jacques Lacan through Popular Culture*. Cambridge, MA: MIT Press.

Žižek, Slavoj. 1991b. *For They Know Not What They Do: Enjoyment as a Political Factor*. London: Verso.

Index